ECHOES ACROSS CONTINENTS

A Memoir of Resilience Through Tumultuous Times

KRISHNA DAS RAY

the three
tomatoes
The Three Tomatoes Book Publishing

Published: February 2025

ISBN: 979-8-9916508-2-3
Library of Congress Control Number: 2024920907

For information address:
The Three Tomatoes Book Publishing
6 Soundview Rd.
Glen Cove, NY 11542

Cover design: Susan Herbst
Interior design: Susan Herbst

This work depicts actual events in the life of the author as truthfully as recollection permits. While all persons within are actual individuals, some names and identifying characteristics have been changed to respect their privacy.

Advanced Praise for Echoes Across Continents

"At the intersection of the personal and the political, this self-portrait recounts the life of a brave, brilliant, and resourceful individual who navigated extraordinary currents of social change, prejudice, and violence. He lived history and offers us the personal perspective of an eyewitness to events that profoundly altered the British Empire, creating new countries but at the same time causing hardship and tragedy. Remaining true to his moral values and family, this physician's dedication to equitable treatment, truth, education, and hard work, stands, with his children and the many people he helped, as his legacy and offers us profound lessons that are still valid today."

~Roseann O'Reilly Runte, Past President
of the Canada Foundation for Innovation,
author of Canadians Who Innovate: The Trailblazers

"Dr. K.D. Ray's is a profound and monumental memoir of a courageous man distinguished by his character, righteousness, conviction, and compassion. From his youth to his lifelong devotion to his patients and his enduring love for his wife Rachel, who stood by his side for over sixty years, Dr. Ray's life is a testament to his unwavering principles. Readers witness a quiet hero who exemplifies the very meaning of life through his encounters and challenges. It is also a sweeping historical saga, touching on the diverse races, religions, nationalities, and countries that have shaped and continue to shape the modern era."

~Michael M. J. Shore, Former Judge of the Federal Court
and Court Martial Appeals Court of Canada,
former editor of Seaports and Shipping World Journal
and author of O Canada, Canada: Short Stories.

"Krishna Das Ray was talented, determined, and curious. He savoured his journey through rapidly changing times, beginning in pre-Independence India and ending in Internet-age Canada. His autobiography provides frank insight into key human realms including family, bureaucracy, and medicine. These chronicles provide a flashlight as we navigate our own journeys in the modern world."

~ Audri Mukhopadhyay, Canadian diplomat,
former consulate general of Canada in Ho Chi Minh City

DEDICATION

For my loving wife, Rachel, whose support was
unwavering during our life's journey together
and throughout the writing of this book.

As long as there is life there is death.
As long as there is life there is conflict.
As long as there is life there is hope.
Death is the natural but not the ultimate end of life
as new life takes over.
Conflict is not the end of society
as new boundaries and new societies form.
New life grows with smiles and love
as if yesterday's problems were never.

~ Excerpt from letter to K.D. Ray from his mother

TABLE OF CONTENTS

Part 1: India

Part 2: England

Part 3: Nigeria

~ Part 1 ~

INDIA

~ 1 ~

FATHER'S FAREWELL

IN 24 HOURS MY LIFE changed. Father was found unconscious in his chamber at the courthouse. He was rushed home by stretcher to his bed. It was 1931. I was eight years old, and Mom told me my father was very ill.

Dr. Bose told me my father had suffered a stroke, which paralyzed his right arm and right leg. I wanted to talk with Father, but he could not speak. I felt helpless as I sat by his bed and stared at him. The doctor told me not to worry. He called Hari, our head servant, and told him to take me from the sick room.

Hari, who was literate but uneducated, had started working for our family long before I was born. I knew Father liked him and trusted his loyalty to our family. In traditional India, "family" means the extended family and includes near relatives and servants. But family meant the "nuclear" family to our father. Hari added himself (and no other servant) to my father's notion of a nuclear family and added bhai (brother) after his name, Haribhai. He knew people thought he was not smart, but he didn't care what they thought.

He always stayed close to my father's friends and the government officers when they continued talking after leaving my father's office. If anyone asked Hari a question, he behaved like a fool—making stupid exclamations or mumbling unrelated facts. They called him "Mumble Fumble." My father never encouraged Hari's snooping but never told him to stop when he repeated the unsavory comments to my father.

Hari grabbed my hand and gently squeezed it, consoling me, as he led me to the front of our house. He said Dr. Bose was "a no-good doctor," who didn't know what he was doing. Hari also didn't trust the Scottish surgeon. He didn't think the foreign doctor would treat my father vigorously.

Hari's remark reflected Bengal in 1932, a time of civil disturbances that called for India's independence. Educated, unemployed young Indian men, especially in Bombay and Bengal, even organized terrorist cells to undermine the foreign rulers who held all the power.

As we sat together, he discussed the case that my father had completed when he became ill. The Congress Party had declared a day of hartal (work stoppage). Almost everything was closed; even roads were deserted. Only government offices remained open, where government administrators ordered employees to show up. The Congress Party and their Satyagraha supporters, who practiced nonviolent resistance, picketed all the government offices, including the courthouse of the British District Magistrate, who was the highest-ranking civil administrator and chief officer administering criminal law.

The British Inspector General of Police arrived on horseback. He used his bullhorn to order protestors to clear out in ten minutes. As he counted down the minutes, the Satyagraha organizers told everyone to lie down in front of the buildings. After ten minutes, he led the charge of his men on horseback. The horses trampled protesters who tried to flee; police officers injured other protesters. The hartal ended with significant injuries. Anger and hatred smoldered for days.

Judges in the criminal courts were administrators, not law scholars. Most of them were British, and some of the Indian officers who served as judges were under the influence of the British. Still, Congress pursued a civil case against His Majesty the Emperor of India and asked for damages from this brutal police action.

Hari told me that the British Chief District Judge had pulled a fast one. He was afraid to handle the explosive case, so he handed it over to my father whom, he claimed, he trusted and respected. He reminded my father of his oath of loyalty to the emperor and of his duty to maintain law and order in these volatile times. He also told my father to remember who employed him and determined his career.

For six months famous lawyers and advocates from Calcutta argued for either the complainant or the defense. My father received mail for and against Congress. Hari described some of the letters. Many of them threatened my father and our family if he failed to judge in favor of his people—the Congress. Some came from revolutionaries and included handprints in raktapanja (blood). Other letters reminded my father of the price that he would pay if he was disloyal and sacrificed law and order—hinting at career stagnation. "What a waste of talent," they wrote.

When the testimony ended, my father spent night after night in his office typing out his verdict, which he kept under lock and key. When he was tired, he would rest on his office couch and each morning, he locked the room and took the keys with him. When he finished writing his decision, my father finally went to the court-room and delivered his judgment in favor of the Indian National Congress. His judgment also declared that the government had to pay damages and legal expenses.

The courtroom went silent, but the crowd outside erupted with joy. People shouted slogans and sang patriotic songs. Some people threw stones and people feared violence. My father left through the back of the building and had his driver take him home.

The next morning every newspaper sang my father's prais-es, except the Statesman, the British-controlled daily newspaper, which stated the ultra-liberal judge, who had no respect for law and order, had encouraged anarchy in India.

Father returned to the court to finish his paperwork. He had a bad headache, so he went to his chamber, took an aspirin, and rest-ed quietly on his couch. Hari told me that armed police officers and men still guarded the Court House, and no outsiders were allowed to visit the judges. On this particular day, none of my father's col-leagues came to visit or chat with him. When the court clerk came to usher my father to the courtroom for his next case, my father was unconscious on the couch.

The day after this conversation with Hari, my father was still semi-conscious and couldn't move. He urged me to write to my cousin Jeevan who was an important doctor at the Medical College Hospitals in Calcutta (former name of Kolkata). I wrote a letter that incorporated Hari's concerns. I asked Jeevan to come immediately and look after Dad who was so ill that he could not talk or move his limbs. Hari prompted me to add that his presence was essential because our town lacked competent doctors.

We didn't think that it was a problem that we didn't have Je-evan's postal address in Calcutta. Many letters came to our father without a house number or the name of our street. Besides, my cousin was an important doctor. We were confident that he would get the letter and would soon arrive at our house to give my father the best care and treatment. Father would recover.

But we never received a reply and Jeevan never showed up. Years later when I met him in Calcutta, Jeevan said that he never received the letter. By then, I understood Calcutta was enormous.

That night everyone in our family and household kept vigil and early the next morning Father passed away. My mother sobbed and we wondered if there would be any end to her grief. All of us cried, and Hari wailed and shouted that the British had killed the great judge Atul Chandra—the personification of justice.

Early the next morning, Uncle Manindra met with a lawyer. They reviewed my father's will and sent a telegram to Hem Ray, my father's brother, at their ancestral home to inform the entire family of this untimely passing. By then, the news had spread. A crowd gathered outside our compound to grieve in silence. At 11 o'clock the British police chief arrived on horseback leading a contingent of the police force. With near military precision, the police on horses and others on foot stood at attention as more cars entered the compound. British and Indian administrative officers and judges in black ties and wearing black armbands had arrived to offer their condolences. Reporters also arrived to cover the event and pay their respects.

As police officers played Retreat on their bugles, officers and judges walked single file past my father's dead body, which was wrapped in a white linen sheet that was covered with fragrant white flowers. Only his head was exposed—at rest on a pillow. One by one, each official bowed to my father and walked over to Mom seated on a chair. Her head was erect, and her eyes were shining; she didn't move at all. Normally a petite, fair woman, her perfect bearing almost looked defiant. Each man bowed before her, then walked away. No one said a word.

The priest arrived to complete the funeral arrangements since the orthodox Brahmin cremation needed to end before sunset. When our father's body and our family reached the cremation ground by the river, a crowd waited to pay their last respects at the pyre, which was ready with firewood and fragrant sandalwood to receive my father's body. As per custom, my brother Kumar, who was three years older than I, lit the pyre and the priest chanted verses from the scriptures while the flames burned bright. My father was no more.

~ **2** ~

THE LETTER

THE MORNING AFTER FATHER'S CREMATION, I walked through our garden. I inhaled the sweet moist fragrance of the gardenias and jasmines that collected early mornings before the sun dried them out. I noticed rows of marigolds and other annuals planted for next year. As birds chirped in trees, a large lizard made weird noises and scurried over dried leaves. I stood still until it skittered away.

When I went home, Mom was sitting with Uncle Manindra. Dried tears still stained her cheeks. My uncle, who was the executor of my father's estate, was telling her that she had inherited all of Father's assets, including his life insurance policy. She would also receive Father's salary for the month, but she would not receive a widow's pension. That was reserved for expatriate British officers.

Our grandmother, who lived at our ancestral home, sent a telegram in which she expressed her grief at the irreplaceable loss of her son. She asked us to come home immediately. The Sradh Ceremony or Last Rights had to take place on the 11th day after his death. She told our mother to put her son's ashes in an urn so they could be interred in a memorial built on the ancestral grounds.

The telegram clarified my situation. Our family would leave this town. I would no longer be able to see my friends. I sought solace at the river, which was muddy from the monsoon. I watched the currents making whorls and waves.

I kept on walking and my mood changed. The wind blew sweetly, and I shivered with exhilaration. I wasn't afraid of the dwindling light. Someone in the distance blew a conch shell and temple bells rang. Someone in the heavens was telling me things would be all right.

I returned home at dusk. I wanted to tell Mom that everything would be okay. But what seemed so plausible by the river turned unbelievable in this brightly lit room where Mom looked so sad.

I went into the bedroom that I shared with my older brother Kumar. He looked troubled as he asked why we had to go to the ancestral home. It didn't have electricity or piped water. The road from the railway station to the village wasn't paved. And since we were traveling in the rainy season, no one with a horse carriage or motorcar would take us to the village. He knew all this because he'd been there. I didn't respond. I didn't want to start an argument.

An emissary from our ancestral village arrived at our house with a lengthy document elegantly created by a calligrapher, signed by our grandmother, and witnessed and endorsed by our father's brother Uncle Hem who was the new head of our family. If the letter had a title, it would have been for the Rebel Angel, Her loving Son. She offered her sorrowful love to her daughter-in-law and two wonderful grandsons. She discussed her sad days caused by the premature demise of her husband (our grandfather) at the same time of life. Cerebral strokes were a curse on our family.

She regretted that our father spent his last days alone—away from his near and dear ones, including her unfortunate self. How she had worked for the success and happiness of this eldest son, our father, who was such a brilliant student, even at the Law College of Calcutta University.

Her son was a good Brahmin who naturally followed the customs and rituals of the great Hindu religion, until law school when he became a disciple of Sir Mahitosh Mukherjee, the chief Justice of the High Court and Vice Chancellor of the University. That man's social ideas violated all Hindu customs, and he turned her angel into a rebel. He was probably the underlying cause of her son's premature death.

A great change came over our father when he returned home for the holidays. He argued with her and the Pundits (or religious scholars) over the scriptures and dared to challenge them over their authenticity. Our father's beliefs had created sorrow in the house.

She was devastated when her son approved Sir Mahitosh's decision to arrange an unorthodox widow marriage. At that point, our grandmother realized her elder angel had become a "rebel Angel."

She still loved her son, so she sought advice from the Pundits. They concluded that she could bring him back to his orthodox roots by arranging his marriage to a Brahmin girl from a high-class orthodox family. When our father came back home for the Durga Puja holidays, he was not pleased with this news. He wanted to postpone the wedding until he received his final degree, which would take four more years.

Our grandmother was petrified. She believed Sir Mahitosh would talk him into marrying a widow, so she used her strongest weapon in a duel with him. She went on a fast and she told her son that she would even refuse to drink water if he rejected this arranged marriage. She would fast until death.

She reminded our mother that everyone in the village implored our father to honor his duty to his mother. His university education was for the benefit of the village. He could not abandon his mother and the village.

Our father succumbed and apologized to our grandmother, who broke her fast. He agreed to the arranged marriage and married our mother. The recitation of these events, she wrote, should make our mother grateful to our grandmother—forever!

Our grandmother recalled the great wedding. Our mother's father was a Maha Mahopadhyay Pundit or Grand Teacher of Learning, and so was her grandfather. However, the family was poor and depended on yearly stipends and gifts from local zamindars or landowners and businesspeople. Our grandmother willingly paid all the wedding expenses and covered the travel expenses for our mother's family and her relatives.

After the wedding, our mother stayed at the ancestral home where she received loving care from our grandmother while our father returned to Calcutta and received his Bachelor of Law degree and first-class honors for excellence. But then our father participated in another widow marriage organized by Sir Mahitosh.

Our grandmother was grief-stricken. She wrote to her son and made our mother write him long letters telling him to mend his ways to ensure their future happiness. She was furious when she learned that our mother supported our father's views. "That was my luck!" She lamented in the letter. Her son and daughter-in-law defied her.

The local Brahmin Society heard about our father's support of this second widow marriage. The society called a meeting and said that our father would be punished unless he changed his ways.

She urged her son to come home immediately, and she instructed her daughter-in-law to tell him to break with Sir Mahitosh. But her son lacked remorse. He told her that he would only return after he arranged for his admission into the master's degree course at the Law College.

When her son finally came home, our grandmother reminded him that the last Mughal Viceroy of Bengal, Bihar, and Orissa had awarded our ancestors the family's landed property in 1738. They were supposed to serve as the sevak or servant of God Vishnu and accept that our ancestral property belonged to God. Our family was to care for the Vishnu temple and perform daily pujas in Vishnu's honor. Our grandmother said that since our family was a servant of God, we received a significant reduction in rent and taxes from the government.

Our grandmother reminded her eldest son that one day he would be in charge of the family estate. But she told him that if he refused to follow the recommendations of the Brahmin Society, he would be excommunicated from the religious fold. He would bring shame on the entire family, and he would lose his inheritance.

Our father told his mother that he would return in a few days. He went to visit Sir Mahitosh, who served as the Chief Justice of the Calcutta High Court and presided over the Judicial Council, which appointed all the judges. Our father told him that since he was married, he could no longer afford to continue his studies and become a Doctor of Law. Sir Mahitosh was disappointed. Our father was his favorite student. Instead, our father applied for a judgeship in a lower court. He got the job.

The newly appointed judge went home. A few days later, he and his wife left for good so that he could begin his new job. In the letter, our grandmother reminded our mother that this act of defiance made her an unhappy woman for the rest of her life. Our father lost his right to the family estate, and he never carried out any of his duties to the family —and she, the unfortunate mother, was left to suffer.

Our grandmother advised us to come home quickly so that our father's Sradh Ceremony could be performed for the departed soul of her beloved son. She promised that if we behaved properly and didn't let ourselves be led astray by undesirables, we would find love in our ancestral home, and we would acquire, one day, everything our father had lost.

~ 3 ~

GOING HOME

THE EMOTIONALLY CHARGED LETTER FROM our grandmother annoyed our mother. She wondered why she needed to dredge up the past. Why did she want to fill our mother with guilt when her husband had just died?

Mom didn't know what to do. She knew that our father never wanted his own family to live in the ancestral village. The school only went to the sixth grade; Kumar was already at that grade level. She would never agree to send us to boarding schools. Our father hated them. Most importantly, she worried about the people living in the village. We would never enjoy their company.

Mom told us that our grandmother and Uncle Hem never did anything to earn her trust. But she knew that they were powerful. She worried that they would not let us leave after the ceremony.

Uncle Manindra said we should, in all fairness, go home for the ceremony. He reminded his sister that our father's death was also a great loss to our grandmother. Uncle Manindra assured Mom that since he was the sub-divisional administrative officer for that part of Bengal, he would send someone to watch over us and make certain that we were safe. Mom told our grandmother's emissary that we would return to our ancestral village two days before the ceremony.

By late afternoon, our family was settled in the first-class compartment of the train with our father's urn and Uncle Manindra, who stayed with us for most of the journey. Morning brought relief. When Uncle Manindra left the train at his station, he reminded his sister not to worry.

Uncle Hem, our father's brother, waited with his entourage at our train station. He expressed his sorrow and said that our grandmother was heartbroken. The head of a village and three boatmen bowed to our uncle and our family before leading us to the family boat.

Every spring the rivers and canals overflowed with water that inundated the lowlands making boat travel the most reliable form of transportation this time of year. As we made our way through the canals, the setting sun spread a rich red color across the water's surface. Even the edge of the black cloud looked as if it were on fire. I breathed the heavy fragrance of the flowers and closed my eyes. Our magnificent boat ride had ended as we entered another canal that led to our ancestral home.

About fifty women reciting verses and wailing over the loss of our father sat at the entrance of our family compound. They kept up their noise while we were led into our quarters. I then heard a woman tell the mourners that they were done for the day and the wailing stopped. The woman told the mourners to return the next morning. As I mulled over this fake performance, a servant showed our family to the bathroom. Kumar was right—there was no piped water. We had a cistern and small jugs for our use.

After we washed up from the journey, we met our grand-mother and Auntie Vasanti in the sitting room. They wept after they said that we resembled our father. Our grandmother thanked her daughter-in-law for coming home. She told us to go rest in our bedrooms.

Gentle sun rays woke me up early in the morning. A maid-servant gave us breakfast and then I went outside to explore the grounds. A man stepped forward in the compound and offered a pranam or respectful greeting before he led me inside an old brick and stone building and introduced me to Nayeb Babu, the general manager of our estate. He was happy to see me. He had known my father well and hoped we would stay here until I finished the village school.

Nayeb Babu arranged for a clerk to show me around the prop-erty. There was a lovely flower garden where I noticed a rectangular pond about the size of a small lake. A handsome pavilion graced the far end of the pond. Its brick and cement floor had steps that led into the water so that family members and their guests could im-merse themselves. The clerk said that our father often sat in this pa-vilion and watched theatrical and musical rehearsals. The other end of the pond had a simple set of stairs for public access to the water.

A private road near the pavilion led to our small orchard. An-other private road intersected with the public thoroughfare that led to the railway station and other villages. Bamboo trees and tall grasses created a natural screen that concealed our property from the road.

The clerk explained that the old building where I met Nayeb Babu once served as the family's main residence until a severe earth-quake damaged the structure. Although the building remained rea-sonably sturdy, the family moved into new private quarters on the compound. Units were added as the family grew.

Our great-grandfather officially divided the compound when his two surviving sons wanted separate living quarters. To prevent squabbling, our great-grandfather chose each dwelling's location and authorized the construction of two similar residences. But the family compound remained one unit because of its indivisible connection to Lord Vishnu, who truly owned our estate.

After our great-grandfather's death, our grandfather became the chief sevak of Lord Vishnu and general manager of the entire estate. He had a brick and stone canopy constructed in front of the old Vishnu temple near the former family residence. Every afternoon, worshippers gathered here for puja and lunch, which was God's gift to his guests. During festivals, priests also distributed sweets to people who came to sing, dance, and offer prayers to Lord Vishnu.

The stone temple with its handsome teak doors had a garden that supplied flowers for the daily puja. From an opening in the garden, I saw four similar buildings erected around a single courtyard. Three buildings were residences for our extended family and the fourth building was for the kitchen and storage. Our grandmother also had her vegetarian kitchen attached to her private building. These four structures with their corrugated, metal roofs and their wood-brick-cement walls and floors were designed to withstand earthquakes.

By midmorning, I thanked the clerk for the tour and headed back to my temporary quarters. I went inside for lunch in our grandmother's kitchen. For eleven days after a parent's death, we children had to eat vegetarian meals. Soon the 11th day would be here: the time for the Sradh Ceremony.

~ ~ ~ ~ ~

The day before the ceremony workers erected two large canvas *shamiyanas* (tents) in our compound. Servants scurried around to find everything on a long list prepared by our temple priest, who had also hired an assistant who hurried to nearby temples to find more items before the pundits arrived.

Our grandmother's cooks in her vegetarian kitchen were busy creating a huge vegetarian meal for all our guests. Relatives from distant villages and towns were attending the ceremony. About 200 local Hindus and Muslims also wanted to pay their respects.

On the morning of the ceremony, the local barber and his wife shaved off every strand of hair on Kumar's head and my head. The barber's wife hacked off our mother's lovely long hair. She looked terrible.

I wondered why this ritual required such cruelty or did the mother of the rebel angel order the humiliation of our mom as an act of penance? Heads shorn, the three of us immersed ourselves in the pond. Kumar and I put on saffron *dhotis* with a shawl over our shoulders and Mom put on a plain raw silk sari.

Our temple priest, who appeared at the top of the pavilion staircase, uttered some sacred stanzas in Sanskrit before he led us to a shamiyana where our relatives and visitors sat near four Brahmin pundits with white scarves draped over their shoulders. Each pundit sat on a small wooden stool in a different corner of the tent with a folio on his lap containing religious leaflets.

Our priest led us to polished wood seats at the center of the tent where we faced a square pit that held a large earthenware vessel. A separate basket held firewood; another held *samagree* (mixture of dried leaves and grains). There were also two brass bowls: one held *ghee* (clarified butter) and the other held powdered incense.

Hindu custom dictated that Kumar, the eldest son, and our mother would perform some rituals under the guidance of the priest who would recite the holy scriptures. I had nothing to do but feel sorry for myself as I suffered the greatest loss in my life.

After our priest put wood into the earthenware vessel, he poured in the ghee and used a lit stick to ignite the fire. He added the samagree and incense and declared that the sacred fire was ready.

This ceremonial creation of the sacred fire has been practiced in Hinduism since the Vedic Era, which was around 1500 BC. The fire is considered pure because it burns away all impurities as flames leap into the sky. Devotees believe that *Agni* or the God of Fire carries the prayers offered by the *Yajna* devotee to the Supreme God.

I listened to the entire ceremony, but I couldn't understand the Sanskrit verses. When the priest occasionally translated some of the rituals into Bengali, he touched my heart.

The four pundits in the four corners of the tent read aloud from the *Ramayana* and *Mahabharata*, the two famous Sanskrit epics. As each learned pundit explained the meaning of different verses, crowds sat, enthralled, at their feet.

After our priest sang the hymn *Peace on Earth*, he sprinkled sanctified Ganges River water on everyone under the tent and on a cow and calf that we were donating to the village temple. He also sprinkled water into the air so that friends and relatives who could not attend the ceremony received this water's blessings. As everyone stood up, I felt peace flow through the deeply tranquil tent.

While the priest, pundits, relatives, and some guests enjoyed a dinner served on bronze *thalis* (plates) in our living quarters, Uncle Hem invited everyone else to stay in the tent where dinner was served on green banana leaves. Muslim workers were provided their own eating area behind the kitchen, but everyone enjoyed the same tasty vegetable dishes and sweetmeats.

Peace descended with nightfall after most guests had left. When I slipped into bed, I felt different. So much had happened to our family in two weeks. It felt like the past was floating away.

Early in the morning, our temple priest started the morning puja by ringing a temple bell in the inner sanctum to awaken the Deity from His sleep. Then he sang a hymn and picked up the Deity, which was an ancient black fossil from the Himalayas, and anointed him by rubbing him with homemade butter. After our priest carefully washed the Deity, dried it with muslin, and put Him on His throne, the priest placed a gold crown embedded with a large sapphire on the top.

During the puja, the priest recited Sanskrit verses before he performed *pranam* by bowing and touching the floor with his head. Finally, he placed a breakfast of fruit and thickened milk on a silver platter for the Deity. This entire ritual took about 45 minutes—and it was performed three times daily.

For Kumar and me, all three pujas on this day were special. After the priest distributed Lord Vishnu's mid-day vegetarian meal to the devotees—an act that completed the ritual that blessed all the food in our house, Auntie Vasanti escorted the two of us into our family kitchen. There, we were served delicious dishes that included fish and lamb. Our eleven days of vegetarian meals had officially ended.

~ 4 ~

GRANDMOTHER: FACE-TO-FACE

THE NEXT MORNING MOM TOLD Kumar and me that our father's good friend Tayab Mian was coming to see us. Our father had often spoken of Mian Sahib, and the two men always exchanged greetings every Durga Puja and Ramadan.

When Kumar and I walked into the public meeting room, Sheikh Hashim, the chief headman of our estate, greeted us. Soon another man entered with an entourage and created a stir. Tayab Mian had arrived. Everyone stood up and said *salaam* to him; but Kumar and I said *Adab*, offering our special guest the proper Islamic greeting that our father had taught us.

Mian Sahib hugged us and tears were visible in his eyes. When Uncle Hem entered the room, the two men exchanged greetings. Our uncle invited our honored guest to sit in a chair before he sat next to him.

Mian Sahib brought gifts for our family. He explained that he arrived after the funeral because he thought it was more appropriate. Uncle Hem agreed and asked our guest, who lived only three miles from our village, to visit more often, especially since we children would be living here now.

When our uncle left the room so that Mian Sahib could be alone with us, he told us to consider him our close friend. He asked if it was true that our mother had decided to stay at the ancestral home.

Kumar asked our guest if he thought this was a good idea. Mian Sahib said it would be impolite to answer, but Kumar wanted his opinion. He told our special guest that he was our uncle. Mian Sahib's heart melted.

Mian Sahib said that he knew our father was against boarding schools. He wanted us to go to school near our home. Mian Sahib, who had attended the same missionary-run boarding school with our father, also disliked boarding schools. He recalled the good times he and our father shared—the games they played, the theater, and the music they enjoyed at his home and here.

He told us he was happy to meet us. Whenever we wanted to visit him, he promised to send his boat to take us to his home, which he said was called "Mian Bari" (or Mian's home) on the big river. At the end of our visit, we knew our father's friend genuinely cared for us. We were sad to see him go.

Our grandmother arrived as we recounted our delightful visit with Mian Sahib to our mother. She said that Mian Sahib had been a pest when our father lived here. Twice, she said that he had been a bad influence. She didn't want us to develop a close relationship with this man. She quickly left the room, but the unease she brought with her lingered in her absence.

The next morning Kumar and I went to visit Auntie Mira and Uncle Swapan who was our father's first cousin. Our uncle was away when we arrived at their home on the compound, but Auntie

Mira was happy to see us. She asked about our former home and our father's last days. She told us that our father had never needed to abandon his ancestral home.

Her words surprised us. We reminded her that the Brahmin Society's ruling against our father had humiliated our grandmother.

Auntie Mira said that while our grandmother had forced her son to give up his plans for his master's and doctorate of law, she could never force him to give up his principles. Our grandmother fell into her own trap. She had no choice but to accept our father's decision to leave the village with his wife.

Auntie Mira said that when she had married into the family, she had insisted on separate living quarters because our grandmother was so domineering and had made Auntie Mira's life so difficult that she avoided the woman. She told us our mother needed to know these things.

On another morning, Uncle Swapan came to the estate office building to collect the honorarium stipend that was owed to each male member of the family. He told Kumar there was probably a provision that authorized a stipend to widows and surviving children of a male family member.

Kumar asked if our mother qualified since our father had left home. Uncle Swapan said that he thought the Brahmin had withdrawn its ruling. But anyone who was denied an entitlement could take our grandmother to court. But it would be messy, expensive, and time-consuming.

After lunch, Kumar and I met a new postman Abdul, who was a friend of Uncle Manindra. He opened his bag and gave Kumar a letter from our uncle for our mother. Abdul told us that walls have ears and eyes; almost everyone in the village was loyal to our grandmother.

When Kumar gave the letter to Mom, she hurried into her bedroom and closed the door. Her brother wrote that if she wanted to leave the village, she should write to him and give her letter to Abdul, who was reliable and trustworthy.

Mom told us not to talk about the letter to anyone. We told her what Uncle Swapan said about the estate rules and the stipends. Mom said, "Time will tell." Kumar hoped her last words would prove correct. He wanted to leave the village. He was in the sixth grade. He was worried about his education.

~ ~ ~ ~ ~

The next morning Mom asked me to give a letter for Uncle Manindra to Abdul. She had written that she didn't want to live in the ancestral home. It would take time to resolve the issue of the stipends with her mother-in-law, but she asked him to be ready for our departure.

Days turned dull until Uncle Swapan showed Kumar and me the village, which was home to Brahmin families who weren't particularly prosperous. We noticed some men gesturing wildly in front of a house. A man stepped forward and said that last night thieves had broken into his bedroom and stole half of his stored jute, which was his main cash crop. The man was devastated. He had thought that his bedroom would be safe. He would be unable to pay rent and all his other expenses.

Kumar felt sorry for the poor man. He said that it must have been uncomfortable sleeping with all that smelly jute and then to have it stolen. What a shame!

"You're talking rubbish! Where were we supposed to put it? We don't have a warehouse with guards like you people." The man glared at Kumar. Uncle Swapan hurried us away.

Our uncle pointed to two modest houses squeezed onto a single lot. He said the land used to belong to us; but we gave the rights to the priest and Nayeb Babu, who are Brahmins. We also gave them land for fruits and vegetables. At their deaths, the properties would revert to the family.

We approached some men sitting on a bench. One man claimed that our father behaved like a big shot, but he never did anything good for the village and never respected anyone from the area.

Another man described what happened when he went to our father's house on behalf of a prosperous trader who was involved in a legal dispute that our father would judge. The man said that when he told our father that the trader would give money for his help, our father behaved in an uncivilized manner—he ran him out of the house. The man said our father claimed that the trader was lucky. He could be reported for bribery, which was criminal behavior. The man said our father was arrogant! Just because he was the judge!

One of the man's friends noticed that we were listening. The man didn't care. He was glad we'd heard what he said.

We walked across a bridge and headed through the part of the village inhabited by washermen, ironsmiths, oilmen, weavers, and other lower-class workers. We came to an immaculate small house and gymnasium at the end of the road. Uncle Swapan said that a man from a family of weavers managed this place, which was the pride of the village. The man had left home after elementary school. He wandered for years following different gurus before he joined an ashram where he learned yoga and studied Gandhi's teachings. When he came back to his village, he carried his own spinning wheel.

The man approached the village elders, including Uncle Hem, and asked for their patronage so that he could establish an ashram. The elders, who were inspired by his sincerity, gave him land and money.

Soon the villagers, who trusted the young man and called him "Sadhu" (honest man), decided that he was a good leader for their children. Everyone called him Sadhu and forgot about his humble origins.

The three of us walked into the ashram and once we met the well-known Sadhu in his clean homespun clothes, Uncle Swapan left us. He said that he would return in an hour.

Sadhu showed us around and said that he had received God's blessings. People had given him all the money and materials he needed. Kumar told Sadhu that he took good care of the place. The holy man turned modest. He said that he merely followed God's wishes.

When we sat in his home, which he called "Humble Cottage," Sadhu listed all the gurus he had met while traveling to ashrams. He said that many of them wanted him to stay, but he preferred to come home and serve his people.

We went to the gymnasium. Sadhu asked if I knew how to use the parallel bars. I said no. Sadhu picked me up and placed each of my hands on the bar. He held me tight from behind and told me to pull myself up. I felt his body press against me, and I felt something hard push against my bum. I remembered something Hari once told me when he refused to let me sit on his lap. I should only sit on the lap of a parent or grandparent. Bad people, he said, took advantage of young boys. I should never let anyone press his body against me.

I was only eight as I dangled from this bar, but I could identify that firm thing he pushed against me. I shouted: "My leg hurts!"

Sadhu loosened his grip and I fell to the floor, rubbed my ankle, and cried. I wanted to look at Sadhu's face, but he hurried to get a jug of cold water. I soaked my ankle and waited for Uncle Swapan to return.

I limped all the way home. At night, Kumar asked me what really happened. I said I sprained my ankle. Nothing more.

One day Grandmother paid a visit to tell our mother that she had arranged to have living quarters refurbished in an empty block. She'd also authorized our entitlement. Mom would receive her stipend. She would have enough money for us to pursue our studies.

Grandmother assured her daughter-in-law that the love she received after her marriage to our father remained alive in Grandmother's heart. If our mom behaved correctly, she would discover this. But if she let herself be misguided, she would never get to know what she gave up.

Mother thanked our grandmother. After the woman left, Kumar was worried. Didn't our mother understand that this place was bad for his education?

Mom told him to be patient. Later in the day, Mom gave me a letter for Abdul to post to her brother Manindra.

The next morning Mom told her mother-in-law that we were moving to the district town of Mymensingh. It offered the best education for her sons.

Our grandmother's eyes turned cold and flinty. "I have been the gatekeeper of this house for many years. I always try to keep the peace. But people plan, cheat, and tell lies to do what they want to do. The truth always nails them in the end. They suffer because they get no mercy from me. Think carefully before you say another word and be prepared to face the consequences of your decision." Grandmother hurried from the room. We didn't see her again for days.

Our mother went to Auntie Vasanti and asked her to arrange for the family boat to take us to the railway station. Our auntie said she'd get back to us. Two days passed—nothing happened.

Kumar went to Nayeb Babu to ask about the boat. His face grew long; he took a deep breath. He said that it was puja season. All the boatmen had vanished.

I asked Auntie Mira to help. She said that she and her husband could do nothing. She lowered her voice and said that she wanted to tell me something, but I could repeat it only to my mother and Kumar. I gave her my word. Auntie Mira said that no boat or any other transport would take us to the railroad station until my brother and I turned eighteen.

I left Auntie's house and searched for Sheikh Hashim. Someone told me that he was carrying out his duties in other villages.

I told Mom everything. But she had her own plans. She gave me a letter for Abdul to post to Uncle Manindra. Three days later, Abdul brought a response that said everything would fall into place. His sister should get ready to move. Mom told us to stay calm but watchful.

A few days later a crowd surrounded some men tacking a large poster onto the wall at the post office. The poster announced an upcoming meeting of three Sub Divisional Officers from the district in our village.

A few days later Mian Sahib came to our public meeting room with a new government officer for our area and two police constables. He introduced the officer to Uncle Hem. The government officer discussed the general condition of our village and asked Uncle Hem if he would hold a public meeting with the Sub Divisional Officers so that the villagers could suggest local improvements and voice their complaints. He wanted our uncle to act as the facilitator because our villagers respected him. Our uncle agreed and the visiting officials got up to leave.

Mian Sahib suddenly asked Uncle Hem if my brother and I could go with him to visit Bajitpur, the nearby company town. He would make certain that we returned before evening. Our uncle sent someone to ask our mother, and she agreed.

Mian Sahib invited us into the handsome rest house, which was used by visiting European officers or senior government officers. There, sitting at a long table, was Uncle Manindra. He was speaking with the Sub Divisional Officer who oversaw our village and other officials. Before Mian Sahib said goodbye, he told Uncle Manindra that his boat and boatmen would be waiting at our village. Our uncle was pleased.

After he left, Uncle Manindra told us that Mian's boat would take us back to our mother. The boat would remain overnight and tomorrow we would leave our ancestral home while Uncle Hem held the public meeting with the Sub Divisional Officer of our area and the lower-ranking officers. Uncle Manindra asked us to relay important instructions to our mother.

Mian Sahib's boat brought us back home before evening. We raced to Mom's room, closed the door, and gave her the messages from her brother. Our mother smiled.

That evening Mom told our grandmother and Auntie Vasanti that Mian Sahib had offered to send his boat tomorrow to take us to the railway station. Our grandmother didn't believe her. Auntie Vasanti said that she and her husband were surprised by her rash decision to leave the ancestral home. She thought that the entire family should decide when our mother left, not Mian Sahib.

Mom said her mind was made up. She was leaving with us the next day. Our mother knew that the daylong public meeting in the family compound provided us with our one opportunity to get away.

The meeting began early the next morning, but Mian Sahib's men did not come for us. We grew anxious as time slipped by. Finally, men arrived to carry our luggage to the boat. They were late because Uncle Hem had sent an apology to Mian Sahib that begged forgiveness for the family members who had taken advantage of him by asking for favors. Uncle Hem told Mian Sahib that he would take care of his brother's family. There was no need for this hasty departure.

Mian Sahib didn't trust Uncle Hem. He wrote back to our uncle and said that there was no reason for an apology. He was doing what was right for his dear departed friend.

At last, it was time to leave. Decorum had to prevail as we headed from the family estate. Uncle Hem, who was busy conducting his public meeting, could do nothing to keep us from going away. Kumar and I said goodbye to our father's family and walked with Mother to the boat. Only one member of that family betrayed her true feelings. As I left the compound, Auntie Mira waved goodbye and her self-satisfied smile betrayed her contempt for that woman, our grandmother.

~ 5 ~

NEW BEGINNINGS

UNCLE MANINDRA MET US AT the railway station. He told our mother that he would come to visit us in Mymensingh in two weeks after he sorted out her finances. He got us settled in our train compartment, then kissed his sister goodbye.

By evening, we reached the district town of Mymensingh. My mother's sister Beena and her husband Bidhan received us at the railway station. Uncle Bidhan led us to a horse carriage, and we trotted into Mymensingh to their poorly furnished, big old house.

School began in two weeks and Auntie Beena said the competition on the town schools was fierce. We had to find a small house to rent and get enrolled—fast. Our two best options were the over-enrolled private secondary school or the all-male government school. Everyone decided that Kumar and I should take the exam for the government school. We were admitted.

Before we could begin searching for a suitable house to rent, Uncle Manindra arrived. He had sorted out Mom's finances. He told her that if she carefully controlled her expenses, she had enough money to manage. If the stipend from our grandmother material-ized, which we still considered unlikely, our situation would im-prove.

The next morning, we found a small rental that was near our school. It was perfect with two bedrooms, a small living room, and a study. The house also had a courtyard with a magnolia tree that reminded me of the magnolia in my father's garden. We moved into our new home and hired a cook who would cook chicken and lamb for Kumar and me, do all the food shopping, and help our mother with her chores. Mom would prepare her own vegetarian meals.

Our government school was a brick British Colonial building set inside a walled-in compound. I felt safe inside here and import-ant. The school also had two well-furnished hostels, one for Hindus and one for Muslims, and a well-equipped gymnasium and fabu-lous fields set up for football (or soccer), cricket, and field hockey.

Once Kumar and I began school, I loved playing football and cricket. These activities helped me meet other students and I also believed that playing sports taught me the importance of good ca-maraderie.

Kumar, who was a loner, thought that our new school spent too much time and money on sports. He believed sports were hob-bies and he frowned upon students who wanted to play sports pro-fessionally.

After Kumar and I completed our first year at our school, Kumar stood second in his class and received a scholarship. I was the family's embarrassment. Our relatives always felt sorry for our mother. But nothing they said changed my lousy academic perfor-mance. Football, cricket, and even hockey ranked higher than good marks in my mind.

But then, when I was in the seventh grade, everyone gathered at our home when Kumar and I received our examination results. Kumar glowed, enjoying the usual round of congratulations. As I handed my report card to Mom, everyone prepared to let loose with often repeated warnings that I'd end up, not in college, but in vocational school, Mom gasped. I stood first in my class.

Speaking like an oracle, Uncle Bidhan said that he knew I could do it. I soaked in the joy of the moment, and I stood first every year thereafter. Both my brother and I won university scholarships for college.

Once I met Uncle Bidhan, I soon realized his Grandfather Ram had been a powerful influence that molded our uncle's character and life. At age seventeen, Ram, who had already learned Farsi, joined a Christian Mission near Calcutta where he studied the Bible in English, along with mathematics and literature.

He left the mission and went to Calcutta, where British officers were impressed by his enterprise and his knowledge and hired Ram to be the *Munshi* (or secretary of the district in charge of collecting revenue) in Mymensingh and offered him a good salary and benefits.

He ruled efficiently—and with an iron fist, and filled the coffers of the district treasury, which pleased the district magistrate and officials in Calcutta. He also took advantage of a "sunset" clause that allowed properties to be put up for sale if property owners and landowners failed to pay their taxes and rents before sunset fell on the due date. Clever Ram kept the most current list of forfeited properties, and he purchased two of them—a handsome riverfront property with extensive land where he lived and a four-acre property in town for his extended family—before they were listed on the auction block.

Ram became one of the richest, most powerful men in the district. He looked invincible. But all men are mortal and susceptible to disease. At the age of forty-two, he died of cholera, purging, and vomiting until his very last breath.

Ram had left behind only one son, Harinath, who lived in the riverfront country home where he administered the estate. But Ram also had two brothers. Ram had given much more of his holdings to his son. He left no will and this unequal distribution led to family squabbling and bitterness. Ultimately, some relatives poached the son's land to resolve the unfairness, and it turned into a court case. Ram's nephew who was the Nazir or chief clerk of the court manipulated the outcome so that Ram's son, who was Uncle Bidhan's father, lost a big chunk of his land.

Uncle Harinath determined that his son Bidhan had to stay in Mymensingh to protect and regain the family's properties.

When our family arrived in Mymensingh, Uncle Bidhan was an exhausted middle-aged man who was addicted to reclaiming his grandfather's property. He was stuck in the past.

My mother's family also influenced my life. For generations, her family had been extremely well educated—achieving the highest level of Sanskrit education and Sanskrit literary education. They owned very little landed property or financial wealth. For hundreds of years, material wealth was donated to great scholars. Hindu kings gave scholars gifts and scholarships which enabled them to excel as teachers.

But when my mother was a child, times had changed. Hindu kings no longer honored scholars or provided them with money. The highly educated depended on the generosity of rich merchants and landowners. Their poverty created inconveniences and drew ridicule from better-off relatives and friends.

Mom's father Omkarnath realized that his children needed a modern liberal education in an English medium school so they would have modern knowledge to succeed in the modern world.

Grandfather Omkarnath sent all three sons to English medium schools in great financial hardship. All three sons, who were excellent students, earned top scholarships in their schools and continued their studies in colleges and universities. All three had successful careers.

He also sent his daughters to school. But Mother's sister Beena, who only studied through the sixth grade, married Uncle Bidhan who had ended his education after secondary school, which disappointed our grandfather. He waited until our mother completed her secondary education before he allowed her to marry our father, the well-educated, eldest son in a rich family. I suppose it could be said that my grandfather's plan backfired since my father turned his back on his own family's wealth. But he pursued a good job, and this made our grandfather happy.

After our family settled into our new life in Mymensingh we received a registered letter from Uncle Hem. The envelope was sealed with our grandmother's wax insignia. Uncle Hem stated that he was writing on behalf of our grandmother, the chief sevak of Lord Vishnu. Our grandmother regretted informing her daughter-in-law that she and her children were no longer entitled to stipends or benefits from the properties of the Deity. Such stipends and benefits are only given to members of the family who offer their services to Lord Vishnu.

The letter stated that once Mother's two boys turned twenty-one years old, they could present their case to the chief sevak of the estate who would determine if their status should be changed. Uncle Hem concluded the letter by saying our grandmother wished to withhold further comments for now. Uncle Hem signed the letter as the general manager of the estate. Nayeb Babu duly witnessed it. There was no signature from our grandmother.

~ 6 ~

HARD LESSON

SPORTS WERE MY OBSESSION. I played during the day; I dreamt about playing at night. I practiced every day, but Sunday. I longed to get on the school football team to kick the football down our field to score the game-winning goal!

In fifth grade, Amal, who was the son of a bank manager, joined our class. He struggled to make friends, so I befriended him. Amal had played football in his former school and asked if he could play with us. I introduced him to the school drillmaster, who was in charge of sports. He put Amal on our afternoon team, which played football until the school gates locked at 5 o'clock. Soon we became best friends.

That summer the selection committee planned to choose sixteen students from the seventh through tenth grade to be on the football and cricket teams. Bimal, who was a tall muscular tenth grader, was the football team captain. Easily offended, he also had a towering ego.

Some students who were already on the football team warned

us that we'd pay dearly if we got on the wrong side of Captain Bimal. They insisted that he had power over the team selection committee. The committee always listened to the captain's recommendations for the team.

Imagine our relief when this easily offended powerhouse told Amal and me that he wished he had more boys who were willing to work so hard. He would coach us on the hostel grounds after school. We eagerly accepted his help. We wanted to be on that team.

One afternoon when it looked like rain, I skipped practice and went home. Since Amal went home by car, he stayed for the extra practice.

The following day Amal arrived in the classroom. He looked shaken and sat down quietly. I asked him what was wrong. Amal told me that he wasn't going to football practice anymore, and I shouldn't either.

We went to my house after school, and Amal told me that Captain Bimal continued to coach Amal when the rain turned torrential. The two of them got drenched and Amal slipped and was covered in mud.

The captain told Amal to go with him to his hostel and have a shower. He could put on some dry clothes before he went home.

Amal was in the shower when the door flew open, and the captain joined him. Amal was shocked. "Don't worry," he said. "The team always showers together." The captain laughed and soaped himself before he soaped Amal's back. When they left the shower, he grabbed a towel and dried himself and my friend. He smiled and told Amal that getting onto the team was a done deal for him because he was very fond of him.

The captain's arms gripped my friend's body like a vice. He pushed him into his bedroom and face down on the bed. He thrust himself inside. Amal was in horrible pain, but he couldn't move. He felt a spurt of fluid gush into him. The captain released Amal, gave him a dry towel to wipe himself, and tossed him some dry clothes.

Before Amal could run away, Captain Bimal said that these things occurred all the time in sports. He warned Amal that he'd get in trouble if he told anyone what happened. Bimal laughed and added that no one would believe him even if he did open his mouth. Worse, Amal would never get on any team.

Amal felt so dirty that he couldn't look at his mother. She would know that something bad had happened to him.

I was at a loss for words. I felt Amal's pain, his anguish. I also knew that this could have happened to me. I could have been in that shower and pushed onto that bed. We both gave up our dream to be on the team. We both abandoned our goal.

~ ~ ~ ~ ~

I drowned myself in classes and classwork. At the end of the year, my report card again made my mother's family very happy. I stood first place in my class and received a coveted academic scholarship. Occasionally, Amal and I batted around a football but we tried our hardest to bury memories of that incident.

During my final years at this school, other doors opened. Without football and cricket in my life, I had plenty of time to examine our neighborhood and our town. Middle-class Hindu families lived exclusively in our part of Mymensingh. Hindu settlers, who moved from their villages in search of work, were drawn to Mymensingh because of its government offices and commercial establishments that provided employment. Families, who pursued college degrees or acquired important skills and professional training, became doctors, lawyers, teachers, or engineers—gravitating to good professions. They convinced traders from their villages to migrate here. Hindus ended up owning most of the businesses in Mymensingh and most of the real estate. They created rental properties for low-income people.

I always wondered why Muslims refused to embrace changes, which led to discrepancies in education and wealth between our two dominant religious communities. Many people believed that when the British defeated the Moghul Empire, which had ruled for centuries over most of India, the British defeated the deep-rooted pride of Muslim leaders and Mullahs.

Hindus, Christians, and Parsees eagerly accepted the benefits that came with the British. They sent their children to British or Christian missionary schools and colleges. They traded with the East India Company and other private European traders. But Muslims refused to send their children to Western institutions.

Some Muslim leaders realized the folly of this decision. They begged fellow Muslims to embrace these changes so that they could catch up with everyone else. Some mullahs also realized that Muslims needed education to compete in the modernizing world.

Most Muslims still lived in villages, but families slowly migrated into new settlements on the periphery of Mymensingh. But the resettlement of Muslims happened so late that they continued to lag behind the other communities, at least for now. I always believed that over time they would catch up with Hindus.

We lived in Uttar Para at the northern end of Mymensingh where I met some other students from our neighborhood who didn't attend my school. Many of them were politically active. I associated with some political students who supported the Congress Party. I attended some meetings, read books, distributed pamphlets, and-felt pleased with my political growth as I learned about India's political history and its current struggle against British rule.

During this time of my political awakening, the Congress Party faced serious challenges. In 1935 the British granted provincial autonomy and created a quasi-federal government in India, which let them take advantage of their old policy of divide-and-conquer. They also declared that provincial and federal legislatures would compensate Muslims who were in the minority with extra seats in the government.

Muslim leaders, who wanted special treatment for their community, rallied behind Jinnah and pushed the Muslim League to field Muslim candidates, who would dilute the strength of the Congress Party, which claimed to represent all Indian people. The Congress Party leaders realized the British declaration could push apart India's communities and lead to the formation of two separate countries in the subcontinent.

In the 1937 election, the Congress Party won the majority of the seats in the central government. Its inclusive-oriented Muslim candidates defeated secularist Muslim rivals. But in our province of Bengal, a Muslim party won the right to form our provincial government.

Muslim control of our province affected our government school where most students and teachers were Hindu. Muslim ministers in the new provincial government made radical changes to policies that governed education and economic growth. They appointed a qualified Muslim as our new headmaster and appointed a politically active administrative assistant as the new secretary of the school.

Every year our government school awarded scholarships for academic achievement to two students, irrespective of religion, from each class. Local merchants and successful professionals also gave stipends to qualifying government school students. Only the Haji Mohammed Mahashin scholarships were restricted to Muslim students.

Our new Muslim-controlled provincial government decided to encourage Muslim enrollment in our school by creating six new scholarships that were reserved for Muslims at each grade level. Suddenly, Muslim students shifted to our school without taking the school's entrance exam. Luckily, I remained the best student and still received the top academic scholarship.

There were other changes. Our lunchtime kept changing to accommodate the continually shifting time of obligatory Muslim prayer. Teachers were forced to list the number of Muslim students in their class and the number of non-Muslim students. All students had to listen to Muslim religious and political leaders who visited our school.

And things did get personal. A Muslim boy in my class asked if I kept flowers that I received during puja inside my schoolbooks. I showed him some dried marigold petals tucked between some pages. He picked up the petals, dropped them on the ground, and stamped on them as he laughed.

~ 7 ~

AN ERA ENDS

AFTER YEARS OF SILENCE, MY mother received a letter from Uncle Hem. Our grandmother had died. Hem Chandra, who became the chief sevak of Vishnu, asked us to come home to attend the Sradh ceremony. It was our duty as members of the family.

I was a student at the college in Mymensingh and Kumar was studying for his bachelor's degree at a college in Calcutta. We sent him a telegram to come home so that he could go with us to our ancestral village.

When we arrived in the afternoon everyone was busy getting ready for the ceremony. I walked to the memorial grounds to see the small brick and stone mausoleum that was built for my father. I stayed there for a while feeling comfortably close to this dear man. Then I walked to the pond and sat down on a pavilion step. Grandmother was gone. An era had ended with her.

On my way to my bedroom, I saw Amar, one of my cousins who had taunted me years ago. He was a student in the town boarding school and had returned to the ancestral home with his younger brother Manah. Amar and I found Kumar and the three of us went to visit Uncle Hem, who was in mourning in his room.

Uncle Hem launched into a litany of problems threatening the financial wellbeing of our estate. Many tenants had stopped paying their bills after the goddamned Muslim party formed the provincial government.

He also informed us that Tayab Mian was dead, and his son was a good-for-nothing Muslim League leader. "Oh, well," he said. "Our property really belongs to Lord Vishnu, so it's not easy to transfer any titles in our estate. But I'm wasting my time. The three of you don't care."

The day was nearly over, and my mind was spinning. Mian Sahib was gone. Our grandmother was gone. I sat in the bedroom thinking about all the profound changes until it was dinnertime.

The next morning, I went to visit Auntie Mira. She said that she was surprised that our mother had agreed to attend the ceremony.

I said that our mother probably came because our grandmother had cared for Mom like a daughter when she first married our father.

Auntie Mira laughed. She asked me if my mother or that woman told me this. I said that my mother rarely mentioned our grandmother.

Auntie Mira told me that our grandmother was always annoyed that her son's wife had finished secondary education. Grandmother believed that women in her family should never go beyond grade six.

The next morning was the Sradh ceremony. Once again, I got swept up in the powerful Sanskrit rituals. Once again it was a moving event.

KRISHNA DAS RAY

The following morning Tayab Mian's son Kulub came to visit. The nice-looking man, who was in his late twenties, invited my brother and me to his home for an outing. Kumar had arranged to visit some people in the village, including Nayeb Babu. But I accepted the invitation.

As we traveled in an old horse carriage that bumped along a rutted road, Kulub told me that he had already made the greatest mistake that could be made in a lifetime. He discontinued his education after the secondary level.

Once we reached his home and entered the drawing room, I noticed that the well-furnished room needed fresh paint. Kulub said that he couldn't afford to spend any money on his house. I asked him what happened.

He said he was paying for the extravagances of his father and his grandfather. His great-grandfather, who was shrewd and hardworking, acquired a vast property and lots of respect. But his great-grandfather's son and grandson never tried to preserve the family's wealth.

He was in debt to his neck and was desperate to find a way out of his financial mess. He said that if he were well educated, he could go to the provincial capital and achieve any goal with the help of family connections. However, his limited education eliminated this option.

When I suggested that he continue his education, he said that he had attended a third-rate school in the local town and had failed his matriculation exam. He couldn't get into a good college in Calcutta, so he ended his education. If he had known that his family's property was debt-ridden, he would have worked harder in school. He only learned about these debts after his father's death.

I asked him why he went to the local town school. Kulu blamed

45

his father. He asked me if I knew why our fathers who had attended boarding school wouldn't let us go to them. I sensed he knew the answer and waited for him to continue. He said that everyone had always claimed that Catholic boarding schools offered the best education, but no one discussed the other things that happened there.

He reminded me that his father was a good-looking young boy. He recently found out from his mother that his father had carried a shameful secret through most of his life that he had only shared with my father and finally shared with his mother. His father told her that a British schoolteacher had systematically raped him while he boarded at the missionary school.

This terrifying experience made his father sacrifice his son's chance for a good education. He was stricken by his lost opportunity. He insisted that his father could have sent him to a Protestant school, which he believed had high moral standards and provided better supervision of their students.

I asked him why he decided to become the president of the local Muslim League. He said it was his only way to survive. The organization had influence throughout the province. He admitted that the present government party, which he called the party of peasants and laborers, was no good. It could never form a national government, even if Pakistan came into existence.

Kulub was convinced that this party worked against landlords and probably businesspeople. So obviously, he could not join the government; but through his Muslim League contacts, he could get agricultural grants and loans from the government for the development of his land. He had hoped that these benefits would let him repay his loans and get rid of his debts.

I felt sorry for Kulub, but he seemed politically astute. I thought that he would find his way out of this mess. But it was apparent to me that times were changing.

Dusk was approaching. Kulub and I said goodbye.

When I returned to our ancestral home, Kumar was sitting quietly in our bedroom. He said he'd had a difficult day questioning family members about the laws that governed our estate. People insisted that they didn't know the answers to his questions, but he thought that they just didn't want to discuss family matters with him.

Kumar assumed that he would have to wait until he turned 21-years-old and finished law school. Then, he would be armed with enough legal knowledge to get the right to see all these mysterious documents. He would unlock the secrets.

~ 8 ~

DOLLY

ONCE WE RETURNED TO MYMENSINGH, Kumar left for Calcutta, and I immersed myself in my last year at our local college. In 1941 Japan's declaration of war brought World War II closer to India and created a visible shift in our daily lives.

Cities performed Civil Defense Drills and the British recruited soldiers from India. The Indian Railways became busy with war-related transit. The government created the Department of Procurement for Ration Shops and introduced rationing. And while the Central Intelligence Department listened for traitors, we listened to the latest war news from radios that blared through loudspeakers in the cinema houses, public offices, and shops.

One day Uncle Bidhan came to our house to speak privately with my mother. He asked if she would be willing to move into his house when I shifted next year to Calcutta to study pre-med or engineering. He worried about the riots between Hindus and Muslims in Mymensingh and thought she would be safer living with him and her sister.

He was also motivated by his financial situation. His life-long pursuit to get monetary damages for his father's lost properties would not be settled in court for years. He owed lawyers lots of money and the bank loan officer would charge exorbitant interest for another loan. He asked Mom for an interest-free loan, which he promised to repay when the financial settlements finally materialized. In return, he would give her a nice bedroom, den, and kitchen in his house so that she could live in comfort and safety.

Mom told Uncle Bidhan that she needed to consult with Kumar and her two brothers. I contacted Uncle Ashok who came to our house and discussed the offer with us. He thought Mom might be better off living with her sister, but she should ask Bidhan to take out a mortgage on one of his properties to protect her loan.

Uncle Ashok also mentioned that he had received a letter from Bareen, who was their second cousin. He and his wife planned to go on a pilgrimage during the puja holidays. He needed a place for their daughter Dolly to stay while they were away, and they thought that Mom's home would be perfect for her.

Kumar planned to stay in Calcutta during the holidays, so his room would be empty. But Mom was nervous about taking on the responsibility of a young girl. Still, she couldn't refuse her cousin, who had been such a good friend.

Mom heard back from Kumar about Uncle Bidhan's request for a loan. He didn't want her to lend him the money, but for her safety, he would accept her decision to move in with Auntie Beena and Uncle Bidhan. Uncle Manindra arrived and talked with Mom and Uncle Bidhan.

Mom finally agreed to move into Uncle Bidhan's house and to provide the interest-free loan, but she insisted that Uncle Bidhan mortgage one of his properties to secure her money.

Before the Durga Puja season, Bareen and his wife brought Dolly to our home. Uncle Ashok also arrived, and our house was crowded with conversations and guests. When my uncle and Dolly's parents finally left, I joined the young girl and my mother for dinner. Dolly was such an attractive stranger that I ate quickly and rushed back to my book in the den. But I couldn't relax. I listened to the chatter in the other room until I fell asleep.

Early the next morning, I visited a friend and didn't return until late in the afternoon. Mom was sitting in a chair, sewing. Dolly hummed as she leafed through a magazine. Mom asked me to talk with her.

I felt awkward and shy. I steeled my nerves and asked if she would like to go for a walk. Dolly looked at me with her devilish smile. "No thanks," she said in a perky voice. "I'm perfectly fine." She lowered her eyes and buried herself in her silly magazine.

I sought comfort in the den and plopped myself into a chair as I tried to figure out this fifteen-year-old girl. She was pretty, and slim, had gorgeous big eyes, a winsome flirty smile, and a smooth silky complexion. Her appealing looks, especially that devilish smile, made me uncomfortable. Was it because I wasn't used to having a girl staying in the house? I was fifteen — the same age as my cousin; but I was too young to understand this confounding girl.

The next morning, Dolly asked in her sweet innocent voice if I would take her for a walk. When we started along the road, she took hold of my hand. She said that she always held her father's hand when they walked together. "You don't mind, do you?" Dolly flashed her devilish smile. This girl, who had taken over my bedroom, continued to jabber as we leisurely continued our walk.

Mom asked jokingly if our walk had been peaceful. Dolly nodded and looked at me. "The streets weren't so quiet, but this gentleman never spoke a word."

That afternoon Auntie Beena and her two sons came to meet Dolly. Uncle Ashok and Uncle Bidhan arrived and launched into a discussion of our political situation. Uncle Bidhan surprised me when he said that the British should stay in our country. He insisted that Congress *wallahs* and other Indian politicians didn't know how to run a country. He said that his family had acquired all its property because of smart British policies.

Uncle Ashok said quietly that the people of India should form their own government, not foreigners. When Uncle Bidhan began to object, Auntie Beena told him to shush. She had heard enough politics for the day.

A few days later, I took Dolly to my college library. When I offered to sign out some books for her, she surprised me with her choice: *Poems on Various Subjects* by Samuel Coleridge.

On our next outing, I took Dolly to hear the famous sitar player Ustad Bairam Khan play a morning raga at his riverfront villa in Mymensingh. Once we sat down on the lawn, we enjoyed the morning breeze and the red glow of the sun rising above the river as we listened quietly. Nothing disturbed the exquisite melody or rhythm. Dolly leaned against my body and her long hair, and her head rested against my left shoulder. She closed her eyes and looked so happy.

During this recital, we sat with an impressive crowd where nearly everyone was Hindu. Yet everyone appeared to hold this famous Muslim Ustad Bairam in the highest regard at a time when political elements were trying so hard to split our two communities apart. It was wonderful!

The Durga Puja season finally began, and Dolly and I had fun during these days. She prepared a few sweetmeats and sang songs in our home. Whenever we went into the streets to admire the elaborate *pandals* (handmade displays), Dolly held my hand. She needed my protection. The crowds were huge.

Soon, Mom heard from her cousin Bareen and his wife that they were coming in a couple of days for their daughter. That night Dolly asked me to visit her on our verandah. She needed fresh air.

Moonlight glistened on nearby trees and Dolly's pretty face as tears slipped down her cheeks. She asked if I would miss her. I felt a rush of blood as my emotions overwhelmed me. "Miss you? I shall miss you more than anything in the world."

Dolly turned to me and put her arms around me. She pulled my head down and we kissed again and again. Dolly said that she had acted from her heart. We went back inside the house, and she left for her bedroom.

I thought I'd have another private moment with Dolly. But it didn't happen. The night before Dolly was supposed to leave our house, I was unable to sleep. I quietly left the den and saw light coming from Dolly's bedroom. I went to the partially opened door. I heard her singing softly and peeked into the room. Dolly was dancing with a pretty silk scarf in her hands. She was lost in the moment--gently moving and singing sweetly to herself.

I felt guilty for invading Dolly's private world. I tiptoed back to the den and slipped back into bed. As I drifted toward sleep, I was overcome with the feeling that I was dancing with lovely Dolly and our eyes were fixed on each other. I did not know how long we danced, but the next thing I remember was Mom calling me, "Get up, it's late!"

~ 9 ~

CALCUTTA

KUMAR PASSED HIS BACHELOR OF arts examination with honors. He applied to law school and applied for his master's degree in economics at Calcutta University. He was accepted into the programs and decided to pursue both degrees. I was hoping to attend either the government medical college or the government engineering college. But first I had to take some science exams. Only the best applicants would receive an invitation from the selection committee to appear for the oral interviews that determined who made it into the programs.

Arup, the young boy from our ancestral village arrived at our house in Mymensingh. He had been accepted at our district college. I was thrilled for him. College was a brave decision for Arup—and his mother who had hoped her son would continue his education beyond secondary school. I helped Arup find an affordable room near the college campus. He was set.

Arup helped me move my mother into Uncle Bidhan's house. Days later I received word from the Medical College that the selection committee wanted to interview me. Uncle Ashok came to visit me before I left for Calcutta. He was the father figure I needed at this stage in my life. Uncle Ashok told me to always remember my mother. She loved me and had looked after me without expecting anything in return. She would be lonely when I left. Tears collected in my eyes. I knew Mom was not well.

Uncle Ashok told me not to worry about her. He would watch over her. He wanted me to concentrate on doing my best at college. He was certain that I would be successful, not just in school but in my profession. On the day I left for Calcutta, he accompanied me to the train station and settled me in the train compartment. He hugged me and said goodbye.

When I arrived in Calcutta, I crossed the train platform, entered the big hall, and saw Kumar. I was so relieved! The hall was packed with people, including soldiers whose presence reminded me that the long war continued.

Calcutta's streets were jammed with cars, jeeps, city buses, trucks, and electricity-powered trams that ran on tracks. My brother took me to his impressive law college hostel, which was in a compound across the road from the enormous medical college and hospital complex.

For the next few hours, Kumar and I talked in his large room until my mother's cousin Jeevan arrived. He was the doctor whom I had hoped to contact when my father was dying. I planned to stay with him until I went through the selection process. Jeevan told us that he'd return late in the afternoon to take me to his house.

Kumar gave me a tour of his college. We strolled by large colonial buildings, vast playing fields and courtyards, and the famous college square where artists displayed their work. We lingered at sidewalk bookstalls looking through the old and new books before

Kumar took me for lunch at the coffee house where everyone mingled together and enjoyed simple food. My brother said the noise and smoke created the character of this place, which was known for its serious discussions about literature, music, and philosophy.

Soon I was sitting with my cousin Jeevan in his car, heading to his house in Calcutta's suburbs. He was married and he and his wife Leena had one small boy and a girl who were eager to meet me. My cousin's residential neighborhood, which was near the Great Lakes, was quiet compared to noisy downtown Calcutta.

Jeevan came from our mother's village. He had been an excellent student and worked hard in his free time to earn money to supplement the academic scholarships that he had won through merit. When he was in medical college, our father assisted him financially.

The night before my interview, Jeevan advised me to get a good sleep, so I'd be well rested in the morning. But tomorrow's ordeal terrified me. As I lay in bed, the minutes and hours crawled by. Morning arrived like a snail.

My cousin supervised my appearance, so I observed college tradition and wore a shirt and jacket. He advised me to wear pants and one of his ties and tied the knot for me—something else I would have to learn.

The waiting area outside the interview room was crowded with hopeful candidates and bristled with anxiety. The school administrator called my name and accompanied me into the interview room.

When a board member asked me why I wanted to be a doctor, I said that I had lost my father to a stroke when I was eight years old. Doctors, including the civil surgeon, couldn't save him. From that day, I wanted to try to save other lives. I hoped to make a reasonable living if I became a doctor, and I promised to work hard if I was offered the chance.

A British doctor said that I'd given the most sensible answer he'd heard all morning. My nervousness vanished and the interview ended. The worst part of the ordeal was over.

After the final interviews were concluded the committee made its selection. The chairman came out to call out the names of the people who had been selected. I held my breath. I heard my name.

Jeevan sent a telegram to my mother, and he called Kumar. The three of us met in the college common room. The first thing my brother said to me was that he appreciated my success, but it was going to be an expensive five-year undertaking for our family.

My brother was right. Still, it didn't feel good to hear Kumar calculate my college expenses and their effect on the family. No one had questioned him about his college expenses, which were just as costly. Mom had also told us that there was sufficient money in the bank for our education. But I said nothing to Kumar. I made it my goal to get one of the scholarships awarded after our first year to the five best students in each class.

Jeevan excused himself and said that he would pick me up later so I could meet some of the other selected students.

One student made a special effort to meet me. He said his name was Champak, but people called him Champ. His father was a well-regarded professor at a private college, but his pockets weren't deep. Champ needed to find an inexpensive hostel close to the college.

I remembered Kumar's unfair words. I told Champ that I also needed an inexpensive place to live.

We found out about a Hindu hostel that was near the college complex and close to the Esplanade and Maidan. The rooms were sunny and clean, and a doctor from the college hospital collected the rent and acted as a liaison officer between the college authorities and the management committee, which was elected annually by the students and prepared the annual budget for projected expenses. The students in this hostel also determined the meals that they ate each day, which was a plus!

This hostel was so popular, that Champ and I signed up immediately. I was also relieved to learn that we could move into our room in three days. I was in medical college. I had an inexpensive new home. I had my first medical school friend—Champ. It was 1932. I was eighteen-years-old, and life felt good.

~ ~ ~ ~ ~

I began my first year at medical college in the Department of Anatomy with osteology, which is the study of bones. In this course, we had to learn how bones, muscles, fascia, and ligaments worked and how they were attached to the body. Once we learned about a part of the body, we were supposed to dissect it.

But finding human bodies to dissect had turned difficult. Our department had orderlies called domes, who were lower-class Hindus permitted to handle dead bodies, and the department also had some funds to purchase them legally, but legal bodies were in short supply. Every year the domes struggled to collect enough unclaimed bodies from the hospital morgue for use in the anatomy department, but they faced fierce competition. Religious organizations also wanted the dead so that they could bury or cremate them, as per their religious traditions.

Since Hindus cremated their dead, some domes began digging up fresh bodies from Muslim burial grounds under the cover of darkness. But Muslim organizations stopped the defiling of Muslim graves. Still, these burial thefts continued. It became a lucrative Muslim monopoly that drove up the price of each body.

Medical students also needed to buy a bag of bones. We could buy them commercially, but most of us purchased them half-price from the domes who cleaned, boiled, and bleached the bones before packing them into a bag.

My coursework consumed me. But some evenings and weekends I explored the Maidan, Eden Gardens, and Curzon Park or I walked to Victoria Memorial and its gardens and studied these contributions to the city from the British Empire. At night I always had to return to the hostel before dark. Partial blackouts were in force because of the war.

During this first year at medical college, I missed going to public libraries and reading books on philosophy, literature, and history. I spent all my time studying medicine, so I lost the part of my life that had inspired me. But my heart still belonged to the books that Uncle Ashok had recommended — books that focused on the mysterious aspects of life that kept me spiritually content.

Six months into my first year of medical college, I received a sad letter from my mother about Uncle Bidhan's youngest son, Satchidananada. Uncle Bidhan had forced him to leave college for a while and sent him to live at the family's riverfront property to keep an eye on all the employees and watch over his frail grandmother.

When the grandmother passed away, Satchidananada wanted to go back to Mymensingh and continue his studies, but Uncle Bidhan told his son that he had to stay and fulfill his duty to the family and manage the complex estate.

He often traveled with some faithful employees to different areas of the extensive estate, where he met with village heads and worked hard to settle disputes over rent and taxes. During one of these village visits, he complained of abdominal pain and began to vomit. The village doctor, who had never attended medical school, said he had cholera and treated him. Nothing he did worked, and he died that night.

The doctor's diagnosis was right, but his treatment was flawed. Satchidananada had died of dehydration, which was a common complication. As I read Mom's letter, I thought how ironic. Uncle Bidhan's grandfather, the Munshi, had died of the same terrible disease.

Auntie Beena and Uncle Bidhan were devastated

~ 10 ~

FAMILY WOES

MY MOTHER'S COUSIN MALATI LIVED in South Calcutta with her husband Umesh, a well-known professor of philosophy at the Presidency College. They asked me to come visit them. I took the tram and got off near a handsome three-story house. A servant opened the door and led me upstairs to the first-floor lobby. Auntie Malati took me into a large airy room where Uncle Umesh sat around a teak table chatting with a group of friends while they enjoyed cold drinks and savory sweetmeats.

Uncle Umesh, who had suffered a stroke, received a good pension from the government. Many Brahmin Pandit families, including Umesh's family, struggled with poverty; but Uncle Umesh was extremely bright, and his family's poverty drove him to succeed. He became a successful professor and businessman. He amassed a fortune.

Uncle Umesh told his friends that my young mind would be a good addition to their discussion about the current war and the Muslim League's recent Lahore Resolution that called for the division of the subcontinent into Pakistan and India.

For much of the time I participated in a lively conversation with Professor Ghose, who was one of my uncle's friends. Professor Ghose supported Hitler and believed that this dictator could make our nation great again. He considered these Aryans our natural allies and reminded me that Germany had adopted our ancient Aryan symbol of the Swastika for their national emblem.

The professor's opinions astonished me, and we argued back and forth until Uncle Umesh winked at me.

Later when the visitors had left the house, Uncle Umesh said that he felt sorry for Professor Ghose. Normally people never questioned him, but today I took him on.

It was late and Auntie Malati told me to spend the night. During dinner, I met most of her grown children. Her married daughter lived with her husband, but all four boys still lived in the house.

After a lovely meal, I went to my bedroom and walked out to the moonlit balcony. I remembered my pleasant evening with Dolly on our verandah back in Mymensingh. I looked at the moon hoping for a message. But I received nothing. I went inside and slipped into bed. I fell asleep dreaming about Dolly.

When I got back to school, I received a letter from Uncle Ashok who told me that Mymensingh's district board and town hall were each awarding a scholarship to medical students from the district. He encouraged me to apply and included the applications. I also needed a professor's recommendation.

The next day I met with Dr. Sinha, the professor of anatomy, who was also from our district. He wrote a reference for me, but he told me not to have high hopes for either scholarship. They were never awarded on merit. The people on these boards gave them the sons of cronies so that they held on to power. I posted the applications to Uncle Ashok and hoped against hope.

After I took my exams, I went home to see Mom who was so glad to see me. I'd been away a year and everyone in that home still grieved over the loss of Satchidananada. Uncle Bidhan walked with a stoop and his face was joyless. Auntie Beena had also aged.

That evening, I had tea with my cousin Sadananda, Uncle Bidhan's oldest son, and his young wife Meena who lived in another part of Uncle Bidhan's house. I wondered why neither Sadananda nor Meena had a sparkle in their young eyes. They'd been married only 10 months.

I told Mom that everyone was so morose that it must be difficult for her to live here. Mom said it was harder for them than for her. Her voice sounded weak and tired. I studied her carefully. I noticed that she looked unwell.

Uncle Ashok arrived later that evening and I finally saw my first genuine smile. He said that he had submitted my scholarship applications. He had talked to a couple of people on my behalf at the town hall and Uncle Bidhan had promised to talk to a few members of the district board.

I told him that I was worried about Uncle Bidhan and his family. Uncle Ashok said that he felt that Bidhan was realizing that his dream to restore his grandfather's legacy would fail. He also thought Bidhan worried about India's communal problems and feared that possibly all Hindus would have no future in this part of the country. Poor Bidhan would have lost not just his beloved son but also his beloved estate.

Later I went to talk with Meena. I told her that her husband seemed depressed, and I offered my help. Meena said that she thought that Sadananda had been envious of his younger brother who had been an extravert and loved life. Meena said that she was a lot like Satchidananada and had always enjoyed his company. Her husband had become suspicious and finally suspected an intimate relationship, even though nothing had happened. Still, her husband had accused her of infidelity. Uncle Bidhan had sent Satchidananda to the ancestral home for a year to resolve the friction that resulted in his death. As I listened to Meena, I felt so sad for everyone in Uncle Bidhan's family. The loss of their beloved son had drained the joy from everyone.

The next morning, I strolled along the river. I needed to think, and the river always soothed me. When I returned home, I asked Mom about her health. She admitted that she occasionally felt palpitations and shortness of breath when she walked for a long time.

I went to a reputable physician's office and told my name to a reluctant receptionist. I added that I was a student at the medical college in Calcutta. I explained that my mother was having heart problems. She needed expert medical advice before I went back to school.

The receptionist said that the doctor had attended the same college. She told me to sit in the waiting room. When the doctor came out of his office, he asked me about college and its hospitals before he finally asked me about my mother.

I told him that I was worried about her heart and that I wanted her to be in competent hands before I left for Calcutta. The doctor came to see my mother early the next morning. He asked everyone to stay outside her bedroom except Auntie Beena. He finally called us in. He reminded us that my mother had suffered from rheumatic fever as a child. The illness had affected her heart.

One valve of Mom's heart was compromised, and another valve could deteriorate over time. If her lesions worsened, fluid

could collect in her legs and abdomen, and she could have congestive cardiac failure. Already, my mom had a small amount of fluid
collecting around her ankles. She also had atrial fibrillation, which
could produce cardiac failure if it wasn't treated properly.

The doctor prescribed Digitalis, but he said that the drug was
scarce because of the war. It was shipped to India from the United Kingdom and the United States. If the swelling spread, Mom
would also need diuretics. The doctor assured me that he would be
available day and night. He also wanted my mom to visit him each
month for a check-up.

I walked the doctor to the front door and asked him his fee
for the visit. He patted my shoulder and told me not to worry. He'd
not forgotten his student days and the fact that his parents weren't
rich. I felt so grateful to this doctor, but I also felt a sudden and unexpected fear for Mom.

~ ~ ~ ~ ~

Arup, the young college student from our ancestral village, came
to see me while I visited with my mother. He had finished his first
year, but he had to give up his college studies. His mother was very
ill, and he had to care for her. She also needed their money to pay
for her remaining days.

Arup assumed that at some point he would need to search for
work in Mymensingh or, more likely, in Calcutta, which probably
offered better jobs. He hoped I would help him if he needed to come
to Calcutta.

I invited Arup to go hear Ustad Bairam Khan play ragas at
his riverside villa. I thought that it would cheer him up. Early the
next morning Arup and I walked to the riverfront villa. The sky was

clear, and the trees and shrubs looked vivid against the river.

As Arup and I sat on the grass, I noticed the crowd was smaller than usual.

The two of us relaxed and listened as the tabla player added his hypnotic rhythms to Ustad Bairam's haunting raga. We became absorbed in the music until someone shouted, "Allahu Akbar."

Heads turned toward the compound entrance where a group of men with knives and sticks were trying to get into the grounds. The guard slammed shut the compound gates. We Hindus who were listening to the music were terrified as the men kept repeating their religious cry and argued defiantly with the guard.

Ustad Bairam and his tabla player stopped their music and went to the gate. Ustad told the men that the young people in the audience, who were not politicians or religious bigots, had come to enjoy the music that was played by Muslims. The audience showered them with respect.

The Muslim men said that no infidel was leaving the compound alive.

Ustad Bairam said that they would have to kill him first.

The Muslims said the Ustad was Shia—the friend of the infidels. Only his fame as a well-respected sitar player kept them from taking his life. The angry men shouted "Allahu Akbar" as they started to scale the wall and climb the gate.

Guards from surrounding mansions raced to the villa. They drew their guns and fired into the air. The pack of knife-wielding men decided against martyrdom and ran away. The audience, including Arup and I, rushed from the compound and the neighborhood. When we finally felt safe, we slowed down and continued home—in silence—consumed by despair.

The next morning, I went with Uncle Bidhan to check the

status of the Sonapur estate at the taxation and revenue office. We were shocked to learn that the land tax on this estate, which was recorded separately from the rest of the riverfront estate, had not been paid. The government had appropriated the property. It would be sold at auction.

Uncle Bidhan knew that it would take years and much money to reverse this government appropriation. He decided to see his cousin Jadunath, who was the current Nazir of the civil court. He had the authority to resolve this problem without litigation.

With tears in his eyes, Uncle Bidhan told his cousin the reason for his visit. By the time he finished telling his story, he looked like a broken man.

Jadunath was sympathetic. He was convinced that someone had betrayed Bidhan. He promised to find a way to nullify the government's action. The property would not go to auction.

Jadunath asked the head clerk in the revenue office to bring out some files. After carefully reviewing them, he asked the head clerk to help him unravel the mystery. Thirty minutes later they told Uncle Bidhan that a couple of his estate officers had withheld the payment of the annual land tax to the government. The property had originally belonged to the Mirza family who had first tried to get the property when Satchidananada was alive, but Bidhan's son had foiled their efforts when he went to Sanupar. The Nazir believed that estate officers who were working for the Mirza family had withheld the money.

Uncle Bidhan had always wondered how his boy had come down with infectious cholera. Satchidananada had always been so careful about his food and drinks. He had wondered if someone had tampered with his son's food.

All these disclosures stunned Uncle Bidhan. The head clerk

searched the files and discovered that Bidhan's estate had never been notified about the upcoming auction of his land; therefore, the government could not sell the property.

But Uncle Bidhan had to pay all the back taxes before the end of the day so that the cashier could enter the full payment in the register on this date. The head clerk told the Nazir and Uncle Bidhan that their meeting and their findings had to be kept secret; he believed a collaborator was working in the revenue office.

My uncle was still worried. Where could he get this amount of money before the end of the day? He asked if I thought my mother would write a bank check to protect him. I thought that she would. He hailed a horse carriage, and we raced home.

Mom wrote the check, and we took the horse carriage back to the revenue office. Within minutes the head clerk gave Uncle Bidhan an official receipt that stated his property had no outstanding taxes.

Uncle Bidhan and I knew the date of the intended auction of the Sonapur property. We were also the only ones who knew that the sale had been canceled. A couple of days after the once-scheduled auction, Naresh, the chief officer of Uncle Bidhan's entire estate, came to see Uncle Bidhan. He cried as he told Uncle Bidhan that he suspected someone from his office had conspired with the Mirzas to seize the Sonapur property. Uncle Bidhan quietly asked him to explain his suspicions.

Naresh said that he'd heard a rumor from the Mirza family that Sonapur was auctioned for default by the revenue office. He couldn't imagine how this happened since his office always paid the taxes. He was upset that Bidhan had lost a valuable property with no way of getting it back.

Uncle Bidhan asked Naresh if he was certain that his office had paid all the taxes for the current year. The chief officer said yes;

they had been paid.

Uncle Bidhan informed his chief officer that his answer was not correct. He told Naresh that last year Satchidanada had discovered that the taxes were in default and had arranged for their payment. He had gone to Sonapur to investigate.

Uncle Bidhan asked Naresh if he knew how Satchidanada had contracted the deadly cholera during his visit. He asked if the servants had boiled the water before they offered any drinks to his son. The chief officer said he didn't know. The servants had been newly recruited. They didn't always follow the rules.

My uncle asked his chief officer again if he was certain that his office had paid the taxes this year.

The chief officer was adamant that no such error could have occurred. But something had gone wrong, and he was sorry for Uncle Bidhan's loss.

Uncle Bidhan told his chief officer to go home. There were important tasks for him to do at the estate office. My uncle said he would try to find out about the horrible auction. After the chief officer left the house, Uncle Bidhan said that he had just spoken with the person who was at the root of this mischief.

~ 11 ~

BENGAL'S GREAT FAMINE

THE NEXT DAY I LEFT with a heavy heart for Calcutta. I worried about Mom. I felt sorry for Uncle Bidhan and his daughter-in-law Meena, and I had a deep longing for Uncle Ashok's company in Calcutta.

While we medical students waited for the results of our annual exam, I kept busy helping Champ canvas for a position on the Student's Union Executive Committee. I also discovered that my cousin Jeevan had changed jobs. He had been appointed the Director of Public Health for the provincial government. His new position, which provided a jeep and driver, demanded lots of travel throughout Bengal to inspect and advise local health departments.

Jeevan's new job forced him to surrender his dream to be both the Director of the Health Institute and the Professor of Hygiene at the Medical College. But, as the father of three children, he probably needed to be practical. His new position gave him a significant pay raise. He would make more money than a family physician.

One afternoon I received a letter from Uncle Ashok. I didn't win either scholarship. He told me that the successful applicants had influential friends in high positions. Professor Sinha had been right.

One night Champ told me that he had heard our examination results would be posted the next morning. By 9:30 am I was in the common room along with a crowd of other students. I was stunned when I saw the results. I was one of five students who won a scholarship for the next year.

Champ, who received good marks in two subjects, did poorly in everything else. He grew suspicious. He said I got the other questions from someone else, and I had failed to share them with him. I insisted he was wrong. But Champ turned against me and told everyone I was untrustworthy.

I changed roommates the next month. Meanwhile, Champ was elected to the Student's Union Executive Committee. He had discarded my friendship, but I had kept my promise and had canvassed on his behalf.

In the second year of medical college, we all worked hard and became accustomed to hands that reeked from bleached human bones. I lived with the odor and immersed myself in my studies.

Meanwhile, the war raged, and European, British, and American troops arrived in Calcutta. Unrest between Hindus and Muslims also escalated. The British government established the Cripps Mission and its members, who came to India, offered India dominion status in March 1942 saying that this status would be implemented at the end of the war. But India's National Congress Party and the Muslim League rejected the British offer.

In August of 1942, the Congress Party passed the "Quit India" resolution that demanded an immediate end to British rule. The British refused the demand. Widespread civil disorder and violent disturbances erupted in the fall of 1942. The British government sent out the police and the military, which used excessive firepower, including aerial bombardments, to suppress the violence. The British forces killed and injured thousands of people and imprisoned the Congress Party leaders, including Gandhi. The people of India were outraged.

The Bengali leader Subhas Bose, who had secretly moved to Germany, went to Burma and formed the Indian National Army, which received help from the Japanese and the Germans. His fledgling army included Indian prisoners of war and deserters from the Indian army along with Indian volunteers.

Bose's Indian National Army planned to defeat the British forces in Burma and Assam before they marched victoriously into the heartland of India. He claimed Indian soldiers would abandon the British and join his rebel forces.

Our national leaders, including Nehru and Patel, opposed Bose's plan and his alliance with the German dictator and Japan's imperials. They told his rebel forces to stay out of India. But Bose's dedicated followers said that they would support their charismatic leader even if he made a pact with the devil.

Then suddenly everyone stopped talking about Bose. We were unexpectedly thrown into a living nightmare called the Bengal Famine of 1942 and 1943.

Famines, which were normally the result of crop failure, often occurred in parts of Bengal during droughts and flooding. Since many parts of Bengal produced two annual crops, the government usually responded effectively and delivered food to help people get through a shortage until the next harvest.

This famine was radically different. The British government knew that other areas of the province had enough food to feed the Bengalis who suffered. But rich grain merchants, who were friendly with the government, hoarded their stockpiles and waited for prices to soar.

The British were also preoccupied by recent events of the war. The Japanese had just defeated the British forces in Hong Kong and Singapore and the British worried about a new Japanese offensive along Bengali's eastern coast. They knew that Bengalis were already strongly anti-British, and they rightly assumed that the British lack of action to resolve the food shortage had turned any remaining compassion against them. So the British acted in its own interest. The government quickly confiscated every boat from the Bengali coastline and every truck and bullock cart. They would let no one help the Japanese.

These appropriations prevented merchants from delivering food and grain from their warehouses to the hungry villagers. As Bengalis starved and died, long columns of weak Bengalis abandoned their homes and began desperate and hideous walks to Calcutta. Many unfortunate souls died on the road and many who made it to a town, or a city were too sick to survive.

Volunteer organizations had built shelters and opened soup kitchens, shaming local governments into making an effort to feed and care for these people, but the government effort was too small and came too late. While the British government insisted the famine was a result of crop failure, Bengalis knew that willful neglect caused two to four million people to die from starvation and disease.

How was it, I wondered, that our twentieth-century government never tried to prevent this catastrophe? Britain claimed it was one of the most democratic countries in the world. Would our foreign rulers allow this to happen to their own people back in Britain? I remembered that they had allowed the starvation and death of people in British-controlled Ireland. It seemed the principles of democracy existed only for the British.

Calcutta reeled from the famine. The railway station became an unintended refuge for the starving and so did every shelter, road, and empty lane. Many of these people contracted infectious diseases and suffered miserable deaths.

The dead and dying littered the streets. There were too few municipal workers to cart away the bodies for mass burials or mass cremations. A paucity of medical facilities and a shortage of basic drugs also made it impossible to save lives or reduce the suffering.

We Indians, who had no say in the matters of war and peace, had to accept the consequences. Not only the poor suffered. Average middle-class Indians had to live with rations and much of the available food in rationing shops was substandard. Employees often added gravel to rice, powdered stones to flour, and inedible oils to cooking oil to cheat customers. The middle class was forced to go to the outrageously overpriced black market run by greedy merchants. Non-government agencies struggled to get the basic grains and pulses that were at the heart of the Bengali diet.

The increasing size of the military also contributed to the woes of the starving. Soldiers and sailors, who served on the frontiers, needed food. These men remained the government's priority.

The Japanese also bombed Calcutta and nearby docks. One night an explosion near our hostel shattered our sleep. Black smoke poured from a house close to our building. Buildings were destroyed. Neighbors were killed. Unruly mobs set army trucks on fire and stoned police and soldiers. The soldiers retaliated and shot people before our eyes. Clashes between Hindus and Muslims caused more injuries and deaths.

I walked along the streets to the Calcutta railway station. I volunteered for non-governmental organizations and treated the starving and the weak. In the evenings many of us students listened to German and Japanese shortwave broadcasts. We listened to the All India Radio and the BBC. They all spouted propaganda.

One day I received a letter from Mom. Haribhai had died. He had been demonstrating in front of the magistrate's office in the town of Karimganj, protesting British rule and calling for India's independence. He was shot to death. Poor Haribhai was unarmed.

He had never spent the money my father left for him. Over the years, the accumulating interest had doubled the amount of money in his account. Haribhai had established a trust called "Milk for Children" in memory of our father. He had collected money for this trust and arranged to have all his assets transferred to the trust upon his death.

I mourned the loss of Haribhai—a decent man who died with honor for his country.

~ 12 ~

CHANGE IN THE AIR

ARUP WROTE ME A LETTER to say that he was coming to Calcutta to look for a job. I went to the train station to meet him. I couldn't imagine him negotiating Calcutta during this tortured time of famine and war.

He was overwhelmed the moment he stepped from the train into the station. All he saw were the starving and dying. He told me our Uncle Hem was donating grain to the poor, who were predominately Muslim, so even the poorest villages attached to the ancestral estate had food. No one was suffering.

I discussed Arup's situation with the managing committee at our hostel and the committee agreed to let him stay with me as long as my roommate agreed, and I supplied all of his food. So Arup stayed in our bedroom.

He talked about the village and said that Hindus were beginning to worry about their future. He had also visited with my mother before leaving for Calcutta. He thought that she looked healthy.

Arup found a job working as a procurement supervisor in a

ration office and the interviewing officer told him that his job might extend beyond the war. He had also found a small room near the ration shop, which eliminated the cost of transportation.

On Saturday morning, Arup and I volunteered at a huge relief area under a canopy in front of a popular Kali temple. We joined about 60 volunteers who were trying to feed and nurse nearly 100 starving village refugees. It was a monumental scene of human suffering.

A local volunteer said that fifty people had died in two days. So many of the starving were skin-covered skeletons and unable to swallow water. A young woman sat on a mat coaxing her listless infant to suck her breast, which looked like an empty pouch of skin. A nurse examined the baby. She gently told the woman that her baby was dead. She asked if she could take it away. The young mother lacked the strength to speak, but she refused to give up her baby.

I immersed myself in my duties and worked like a machine without emotion. Arup was overwhelmed. He raced outside and stayed in the fresh air until he could calm down his emotions.

Later, I checked on the young mother and her dead baby. Two men had arrived with an improvised stretcher. The woman had died. No one was there to comfort her; no one shed any tears for her or her baby.

Arup and I returned to the hostel. I ate very little supper and went to bed. The faces of the young mother and her baby haunted me. Maybe a year ago she was newly married, happy and healthy, expecting her baby. Maybe she never knew about the war and how the British had prevented the transport of food to her village.

Soon we medical students were busy studying for new exams. But Japanese planes continued to bomb Calcutta, and another bomb hit a nearby building killing some people and injuring others.

This year's written and oral exams were exhausting and this time I received no help from Champ. I planned to stay in Calcutta until I received my test results, but Uncle Ashok sent me an upsetting letter. Mom was sick again—experiencing palpitations and swelling in her legs and abdomen. He wrote that Digitalis was unavailable in Mymensingh. He needed me to get the medicine in Calcutta and get home with it as soon as possible.

I went to several drugstores, but no one had the medicine. Desperate, I went to the college hospital pharmacist. He gave me his personal card on which he wrote my name and the address of a druggist who had a shop in a building filled with numerous small pharmacies that sold medicines at black market prices.

The druggist was in a risky part of Calcutta, so I asked Arup to go with me. The pharmacist scrutinized the personal card before he said that unfortunately, I needed a hard-to-find drug that was expensive. He only sold it to people who were introduced to him by trustworthy pharmacists. He offered me two bottles of Digitalis and I paid him his exorbitant price.

On the way to the hostel, Arup said the guy told me a pack of lies. Everyone was taking advantage of every shortage. He said that he had been transferred to a new office that procured food for the army. They used novel ways to make money off gifts that came to foreign soldiers. They created fake invoices and sold some of these gifts of food and clothing. When I asked Arup if he was involved in the scam, he said that he was a small fry. But I wondered if Arup knew about this corruption before he took the new job.

~ ~ ~ ~ ~

I took the next available train to Mymensingh. Mom was in bed when I arrived home. Her swelling had gone down, but she still had palpitations.

I told the doctor that I had obtained some Digitalis on the black market. He was disgusted that we were at the mercy of greed.

Luckily, I found a Brahmin widow who was willing to stay in our house and look after Mom, an arrangement that pleased both of them. During the day I sat with Mom and Uncle Ashok came in the evenings. I also visited with my cousin Sadananda and his wife Meena. They had a lovely new baby, but I still failed to detect any warmth in their relationship.

One night while I was staying with Mom, I woke up to frightening shouts of "Allahu Akbar." Everyone raced outside as police cars, sirens wailing, and jeeps and vans with more police sped down the street toward the edge of town. The chief magistrate and his senior officers followed in their cars; so did a truck filled with armed soldiers. The shouts of Allahu Akbar wrenched the air for over an hour.

We were frightened and feared the worst until the police officers returned and told everyone to go back inside. Everything was all right.

The next morning, we heard that religious and political Muslim leaders had told Muslims in nearby villages that Hindus had killed a pig, which was a sacrilege, inside the main Mymensingh mosque before they destroyed the shrine. They also told them that Hindus were in the process of destroying a second mosque. They asked Muslims to go kill Hindus in Mymensingh. Muslims from these neighboring villages had gathered at the edge of Mymensingh ready for Jihad and their great revenge.

The magistrate had enlisted the help of influential Muslim leaders and the Imam (religious leader) of the supposedly destroyed mosque. They stopped the Muslims who were prepared to march into our town. The Imam told the Muslims that the mosques were undamaged and undefiled. The Imam gave the crowd a fatwa (religious ruling) to go back home. Before the crowd retreated, the Imam asked all Muslims to be ready to serve Allah if they ever got a call from him or from the president of the Muslim League in the future. They should not listen to anyone else.

The next morning Uncle Bidhan insisted that if the British officers hadn't been in Mymensingh, Muslims would have killed all the Hindus. He worried about these conflicts and asked me how he could protect his family.

I told him I thought it would be unwise to let anyone know he was afraid to live here. But I suggested he sell a few prime properties that were far from Mymensingh.

I also told him that I believed that all of East Bengal would go to Pakistan in a few years. If he could sell enough land to build a house in Calcutta or any Calcutta suburb, he would have a valuable asset if they lost their family estate. I advised him not to wait to sell his land after the creation of Pakistan. No one would buy property from Hindus. I also told him to put the Calcutta home in Auntie Beena's name, so that the property would provide her with financial security when she was older.

The next day as I walked in our neighborhood. I sensed the shift that was taking place everywhere. People understood intuitively that something profound was happening. I walked along the lovely river, but I stayed near the senior service quarters where I knew I was safe. I took comfort in knowing that Mom was recovering. This was a sliver of good news. But the time had come for me to return to Calcutta.

~ 13 ~

THE WAR ENDS

I DID WELL ON MY medical exam. I kept my scholarship. I told Kumar the good news about our mom and my renewed scholarship, but he soured my mood. He warned me that I must never again allow a gap in Mom's treatment. He was also annoyed that I'd convinced her to give Uncle Bidhan a check to solve his tax problem.

Kumar told me about his new friendship with a law student named Alok whose family lived about ten miles from our ancestral estate. He said Alok's father Jagdish, who was a lawyer, knew that we owned good agricultural land near their property.

He also knew that Alok's family had been considered our family's enemy, but he appreciated this new friendship. Alok and his father were going to help Kumar get some information about our family estate and our family's other properties in the district. Kumar worried that our father's family could lose the estate and all its land if the district became part of Pakistan.

I hoped my brother's new friends were honest. I didn't want them getting their hands on our land. But I also felt that Kumar's concerns were realistic. We could lose everything if the district was swallowed into the new country of Pakistan. If my brother could sell some land with the help of his friends, it could help the entire family.

A few days later I heard that Arup's mother was very sick and wanted him to come home. He took a leave from his job and went home immediately. This young man from the village had developed such self-confidence. He had also turned debonair—with his nice haircut and fashionable clothing that included a silk scarf tied elegantly around his neck. He'd changed so much.

The next day Arup and I bought two more bottles of Digitalis from the greedy pharmacist, and he would deliver them to my mom on his way home to our ancestral village.

In my third year of medical college, I started clinical medicine. The new students sat with all the medical students in the third through fifth years of study in a big auditorium and listened to each lecture. There was no such thing as an introductory lecture. We had to sink or swim.

We also had our first contact with patients when we split into small groups and made clinical rounds with our professors and other consultants in the hospital wards. We rarely received any individual attention from our professor, and we often struggled to hear him or understand his British accent as he explained a patient's problem and treatment. We straggled behind the sister on the ward, who pushed a trolley with the patients' records, the senior registrar (resident), middle registrar, junior registrar, senior houseman (intern) and two junior housemen, and members of the consulting staff. Luckily for us, the consultants, who were usually Indian doctors, were less formal than our professor of clinical medicine. We could freely interact with them.

Once weekly, our professor also held a clinical session where he would stand by a bedridden patient and discuss the medical issue. He would grill us and demonstrate the proper way to examine a patient suffering from a specific condition. Unfortunately, these valuable sessions were rare.

Since our school followed the British teaching system, we continued learning the basics of medical science from the registrars in their tutorial classes. We also soaked in knowledge from books, and we searched for sympathetic consultants, who agreed to help us.

Patients in the paying wards didn't want medical students poking at their bodies. However, if our assigned patient was cooperative, we were fortunate because paying patients were normally able to describe their symptoms and tests. The general ward patients were often illiterate and couldn't explain or even identify their ailment.

We also had to be careful not to interfere with the work of the nurses, who were typically Anglo-Indians, although the superintendent of nurses and the sister tutors were British. Most nurses were highly intelligent and efficient, but they disliked us because we often slowed down their work.

Nursing orderlies and servants, who were at the bottom of the employment ladder, did muscle jobs and dirty jobs, such as looking after bedpans. These employees, who generally came from Bihar and Eastern Uttar Pradesh, worked hard for their meager salaries. In keeping with the British tradition, these orderlies and servants were called "coolies" (or laborers). Their work was critical to the hospital staff; yet much to my disgust, the hospital authorities failed to appreciate their value and never tried to improve their pay or working conditions.

~ ~ ~ ~ ~

In 1944, two students, who were card-carrying members of the Communist Party, joined our hostel. Their party had gained popularity in India. Many educated Bengalis appreciated the courage of the Soviet Union army when it fought against Nazi Germany. They were aware that the Russian Communist Party was committed to integrating people of all ethnicities and religions, including Muslims, into their "Patriotic War."

Socially conscious Indians believed these same positive changes could occur in India, without the evils of capitalism that came with the British—evils that harmed the poor. Many people in India were tired of greedy Congress Party elites who poorly managed provincial governments.

Communists, who hoped to turn this large disgruntled, educated middle class into communists or communist sympathizers, installed two communist students into every student hostel. These card carriers, including the two well-mannered and academically strong students who moved into our hostel, began to quietly introduce their doctrine to us.

On June 6, D-Day, we hung around our roof and listened to the radio. I kept a record of the advance of British and American troops once they landed on the shores of Normandy. I wanted to determine the accuracy of the announcements on the BBC and Voice of America. I tallied the mileage. The troops should have made it beyond Russia, but they had just crossed the Rhine River. No one else, it seemed, kept track of this nonsense.

The Japanese claimed that they were winning on the Assam front. According to their radio bulletins, they should have reached the province of Bengal. However, students in the hostel were receiving letters from Assam that mentioned nothing about the Japanese land invasion. They wrote about occasional bombings by Japanese planes, nothing more.

Every morning the Communist Party delivered free newspapers to our hostel that reported local news and news from the European and Japanese fronts. Both of these communist papers slyly claimed that this war between colonial powers had become the People's War. With great effort and sacrifice, the Russians stopped the Germans and forced them to retreat from the Caucasus.

One day I asked one of our card carriers if he could get me an English translation of Marx's *Das Kapital* and a biography of Lenin. He gave them to me the next day. Communist literature regularly arrived in my bedroom. I never doubted who left them, but this student never discussed the books with me. The party's indoctrination was subtle.

The Communist Party of India invited students from our hostel to a meeting to discuss India's economy. The party leaders who came from Hindu and Muslim communities used an engaging style to present their history of the Indian economy. They discussed how our foreign rulers used their leverage to get the dynasties of Nizams and maharajas and other princes of the so-called independent Indian states to accept the sovereignty of the British Emperor, who often ruled against the interests of ordinary Indians.

They admitted that the British introduced Western education and health services, but they also flooded India with cheap products manufactured in their industrialized economy that made our handmade products uncompetitive, especially since the British levied higher taxes on Indian-made goods. The leaders said that our situation was probably worse than the situation in Russia before its Bolshevik Revolution.

I went to more meetings but over time, the Communist Party's expectations turned specific. To participate in the People's War, we people were expected to give the party money and labor. A few students did become Communist Party members and signed up for specific tasks. A few other students, such as I, were sympathetic to the cause, but we only helped from time to time.

I also continued to listen regularly to the radio on our roof. The Allies, who were engaged in fierce fights with the Germans and Japanese, defeated Italy by the middle of the year. De Gaulle had entered Paris, and the Russians had conquered Hungary. The Americans finally captured Manila. Then, at the start of 1945, the British overwhelmed the Japanese army in Burma and the Americans used their submarines and air power to crush the Japanese navy.

One morning, the war came perilously close to us in Calcutta. I was examining a patient when I heard a loud boom. I raced outside with some nurses and an orderly and we saw an air force plane in flames on our hospital grounds.

Military police, who streamed into the area, placed a cordon around the wreckage and tried to extinguish the fire. They pulled two deceased airmen from the cockpit. They were burnt beyond recognition. Military records determined that both were young Australians doing air reconnaissance of the Bay of Bengal.

I pitied the parents of these two young men who would receive devastating news just when people thought that the war was ending. Events moved swiftly. Roosevelt died and President Truman became America's commander-in-chief. He pushed the Allies on every front, and they gained ground in Western and Eastern Europe. Italian partisans captured Mussolini and killed him. Russian forces advanced to Berlin, and Hitler committed suicide on April

30. Germany capitulated on May 7. The next day the war ended in Europe.

In the Pacific Theater, the Allies waged protracted battles, but when American bombers dropped atomic bombs on Hiroshima and Nagasaki, Japan surrendered on August 14. World War II ended. The estimate of war dead was thirty-five million people. An additional ten million people died in concentration camps in Europe, and at least two million died in Bengal. But this last number of the dead in our country was never included in official tallies. Maybe war chroniclers believed that the Indian dead were inconsequential.

While the Western World and Russia celebrated their victory, we Indians, who had contributed money, materials, and soldiers had nothing to celebrate. Instead, we suffered from our battle scars, the catastrophic cost of our famine, and the punitive damages that were inflicted on us for daring to ask for independence. Most of our leaders languished in British jails.

~ 14 ~

NEW PATHS

THE ALLIES' WAR VICTORIES, ESPECIALLY Russia's capture of Berlin, profoundly affected educated Indians. India's Communist Party made full use of its propaganda to win over students and low-wage factory workers who suffered from poor living standards. Its newspapers continued promoting the 'People's War' against British and India's rich landowners and capitalist owners of businesses and factories. The party trained members to infiltrate factories, poor villages, and urban areas that had so many unemployed educated people. The Communist Party was determined to form a communist state in India.

Many of my friends and I wondered about our future living in this complicated political powder keg. I was young and impressionable, and I had read *Das Capital* and Marx's historical interpretation of Europe's economy. But I wasn't convinced that the brand of capitalism associated with Western democratic countries would self-destruct. I rejected totalitarian societies, including communist societies, which forced people to surrender their imagination, creative thinking, and entrepreneurship. Communism lulled people into a state of mediocrity. I believed innovation and inspiration would discover new solutions that would improve the lot of the world. I believed that faith guided people along a path that moved toward enlightenment and social, scientific, and individual progress.

Arup surprised me when he finally returned to Calcutta. He was a happily married man. It had pleased him to see the joy in his mother's eyes when he married the woman that she had chosen for him. His wife Kamini planned to stay in the village with his mother until her demise. Then she would come to live with him in Calcutta.

He also told me that Uncle Hem had a falling out with Manab. His youngest son wanted more control over his education and also questioned his father's management of the estate. Uncle Hem, who was a strict disciplinarian, was so furious that Manab ran away. He insisted that no one, not even his wife, should offer his son shelter or food. Auntie Vasanti gave money to Manab but at great personal risk. Uncle Hem had a terrible temper.

A few days later I was unable to get to the druggist to pick up two bottles of Digitalis. I asked Arup to get them for me and gave him the money. Ten days later he left them in my room with a short note. One month later, the druggist sent me his own note: he wanted the money for the two bottles of medicine that my friend had collected for me.

I was shocked. I looked for Arup in his apartment; he wasn't there. I called his office, but he wasn't there either.

Weeks passed. I needed more Digitalis for my mother and returned to the druggist. He was furious for waiting so long for his money, especially when he had a long waiting list of responsible customers for these foreign-made medicines. I apologized and gave him enough money for four bottles, which included the two new bottles I bought.

Days later, I finally found Arup at his apartment. He made casual chitchat, saying that he had tried to find me several times.

I told him about my uncomfortable visit with the druggist who claimed that he had never received the money for the Digitalis that Arup had bought for me. Arup insisted that he had paid the druggist.

I knew Arup, a newly married man, had returned to Calcutta with very little money. Still, I struggled to believe him. I couldn't believe that he would cheat me.

I asked Arup if he would come with me to the druggist, but he said he'd have nothing more to do with that scoundrel. He offered to pay me back the money when he received his bonus in two weeks.

I told him to forget it.

After this uncomfortable conversation, Arup became a stranger.

~ ~ ~ ~ ~

Kumar received good news. He still needed to take his law exam, but the professor of his economics course had approved the subject for the thesis required for his master's in commerce degree. Kumar believed that his education was finally coming to an end.

In contrast, I had two months of hard work at the hospital, an enormous stack of magazine articles to read, and the ordeal of my annual exams.

My brother took his exam and headed home. He said that he had important things to do for the family. He was fulfilling his role as the eldest son. As always, I did not pry.

Mom wrote me a letter saying that Kumar had reached home safely, but he was extremely busy with a lawyer named Jagdish and his new friend Alok. The two of them were always at the district revenue office. Kumar told her that he was conducting some real estate transactions and would tell me everything when he returned to Calcutta.

A month later Kumar was back in Calcutta. He said he had dealt intelligently with some of our ancestral properties by granting Alok and his father a 90-year lease for a good property that didn't belong to our family deity. Our great-grandfather had acquired this property long after he received the original charter from the last Moghul emperor. He said that the transaction for the long lease was easy business—free of any binding rules.

Kumar insisted that his friends were helping to protect our family's future. This transaction was the start.

I knew my brother couldn't possibly have received the full value for this land, but I understood the motivation behind the deal. Our father's family could lose everything with the creation of Pakistan.

Kumar also worried about Uncle Hem. He was convinced that our estate required a smart, shrewd manager who could turn the family estate into a gold mine by selling off the land before India was divided. Kumar reminded me that he was going through all this trouble on his family's behalf. I should support his efforts.

Finally, I took my exams. When I learned that I did well on them, I hurried home to see Mom.

She didn't look good, but she claimed that she was fine, and said she would live to see me become a doctor in one more year. I hated hearing this talk from my mother and I was relieved when

Uncle Ashok, Uncle Bidhan, and Auntie Beena, Sadananda, and Meena joined us. I felt happy surrounded by my extended family.

Long talks with Mom's doctor confirmed my suspicion that her condition had worsened. Deteriorating lesions on her heart were increasing the possibility of fatal cardiac failure. Her prognosis was not good, and the slightest exertion left Mom short of breath.

Uncle Bidhan also worried about my brother and his business activities in Mymensingh. He didn't think that Jagdish, my brother's lawyer, was honest or straightforward. He assumed that Jagdish was conducting business with my brother that involved land holdings at our father's ancestral estate. He was also aware that Kumar and Jagdish had talked my mother into transferring her investments into an account in Calcutta that would be jointly held by my brother and my mother. Finally, he knew that Kumar had added his name to her bank account. They'd told our mother that these changes would protect her family assets in case she died.

As I listened to Uncle Bidhan, I thought my brother was prudent to transfer my mother's assets to Calcutta. As for selling land, I had advised Uncle Bidhan to start selling his own land and my uncle had told me during this conversation that he had sold some peripheral properties. He was able to repay my mother for the loan, which removed a heavy burden from his mind. This last news pleased me.

Uncle Bidhan said that Kumar should keep me informed about any transactions and changes involving our ancestral property and our father's assets. I was not a minor. Uncle Bidhan was right, but I understood my brother's reluctance to engage me in these family matters. He knew that I was overwhelmed by the demands of medical school. He also knew that I was deeply worried about our mother's health. I chose to believe that Kumar was making prudent decisions on behalf of his entire family.

I thanked Uncle Bidhan for all the information, and I encouraged my uncle to sell more land. I feared that Pakistan would soon become a reality. He told me that he had decided that he wanted to retire in an ashram in Calcutta.

I knew Uncle Bidhan kept his money in a local bank, so I suggested he transfer his funds to the Imperial Bank of India in Calcutta, which would remain part of India. I reminded him that Mymensingh's branch manager, Mr. Sharma, was the father of my good friend from the government school.

The next day we met with him, and he helped Uncle Bidhan open a joint account so that both he and Auntie Beena had access to their money if either one passed away. He also advised Uncle Bidhan to open an additional account at a specific branch in Calcutta where his friend was the manager. This would simplify the identification process.

Auntie Beena had tears in her eyes when she provided her signature at the bank. Her future security was assured. She and Uncle Bidhan also took comfort in knowing their assets would go to their only surviving son.

One morning when I had to get money for Mom from her bank, I noticed Kumar's name attached to Mom's account. It suddenly bothered me. But I decided that time would reveal his true motives.

Before I returned to Calcutta, Mom told Uncle Ashok, her sister Auntie Beena, and me that she knew her health was failing. Her days were numbered, and she longed to see her oldest son married.

She planned to write to him, and she thought her son would grant her request. I promised Mom that after she wrote Kumar, I would speak to him.

Before I returned to Calcutta, I had a chance to speak alone with my cousin Sadananda. He said that he believed in his heart that his father loved the younger son so much more than he ever loved him. He said he had no joy in his life—yes, he loved his daughter, and yes, he hoped God would grant him a son this time. But it wasn't enough.

I asked Sadananda if he liked his job. He said that it suited him. He also knew that he would be transferred to India if Mymensingh were absorbed into Pakistan. He would be safe.

I wondered about Uncle Bidhan's family. Sadananda was the great-grandson of Ram, who had been brave and seized opportunities that allowed him to build one of the largest estates in the entire district. This young descendent only cared about his secure, unchallenging job and his humdrum life that kept him stuck in a joyless marriage with young children.

~ 15 ~

THE GREAT CALCUTTA KILLING

COMMUNALISM WAS ON THE RISE in Calcutta, and so was unemployment since many jobs ended at peacetime. During this time of upheaval, Communist Party demonstrators shouting slogans moved through the streets, as did supporters of Hindu parties and supporters of Muslim religious leaders and the Muslim League Party, which had formed Bengal's government.

Once again, I won a scholarship. I would make it through my last year of college. My brother also accepted our mother's wish for him to marry. But Kumar insisted that he had to read each proposal and see the photograph of each girl that came to his mother. He also wanted to date the girls that he liked before he chose his bride.

I visited with Auntie Malati in South Calcutta. She knew appropriate young women and she soon gave us a stack of proposals. Kumar rejected them. He wanted a young lady with a secondary education, not a university education. Women with a college degree were too independent and didn't make good wives.

During this last year of school, I met Amjad, a young Muslim student, who surprised me with his unusual views. He had two brothers and two sisters and lost his father when he was seven years old. He wasn't close to his eldest brother who oversaw the family property. When Amjad said that he assumed that his brother considered himself the sole owner of the estate and wouldn't act on behalf of all his brothers and sisters, I told him that I understood. This was a common problem in every family with real estate: Hindu or Muslim.

Amjad laughed. I'd survive, he said. I had a good sense of humor.

Amjad's uncle, Fazlul Huq, who had been the first premier of Bengal, had passed laws to alleviate the unfair burden that accompanied heavy debts, and he had reformed unjust taxation and rent laws. None of these laws endeared Fazlul Huq to rich Hindus or rich Muslim landlords and businessmen, but he still had considerable influence and power in the Bengal government.

Amjad was against the quota system at the medical college. He believed that India would eventually be stuck with inferior doctors by passing over more qualified candidates. He also worried that the Punjab Police force, which was entirely Muslim and brought here from a different province to protect Bengali, could easily antagonize the Hindu population in Calcutta.

In 1946 another British Cabinet Mission failed to establish a framework for India's independence that was acceptable to all of India's political party leaders. The mission also rejected the demand for Pakistan, believing that it would compromise the defense of India.

The Muslim League declared that April 16, 1946, would be "Direct Action Day" and called for demonstrations in Calcutta. The demonstrations triggered days of communal riots that became known as the "Great Calcutta Killing."

Hindus said that Muslims started the riots by telling all shops to close for the day. Hindus and Sikhs kept their shops open. When Muslims marched through a main shopping street, some demonstrators came prepared with knives and swords and attacked uncooperative shopkeepers. They set shops ablaze gutting entire streets. Thousands of people were killed and injured—and revenge begot revenge.

Muslims claimed that their unarmed protestors were shouting slogans and carrying flags through the streets when armed Hindu gangs attacked them and other Muslims in the city. Muslims, who were the minority community in Calcutta, suffered disproportionately.

Our Hindu hostel was in a Muslim neighborhood close to the well-guarded medical college and hospital. Fighting erupted outside the walls of the college and hospital and total anarchy ran wild in the streets. We were terrified, trapped in our hostel where its flimsy iron gate was an insufficient barrier. We feared that we'd be attacked and neither the police nor the hospital administrators could save us.

For two sleepless nights, we watched from our verandah as Muslim gangs with iron sticks and long knives roamed the streets. When a lone man in a dhoti and vest walked down a lane, a gang swarmed him and beat him. Finally, when someone slammed an iron rod over his head, the man, with blood streaming down his face, crumbled to the pavement. His legs twitched before he died.

Public transportation stopped in Calcutta. Only police cars, sirens wailing, raced through the streets. Nights were dark and hostile. Huge fires lit up the sky. Were they Hindu or Muslim homes and establishments? We didn't know. A gang dragged a poor fellow trapped inside a ground-floor Sikh restaurant to the street and killed him. They torched the restaurant. We heard screams claiming support for one of the religions and we heard screams of torture.

By the third night, when we were still trapped on the verandah, we heard looters breaking down doors. We stayed quiet and vigilant as they vandalized shops and glass shattered everywhere. People carried off radios, tape recorders, watches, furniture, food—whatever they could find.

Finally, an organized crowd of Hindus with sticks and daggers counter-attacked. They hit Muslims and destroyed Muslim shops. A student from our hostel foolishly shouted in support of the Hindus identifying us to the Muslim gang that prowled our street. They raised their lethal sticks at us just as a police car and ambulance raced up our street and stopped at our front door. An officer quickly escorted us into the ambulance and within minutes we finally stood shaking in the safety of the hospital compound.

That night we heard more screams. But since we were behind high walls, we could see nothing. While we spent seven days in the medical compound, Hindu, Sikh, and Muslim victims of severe burns, open flesh wounds, and fractures crowded the hospital. The dead filled the morgue and covered the floor of the coroner's office. Several newspaper reporters came to the hospital to see the level of violence from the hospital's perspective.

A reporter told me that the provincial government had finally requested help from the central government, which sent in the army to patrol all of Calcutta. This show of strength was stopping the riots.

Days later the fury ended. When I met my brother in his college hostel, he said that Auntie Malati in South Calcutta insisted that I stay with them until everything quieted down in Calcutta.

Once the roads were safe, Kiron, whose wife Shanti had served me breakfast one morning, arrived to drive me to my aunt's house.

We avoided Calcutta's main streets and tried to travel in Hindu areas. Kiron said that most burned shops and houses belonged to Muslims. Hindu houses suffered the same destruction in Muslim areas.

During my weeklong stay at Auntie Malati's house, I sensed tension whenever the family discussed the riots. They seemed ashamed that most of their local Muslim population had vanished. Were they dead or alive? All my relatives insisted that they had never witnessed any arson or murders. I guess this was possible since so few poor Muslims or even rich Muslims lived in this part of South Calcutta. But my relatives always switched the conversation to discuss India's prospects for independence.

One evening when I stepped out to the verandah, I encountered Kiron's wife Shanti who was staring out at the road. She turned around when she heard my footsteps. She seemed tense but smiled through her sad eyes as she walked back inside.

I looked into the night and watched the lights and all the movement on the road. I thought about the riots. I wondered if any Muslim dared to walk on the street to earn money and feed his hungry family.

~ 16 ~

BLAME GAME

FINALLY, WE WERE ALLOWED TO return to our hostels. Before I left my relatives, Auntie Malati handed me four more proposals for Kumar. When I gave them to my brother, he was with his friend Alok, who was praising him for completing all the transactions involving our ancestral property before the communal trouble began. Alok reported that we were lucky; no significant violence had occurred in our district.

Alok and Kumar scrutinized the four proposals and chose one from a business family and one from a middle-class family. My brother told me to arrange dates with each young girl. He would bring Alok, and she could bring her chaperone.

After our college classes resumed, Amjad was distraught. He knew many people who had been killed in the riots and he had worried about my brother and me. A genuinely fine fellow, Amjad asked me to spend a night in his hostel where we talked on the roof.

Calcutta looked so peaceful; it was hard to believe that two weeks ago murders and fires had claimed so many lives. When I told Amjad about the destruction in South Calcutta, he said that Muslims fared worse in North Calcutta. South Calcutta's Hindus actually saved the lives of many Muslim neighbors when rioters came and attacked. But in the north, where most Muslims lived in ghettos, they were unlucky. They didn't have Hindu neighbors. Muslims often hid their Hindu neighbors inside their homes, but the poor Hindus stuck in ghettos were also killed.

Amjad's uncle Fazlul Huq had known that the Muslim Punjabi police force would be unable to save the Muslims in Calcutta. He had rightly predicted that their presence would be provocative. When I left Amjad, I returned to my hostel with a heavy heart.

Days later, I found a Muslim to take me around North Calcutta. I wanted to see the destruction. Ali showed me the big water hoses that were used to remove blood and other traces of incriminating evidence that lay uncoiled on the streets. The dead were dumped from trucks by the sea. He spoke of Muslim survivors, mostly women and children, who lived in two other areas in North Calcutta. But the neighborhoods, which we were visiting, were poor with a mixed population. Some Hindus, whom Ali called informers, had evidently called the Muslim Punjabi police. He added that the Hindus would pay for their sins.

We drove through small Muslim neighborhood pockets where the impoverished residents were massacred, yet in another small neighborhood where Hindus saved their Muslim neighbors, everyone continued to observe intercommunal harmony. In one neighborhood, I saw Muslims and Hindus sitting together singing folk songs. If these people could live harmoniously during the worst of religious riots, why couldn't others get along?

After this troubling visit to North Calcutta, I wondered what happened to the nearby cultural institutes and centers that surrounded College Square. When I walked to the square, I noticed the absence of Muslim artists, who normally hung their paintings and drawings on the iron railing that wrapped around the square. Not a single artist displayed Islamic art or played the music of Islam.

I went into the Coffee House, which was popular with students, left-wing politicians, and newspaper editors and correspondents. I didn't see any Muslim students, nor did I see the Muslim correspondent who frequently chatted with me. A Coffee House attendant told me that Muslim fanatics thought that the correspondent was too partial to Hindus. They killed him.

I finished my coffee and walked to the mosque on the square. The exterior had a gaping hole in one side. Inside, someone had dug a hole in the floor and wrote: "This is the way your Allah fled." I saw no signs of blood anywhere. Had anyone been hurt here? I didn't know.

As I walked back toward the college, I remembered the Hindu temple built on a side street between the college compound and our hostel. It was partially destroyed. Bloodstains streaked the interior and bloodied clothing lay strewn on the floor. If there had been bodies, someone removed them. But no one thought to clean away the blood.

One afternoon he and I entered a building to witness a meeting of the Student Union, where students, local professionals, and business people were discussing the riots, their aftermath, and the cost of restoring the neighborhood. Two eloquent speakers stuck to the agenda, but others shifted the discussion and asked why the central government, dominated by Hindus, failed to send in soldiers or paramilitary forces to protect the Muslims.

A lawyer explained that the law required the provincial government to request help from the central government before it could intervene. The lawyer was shouted down and called a traitor.

Another person raged against Hindus for brutally murdering Muslims and destroying their property. Someone else insisted that the only salvation for Muslims was the creation of Pakistan, with Muslims keeping all of Bengal, especially Calcutta, in their new country. More people hollered that revenge was the sacred duty of all Muslims!

The Student Union formed a committee to address the needs of displaced students. But even this wise action led to shouts against Hindus and religious cries in support of Islam.

I became frightened. Burly men with daggers manned the two gates. I overheard nearby students say that Hindu political parties had sent spies to the meeting to sabotage Muslim plans. One student said that these spies should be killed.

I felt Amjad's tension before he pressed my hand signaling for quiet. We watched a guard drag a man into the bathroom to determine if he was a circumcised Muslim or a Hindu spy.

Suddenly, six men with sticks gathered outside a gate. They made eye contact with Amjad.

"Uncle's men." He whispered.

The men rushed over and yelled at Amjad. "You Bashir, what the hell are you doing? Your uncle, Honorable Premier, is waiting for you. How dare you be late for the big man?"

The six men dragged us to their car and rushed us to the house of his uncle, Fazlul Huq.

The former premier sighed. The anger we had witnessed at the meeting worried him. Fazlul Huq had envisioned India's division and the formation of Pakistan, but the foolhardy division of Bengal? He couldn't understand Bengal's Muslim League leaders. To divide Bengal was unthinkable.

~ 17 ~

KUMAR'S MARRIAGE

A LETTER ARRIVED AT THE hostel from my mother. She said that she would be happy with either of the two girls who had appealed to Kumar. She awaited Kumar's final choice. I told Auntie Malati to arrange meetings between my brother and the would-be brides.

College turned difficult. The riots had set us back at least three months in our courses and clinical work. No one knew when we would take our exams. Then, we faced another problem. Our British government, which was condemned for its negligence during the famine, had a new crisis. Remote villages that lacked doctors had devastating outbreaks of life-threatening diseases.

The government, which was determined to spend a minimum amount of money to solve this crisis, sent senior administrative officers to our college and hospitals to recruit the help of final-year students. The university agreed to a six-month delay in our qualifying examination so that the government could get volunteers from the medical college. Each volunteer would receive a stipend in return for two months of service in disease-affected areas.

Before we left Calcutta to begin our assignments, Arup came to visit me. I asked him why he was honoring me with his presence after so many months.

Arup told me not to be sarcastic. He'd been busy. He wanted to discuss something serious, in private.

Once we were on the roof of our hostel, Arup launched into his fantastic tale of personal misery. A few days ago, he had no choice but to sit down on a dirty toilet seat. Something jumped up and bit his penis. For 48 hours, he had been experiencing a sharp pain in his penis, especially when he peed. He was scared and wanted me to help find him a physician.

I told him that I could take him to a reliable certified doctor, but first, he had to be honest with me. From the description of his symptoms, I thought that he had contracted a venereal infection, which is transmitted through sexual contact.

Arup insisted that he was telling the truth. My voice turned firm. I would only take him to an excellent doctor who would cure him if he provided an honest account of how he got sick.

Arup wept. He said that while he was drinking beer with friends, he'd given in to his weakness. Arup worried about what might happen to his innocent wife and himself if he wasn't cured.

We went to see the doctor and Arup told him the truth. In two weeks, he was cured and freed from his worries.

A few weeks later he apologized for lying to me when he had taken the money that was supposed to cover my mother's medicine. He handed me an envelope of money and begged for my forgiveness. I told him to forget that any of this had happened. He remained my good friend.

Soon, Kumar spent a day with Anjali, one of the young ladies he wanted to meet. His friend Alok joined them for tea. Next, Kumar spent a day with Neena. He saw each of them a second time, but he could not make up his mind.

Anjali's parents invited Kumar and Alok for dinner at their home. Before they sat down to eat, my brother met Anjali's cousin Asha. At first sight, he fell in love with her. After they talked together, Kumar asked Asha if he could meet her again. But Asha lived in Bihar. She and her mother were visiting Anjali for only a week.

Asha's mother asked Kumar if he was requesting a date with her daughter. Kumar sheepishly said yes.

While the two mothers and Asha talked privately about this strange turn of events, Alok and Anjali engaged in their own delightful conversation. They forgot about my brother who sat with them in the room.

When the mothers and the young cousin returned, Asha's mother said that if Kumar was serious, he could have one date with Asha. Only one.

Anjali's mother called everyone to dinner. But Anjali and Alok were so absorbed in their private conversation that they didn't hear her. When Mrs. Sharma asked them again, they blushed.

A few days later Kumar chose to marry Asha whom he had met by chance. Alok declared his love for Anjali. Everyone was happy with this love story that was reminiscent of Shakespeare.

Mom wanted the wedding in Mymensingh, but the communal and political situation in Bengal made this too risky. The wedding was planned to take place a few months later in Calcutta. Unfortunately, Mom wouldn't be able to attend; but Kumar promised that he and Asha would visit her once they were married.

~ ~ ~ ~ ~

Soon, as last-year medical students, we began our volunteer service in villages that lacked electricity and dependable clean water. Their absence created a perfect environment for water-borne diseases.

I remembered an inexpensive water purification system that we had devised in our ancestral village and created one in the village of Karnapur where I worked.

I also had some medicines that treated infectious diseases, common skin problems, malaria, and other simple infections. However, I was unable to treat life-threatening illnesses. Those patients were taken to a distant hospital.

Every day as I treated a long line of villagers, I grew acutely aware of my inadequacies as a doctor. I also realized that my sense of inadequacy would remain even after I received my license to practice.

One day after long hours in the clinic, I was exhausted and quickly fell asleep in my room. Villagers thumping on my door woke me up. A midwife had been unable to help a young lady in labor. She feared that the baby was dead.

I had to help, but I had delivered only five babies at the medical college, and it had well-equipped facilities and assistants on call.

When I saw the woman, I was relieved to hear the baby's heartbeat through my stethoscope. I washed my hands and pulled on a pair of gloves. The baby's mother had a large pelvis, so I could insert my hand and feel the baby's head and the woman's fully dilated cervix.

I pushed my hand between the baby's head and the woman's pelvis. Something moved and the woman started pushing, hard. Fifteen minutes later, she gave birth to a healthy baby girl.

The midwife told everyone I'd saved the baby. Even the sub-divisional officer thanked me personally for my life-saving work. Life turned sweet.

But one day a villager arrived at the clinic carrying his son who was hot from a high fever, his sputum was bloodstained, and his breathing was fast and shallow. The little boy could never survive a trip to a distant hospital, so I kept him with me in the clinic. All day I treated him with my meager supply of medicines. But pneumonia was a killer.

In the evening the father carried his young son home. When I visited the boy later that night, his condition remained grave. When I saw him in the morning, he had died. I felt so bad for the father, who had lost his wife a year ago.

At the end of my stay in November, my new friends organized a banquet in my honor. The man who had lost his son told everyone that he knew from the expression on my face when I first looked at his child that he wouldn't survive. But the man was grateful that I did everything possible to try to save his boy. I couldn't believe the man's kind words. His faith in me had kept him going.

When I returned to Calcutta, Mom had asked her cousin, Auntie Malati, to make Kumar's wedding an honorable Hindu event worthy of the family. Auntie took the request to heart and arranged everything. She didn't need my help.

I missed two days of school in order to attend Kumar's wedding. I hovered around the priests and tried to understand the 4000-year-old Vedic ceremony, especially the vows of the bride and groom that expressed their love and fidelity. The celebration was a success. I just wish that Mom had seen her eldest son married and had met his bride, Asha.

~ 18 ~

REAPPEARANCES

WHEN THE MUSLIM LEAGUE AND princely states boycotted the meeting of the Constituent Assembly in Delhi in December 1946, India was hit with more communal disturbances. The police, who protected our hospital, shut the main doors as large processions approached our compound. But the shouting interfered with our studies and clinical work.

Later, the injured streamed into the hospital, and doctors and students were kept busy in the emergency rooms. Party leaders also trouped into the casualty wards, attracting supporters and the curious. They disrupted our hospital care and our work.

I spent every available hour studying for my final exam. I also attended private tutorial classes, which offered invaluable question-and-answer sessions. These classes weren't free. Luckily, I could cover their cost.

Kumar and Asha visited Mom in Mymensingh for only a short time. My brother disliked staying in Uncle Bidhan's house even though they were given a separate room. He said everyone in that suffocating house was gloomy and morose and Mom's room felt like a hospital ward.

Kumar finally stopped his complaints and announced that as a married man, he had to think of his family and his future. He had earned his law degree and his master's degree in commerce. He and Asha were going to spend a month with her parents in Bihar, Agra, and Delhi. Kumar was thrilled to visit someplace new.

While visiting Delhi, Kumar met with two successful lawyers who had been friends of our father. They offered him tea and told him that he could not expect to be appointed a judge since he didn't get first-class honors on his law exam. They advised him to begin his career as a legal officer in a bank and they offered to serve as referees if he applied for a specific job. Their advice was difficult for Kumar to swallow.

He was talking about this meeting while the two of us sat on the roof of my hostel. Suddenly, he switched topics and let loose with four-letter words aimed at politicians who were pushing for the formation of Pakistan. He was furious because he would lose the family estate to this new country.

Kumar blamed our grandmother, our father, our uncle, and even our mother for our current mess. Their failure to make wise decisions created his economic misfortune. As a married man who had a wife to support, he couldn't risk spending four years of hard work to set up a law practice, which would produce little income. He didn't even have the start-up money.

My brother again berated our father for failing to leave sufficient money for his family. He berated his father-in-law who wasn't rich. He wallowed in his bad luck and spewed venom against everyone for hours. At last, he cooled down and left the hostel. I had sacrificed valuable hours that I needed to study.

For days, clinical work overwhelmed me. I also had to deliver 12 babies—my one remaining medical degree requirement. But each healthy baby filled me with joy.

On Saturday morning I strolled through nearby College Square to the Coffee House. I looked around and noticed a young man reading a newspaper as he sipped coffee and munched on cashew nuts. He looked familiar. As I approached his table, he looked up and smiled.

I said that I didn't mean to be rude, but he reminded me of someone I knew.

The young man smiled and said that reports of his death were premature. He was Suleiman, without the sideburns and goatee.

I was thrilled to see him.

Suleiman invited me to sit with him and told me his story. During the Great Calcutta Killing, he was actually investigating a white-collar crime far away from his home. When he returned to his house, the front door was damaged. He pushed it open and discovered his family huddled together in the corner of the front room. They were mourning the death of his younger brother.

Suleiman said that the Muslim League despised him because of his liberalism and his newspaper articles that objected to the formation of Pakistan. Muslim League officials had put Suleiman's name on their list of nationalist Muslims whom they wanted "eliminated."

The league had sent a Muslim gang to his front door late at night. When his mother opened the door, they rushed inside and yanked a young man from his bed, and dragged him into the street. They told the young man this is what happens to traitors. They killed him. But the gang had killed Suleiman's younger brother, who never identified himself.

Suleiman's eyes filled with tears as he wondered how these Muslim gang members could believe that they would go to heaven for carrying out this order. Suleiman said his brother would go to heaven, not them. He made the true sacrifice by letting himself get killed to save the one they really wanted.

Suleiman no longer lived at home. He had shaved off his sideburns and goatee and lived in a room on the top of a cultural center in the College Square, where he wrote a column called Miana Speaks. The Miana is considered India's most talkative bird.

I told him about my visit with Fazlul Huq. How this extraordinary man accepted that Pakistan would come into existence but feared the division of Bengal. I told Suleiman that Fazlul Huq thought this division was inevitable unless Hindus and Muslims miraculously resolved their differences.

Suleiman thought that the Muslim League would lose the upcoming provincial election. It would be unable to form the government. He thought the former premier, Fazlul Huq, would join forces with another party and form a coalition government.

Suleiman believed this theory because Bengali Muslim students booed and hissed when Mr. Jinnah visited Dacca University and said that Urdu would be the national language of Pakistan. Bengali Muslims were proud of their Bengali language. Suleiman hoped that Hindu and Muslim leaders played their cards right so that Bengal emerged as a sovereign country along with India and Pakistan.

When I left Suleiman at the Coffee House, I thought about his unfortunate younger brother. What was the young boy thinking as he died? He knew the Muslim gang had the wrong brother. Why didn't he try to save himself? He had performed such a noble act.

~ 19 ~

PAINFUL FAREWELL

KUMAR HAD TO GET A job. After failing to get interviews with the government or a commercial house, he sent applications to become a legal officer at a bank. He included the name of one of the lawyers he met as a referee.

He landed a job as a general duty officer at a bank with the promise of a promotion to legal officer if he performed well. He and Asha moved into a nice two-bedroom apartment at reduced rent—a benefit of his new job.

I was overwhelmed, studying late into the night and staggering into the hospital in the morning. Rest was a luxury no student could afford. I felt confident when I took the written exam, but I was scheduled to take the clinical and oral examinations in unfamiliar hospitals. I hadn't studied their particular pathological specimens or any of their patients. The examination dragged on, but I didn't make a fool of myself in front of the examiners.

I wanted to hurry home; I knew Mom's condition was deteriorating. Arup also needed to get home. His mother had just died.

So we decided to journey together. But Kumar insisted that I first visit him so that he could remind me, as if I were a child, to bring the medicine to our mother. Then he added that he had made our mother happy. He had gotten married to please her.

Mom was so sick when I walked into her bedroom. She struggled to sit up in her bed and her breath was short. But her beautiful face lit up with a sweet smile. I put pillows behind her back to make her more comfortable. I sat next to her and told her to stay quiet while she regained her strength. I said that I would talk to her. I told her about the wedding, my exam, Kumar's new job, and my recent visit with Kumar and Asha in their apartment. I assured her that they seemed happy.

All this news cheered Mom. Her housekeeper told me that my mother had lost her appetite and ate very little food. I could also see that Mom's ankles were swollen; her neck veins seemed engorged and dilated.

When the doctor came the next morning, he told Mom that she had to eat. Otherwise, the medications would fail to help her. He told me that she was in chronic congestive failure with fluids in her lower extremities and congestion in her lungs. Her liver was enlarged, and she had an irregular heartbeat. He thought that she could live much longer, but she needed careful monitoring—and she had to eat. He increased her diuretics and added potassium to her regime.

For the first time in my life, I cooked my mother's meals. I assumed that she would feel guilty if she refused to eat what I prepared for her. I went to the market and bought her favorite fruits and vegetables. I made her cottage cheese for protein.

The housekeeper continued to change Mom's bed and gave her sponge baths when she lacked the strength to get into the aluminum bathtub I brought for her. She also helped Mom use the bedpan.

Initially, Mom seemed better. For the first time in six months, she could walk to a chair and sit down, and she could talk for a while without discomfort. The improvements cheered us.

All these days and nights that I cared for Mom represented a special moment in my life. I only left our home to buy food for her. Her religious customs, which disallowed fish, eggs, or meat in her diet, angered me, deeply. Their addition would have improved the taste of her food and her health. But Mom would not eat anything prohibited by her faith.

I often wondered why women, in particular, were forced to bear so many of life's privations and difficulties; but really, how could things be different? Men, who dominate our society and religion, wrote the laws, which, in time, turned into our society's customs and traditions.

While I stayed with Mom, I had a great opportunity to serve this dear woman who had selflessly looked after her two sons until we had left her and our home. Mom spent the last years of her life without us and her accustomed comforts. I received great personal joy from knowing my care made her feel better. She was my sole interest at this time of my life.

After my first month at home, I thought my mother was improving, but her doctor cautioned me. He said that her improvement had no bearing on her prognosis. Her condition remained grave. Any attack of arrhythmia could be fatal.

Days later I received a letter from a medical college friend who said that I passed our exam with good marks. I was eager to attend our convocation, which would occur in three weeks, but I could not leave Mom in her present condition. I wrote back and said that my mother was seriously ill. I would pick up my diploma from the university office.

I told Mom my test results. Her face brightened and her beautiful eyes were shining with pride. She hugged me and said my father would be so proud.

As tears slipped from my mother's eyes, I appreciated all the sacrifices she had made for my brother and me. She had lived these last years in such simple accommodations and had fed herself on the hope that her two boys would be successful in their studies and professional lives.

I stayed with my mother for two more months and did everything I could to make her happy. Small things brought her joy: a delicious piece of fruit or vegetable, a few words that I spoke to her. I looked forward to the smile appearing on her face and the joy expressed in her eyes.

But slowly, Mom turned frail. Her cardiovascular system rebelled against her medications. She suffered uncontrollable arrhythmia followed by cardiac failure. Mom struggled for each breath, yet she remained conscious until the very end.

I sent my brother a telegram telling him our mother's health had deteriorated. A few hours before her death, Mom motioned with her finger to sit next to her. She kissed my forehead and smiled gently at me. She drifted into sleep and never awakened. I grieve again for my dear mother as I write this.

I notified my brother, and then I began to arrange for my mother's funeral. Uncle Bidhan and Uncle Ashok did most of the work. I was too bereft.

Kumar and Asha arrived a few days before the Sradh ceremony. He was furious that I had sent him my first telegram so late. Uncle Bidhan disagreed. He spoke with unusual conviction and told

Kumar that one week ago our mother was better than she had been for months because of my good care. No one realized that her end was near.

After the Sradh ceremony for my mother, I knew that I had to get back to Calcutta. I'd lost my father so long ago, now I'd lost my dear mother. I felt so alone.

~ 20 ~

INDIA'S INDEPENDENCE

BEFORE I LEFT MYMENSINGH, UNCLE Ashok gave me an envelope from Mom. She had wanted me to open it once I was back in my room in Calcutta. He asked me not to fight with Kumar. My elder brother was newly married and under strain because he lacked the money to begin his own legal practice. He reminded me that our father's family had denied us our stipend.

Uncle Bidhan thanked me for looking after him and taking such good care of my mother. He made me promise to ask for help if I needed it and told me to get on with my life.

Once I was in my bedroom at our hostel, I opened the envelope. Mom had written me a short note that said she would love me always. She would always keep an eye on me, so I must never do anything that would upset her. She wished me good health, happiness, and success in life. She had attached a check for 1500 rupees. On another paper, she had handwritten some verses in Bengali, which I translated into English:

117

As long as there is life there is death.
As long as there is life there is conflict.
As long as there is life there is hope.
Death is the natural but not the ultimate end of life
as new life takes over.
Conflict is not the end of society as new boundaries
and new societies form.
New life grows with smiles and love as if yesterday's
problems were never.

While I cared for Mom, I had told her that my next year in Calcutta would be a financial struggle. I had to complete one year of clinical assistance before I received my license. I needed to spend another year in the hostel. Clinical assistants received a stipend for their work, but it only covered the cost of room and board. I told her that I felt uncomfortable asking Kumar for help. Mom said she understood. This check was the proof. Because of her thoughtfulness, I'd be like other junior doctors—short of money, but high in spirits—looking forward to a promising future. I was so relieved. She was such a dear mother!

~ ~ ~ ~ ~

Finally, patients addressed us as doctors and everybody in the hospital treated us with respect. All hospital patients were under the care of consultants, with numerous doctors, from the senior registrar and junior house surgeons down to the house physicians, working under the order of these consultants. The hospital also had a resident surgeon and a resident physician. As clinical assistants (junior doctors) we cared for patients, helped with X-rays and laboratory diagnoses, treated emergency room patients, and assisted the physicians and the resident surgeon in the operating room. We also helped interns. We were busy.

But I soon discovered the nursing sister, who was in charge of each ward and knew the treatment for each patient, bore responsibility for any oversight. Each morning the ward sister accompanied the consultant on his staff rounds. She knew everything that happened in the previous 24 hours and every small change in the patient's condition. Nothing slipped by her.

Nurses-in-training gave out medications and most injections and they did most of the physical work, including servicing bedpans and urinals. Everything moved smoothly except when the wards were overcrowded.

Most nurses were Anglo-Indian, but Indian girls were entering the profession, often against their parents' wishes. Upper-class Hindus looked down on nursing since it involved the use of bedpans. Muslims didn't want their daughters working in male wards. Many Anglo-Indian nurses, who had dominated the profession for generations, resisted teaching the Indian girls; so the Indian girls struggled against hostility and friction. But as more Indian girls entered the profession, Indian society and the Anglo-Indian nurses relented. They all began to work together, in relative harmony.

India's political stalemate finally broke when the British announced power would transfer to India by June 1948. Viscount Mountbatten became the new viceroy in March 1947 and consulted with our leaders. He realized that the Muslim League would only accept a divided India with the creation of Pakistan. Congress leaders agreed to the partition against the advice of Gandhi.

India's independence, which created a separate dominion of India and a separate dominion of Pakistan, became law in July

1947. Cyril Radcliff presided over the British commission that drew up new national boundaries. The assets and debts of the government of India were divided; and central government servants, including soldiers, were allowed to swear allegiance to either country. Provincial employees who served in the provinces of Bengal and the Punjab could work for either Pakistan or India.

With the help of Indian political leaders and civil servants, Mountbatten formulated a proposal for the princes of the native states of India to give up their sovereignty and British allegiance and join either India or Pakistan. All but three princes agreed: the Maharaja of Kashmir, the Nizam of Hyderabad, and the Nawab of Junagadh.

As mass migrations of people began moving between the two countries, the world witnessed gruesome massacres that continued for months. Most of the carnage occurred in the Punjab where Hindus and Muslims were slaughtered as they attempted to journey to their new country. Trains arrived in India's Punjab or Pakistan's Punjab carrying mutilated victims who had dared the dangerous trip.

Violent riots erupted in Bengal and Bihar and other parts of India. Hindus and Sikhs in Pakistan's province of Sind fled to India. Some Bengalis and Biharis escaped to East Pakistan; others who lived in East Pakistan escaped to India's Bengal and Bihar.

The police couldn't stop the violence, so India's armed forces congregated along the Punjab boundary. But their deployment left Calcutta's Muslims unprotected. Most Muslim administrative workers and Muslim members of the security forces had gone to Pakistan.

Mountbatten and the central government worried about communal riots breaking out in our city. He asked Gandhi to go to Calcutta and use his powerful voice to call for nonviolence. Gandhi, who had opposed the partition of India, agreed to intercede in his capacity as a private individual, but he would not go as an emissary of the government. Once he moved to Calcutta he lived in a Muslim neighborhood.

Sporadic violence erupted in Calcutta and some Hindus who had suffered at the hands of Muslims protested outside Gandhi's house, but the presence of the great leader appeared to work. Tempers in Calcutta cooled as the revered leader continued his calming daily prayer meetings.

On midnight August 14, 1947, when India was proclaimed a free country, people crowded the streets of Calcutta. Hindus, Muslims, Christians, Sikhs, Parsees, and every other ethnic community hugged one another forgetting India's history of turmoil and hatred. People distributed sweets, and no one cared who distributed them. After the terrible famine, the violent oppression of a foreign government, the brutal Calcutta Killing, and the privations of war, people were in a forgiving mood.

But independence for India wasn't a simple straight line. When the Hindu Maharaja of Kashmir, who ruled over a majority of Muslims, refused to join India or Pakistan, Muslim tribal forces invaded Kashmir. To avoid certain defeat, the Maharaja joined India. The Government of India accepted his decision, but it promised that the people would have their say in a referendum after the Pakistanis withdrew from Kashmir. But fighting continued until the United Nations Security Council implemented a ceasefire along an artificial line that granted two-thirds of Kashmir to India and the remaining third to Pakistan.

Pakistan refused to withdraw, and India never held its referendum. The beautiful valley of Kashmir became an ugly rift that

adversely affected the relationship between the two newly independent countries and their people.

~ 21 ~

IN TRAINING

INDEPENDENCE USHERED IN CHANGES TO our medical colleges and hospitals. Accomplished Indian professors replaced British-born counterparts as college principals, hospital superintendents, and as professors of surgery, medicine, ophthalmology, and obstetrics and gynecology. Officials at the Ministry of Health sent trained nurses to England for advanced education and additional experience so that they'd qualify for vacancies and positions as nursing tutors. An increasing number of Indian girls applied to our nursing program and tried for staff positions.

For the first time in our careers, we clinical assistants needed to get to know the superiors who would determine our future appointments if we wanted to become house surgeons, house physicians, and registrars. Personal feelings toward each candidate, outright nepotism, and even political influence would play a role in each promotion. Unfortunately, I didn't know any of the new professors; and only a couple of visiting consultants knew me from doing ward rounds. My cousin Jeevan, who was well-known and well-liked, was still in the United States.

I began studying the conduct of senior doctors at the hospital. I noticed that every evening, resident surgeons and physicians became the nighttime bosses; and registrars (residents) and senior housemen (interns) also became important. During breaks, this new crew gossiped in the restaurant. To gain their appreciation, I offered to do some of their work to give them free time.

After a couple of weeks, Dr. Bose, a senior doctor, asked me if I had selected my discipline for future training. I volunteered that I wanted to go for training in medicine, but I knew that all three available positions in this field were probably beyond me.

Dr. Bose said that the top student in medicine and the best student in our class were applying for two of three positions. He thought that I might win the third slot if I applied. However, Dr. Bose thought that I should apply for training in surgery. I'd definitely get the second slot. No one matched my marks. Since I could only apply for one discipline, I had to choose wisely. I decided to go for surgery.

I was selected for this field, but I was assigned to the junior most visiting surgeon. I was annoyed until Dr. Bose told me that this surgeon was highly regarded. He also had a good private practice.

Once we started training, I rarely had time to sleep. I'd brush my teeth, gulp down breakfast, and set off to the hospital. Twice weekly I was on call for surgical emergencies. Even when I wasn't on call, I had to respond to emergencies in the ward. None of us clinical assistants ever had free weekends. When we needed a break, we had to find a doctor to cover our patients.

We were reminded that our work was not a job; we were privileged to train with a distinguished physician or surgeon and lear the art and science of healing.

But the endless job had advantages. Patients and their relatives showered us with respect and token presents. We received low salaries that barely covered our living expenses, but we received free bachelor accommodation in a nice building near the hospitals. We had free nightly meals when we were on call at the hospital and nurses shared chocolates and other delicacies that they received from private patients.

I became friends with many Anglo-Indian nurses and learned about their community. Their fathers were often British bachelors who worked for the government or companies in India. They often had affairs with Indian women who became pregnant. None of the men officially recognized the relationship or took responsibility for the child. Occasionally, when the man left India, he would give the woman real estate or money. A few said that once they were resettled in Britain they would send for their wives and children. But this rarely happened. Most of the Indian women with fatherless children were stranded with no livelihood.

Christian missionaries claimed these children were Christians in distress with British blood in their veins. The missionaries baptized the women and children, who were also educated to the secondary level so that they could pass the Senior Cambridge Examination and support themselves.

They convinced the British government to declare all these children Anglo-Indians. But the government wouldn't call them British children.

Unfortunately, these Christianized people became "others," who were distinct and unlike the rest of India's population.

At Independence, Anglo-Indians anxiously wondered about their status in free India. The Indian government recognized the

Anglo-Indians as a distinct community with English as their language, but it declared that no group in India was entitled to special privileges.

Anglo-Indians realized that they would struggle to compete and struggle to survive. Many of them decided to stay in India, but some wanted to emigrate.

I wasn't surprised that the British treated these women with favor because they were generally lighter skinned than other Indian women. Even in the hospital, fair-skinned Anglo-Indian girls, who were the darlings of the British matron and sister tutor, were awarded promotions and preferred stations on the wards.

But darker-skinned Anglo-Indians, who generally came from the south, were teased, even by other Anglo-Indians. The dark nurses were called "black hag" or "midnight." Color consciousness was so perverse that one dark-skinned Anglo-Indian girl called another darker-skinned girl "midnight." The darker-skinned girl, who was often subjected to insults, shouted back: "Who's talking? You are at least half-past eleven."

Other nurses who noticed my friendships with some Anglo-Indian women suspected I was leading them on. Every evening, one of my many friends usually had delicious chocolates and willingly shared them with me as we talked. But I always kept my distance. I'd been brought up in a very conservative society with strict sexual behavior. I was also ambitious. I was in my second year as a house surgeon. In a year I would start my career as a surgeon, or I would become a general practitioner. I didn't want a serious relationship.

~~~~~

On January 30, 1948, when our government still struggled to care for millions of refugees and many of us continued to grieve over the millions who died during partitioning, Nathuran Godse, a fanatic Hindu, did the unthinkable. He assassinated Mahatma Gandhi as the gentle man walked to his evening prayer meeting in Delhi. Godse's bullet pierced the entire nation; we were consumed with pain.

Acts of violence reached us in the hospital. One day, someone left a suitcase in our emergency room. The medical officer called the police, who opened the suitcase. The Muslim League flag was draped over the dismembered body of a Hindu doctor who worked in the hospital.

The death of the doctor, who had an apartment in a predominately Muslim neighborhood, shocked us. He was considered liberal-minded, and he often defended Muslim causes in discussions.

One day at work our chief surgeon asked me to be his assistant in his private surgical practice. Nurses and the visiting surgeon also recommended my services to private patients in the hospital after they were discharged. These extra opportunities radically improved my financial position. I could buy some new clothes, treat myself to an occasional meal in a restaurant, and even splurge on a movie. But I rarely saw my brother.

Then Kumar called. He needed to see me. I arranged for a house surgeon to cover for me, and I went to visit my brother. He told me that Asha was pregnant. He needed me to arrange for her prenatal care and the delivery of her baby.

I talked to a visiting obstetrician at our hospital who agreed to care for Asha. I booked a quiet, private room for her in the hospital when she went into labor.

Unfortunately, Asha had minor complications when she gave birth to a baby boy. She stayed a few more days before she and the baby went home.

Six weeks later Kumar called. He was frantic. Asha had fainted.

A house surgeon covered for me, and I raced to Kumar's apartment. Asha had a slightly elevated fever; her pulse was fast and her blood pressure was low.

I called the obstetrician who came and examined her. Asha had a serious post-partum infection, which required aggressive treatment. We began an intravenous drip of glucose and saline, injected her with penicillin every four hours, and injected cortisone every six hours. If the blood pressure and pulse rate did not improve within 24 hours, he told me that Asha would need a plasma transfusion to avoid peripheral failure and further complications.

Asha required continuous care. If she remained in her apartment, I had to stay and provide the care for her. But Kumar worried that his wife wouldn't get her medications on time if we put her in the hospital. He insisted that Asha had to stay at home.

The obstetrician wrote a letter to my boss explaining why I needed to be away. I returned briefly to my ward in the hospital. The sister and the staff nurse, who were Anglo-Indian, helped me pack all the required medications and sterilized IV sets. I hurried back to my brother's apartment and began Asha's treatment.

The first night I stayed awake. I worried I'd sleep through and miss a scheduled medication. By morning, I didn't notice much improvement in Asha.

Uncle Umesh called and insisted that I get Dr. Sarkar, who was Calcutta's most renowned doctor, to see Asha. If something terrible should happen to her, my uncle worried that I would be blamed.

I called the well-known Dr. Sarkar, who said that first, he would send a lower-ranked member of his entourage to look at

Asha. This doctor informed me that I needed to get a plasma set for Asha. The entire entourage, including the big man, would be at the apartment at 12:30 p.m.

I had three hours to get the plasma kit, which would only be available from the druggist who sold me Mom's medicine. I hurried over to his shop and raced back to the apartment just before Dr. Sarkar arrived with two of his assistants. He examined Asha and told Kumar that his wife needed a transfusion of plasma, immediately. Dr. Sarkar didn't know where we would get this transfusion. I gave him the kit and we began the treatment immediately.

Dr. Sarkar said that Asha still might not recover, but he wished us good luck and left. When I told my uncle that Dr. Sarkar had refused any payment, he wasn't surprised.

Asha's blood pressure slowly returned to normal, and her pulse slowed. I called the obstetrician who treated her in the hospital. He said that Asha needed to stay in bed and continue with the antibiotics for seven days. So I stayed with Asha one more week, which was an unexpected gift to both of us. We finally got to know and care about each other.

During that extra week with Asha, she told me that Kumar wouldn't let her go to college or pursue a professional career. I told Asha that sadly our community accepted my brother's attitudes and considered them normal. But I didn't.

I told Asha that my widowed mother was forced to accept terrible traditions that adversely affected her. I explained that many of these traditions weren't in our scriptures, but patriarchs in our society had drummed them up later. Unfortunately, both men and women lacked the courage to put an end to them.

~ 22 ~

EYES TOWARD ENGLAND

IN TIME I BECAME THE senior house surgeon at the hospital. Original-ly, I planned to specialize in medicine; but during these two years of training, I decided that the modern developments in physiology and biochemistry pointed to a more stimulating career in surgery.

Unfortunately, I had unknowingly incurred the hostility of Dr. Bhattcharya, the new professor of surgery. I would need his approv-al to become a registrar (resident), which was my next goal when I completed my third year. My direct boss Dr. Banerjee was indepen-dent-minded, but he wasn't a close associate of Dr. Bhattcharya. He couldn't help me.

I talked with my cousin Jeevan, who had returned from Johns Hopkins with his new degree. He advised me to keep my head down and continue to do my work while he snooped around. When we met over tea, Jeevan confirmed that the professor claimed that I had insulted him. I had to accept the consequences. Dr. Bhattcharya might not appoint me to be a registrar.

I told Jeevan that I ultimately hoped to become a fellow at

the Royal College of Surgeons of England. Jeevan explained that surgeons at the hospital normally tried for both the English and the Edinburgh Fellowships, and usually Indian surgeons received the Edinburgh Fellowship. I didn't tell Jeevan that I would be an exception: I only planned to apply for the English Fellowship.

Jeevan thought our family had enough money to support me while I was on this fellowship, but I knew this was only true on paper. I doubted my brother would agree to help me.

When I finally discussed the fellowship with Kumar, he reminded me that only the top students went abroad on fellowships. He also knew that a few students had also failed to achieve their goals. When they returned, their expensive misadventure had ruined their families.

As I listened to Kumar, I knew that I wasn't the top student in surgery. Still, I wanted to try for this fellowship, and I didn't appreciate his remarks.

Kumar finally said that if the geopolitical conditions were different in India and the family estate was productive, he could consider this goal. But right now, my pursuit would tie up too much of our family's limited resources. He told me that I had already wasted two years with my fancy thinking. I should stop now before I completed my third year as a house surgeon. I needed to earn a living.

I was so discouraged when I left Kumar. I talked with Jeevan. My brother's attitude didn't surprise him, but he could offer no solution.

I re-assessed my situation: I enjoyed my work at the hospital, and I believed that I could make a successful career in surgery. I decided that I would pursue my goal. I also reaffirmed my personal resolution to avoid all serious relationships at this point in my life.

Dr. Banerjee, who was sympathetic, encouraged my decision

He also helped me financially by hiring me to assist him with his private cases.

I began making a moderately good living and created a pleasant life for myself in Calcutta. Wealthy patients invited me to music concerts. Another patient paid a famous tailor to make me a fine woolen suit. I'd never worn a fancy garment, but it forced me to spend money on ties and shoes.

I started researching the requirements for the fellowship. The National Board of Medical Registration in England recognized my university degree and my hospital training, so I had no educational barriers. I also discovered that the United Kingdom's new National Health Scheme had created a shortage of junior doctors in the country's hospitals. Openings were available to Indian doctors. The pay was abysmal, but I figured I could survive while I gained valuable clinical experience that would help me prepare for difficult basic sciences and clinical aptitude exams.

Everyone strongly advised me to take the basic sciences exam before I took an exhausting job as a house officer or registrar in a British hospital. Some doctors, who ignored this advice, were so overwhelmed by work that they couldn't study or attend a single preparatory course. They failed the basic sciences exam.

I accepted this wisdom. I would save enough money to get to England and support myself the first year that I was on the fellowship.

Dr. Banerjee continued to be supportive. He encouraged me to apply for the post of registrar at the end of the year. If I failed to get this appointment, he thought he could extend my current position another year so that I could stay at the hospital in Calcutta.

I had made up my mind about my immediate future. But the heart follows its own strong will and doesn't always cooperate. This became true for me—even though the heart that caused trouble didn't belong to me.

Linda, an attractive young nurse on the ward began telling friends that she knew that I loved her. Every evening, she doted on me in front of her friends. She also arranged small evening parties where I was her special guest. People decided that we were a couple.

When Linda and I talked together, she often told me about her family. Her father was a Scotsman who managed a group of British-owned tea gardens in the Himalayan foothills. He married a young woman from a hill tribe and they lived in a handsome bungalow. Linda was close to her father and I assumed that she had a special relationship with him because she looked Scottish.

When her father was 55-years-old, he retired. Linda, who had passed her Senior Cambridge examination, was already a nursing student in Calcutta. Her father, who decided to go back to Scotland, told Linda that if she went to the United Kingdom, she should contact him. Then he was gone. Linda told me that she never heard from him again. She looked straight at me and asked if all men behaved like this.

I felt caught in a difficult situation with Linda. I had never taken her on a date. She came to her conclusions about our relationship from our conversations. I enjoyed her friendship, nothing more.

Then Asha called me. My sister-in-law needed to talk in private with me.

A strange feeling troubled me in the pit of my stomach.

Asha told me that three Bengali nurses whom she'd met during her stay at the hospital had come to see her. They were confused by my inconsistent behavior. They had all heard that I wanted to go to the United Kingdom on a fellowship in surgery. One nurse, who was named Leena, insisted that if my goal kept me from commit-ting, her father would willingly pay all the expenses attached to my fellowship in England. Leena then declared that she loved me and said that she believed that I loved her.

As I heard this, I thought, great! Two nurses believed I loved them.

I told Asha that I didn't know how this girl Leena could imag-ine such crazy things. I had never acted in any way or said anything to suggest that I loved any of these girls.

Asha refused to pass judgment, but she said that something about my behavior attracted women. And if I cared for Leena, why not consider her offer? She was good-looking, she came from a re-spectable landowning family, and her father offered to pay the ex-penses for my fellowship in surgery. Asha reminded me that my brother would never give me money to pursue this fellowship. Here was a solution.

The conversation with Asha made me feel awkward. I didn't want to sacrifice my freedom by letting Leena's father pay for my fellowship. My goal to get a fellowship in England was my first step toward my future career and life.

I knew I confused my sister-in-law. Asha wished me good luck and promised that she would stay out of my personal business. I told her my future would reveal itself in time. Most likely it would surprise both of us.

~ 23 ~

RACHEL

LIFE MOVED ON. LINDA NO longer worked on my ward and whenever I saw her, I never encouraged her interest in me. I also continued to work with Leena, but I knew that she'd heard from my sister-in-law that I wasn't interested in her proposal. I was uninterested in any romance.

At the end of the year, I applied for a post as a registrar. But at the interview with Dr. Bhattcharya, the professor of surgery, who held a grudge, won our contest. I wasn't selected.

I talked again with Dr. Banerjee, who proved to be a man of principle. He would keep me on as the senior house surgeon, but I still needed to go through the formal application.

I had to go back to interview with Dr. Bhattcharya again, and he laughed. He asked if I planned to make a career as a perpetual house surgeon. I told him that I still had good things to learn from my knowledgeable boss.

When I told Kumar about my extension, he thought I was stupid wasting my time and money for nothing. He was convinced I had no future in the surgery department. My brother told me to get married. I had many good proposals available from fine families.

I ignored Kumar and told him I'd come to see him because I needed money to pay board for the one-month gap when I was not working in the hospital. Dr. Banerjee had offered me work in his private practice, but I still needed help from Kumar.

My brother scoffed. He said that if my boss were truly helpful, he would have told me to stop my nonsense and get on with my career.

Asha overheard Kumar. She told him that I had been good to his family, especially her. She reminded him that I'd saved her life.

My brother insisted that I'd done this to impress her. He asked me how much money I needed.

I handed him the bill and said, "It's a small amount."

"Every amount is big if you don't earn money," he snapped. Kumar opened his wallet and threw some banknotes on the floor.

I turned and walked out of the room as Asha scooped up the money and raced after me. She made me take it all—far in excess of what I needed. I promised myself that I would never again ask Kumar for money.

For one month I worked under Dr. Banerjee since I didn't have any official status in the hospital. He gave me a few private cases and some nurses recommended me to a few patients who also needed private care. I made enough money that I finally had time to rest.

One afternoon when I had rare free time, I wandered around to see different surgical wards. As I entered an unfamiliar ward, I saw a fair-skinned young lady in the nurses' station examining patients' charts. She was young and very pretty, with a lovely aquiline nose, large brown eyes, and wavy light brown hair. I forgot all about my determination to stay clear of romance.

When I walked away, a nurse approached me and asked me what I was doing in the ward. I told her that I had wanted to visit the master ward. She explained that the work here was similar to the work in other wards, but this ward had fewer emergencies.

Two days later, I succumbed to desire, and I went back to see the pretty girl. I stood on the ward, staring so long, that the staff nurse told me not to pretend that I had come to look at the ward. My lame excuse would only work once.

The staff nurse looked me straight in the eye. She said that the young lady was not only very young but also very different from the other girls in the hospital.

I wondered why the staff was trying to protect the young girl; and what she meant by different?

I soon learned that the young nurse was Hebrew, and she continued to live in a Calcutta apartment with her family. She had an older sister named Naomi, who was completing her final year in nursing school. The nurses told me that the young nurse was too young for my games. These warnings surprised me. I hadn't even talked to the girl.

One week later, I returned to the ward. The young girl had been posted to another ward and I didn't know her name.

One afternoon while I was busy working, I noticed the lovely young lady in our nurses' station. The staff nurse introduced me. Her name was Rachel Bekhor.

When I returned for evening rounds, Rachel was still in the nurses' station. I visited with my patients before I sat near her and updated the orders while she collected medicines for everyone on the floor. I kept trying to talk to her, but she said that she had too much work to do.

I enjoyed working on the ward with her. She was conscientious and carefully followed written orders. But she was not without fault. Sometimes she failed to follow verbal orders. No one could understand why this happened since Rachel was so responsible about everything else.

One day after the sister tutor gave Rachel some work to do she became flustered. She told me she didn't understand what the sister tutor wanted her to do. I had overheard the order, so I helped her get the work done. When the sister tutor returned, she complimented Rachel, who smiled at me. I felt wonderful.

I helped Rachel whenever I could. I also relied on her excellent nursing skills. Years later I became aware that she was almost deaf but managed because she was brilliant at lip reading. She often gave a sweet smile when she heard nothing.

We enjoyed each other's company. As our friendship grew, I often brought her chocolates in the evenings, and she often brought chocolates for me.

Soon, nurses warned Rachel that I was a flirt, known for misleading girls and conducting infamous relationships. They told her to be cautious.

Friends also told me that Rachel's family was conservative. Nothing would come of this relationship. And while Rachel was pretty, she would look really haggard in a few years.

Rachel was different. She never talked about the other girls or their relationships. She had no close friends at the hospital. After work, she went home to her family. So, yes, Rachel had little in common with the other nurses.

During this time, I assisted Dr. Banerjee with a difficult operation in his private clinic. I also took care of the patient after his discharge. I had some spare money, so I decided to throw a party in the special room on the hospital roof.

All the nurses were eager to attend. I also invited Rachel, but I selected the day she wasn't on duty. She didn't know if she could attend since her parents expected her to stay at home until 9 p.m.

I told Rachel I would start the party at 9:30. I really wanted her to come.

At 9 p.m. everyone arrived, except Rachel. Linda told me that she knew Rachel would never show up. She never came to the nurses' parties. She also said that Rachel had a boyfriend and spent her free time with him.

I gave Linda another drink to shut her up and talked with my other guests. Thirty minutes passed. I felt hollow inside. I couldn't understand why Rachel's absence bothered me.

I heard the rattling of the elevator moving up the shaft. The door opened. There was Rachel wearing a nice pink dress and not a trace of makeup. She was a natural beauty. Later that evening, Rachel told me that I'd chosen the day of Yom Kippur for my party. She could not eat all day and could not leave her family until they had observed all their rituals and broken their fast with a meal.

I was so happy to see Rachel. I loved watching her on the roof, I loved watching her drink lemonade, I loved watching her eat just a few finger foods.

The party continued until midnight. I walked Rachel to her nurses' quarters after everyone had left the party. A few days later Rachel asked if I would like to meet her family. I was thrilled.

~ 24 ~

JACOB

WHEN I WENT TO RACHEL'S apartment, a servant ushered me into the lounge to meet the Bekhor family. Rachel introduced me to her mother, Georgina, a stout middle-aged lady, her father, Yehuda, a tall gentleman with a distinctive nose, her three brothers Joseph, Jacob, and Daniel, and her older sister, Naomi, who worked at the hospital. Rachel also introduced me to her mother's elegantly dressed brother David. We sat and talked together until Rachel's mother invited us to the dining room for dinner.

Friday evenings in a Jewish home were special. Once we were seated at the table, Rachel's father began to recite a prayer, and her mother joined in. They blessed the bread and broke it into two pieces before distributing it around the table. They blessed the sweet wine before they served it to each of us. The dinner was filled with rituals.

During the sumptuous dinner, I also learned some of the rules that defined kosher food, which was the only food orthodox Jews were permitted to eat. Most importantly, orthodox Jews were not allowed to mix meat and milk products. After a meal of meat or fish, they had to wait a certain amount of time before ingesting milk, even if it was a small ingredient in a product.

Separate pots and pans were used for milk and meat. The family could only eat fish with scales, and the birds and animals they could consume had to be slaughtered by a rabbi who certified that the creature was disease-free. Because of Calcutta's limited Jewish population, few animals were slaughtered, so most Jews in this city lived on fish and fowl.

During dinner, we discussed the political situations in both India and Israel, a young new country created by a United Nations resolution that divided Palestine in 1948. Our conversation was always polite, no matter the subject.

After dinner, Rachel and I sat in the family's lounge. She was delightfully intelligent, and the minutes together flew by as we talked about politics and literature. By the time I left her family's apartment, it was nearly midnight.

A few days later, Rachel's brother Jacob came to visit me at my residence. He hoped that I would help him distribute some communist pamphlets to young people to get them to join the party and fight for its cause.

My opinion about communism hadn't changed. I respected the dedication and sincerity of most communists, but I preferred democracy and the democratic process that allowed voters to express their personal choices at the polls. But I knew that communism was a growing force in our country. After the partition of Bengal, the Congress Party won the right to form the West Bengal government. Many people believed that this party, which was prone to corruption, moved too slowly to reduce the economic and social misery of the poor, so I wasn't surprised that Jacob wanted the communists to win the next election.

During Jacob's visit, I was polite to him. I took some of his pamphlets, but I told him I never had spare time. I couldn't help promote his cause.

Jacob, who was tall with Rachel's beautiful eyes, had been a good student. He passed his Bachelor of Science examination. But I thought Jacob lacked ambition. He enjoyed the attention he received from young people, especially the girls, who were drawn to his interest in politics, or his sense of humor, or maybe his beautiful eyes.

Jacob returned a few days later with more pamphlets. We enjoyed some snacks while he talked about his family. He admitted that he wanted to continue his studies and pursue an academic career, but he could not afford an advanced degree.

Jacob had already been honored with early admittance into the Statistical Institute of India; but when he mustered the courage to ask his father to pay for this school, his father said that he would not spend money on any newfangled subject that lacked scholarly value.

Jacob wasn't bitter. He knew his father had been financially ruined during the First World War. But he regretted that he couldn't take advantage of this opportunity. He didn't ask anyone else for help, and he knew that it was hard to get a good job that would cover the cost of the program.

I realized that Jacob was truly kind and compassionate. He genuinely cared about the poor in India. He studied their needs and read about the political and socioeconomic conditions of India.

The Communist Party recruiters recognized that this indignant rebel would be a committed reformer. They invited him to their party headquarters and taught him the communist belief that socialism would solve the evils of capitalism. Jacob was perfect for the party; he lived up to the party's expectations.

India's elite enjoyed armchair discussions about communism, but few politicians, capitalists, and members of the landowner class would ever allow changes that turned India into a communist country.

When Gandhi was alive, he had renamed the untouchables "Harijans." This term means God's children and Gandhi's motivation went beyond the name change. He insisted that all Harijans should be treated as children of God. Ruling politicians accepted Gandhi's pronouncement.

Dr. Ambedkar, who was a highly educated and well-respected member of the Harijan community, was a member of the constituent assembly and the minister of law in the central government. When the assembly declared universal suffrage in India, this opened up the electoral process to Harijans. Most politicians, who assumed they were powerful enough to influence or even buy the Harijan vote, applauded the declaration.

Dr. Ambedkar was emboldened. He tried to enact additional parliamentarian laws that called for profound social changes throughout our society. His actions outraged politicians. Dr. Ambedkar resigned. But he continued fighting for his beliefs and his people, who wanted far more than their new classification and their right to vote. They wanted all the rights granted to everyone else.

Such demands from the untouchables didn't amuse high caste Hindus. However, they discovered that they could not control the vote of the Harijans.

The Congress Party started to crumble under the weight of thousands of small, mostly non-violent, social revolutions. The communists helped fuel many of these protests for change, so the Congress-controlled government was determined to suppress this radical group.

I agreed with Jacob that India's social and economic progress moved slowly, but I reminded him that each of us had a voice in our government. If the communists came to power, they would dictate the course of events. Jacob didn't agree, but we enjoyed our talks, and he continued to visit me.

I often spent Friday evenings at Rachel's house, and usually, we talked long after dinner. One night when I left her home some-one in the next apartment opened the door and said," There goes the stupid quack."

A stocky man about forty years old stepped back inside the apartment and shut the door. His words troubled me, but I didn't tell Rachel about the incident.

After Jacob attended the annual meeting of the Communist Party in Bombay, he came to see me. The party had paid for his trip and had invited him to speak at the gathering where he met par-ty leaders from India, the United Kingdom, and the Soviet Union. Jacob didn't think any other party in India would ever bestow him with such an honor.

We met my friend, the reporter Suleiman, at the Coffee House. He told Jacob that the central government was nervous about com-munist party activities. He thought that the government might start authorizing raids on party offices and homes and arrest party mem-bers. He asked Jacob if he had heard these rumors. He hadn't heard anything. I told Jacob to be careful.

When we were alone, I asked Jacob about the stocky man who lived next door to his family's apartment. He said that his father held the lease on that apartment, and he rented it for extra income.

Their tenant Leo was an Anglo-Indian bachelor. His mother often cooked food for him. During the war, Leo managed a canteen for the British army where he could purchase hard-to-get canned foods from the West at a low price for Jacob's mother. But Jacob said that he had no patience for this ignorant and haughty man, who pretended to be British. Jacob asked me why I asked about the guy.

I told him what happened that night outside their apartment. Jacob thought for a moment and said Leo was a racist with an inferiority complex. Most likely, he didn't like my friendship with Rachel. Jacob quickly volunteered that he was glad I was spending time with his sister. He thought everyone in the family was fine with it, too.

Early one morning Jacob, looking disheveled and exhausted, appeared at my residence. He needed to have a private conversation. I promised I would keep our talk secret.

Jacob assured me that he had never done anything violent or criminal; but yesterday evening when he started walking up the street to his apartment building, he saw police cars stopped outside the front doors.

Jacob remembered what Suleiman had said at the Coffee House. He hurried to his friend's house, who hid him in his bedroom.

His friend told Jacob that the police had raided several communist homes and had taken some party members to the police station for questioning. His friend was not a communist, but his friend's father hated communists. Jacob snuck away before sunrise. He knew the police were looking for him and he couldn't go home.

Jacob had followed back roads until he reached the medical college hospitals. He noticed that the guard at our gate was asleep, and he hurried into our residential hall.

I told Jacob that he was welcome to stay in my bedroom until mid-afternoon, but then doctors would be in the halls. Friends could barge into my room. He wouldn't be safe.

I thought of Suleiman and called him. He had just returned from covering these nightlong police raids. After he slept a few hours, Jacob was welcome to take refuge in his place.

I went to the dining room, put my breakfast on a tray, and returned to my bedroom. I told Jacob to eat up.

I left for the ward and ate my breakfast in the restaurant. At 11 o'clock, after I finished my rounds, I left instructions for my junior doctors and explained that I would return in three hours.

I asked the door attendant at our residence if he could do a quick errand for me. I tipped him and promised to watch the door until he returned. The minute the attendant left our building, I told Jacob to hurry downstairs and go to College Square where I would meet him in a few minutes.

Once the attendant returned, I met Jacob at the square. Soon we were standing with Suleiman in his small apartment. Suleiman invited the young boy to stay with him for one week. But Jacob was not to contact anyone, except me—during his stay. The young fugitive had a temporary refuge—for now.

~ 25 ~

FROM BAGHDAD TO CALCUTTA

RACHEL WASN'T SMILING WHEN I returned to the hospital. I asked her what was wrong. She was worried. I told her that Jacob was all right. I asked her to get Naomi, who was on another ward. We needed to talk.

When I informed the sister on the ward that I had to tell Rachel something important, she said that Rachel could have no more than 30 minutes with me; but I owed her one. I told her I owed her so many debts that I'd never be able to repay her.

The three of us slipped into an empty room and I told them about Jacob. Naomi said that a police detective had visited their apartment last night. He had wanted to question Jacob. The detective asked their father how he could let his son mix with such hooligans. The detective said he'd come back and left.

Rachel's brother Joseph had already seen a respected Jewish lawyer who advised the family to deny any relationship with political parties. The lawyer said they should tell the police that young Jacob was unemployed, which left him with too much idle time. He was curious about politics, but he had no political party affiliation, and he wouldn't have one in the future. The lawyer had offered to prepare an affidavit on Jacob's behalf if they needed one.

Naomi told me that Mrs. Bekhor cleaned out her son's bedroom and burned every political pamphlet, poster, and letter that linked him to politics. She filled his room with religious books and pictures; Jacob wouldn't recognize the place.

Naomi said that she wanted proof before she could tell her mother that her brother was okay.

I told Naomi that Jacob was with a friend, but I couldn't give her the address or the telephone number. I agreed to call him, and she could speak to Jacob briefly, one time. I asked them to leave the room while I gave the hospital telephone operator the phone number to dial.

As soon as Jacob came to the phone, I called Naomi and Rachel. Naomi spoke to her brother for two minutes. Then I told her to hang up. We all returned to our work.

During the next few days, I spent time with Jacob at Suleiman's apartment. His frightening episode with the police had cured him of his romance with politics. But Suleiman's work as a journalist intrigued the young boy. He asked if he could tag along with Suleiman for a couple of days.

The two days that Jacob spent with Suleiman taught him a lot about politicians, even communist politicians. He learned how they "liquidated" undesirables—supposedly, on behalf of the unfortunate in our society.

Jacob said he wished he could begin a professional career, but his father thought like a Neanderthal. He also recognized that his father's financial shortfall and his own personal impetuosity were closing the doors.

Suleiman promised Jacob that he'd talk to a few professor friends to see if there was a good path for him to follow.

During the time I spent with Jacob, he told me the fascinating history of his family. Rabbi Shlomo Bekhor Hussein, who was their grandfather, had been a well-known scholar and the chief rabbi of Iraq. An astute businessman, he had established a school for religious studies in Baghdad, started the first printing press in Iraq, and owned considerable real estate.

When the rabbi was elderly, he became absorbed in the scriptures and teaching. He let his eldest son Joshua manage his business interests. Jacob and Rachael's father Yehuda, who was the younger son, won a scholarship to continue his studies in France, but his mother didn't want her son to leave Bagdad.

World War I began after Shlomo's death. Iraq, which was part of the Ottoman Empire, was allied with Germany and Austria. The rulers of the Ottoman Empire decided prosperous Jews of Iraq supported their enemies: the Anglo-French allies. They began arresting Jews and confiscating their property. Yehuda, who was about 20 years old, fled Baghdad with a small amount of money. When he reached a port on the Persian Gulf, he boarded a boat and sailed to Bombay.

He located a cousin Neim, who worked for a small business. Yehuda got a job in a shop and made do with the lousy pay while he spent his idle moments learning English, which he believed was the ticket to a successful business career.

After the war, he returned to Iraq, where he married Georgina Kassim. He tried to get back the seized family property, but the government had sold off their share of the real estate at auction and had also confiscated all of Shlomo Bekhor's assets that had been held in British Banks. These assets were gone for good.

Yehuda decided to return to India with his wife Georgina and her brother David. The three of them sold their belongings and hoped they had made enough money to begin successful new lives.

Yehuda's cousin Neim, who welcomed them in Bombay, convinced them to board a train and go with him and his family to Calcutta to start a new business. As much as Georgina loved Baghdad and its Tigris River, Calcutta appealed to her. She appreciated her first flush toilet and the comfortable house.

The extended family rented a house in a Calcutta area called New Market, which Neim thought was a great neighborhood in which to start a new business—and he knew the perfect business. He painted an optimistic picture of India's tea and coffee trade and impressed them with his knowledge of suppliers and would-be clients. He was eager to put his expertise to work. His only hurdle was insufficient capital.

Yehuda and Georgina agreed to provide most of the capital, but Georgina wanted to put aside money for her brother David to continue his studies. Her request angered Yehuda and Neim. They told her that if she didn't trust them, she should go back to Baghdad. They needed all the money to start the business. Georgina relented.

They rented a shop in New Market and Neim ordered the merchandise. A year later their new business was barely surviving. The family borrowed money, and they limped along for five years. They were finally forced to sell the business to pay off their debts.

Georgina's brother David never continued his education. Lack of money was one problem, but he had also failed to pass a single entrance examination to a good school.

The family split up when the family business was sold. Neim worked for a Jewish merchant who sold textiles. Yehuda stayed in the coffee and tea business earning just enough money to support his growing family. His young daughter Naomi and young son Joseph became students at English-medium schools run by missionaries.

The Bekhor house observed orthodox Jewish customs, but Georgina wanted her children to have a modern British upbringing. Yehuda was a poor businessman who lacked drive. While his contemporaries made money, his finances never improved. He blamed his suffering on fate and everyone he knew. After all these years, he still hoped he would reclaim his lost wealth and lead the life he deserved.

His wife's brother David, who lived in their home, did nothing to help the family. He refused to work hard, and he went regularly to the synagogue and joined the Mason's Lodge, where wealthy men occasionally got him odd jobs. David used his meager income to buy fashionable clothes so that he looked like a man of substance. Yehuda resented him. His wife felt sorry for him. Her husband's business venture had consumed her brother's share of money and had torpedoed his career.

Georgina was hardworking with a great business sense. She thought her husband should add a small eatery to his shop. Mr. Bekhor said this idea was beneath his dignity.

The couple had three more children: Rachel and two boys Jacob and Daniel. Life turned difficult for Georgina since her husband refused to help with their children's education and upbringing. She was exhausted by her responsibilities, and her husband remained oblivious.

Early one morning Yehuda saw Naomi studying for her Senior Cambridge examination. He told his little girl that she didn't need to study. It wasn't important. Naomi felt sorry for her father. He was stuck in his old world, and he couldn't understand the new world unfolding around him.

Naomi and Rachel realized they had to earn a living to create the life they wanted for themselves. When Naomi completed her examination, she talked to a married nurse who lived in their building. She took Naomi for an interview at the nursing school. She was accepted immediately.

Naomi only told Rachel her good news. They both knew that their parents, especially their father, would be opposed to this modern turn of events. Naomi waited until she was officially enrolled before she informed her parents.

Naomi's father was aghast. He went to pray at the synagogue, and he asked his wife to fast for atonement. They both begged their daughter not to enter this dishonorable profession.

Naomi reminded them that the family lacked the money for her brothers to continue their studies in college, which was something most Jewish families wanted for their children. So surely, they would never pay for their daughter's further education.

Her father offered to arrange a good marriage for Naomi. His suggestion stiffened her resolve. She became a student at the nursing school. Two years later, Rachel followed her sister's footsteps. Her parents were angry with her, but Rachel shared her sister's determination. Nothing would stop her from pursuing her goal.

~ 26 ~

TWO GENERATIONS

DAYS LATER SULEIMAN CALLED ME. He had learned that an international computer company in collaboration with the Government of India was offering a six-month long, all-expenses paid training course in Bombay for students to learn computer technology. He had talked to the head of the university physics department who had agreed to serve as a referee on Jacob's behalf. Suleiman thought that Jacob would qualify, but he could not have a police record.

We talked to Jacob who asked for two days before he made his decision.

Later, when I saw Naomi at the hospital, she said that she was leaving her hospital job to work in an excellent nursing home, where she'd make better money. She also mentioned that her parents wanted to meet with me as soon as possible.

I offered to visit on Saturday.

When I told Rachel my plans, I noticed her concern but she promised to join us later that evening.

When the servant opened the door on Saturday, I understood

Rachel's hesitation. The house was quiet. Mr. and Mrs. Bekhor sat in the lounge beside a table with a big plate of roasted pumpkin seeds. They were peeling the pumpkin seeds, one by one, eating them leisurely.

Mr. Bekhor asked me to sit down.

Mrs. Bekhor explained that Saturday was their Sabbath, the day that God blessed for resting. It was not the best day for a visit. From Friday sunset to Saturday sunset, Jews did not light any fire, did no cooking, and shunned all physical activity. They ate cold food and didn't smoke or drink alcohol. She said that Mr. Bekhor could manage the prohibition against alcohol since he drank after sunset, but the inability to smoke made him irritable.

From the moment I sat down with the Bekhors, they peeled and ate their mound of roasted pumpkin seeds—one by one—keeping busy to pass the time. But this simple activity was inadequate. Mr. Bekhor's mind moved at a fast clip as he reviewed individual injustices that he had suffered throughout his life.

He complained about his father's decision to retire from his successful business to teach the Torah and Talmud. He railed against Iraqi neighbors who pilfered his father's estate. He complained about his older brother's self-serving deal with Ottoman officials.

How he suffered, lamented Mr. Bekhor, while others enjoyed what was his. He left the room and returned with a typewritten letter from the Bank of the Middle East. He made me read the letter. It explained the bank's inability to repay him his deposits that had been confiscated by the Ottoman authorities.

"Where was the justice?" asked Mr. Bekhor. I had no answer.

Mr. Bekhor talked about his sorry state of affairs until finally I asked him why he wanted to see me. He said he wanted to know the truth about his son, Jacob. He insisted his son was a good boy; and if he followed proper food habits, he was certain Jacob would become a man of good character.

I told Mr. Bekhor that Jacob was a good fellow, and he would be home in a few days.

He asked me to tell his sons to start working. It was their duty to look after their elderly parents. He switched the talk to Joseph. He was no good. He wouldn't help his father in the shop. He only wanted to play his violin! How would he ever make a living?

Joseph walked into the lounge and told his father to stop all his talk. His blood pressure would go up.

Mr. Bekhor stormed off to his bedroom, with Mrs. Bekhor trailing behind him, apologizing in his wake.

I tried to talk to Joseph about Jacob, but Joseph veered the conversation back to himself. He said that he had to find a job and leave this house. There would never be any meeting of minds.

I asked Joseph why he didn't try to work for his father. He insisted that his father always vetoed any changes he suggested. The shop would never prosper. He had asked his father if he could prepare samples of their teas to give to retailers in Calcutta and other cities. He believed his father could establish his own brand and develop a successful product line, expand the shop, and make good money. His father called Joseph a lunatic with grandiose schemes. Joseph said that he also brought up his mother's plan to add a small café to their shop. His father hated the idea.

Joseph had given up. He refused to work in that unsuccessful, outdated shop.

Joseph's parents returned to the lounge. Mr. Bekhor sat back down, still fuming, and demanded a cup of tea. Mrs. Bekhor gave him some iced tea. He wanted hot tea, which was unavailable on the

Sabbath. He dumped the iced tea on the floor.

Meanwhile, Jacob decided to apply for the computer science training. He and I went to visit the well-respected Jewish lawyer who had agreed to write an affidavit on behalf of Jacob. Five days later Jacob appeared with the lawyer at Calcutta's central police station. A detective grilled Jacob and the police superintendent gave him a strong warning: One more tangle with the law and he'd go to jail.

Suleiman got Jacob the application form and excellent referrals for the training program. Jacob completed the application process; and while he waited for the results, he went home to spend a few days with his family. He was accepted into the program. By the time he left for Bombay, the Bekhors were so grateful. They called me a true friend of the family.

~ **27** ~

LOVE

I NEVER BECAME THE REGISTRAR at the hospital, but doctors and nurses treated me as if I had achieved this rank. Our ward worked efficiently, everyone got along, and patients seemed satisfied with their treatment and care. I felt secure.

One morning an elderly woman with bowel cancer was transferred into our paying ward from a district hospital. She was also diabetic and suffered from hypertension. I liked the lady. She was kind and intelligent.

Her husband, who was a powerful member of the legislature, and his entourage visited her frequently before her operation. However once the woman underwent extensive surgery to remove the cancer, we knew that any complication during her post-operative period would interfere with her prognosis.

I soon heard from the nurses that the politician-husband and his cronies were visiting the woman and making so much noise they even disturbed other patients. The nurses asked me to leave a note on the woman's bedside table that restricted her to two visitors at a time. The husband ignored the restriction and stayed beyond the authorized visiting hours.

The elderly woman, who was in severe discomfort, told me that her visitors exhausted her. Other patients also complained about this boisterous collection of men. The next day I was in the ward when the husband arrived with his buddies.

I told the man that his wife was only permitted two visitors at a time.

The man asked if I knew who he was.

I told him I was in charge of the ward, and the welfare of patients came first. He had to follow the rules.

"To hell with you and your rules," he snapped. The husband ripped up the note. I stopped him and his entourage as they tried to bully their way into the room.

"This is a hospital," he shouted. "Not a prison." The man stormed out of the ward and headed straight to the hospital superintendent's office. He complained that I'd insulted him and showed him no respect.

The hospital superintendent assured the husband that the professor of surgery, Dr. Bhattcharya, who was the head of the department, was coming to the hospital the next morning, and would investigate the complaint and take proper action. The superintendent promised to keep the politician-husband informed.

I was worried. But luckily some helpful Bengali nurses told the elderly woman that this episode could destroy my career. Such a pity, they said. I was such a conscientious doctor. I'd stayed with her until the anesthesia wore off. I'd visited her repeatedly to check on her condition even when I was extremely busy with other patients. She told the nurses that I must have had a good mother to turn me into such a wonderful man.

I told my boss that the professor of surgery might call. I was too late. The investigating team was arriving at 11 o'clock.

When I visited the lady that morning, she began singing a Bengali song, which, in English, said, "If any boy is so good, how good must be his mother."

I told the kind woman that I thought I had my mother's blessings, but unfortunately, my mother passed away a few years ago. The elderly woman understood the depths of my loss. She said I had her blessings as well.

At 11 o'clock, Dr. Bhattcharya, arrived with the politician husband and two of his cronies. The resident surgeon and his entire staff trailed behind them. They were an imposing group of witnesses to my downfall.

Dr. Bhattcharya glared at me and said that the hospital was not a prison.

I nodded and kept quiet. I also hung back while the group crowded around the elderly woman. Dr. Bhattcharya asked her how she was feeling. She said she'd be dead by now, except that some good doctors and nurses were taking excellent care of her.

Dr. Bhattcharya said her husband had complained that a junior doctor had been rude to her husband and suggested that this doctor must have caused her great stress.

The elderly woman insisted that all the doctors had been good to her, especially one doctor. She started singing, "If any boy...."

Dr. Bhattcharya looked at the politico husband, who pointed his finger at me. "He's the offender."

The lady scoffed. "What's the matter with you? He's the dearest boy! You want everyone to say 'yes, sir' to everything you say. But this doctor works hard; he won't do that." The lovely old lady yawned and said she was tired. She wanted everyone to leave her in peace.

As Dr. Bhattcharya passed by me, he said that I might get my way with an old woman, but one day I'd be caught. If this inquiry had gone against me, I would have had a stain on my career for years. I decided I needed to control my temper. The price of speaking out was too high.

The next day I received an unexpected letter from Dolly. We rarely corresponded, but she wanted me to know that she had received her Master's degree in philosophy, which ended her university education. She expressed her eternal love for me and said her feelings for me were irreplaceable; however, she added, that she had done her research in the world of Brahmin tradition. No marital relationship was allowed between any couple separated by less than seven generations. We were third cousins. Dolly knew that we could never be husband and wife. Neither our society nor our families would accept our relationship. Dolly said she had agreed to marry an intelligent, highly qualified man. She'd met him and decided that he would be a good life companion.

Dolly hoped I would meet a special person with uncommon talents. She ended by saying she'd love me until the end of her life.

What a letter! I was neither happy nor unhappy that Dolly was getting married. For hours, I kept thinking over her words to me, and finally, I concluded that Dolly would always be in the background of my life, but that was it. Life would go on.

I destroyed the letter and wrote back my congratulations to my lovely cousin on getting her Masters. I added that I was glad she was getting married. I mailed the letter and didn't know if I'd ever see her again.

I didn't want Rachel involved in my patient problem at the hospital, so I hadn't seen her in a while. When we finally got together, she knew every detail about the foolish event with the political husband. Nurses talk, she reminded me.

Rachel said things were better at home since Jacob was back with the family. She laughed and added that her younger brother had hardly recognized his bedroom.

Days later Naomi called to say her mother wanted to see me. When I arrived at the apartment, Mrs. Bekhor thanked me for looking after Jacob. She said that she wanted my assurance that everything was properly arranged for Jacob so that he could begin his training in Bombay. She also wanted to be certain that he'd be able to get a good job once he completed the program.

I told Mrs. Bekhor not to worry. Everything would work out for her son.

When I left the apartment, I was surprised to see Rachel approach the building. She was supposed to be working. Rachel explained that she wanted the night off and switched shifts with another nurse. She wanted to see me.

I suggested that we go to the movies near our hospital. From the theater, we went out to eat. It was so lovely to spend time with Rachel. When we held hands as I walked her back to her residence, I was overcome with strong feelings. I remembered walking with Dolly along the riverbank in Mymensingh. But this moment was all about Rachel. Just Rachel.

~ 28 ~

NEW HORIZONS

ONCE JACOB WENT TO BOMBAY, I turned my attention to Joseph who wanted to try to become an Indian Air Force pilot. If he were selected, Joseph thought he could become an officer over time.

Joseph's father hated this plan. He said that joining the military was crazy. When he was growing up in Iraq under the Ottoman Empire, his relatives had paid bribes to keep him free of mandatory conscription. In India, military service was voluntary. Why on earth, he asked Joseph, would he, a Jew, want to join the army or air force?

But Joseph was determined; so, his mother, who also hated the plan, went on a hunger strike. She would rather die, she told her son, than see him become an air force pilot. Joseph gave up his dream.

Finally, Joseph found a job as a supervisor at the British-owned Imperial Tobacco Company. The title was greater than the job. Joseph would have to spend time in Andhra Province in the south of India and purchase quality tobacco from producers in rural areas. Transportation and hotel accommodations would be difficult and rustic, he would have to learn Telegu, the local language, and he needed to live periodically in Andhra. Joseph took the job and went off to Andhra in the south. Yet another member of the younger generation of the Bekhor family had started life on his own.

Meanwhile, my future was one big question mark. Unless I pursued post-graduate training and studies in England, I would never become a surgeon. Studying in the United States was not feasible. Training would be expensive, and our Indian degrees didn't count for much.

I stuck to my original plan to go to England and become a Fellow of the Royal College of Surgeons. However, I needed to raise money to support myself during my first year in London. I talked to Kumar, but he was against my expensive plan and wouldn't help me. While I tried to come up with a solution, I continued working hard at the hospital.

One Friday evening after I ate dinner with the Bekhors, I talked with Joseph, who had recently returned from his first trip to Andhra. He said that his work was okay; but he had decided that since he lost every fight with his parents, he would save money so that he could move to the United Kingdom and try for a music career, which was his true goal.

I asked Joseph how his parents reacted to my friendship with Rachel. He said that he knew his parents liked and respected me, but they objected to my religion, which eliminated any chance of a relationship.

He also told me that once Rachel completed nursing school their mother wanted her to go to England for more training. But he was shocked when he heard his mother say in Arabic that the real purpose behind the trip was to get Rachel married there. Her niece Miriam's elder brother, Isaac, who was a photographer, lived in London. They thought that he would be a suitable match for their daughter. But for their plan to work, they needed Rachel to stop fooling around with me.

My head was spinning when I left the Bekhor's apartment. Yes, I planned to pursue my career in England. But Rachel... My brain and my heart knew I also needed to pursue her.

The next morning, I told Rachel about a Christian nurse named Sally who was applying for midwifery training in England. I thought that this program might be good for her.

Rachel and I went to talk with Sally. She told Rachel that the midwifery course was an excellent opportunity with favorable arrangements. She only had to pay for her travel expenses to the United Kingdom. The governments of India and Britain would cover everything else.

Sally offered to get Rachel the information and an application form. She had time to decide; the course didn't begin for a year. Sally hoped Rachel would apply and be there with her.

On our way back to the ward, I told Rachel that the training in England could be good for her. She could stay in England or come back to India. As a state-registered midwife, she'd increase her pay in this country.

Rachel decided to apply, but she didn't tell her mother about the course until she was accepted. Her mother was delighted, and she never knew that I was aware of Rachel's plans.

One afternoon Rachel finally asked me about my future plans. I told her I wanted to become a Fellow of the Royal College of Surgeons of England. My anatomy professor had already granted me permission to study in his laboratory for a few months, which would help me prepare for the fellowship,

~ ~ ~ ~ ~

The Royal College of Surgeons informed me my fellowship papers were in order. I was eligible to apply for this course which would prepare me for the pre-clinical part of the FRCS examination. Now I needed money to get to London and through the first year. I visited Uncle Manindra, who was posted near Calcutta. I hoped he could convince Kumar to give me the money.

Uncle Manindra was surprised Kumar opposed my plans. He was confident our family account had sufficient money for me to pursue the fellowship. He said he'd go talk to my brother.

I returned to Calcutta and immediately started studying in the anatomy lab with two other doctors who wanted to go to England as fellows. Dr. Saha, who was married and had a child, had worked for eight years as a medical officer in the railways. He had been the top student in surgery in his class. His family was wealthy and could afford Saha's goal to become a fellow at the Royal College of Surgeons. My friend Amjad, who had completed ENT surgical training and one year of general surgery, was the third member of our group.

The three of us received some human bones from the department and spent hours studying osteology. We soon developed a close relationship with the bones and each other.

Right after we started studying physiology, I received bad news from Uncle Manindra. My brother told our uncle that he refused to destroy the entire family to satisfy the whim of one family member. He also insisted I was trying to influence Uncle Manindra in order to create a rift between my brother and all his relatives.

I tried to borrow the money from Uncle Manindra, but I received a letter from him that said with retirement on the immediate horizon, they were in no position to lend me money.

In desperation, I wrote a long letter to Uncle Hem explaining the importance of my career goal and my brother's complete unwillingness to help me.

I continued with my hospital work and my studies in the anatomy lab. During the evenings, I tried to relax with Rachel. Occasionally, we ate together or went to the movies or discussed books we had read. I looked forward to our hours together. Soon, Rachel would end her nursing course at the hospital. I would see her infrequently when she began working for a few months as a private nurse to earn money for her trip to England.

One Saturday afternoon I hired a taxi, and Rachel and I went to the Ram Krishna Mission in Belur, which was beautifully built in the less florid, North Indian tradition. The temple, which was also popular with foreigners, was nestled on the banks of the Hooghly River. The setting inspired us to rent a small country boat rowed by boatmen.

The experience on the Hooghly was magical. The sun had a red glow that spread through the sky and a gentle breeze soothed us. The view was overwhelming, and my hand had slipped onto Rachel's shoulder until she gently moved it away. That evening Rachel and I decided to walk back to our homes, which were just a short distance away.

Finally, I heard back from Uncle Hem, who was relieved that I had never forgotten my roots. He said East Pakistan was particularly difficult for non-Muslims, especially Hindus. Law and order had suffered, and tenants on the family's property often neglected to pay their taxes or fulfill their obligations to share the produce from their crops. The estate's income had depreciated by 50 percent.

Uncle Hem said that two years ago he would have happily paid all my expenses, but he would try to cover the core amount of the fellowship. He also said that my brother's attitude didn't surprise him. He knew Kumar had inherited genes from the maternal side of my family, who eagerly received from others with their hands in the supine position, but they never learned how to turn their hands over to give. Uncle Hem told me to study hard and get ready for my journey.

Uncle Hem's response shocked me, and I knew that his offer was genuine. It would be beneath his dignity to go back on his word. But I needed to raise more money. I approached Jeevan who was so successful. My father had helped my cousin when he was young. I hoped Jeevan would return the favor. My cousin promised that he wouldn't let me down since he was certain I would repay the loan. Finally, I believed I would begin the next stage of my career.

One day Rachel called from her new job at the nursing home and asked me to come see her. When we met, she told me that her Mom and Dad were happy about her upcoming trip, but Naomi and Miriam were unusually glum. Rachel was also aware that conversations often stopped in her home when she walked into the room.

Rachel had to get back to her patient. As I started to leave, I told her I was glad she was going to England because it looked like I'd be there by the end of the year. I asked her not to share this information with anyone. I loved the sweet smile she gave me when I finally left.

One evening Linda asked me to come see her in her ward after my evening rounds. We stepped into an empty room where we had a drink and some light food. Linda asked me what I was doing after I finished my work now that the Hebrew girl was gone. She told me she heard Rachel was leaving India and giving up nursing to marry a Jewish boy in England. This was the real reason she was going to London. Linda added that a matchmaker was arranging Rachel's marriage.

A few nights later the great Scottish sister tutor was retiring and planned to return to Scotland. The nurses threw her a big farewell party and Linda, dressed in a lovely sari, looked quite pretty. I brought Joseph as my guest since Rachel was working. When I introduced him to Linda, I told her we had to leave before the dinner. Linda was disappointed and kissed me goodbye.

I was so embarrassed, but Joseph's face lit up. His happiness surprised me until he said that his parents had finally told him about their plans to get Rachel married in England. They'd started corresponding with Miriam's brother Isaac and they had urged him to court her, with their blessings.

Joseph said he had dreaded talking to me about the futility of my relationship with his sister. He had also failed to talk to Rachel about her parents' disapproval of me. She was so bull-headed, and bad-tempered, and she never listened to anyone. This was why her parents had not told her the real reason they were sending her to England. Rachel had to marry inside her community.

Joseph tried to boost my ego. He told me I was intelligent and educated. Rachel, he insisted, was not up to my standards. I could do better, he said. Linda was a much better match.

At the hospital, Linda paraded around a photograph of the two of us that was taken at the party. She told everyone we were back together. I tried to stop all the gossip, but it continued.

One evening Saha invited me to his family's large ancestral home in Calcutta to meet his wife and son. Joya, who was educated, didn't want to work and preferred caring for her husband and son. She supported her husband's goal to become a fellow in England, but she was going to stay behind with her in-laws since Saha would be so busy with his studies.

Saha was so fortunate. His goal was unobstructed. But Amjad and I shared the same problem. Neither one of us had enough money to be confident about our future.

The next time I visited with the Bekhors in their apartment, I didn't feel the tension that had slipped into place after the riverboat trip. Everyone smiled at me, and Mrs. Bekhor volunteered that they had gotten Rachel's British Indian passport from the British High Commission. She was so eager for her daughter to meet her cousin in England.

Naomi arrived after completing her shift at the nursing home. She said Joseph had told her that Linda and I were an item. She quickly asked if Joseph had talked to me about Rachel.

I nodded.

"So, you know what my mom is planning?"

I told Naomi that it was strange everyone knew about this plan for Rachel except the person who should have known first: Rachel.

Naomi said that her sister was kept in the dark because, and here came the familiar litany—Rachel was stubborn, bad tempered, and angered easily. And yes, admitted Naomi, she respected her sister's honesty and reliability.

I told Naomi that honesty and reliability made Rachel trustworthy, which was an admirable trait. As for being obstinate, this quality could be both good and bad; and I dismissed all the talk about a bad temper. I never witnessed it in Rachel.

Joseph arrived and simply said, "Out of sight will soon turn into out of mind for you and Rachel."

After such a completely unappetizing conversation, we went into the dining room for the Friday night Sabbath dinner. Mr. Bekhor began his familiar chant, the bread was broken, and David offered the wine, which was blessed and served to all of us.

The next weekend Jeevan's wife Leena invited me to Sunday dinner at their house. I was thrilled. My money problem would soon end. As Leena walked me around the lovely grounds and their handsome house in South Calcutta, the phone rang. Jeevan had to leave unexpectedly.

Leena brought up the loan. She said that they were grateful that my father had helped Jeevan, and they wished they could do the same for me. But their house cost more than they expected, and they couldn't help me.

I told her I understood, and we said goodbye.

I was in such a crazy situation. The three people I thought would help me and could afford to help me—my brother, Uncle Manindra, and Jeevan—had backed out. The uncle who agreed to help me was not on my original list, and he was in a difficult financial situation. How strange!

I couldn't believe my misfortune. I still needed to find one or two other people to help me, or I'd be forced to give up my dream for this fellowship. I was at a loss. Crushed and disheartened.

~ **29** ~

MONEY QUEST

TIME MOVED ON. BEFORE RACHEL could leave for England, she had to go with her mother to see Mrs. Cohen, the widow of an important Jewish judge in Calcutta. The Cohens, who were originally from Baghdad, were widely respected for their philanthropy and business success, but not by Mr. Bekhor.

Mr. Bekhor insisted they had pilfered some of his father's property in Iraq so they could sell it to get money to move to India. Mrs. Bekhor, with her humble background, felt differently. She thought the Cohens were upper class, with an illustrious pedigree that extended back to the Bible. More immediately, she appreciated the help they offered her and other less fortunate Jewish families in Calcutta.

When Rachel agreed to visit the widow, she didn't know her mother had asked Mrs. Cohen to remove Rachel's impure ideas regarding a relationship with me. Rachel sat and listened politely as Mrs. Cohen extolled the greatness of the Hebrew race. She reminded Rachel that God had instructed all Jewish women to keep the

Sabbath and follow every Jewish ritual and traditional observance. Mrs. Cohen said Rachel had to marry a Jewish man and raise her children to be Jewish. If she married outside her religion, she'd bring God's wrath on her people.

Rachel kept her mouth shut. She knew Mrs. Cohen had signed the written security guarantee in which she promised to cover the cost of Rachel's return trip to India. Without this guarantee, Rachel couldn't go to England.

The day of Rachel's departure arrived. Mr. Bekhor panicked: his unwed daughter was setting off to a distant land. How reckless! No single girl should make such a foolish trip! He ranted and wept as he held his precious Rachel in his arms. He became so distraught that he couldn't accompany her to the station.

Once we reached the train platform, I stood behind Mrs. Bekhor while she fussed over her daughter. Rachel looked at me through her liquid brown eyes that were filled with trust. She seemed to be sending me a message. Finally, Rachel boarded the train, and it chugged out of the station. Rachel was gone.

Sleep eluded me. Random memories swirled through my mind. I remembered meeting Rachel, and I remembered her sweet reaction to meeting me. How she slowly learned to trust me. How her family dreaded our relationship. And I remembered how her family secretly arranged for their nephew in England to court Rachel with their blessings. I'd done everything I could to help the family. Yet...

Did I really love Rachel? I didn't know. But I knew she made me happy when I was with her and I knew I'd do anything for her without any reservation.

I saw a vision of Dolly standing at a distance from me. She was pleased with my relationship with Rachel. She seemed to encourage me to follow Rachel to England.

Work at the hospital kept me busy. One day I discussed my goal to get the English fellowship with my boss. He'd heard about the study group in the anatomy laboratory. He also knew that I was struggling to raise the money to go abroad and survive the first year. He offered to help. He was the private surgeon for some foreign and Indian companies in Calcutta. He asked me to assist him with his cases. He also said that he needed my help with follow-up care.

I remember one case in particular involving the manager of a British company, who was in a bad car accident. He had suffered a concussion and compound fracture of his right lower leg with extensive lacerations and loss of tissue. After he left the nursing home, I took care of him in his home.

One day my patient said that he was infuriated by our government's proposal to introduce minimum wages. He insisted that communists had demanded this proposal, which would force the closure of factories and mills. Workers would lose their jobs.

My patient, who had lived in India for years, insisted workers were paid decently and earned extra money when they deserved it. Why did they need a minimum wage?

His perception of the poor shocked me. I knew that these workers ate simple cheap meals and lived in miserable crowded shacks to send some of their meager earnings to poor relatives in Bihar.

I thought it was critically important to increase their wealth, as important as improving our country's infrastructure and education and health systems. Only ten percent of our population was literate. Our country's farming methods were backward, with illiterate farmers using outdated tools.

I also knew that India's poverty had increased during the last

40 years of British rule while most other nations had increased their wealth. This British manager was wrong. If business people from rich countries thought India's abysmal living conditions were normal, they would never help us improve our world standing.

One day my cousin Sadananda called me. He had accepted India's offer of partitioning and had transferred his job and his family from new East Pakistan to Calcutta. He lived in the suburbs, but he rarely called me.

Sadananda said his father, Uncle Bidhan, who was coming to Calcutta, wanted to see me. I was thrilled. When I saw him, Uncle Bidhan looked much older. He said life in East Pakistan was lonely and dangerous, but he hoped to move to Calcutta next year.

Uncle Bidhan had followed my suggestions. His son was going to build a house for his young family and his mother, Auntie Beena; and the house would be in her name. He'd also made out a will that named his son the ultimate beneficiary after the death of Auntie Beena. I was relieved to hear this.

Sadananda wanted Uncle Bidhan and me to help him select the plot for the new house. His real estate agent took us to a middle-class community under development in a safe Calcutta suburb. We made our choice and arranged for Uncle Bidhan and Sadananda to meet with a lawyer to finalize the contract.

On Monday Uncle Bidhan and I went to the Calcutta branch of his bank and sorted out the financing. Once everything was arranged, Uncle Bidhan was so happy and grateful that I'd helped him yet again.

After a while Uncle Bidhan wanted to sit and talk. He'd been so busy with his personal affairs that he was eager to learn about me. I told him that I wanted to become a fellow of the Royal College of Surgeons, but my brother wouldn't give me the money.

Kumar's behavior didn't surprise him.

I told him Uncle Manindra and my cousin Jeevan said they couldn't help either.

Uncle Bidhan was disappointed. He wondered how they could forget that they went to my father for help when they were studying, and my father had helped each of them. He asked how much money I needed; then this dear uncle made an offer. He couldn't come up with the entire amount, but he'd loan me a significant portion and he'd talk to Uncle Ashok about loaning me the rest. If Uncle Ashok couldn't help, my uncle would find someone else.

Uncle Bidhan insisted we return to the bank. He bought a bank draft in my name and put it in my hand. What a wonderful man!

A few days later, I received a letter from Uncle Ashok. He was sending me money. I couldn't believe it! My money problem was nearly resolved.

Life was so strange. How odd that my brother, who acquired two postgraduate degrees at considerable cost to our family, seized control of the money left for both of us and wouldn't give me my rightful share. I thought about Uncle Manindra and my cousin Jeevan, who were in a position to lend me money; yet they had turned me down.

I never planned to ask for help from Uncle Hem and I never imagined he'd come to my rescue. But this man was the one who held his hand out to me. I never considered approaching Uncle Bidhan or Uncle Ashok. Neither man was in a position to help. During much of my life, I'd watched Uncle Bidhan struggle and fail to reclaim his family properties and assets. But my two dear uncles, who loved me, took the risk because they believed in me.

It was difficult to get money from East Pakistan to Calcutta.

But Uncle Ashok had said in his letter to me that lending me this money was the right thing to do. God would show him how to get the money to me.

~ 30 ~

MARKING TIME

As SOON AS I TOLD my boss Dr. Banerjee that I had the money for England, everyone seemed to hear my good news. My brother called and said I had to get married. He had good candidates. "Don't be stupid," he said. I could still end up short of my goal. I had no interest in talking with Kumar. My life was moving on.

Jacob, who had returned from Bombay, came to visit me. He had signed a three-year contract with a British computer company that had an office in Calcutta. He was excited about his future. He said his mother wanted me to come for dinner on Friday evening.

I told Jacob my latest news from Rachel, who had begun her midwifery training at Leicester General Hospital. As I spoke about his sister, Jacob looked uncomfortable. He asked if I knew his parent's matchmaking plans for Rachel.

I said I was aware, but I doubted that Rachel would be interested.

Jacob disagreed. He said his sister would get lonely in England. Once Miriam's brother started to court her, she'd be receptive. He doubted I'd see her again. She'd be married in six months.

At the Bekhor's apartment on Friday night everyone was cheerful. As Mrs. Bekhor showed me a photo of Rachel and her cousin Isaac, she said that he was a bright young Jewish man with a successful photography studio. She hoped they liked each other.

"It would be up to them," I said.

Days later I received a letter from Rachel that dwelled on her radically changed hospital diet of fried fish and roasted chicken. She was grateful for the bottle of tomato sauce. She included a picture of a young man. She asked if I liked the photo of her cousin, who had been so kind to her since her arrival.

I wondered if Rachel was teasing me or if she was preparing me for things to come.

I wasn't leaving for England until December, so I needed a job for six months. Unexpectedly, the assistant emergency doctor, who was Muslim, decided to go to East Pakistan. The new country needed physicians.

I went through the interview process and stood before the professor who enjoyed humiliating me. I assured him that this would be the last time he interviewed me. I had been accepted for the primary FRCS course in London.

I received the job and permission to stay in the residence hall. I could keep my expenses low during my final months in Calcutta.

Rachel continued sending letters with photos of her taken by her photographer cousin. The photos so unnerved me that I dreaded her letters. Then, the letters stopped; and this made me feel worse.

I finally went to see the Bekhors. Rachel's mother was distraught. Her daughter had been found unconscious in her bed. It had been so cold Rachel had left on her gas heater and everyone assumed that she was overcome by gas fumes when the pilot light blew out.

Mrs. Bekhor said doctors had conducted numerous tests and shaved off her lovely hair. She still suffered from headaches and Mrs. Bekhor worried that Rachel had a brain tumor.

Miriam and her husband, who had separated for a while, had reconciled. They were moving to England.

Mrs. Bekhor believed that Miriam would find happiness once she escaped her husband's cursed family. She also assumed her niece would be a great comfort to Rachel. The woman sighed. "Of course, only God knows if Rachel will survive if she has brain cancer."

I was glad to leave the gloomy apartment. The Bekhors were decent people, but they were so narrow-minded that every small change terrified them. They were trapped inside their bleak world that left them deeply morose.

I worried about Rachel. I'd heard nothing from her for a month. Finally, Rachel sent a letter. She said that she felt better, and her consulting neurologist had ruled out a brain tumor. However, she still suffered from headaches and nausea, and brain wave changes might indicate epilepsy. She said she didn't have any new photos to send me. I wouldn't recognize her without her hair. I was relieved she still had her sense of humor.

I talked to a neurologist at our hospital who said brain wave changes were often a residual symptom of gas poisoning. He felt confident that when her doctors in London repeated the EEG in a month, they'd see radically improved results. He also thought the headaches and nausea would eventually disappear. I visited Mrs. Bekhor to share his opinion with her. I saw Miriam, who was eager to move to England.

Two weeks later, I received good news from Rachel. Her headaches and nausea had disappeared. She'd been discharged from the hospital. I also received a letter from Uncle Ashok, who instructed me to go to the Calcutta branch of his bank to collect a bank draft to cover the loan. I received the check from the bank and deposited it into my new Lloyds Bank account that would send money to me in England. Now, all I needed was the loan from Uncle Hem.

~ **31** ~

THE TRANSFER

OUR STUDY GROUP IN THE anatomy lab advanced to physiology and chemistry, but Amjad was anxious. He hadn't received any financial help from his brother, who lived in East Pakistan with his uncle Fazlul Huq.

Amjad wrote to his brother and explained he was studying hard in Calcutta to get an important British fellowship. His brother insisted that Amjad return to East Pakistan and convince him, face-to-face, why he had the right to use the family resources to become a surgeon when East Pakistan had such a critical need for general practitioners.

Amjad was devastated. He realized he had to go to Dacca and discuss his career with his uncle Fazlul Huq, who had become politically prominent in East Pakistan.

Even the Saha family, which had enough money for Dr. Saha to do post-graduate work in England, began questioning the expenditure. All of Saha's brothers, who had joined the family grocery business, had prospered. The family knew their brother Dr. Saha, the only family member with an advanced degree, was well educated, but they wondered if he was intelligent. What if he failed in England?

One day Arup came to my residence. He told me Nayeb Babu, the manager of our family estate, was coming to Calcutta to see his son. Arup, who was friends with the son, said that Nayeb Babu wanted to see me during his visit. I wondered if this was how Uncle Hem would get me money.

Days later Arup brought Nayeb Babu to see me. I was delighted to see this man after so many years. Our estate manager handed me an envelope securely closed with the family seal. He said that it contained a private letter from Uncle Hem. No one else could see it. He asked Arup to leave the room.

I broke the seal and read a short note from Uncle Hem, who briefly narrated my father's failure to achieve his personal goal because of family differences. At the sunset of our family's estate, Uncle Hem said he wanted to help me achieve my goal. He wanted me to succeed.

The letter contained another note from a well-known business establishment in our ancestral district that was written in code. It included an address of an affiliated office in Calcutta. Uncle Hem was relying on *hundi*, the ancient Eastern business practice used to make money transfers.

Uncle Hem wished he could do more for me; but Nayeb Babu explained my uncle had struggled to come up with the money he was sending me. The ancestral village was experiencing very hard days. I was overcome with gratitude for Uncle Hem. He wasn't a noble landlord, but he was an honorable man. His help made my dream come true.

I thanked Nayeb Babu and offered him something to eat and

drink. But I knew he was a conservative Brahmin. He wouldn't swallow water from my faucet.

I took the next morning off from the hospital so Arup and I could get the money. We entered a building, and I told the man at the front desk that I needed to see the officer who handled East Pakistan. He led us to a back room where a man sat on a low platform covered with cotton mattresses and huge pillows. The man invited us to sit.

I handed him the *hundi* and he peered down a page in a huge accountant's book. "Ah, here it is. How do you want your money?"

I said I was afraid to carry a big amount of cash in Calcutta. He nodded and offered to give me a company check, which, he said, every Calcutta bank would honor. My heart thumped as I watched the man write out the check, and I felt such relief when I held it in my hand.

Arup and I raced to the Lloyds Bank, where I deposited the check. The next morning, the check had cleared. I was a happy man.

Soon, my brother heard the news of my good fortune. He made a rare visit to my residence and demanded to know who financed my adventure and how much money they gave me.

My brother's use of the word adventure offended me. I asked him why I should tell him my private business.

Kumar said I lacked self-respect. I had willingly begged people to help me, and I had begged all the wrong people, like Uncle Bidhan. He insisted Uncle Bidhan loaned me money because he'd borrowed money from us. Kumar claimed Uncle Ashok gave me money out of pity. He said these loans were a disgrace.

I'd heard enough. I told Kumar these loans were my personal business with my uncles. If he wanted any more answers, he had to go grill them. I told Kumar I had important things to do. My brother stormed out of my room.

~ ~ ~ ~ ~

Days later Jeevan was waiting for me in my room. He asked if I'd completed all the arrangements for my fellowship. I told him that I'd raised the money, but not from the expected sources.

Jeevan asked if I had everything else organized.

I said I needed a guarantee so the passport office would process my application.

Jeevan asked for the form and looked through it. Without saying a word, he signed his name as the guarantor and gave me back the form. He said in a soft voice that he was sorry this was the only thing he could do for me.

As I thanked him, I knew that I had just witnessed the fragile side of my cousin.

I was busy at work during the days; but I had time in the evening to chat with doctors and nurses, including Linda, who seemed happy that I was trying for the fellowship in England. She wished me success and encouraged me to marry a nice young lady in England. Linda said that she had heard that Rachel was hitched. "It didn't take her long," she added. "He must be a Jew."

Leena also told me that Rachel had a boyfriend in England. If I didn't believe her, I'd get the truth from Sally. I realized that this Christian nurse was the source of the juicy yarns. Sally, who was never a great friend of mine, probably told these stories about Rachel to get back at me.

I received a letter from Rachel. She had finished her preliminary course, and she planned to leave the hospital in Leicester to work in a maternity hospital in the London suburbs for the second part of her training.

Rachel also wrote about Miriam who was living in a rented apartment with her husband Jonathan in London. Miriam, who had passed her Cambridge exam, had become a shorthand typist and earned more than her husband. Rachel mentioned nothing about Miriam's brother Isaac. She also said nothing about her own health and recovery. I was happy Rachel hadn't forgotten me, but I worried about her physical condition.

I went and saw Mrs. Bekhor, who was furious with Isaac. She said he had been so kind to Rachel when she first arrived. He had visited her every weekend and Mrs. Bekhor was certain that the happy couple would have a future together.

But when Isaac saw Rachel at the hospital, her shaved head and the tubes poking out of her appalled him. He told his sister that Rachel's condition unnerved him, and her abnormal EEG scared him. Isaac never visited Rachel again. He told Miriam that he never had romantic feelings for Rachel. He just wanted to be friends and help her feel at home in England.

"Such a liar!" said Mrs. Bekhor. "Why is God punishing me? This boy is no good, like his father."

I asked if she had heard anything from Rachel about Isaac.

She announced that Rachel had stopped writing to her.

I felt sorry for the poor woman. She loved her children, but none of them could remain close to her. She was so determined to get them to follow all the orthodox Jewish customs and food habits that she drove them away.

When I finally escaped the Bekhors' apartment, I was convinced that living near this woman would be a nightmare. She spewed out misery, irrespective of the truth.

I wrote to Rachel and encouraged her decision to work at the new hospital. I wrote that I wished I was there to boost her spirits, and I assured her that all my arrangements were finally in place. I hoped to be in England by the end of the year. I closed by saying that I hoped she would want to see me when I arrived.

I continued preparing for my departure. I visited Jeevan's tailor who fitted me for some winter clothes for England. Since my cousin was a regular customer, the tailor agreed that I could pay him when I returned from England.

Our study group would soon lose one of its three members. Amjad had to go back to East Pakistan. He knew he would have a tough time when he met with his brother, but he trusted that his Uncle Fazlul Huq would come to his defense. Amjad still hoped he would get to England. He would just arrive on an East Pakistan passport.

When I went to say goodbye to Kumar and Asha, my brother insisted I was wasting money and productive years on this wild goose chase. He yacked until I finally interrupted him. I said that I had received very little help from him to pursue my fellowship.

Kumar snapped back that letting me go was his help.

I said goodbye to my relatives in South Calcutta, including Auntie Malati and Uncle Umesh. I saw Kiron's wife Shanti, who was still at college studying to become a teacher.

I received another letter from Rachel. She had moved to London. Rachel still said nothing about her cousin Isaac. The letter made me smile. Rachel had moved to London. I would see her soon.

~ 32 ~

FAREWELL, CALCUTTA

FINALLY, I RECEIVED MY PASSPORT. Saha and I booked our passage by boat to England and secured rooms in the inexpensive Indian YMCA, which was safe and close to the university in central London. Saha and I also said a sad goodbye to Amjad, who left for Dacca, where he planned to meet his Uncle Fazlul Huq.

We soon received a letter from our dear friend who said that he was with his elderly brother Altaf, who was the head of the family and treated Amjad like a dependent. He believed that Amjad was not part owner of the family property and unfortunately, all the prominent villagers shared his brother's view.

Altaf believed that Amjad's dream to pursue a Western lifestyle in England was selfish. He was willing to help his younger brother start a medical practice in the village or the local town. Amjad could also become an important politician like his Uncle Fazlul, who never went to England but became the premier of Bengal. Altaf added that the only man from the village who ever went to England was killed there.

Amjad planned to stay with Altaf before returning to Dacca to see his Uncle Fazlul, who was his only hope. Maybe he could get him to change his mind.

I felt bad for Amjad, but I had no way to help him. Sometimes the extended family looks great to an outsider, but the patrician often treats other family members as commoners who have to follow his rules and not question his authority.

I went to the Bekhor's apartment to say goodbye. Mrs. Bekhor, who received all her news about Rachel from Miriam, said that Isaac heard that Rachel suffered from nerve problems and possibly mental problems. This was why she became unconscious in her apartment. He insisted that he was right to avoid a relationship with Rachel.

"What a pack of lies!" said Mrs. Bekhor.

I received another letter from Amjad. He said that his brother had made him come to his office and meet a bearded middle-aged man who traveled with a large retinue.

Altaf told him that their late father had given his word to this bearded man that Amjad would marry the man's daughter when they both came of age. The man said that his daughter was beautiful, and he had made certain that she passed her primary school exams so Amjad could have an educated wife. He announced that this agreement between the two honorable men was legally binding. He wouldn't leave the office until the wedding date was settled.

Amjad felt sick. He told his brother that he would be back in five minutes. He needed to take some medicine for a severe headache. He Amjad hurried to the main house and saw his sister. He told her about their father's agreement with the bearded man. She asked him to stay calm. Maybe there wasn't an agreement.

Amjad reminded his sister that their elder brother could easily produce several friends who'd claim they had witnessed the promise when it was originally made between the two men.

His sister said he should tell their brother that this news was so sudden and overwhelming that he needed two days before he could give his final yes.

Amjad described how he returned to his brother's office and followed his sister's advice. He also asked his would-be-father-in-law to stay as the family guest during this two-day wait.

His elder brother smiled. He said his college-educated brother was finally shedding his Calcutta attitudes, which were so alien to their Islamic culture.

Amjad's sister gave her brother some money and told him to flee. That night he snuck out of his house and hurried to the river. Without revealing his identity, he convinced a boatman to take him across the river. He paid him handsomely and walked to the railway station where he took the next available train away from the district and on to Dacca.

When Amjad reached his uncle Fazlul Huq, his uncle assured him that he was safe now and he was welcome to stay in his house. He had never heard about this marriage contract from Amjad's father Mujbur, who normally discussed important matters with him. But he needed to resolve this issue; then he promised to get Amjad the money for his postgraduate studies and arrange for his passport. But it would take time.

~ ~ ~ ~ ~

The days before my departure were magic. The nurses, including Linda and Leena, held farewell parties for me, and Arup invited me to his apartment for a final evening together. His wife Kamini made a wonderful meal, and we all discussed the great changes in India that were reshaping our future.

The next day I asked Arup to take one last walk with me through some of Calcutta's lovely squares and parks before we headed to College Square, my favorite haunt. When we reached the mosque, I was relieved to see that Muslims were finally using their shrine again. I hoped all the wounds inflicted on the human heart could be repaired like this structure.

Arup and I entered the Coffee House and enjoyed a good meal with Suleiman. I felt so peaceful as I sat with my two good friends. I forgot all the communal horrors we had recently experienced.

When I returned to my residence, a letter from Uncle Ashok was sitting on my table. Uncle Ashok had told Dolly's father Bareen that I was going to England for postgraduate studies. Dolly's father passed the news on to Dolly, who lived with her husband in Bombay.

Uncle Ashok said that Dolly and her husband wanted me to spend time with them before I left Bombay for England. They had a comfortable guest room in their Marina apartment that overlooked the Arabian Sea. They already knew the date of my departure from Bombay and the name of my boat, but they didn't know when my train from Calcutta would arrive in Bombay. He included their Bombay telephone number and address. He asked me to call and let them know when I would arrive.

The thought of seeing Dolly again filled me with excitement; and, I admit, a bit of apprehension. I sat down and just as I was about to call them, the phone rang. A gentleman on the line said that he was Dolly's husband Debu. He insisted that I stay with them in Bombay before I left for England. I gave him my train's arrival time.

So many people came with me to the Calcutta railroad station.

When we arrived at our train compartment, it was crowded with Saha's wife Joya, and some of his relatives, so I stayed outside on the platform saying my goodbyes to friends, Mrs. Bekhor and Naomi, but not my brother.

Time raced by. Suddenly, as if in a dream, Uncle Hem, impressive in stature and personality, stood in front of me. Everyone stared at him as Uncle Hem gave me a bear hug.

"You will do well," he said. "You have all my blessings." Uncle Hem scanned the small crowd and said he wasn't surprised that Kumar had not come to say goodbye to me. "That boy is nothing like us. He takes after his maternal uncles."

The station bell sounded the last warning. The train was about to depart. Uncle Hem said goodbye. He turned and walked away with his firm sure steps.

I boarded the train and stepped into the compartment as Saha's relatives and Joya said their final goodbyes. As Saha hugged his young boy, I looked at Joya and saw the tears in her eyes that expressed her joy over her husband's ambition and her fear of the unknown. Joya knew that she would have to endure this separation for several years.

I also knew that while there was risk in this journey for both Saha and me, I was fully aware that Saha's years in the medical service of the railway had taken their toll on him. God, forbid, if Saha failed in England, what would be the consequence? I couldn't imagine.

~ 33 ~

GOODBYE INDIA!

WHEN I LEFT CALCUTTA, I was 28-years-old. I carried one suitcase filled with clothing and a bag of books and toiletries. Saha was loaded with baggage. He had Indian clothing so that he could maintain his identity and Western clothes. Since he had heard that British food was insipid, his brothers had packed lentils, mustard oil, fine Indian rice, and several spices and condiments.

We were spending two nights on the train, so Saha and I had splurged on a second-class, small compartment with bunk beds for four people. One passenger was a quiet elderly man, who showed no interest in talking to us. The other passenger was Harsh, who was young and assertive. He was going to England for business training.

When Saha removed some food from his huge stash and we started to eat, the young fellow's eyes followed each morsel as it traveled to our lips. Saha opened another pouch of food. Again, Harsh's eyes tracked each bite. Saha offered the boy a small portion. He gulped it down.

That night I tried to sleep but my mind raced faster than the train. I thought of Dolly. She was such a pretty teenager when I knew her. I assumed she was now beautiful. I hoped she was happy and wondered how I would feel when I met her. I thought of Rachel and hoped she had completely recovered and felt good about herself.

Both ladies were so loving but so different. Dolly was confident, strong, and stubborn; but she was still gentle and kind. Rachel was stubborn, strong, gentle, and kind; but she often doubted her judgment. She lacked Dolly's privilege, which provided the opportunities that let Dolly develop her talents and self-confidence.

I must have fallen asleep. The train jolted to a stop. I looked out the small window. The sun was coming up. I figured we were at a station because hawkers soon moved through the corridors.

All day long the train headed away from Calcutta. By noon of the next day, we rolled into Bombay's train station, which was a huge gothic masterpiece. I stepped outside and stared at the people on the platform. I noticed a young lady waving a silk scarf in her hand. Dolly! I would not have recognized her before I studied her face, which flashed that naughty smile that had once stolen my heart.

Dolly's husband Debu was handsome, with great manners. We shook hands, and then we hugged until Dolly stepped forward. "What about me? You men are brutes!"

Soon, we were in their car and the chauffeur was driving us to the Bombay Gymkhana Club, where Dolly's husband was a member. I slipped into the beautiful men's room and showered before we enjoyed a perfect lunch. Then we drove along the Marina to their flat. The Arabian Sea, with its numerous ships and Arabian dhows bobbing in the waves, was gorgeous.

Their apartment was spacious and beautiful, with a modern

décor. Dolly asked a servant to show me the guest room, which was far superior to any room I'd ever used in my life. I changed and sat with Dolly and Debu on the curved balcony that overlooked the sea.

Debu asked me to accept an honest apology, but he had to leave tonight to go to Pune on business. He was unable to get out of the trip. He had hoped to spend the day getting to know me. But since he was going in a company car, their private car and chauffeur were at my disposal—and Dolly would be here. He knew we had lots of news to share. He said Dolly had told him I was her favorite brother.

Debu told his wife not to say anything bad about him. Dolly cocked her head and smiled. He gave her a long loving kiss and left the apartment.

The mutual honesty and trust between Dolly and her husband impressed me. I promised myself I wouldn't do anything to jeopardize their bond.

Dolly and I stayed on the balcony watching the large red sun dip into the sea and slowly disappear. The sky glowed red. It was beautiful, and the gentle sea breeze made everything feel clean.

Dolly fixed us some tea and a plate of biscuits and sweets. She had made these sweets in our home when she stayed with us.

Dolly talked about life in Bombay. She said her husband was very decent and always treated her with love and respect. But she missed her parents who had only come to see them once.

I volunteered that life had different phases. Maybe this was the time to make an intimate bond with her husband, so their life would be genuinely happy and fulfilling. Dolly was relieved to hear me say that I wished her happiness. She doubted that many people in my situation would have said this. It was one reason she loved me so much.

I told Dolly that of course, I wished her happiness. I also wished God would bless her marriage and she would have wonderful children.

Dolly said we should go for a short drive. The chauffeur showed me around Bombay, and when we returned to the apartment, Dolly ordered food from a good restaurant. She freshened up in her bedroom and I retreated to the bathroom attached to the guest room. When she returned to the lounge, Dolly looked heavenly. I complimented her and she laughed. She asked if I remembered that evening we stood on the verandah.

I nodded.

Dolly reminded me that I had told her she was sweet.

I said nothing. Our eye contact said more than enough.

She poured each of us a shot of gin and added some lime. It was wonderful to sit by the sea sipping the drink and watching her, but I also felt a strong tension between us.

Finally, she asked me why I didn't come to her wedding.

I confessed that I wasn't strong enough to watch her get married to someone else.

Dolly said her decision wasn't easy. She still wondered if she did the right thing.

I told Dolly that her husband loved and trusted her. We should never betray that trust.

Dolly hoped I would be strong enough for both of us.

We ate our dinner on the balcony. The food and the atmosphere were perfect. We stood together by the railing. The moon was up, and Dolly's moonlit face melted my resolve. She cast a spell on me, and I held her hand.

When Dolly moved closer to me, I had the urge to hold her

and kiss her to relive that moment that happened between us at an earlier time in another place. Her face was flushed, and her body trembled. But I moved away. I said goodnight and walked to the guest room.

The next morning, I joined Dolly in the lounge while the servant prepared our breakfast. She asked me if I had slept well.

I said yes, and kept my unsettled thoughts buried for now.

I didn't need to get to the boat until the afternoon, so we went to the museum that had artifacts from the Indus Valley Civilization. We came back to Dolly's apartment for lunch and then I got ready for my departure.

I stood on the balcony with Dolly, and we enjoyed one last long look at the sea and the boats. I told her that I had wanted to say something to her since the morning, but I had been struggling to find the right words. I said I couldn't deny my real feelings for her. I admitted to her that last night's temptation nearly got the best of me. But I was relieved I'd stayed strong.

Dolly told me not to say anything more. She was grateful that I left for the guest room last night because she had felt so weak. She didn't want us to lose respect for each other. She also didn't want her relationship with her husband to suffer. She said she would always love me, but not in that crazy heart-stopping way. She hoped that I would always love her a bit, but she wanted me to get on with my life—and love a wonderful, wonderful woman.

We went to the pier and said goodbyes. I found Saha and we went through all the formalities and boarded the *MV Strathnever*, the P&O vessel that would carry us to England.

We went upstairs to the deck on the port side to watch the activities on the pier. There was so much noise as a crane lifted luggage and goods depositing everything into the hold and on the deck of the ship. People waved goodbye to passengers. I noticed Dolly. I waved and she waved back with her right hand.

Our ship bellowed a long deep wail, and tugs started moving us toward the sea. Dolly stood on the pier. She had removed her beautiful silk scarf from her neck and waved it and waved it.

Soon, the ship turned, and I could hardly see Dolly. But I saw her beautiful silk scarf in the air flying behind the ship before it fell on the churning water. I watched the scarf move with the waves, but soon Dolly and the scarf vanished.

It was early evening. I gazed at the sparkling lights of the Marina until the city lights disappeared. I saw only the stars in the night sky that twinkled as they had twinkled for millions of years over the dark sea.

I closed my eyes. I saw Dolly smiling and waving her beautiful silk scarf, and then I saw Rachel.

~ **Part 2** ~

ENGLAND

~ 34 ~

AT SEA

SOON BOMBAY WAS BEHIND US. I was on my way to England. Saha and I explored this ship that would serve as our home for two weeks. We strolled through the promenade deck and entered a spacious lounge that led to the London Pub, where we could sit and drink. We descended an ornamental staircase to the huge dining room. We went back to the promenade deck and found a cozy library. When we returned to our cabin, we met our two cabin mates, Ravi and Amal, who were mechanical engineers heading to Worcester for additional training.

The bell rang for dinner. We found our table and soon discovered that many of our fellow travelers were students heading for post-graduate degrees in the United Kingdom. The dining room hummed with noise until the chief steward climbed on a stool and bellowed through a megaphone for silence. The waiters moved in drill fashion to the kitchen. They reappeared with dinner—soup, main dish, and dessert.

Most of the people at our table had some form of dietary restriction based on religion. Hindus did not eat beef, Muslims did not eat pork, and some people were vegetarian. Some food on the limited menu was unknown to us at our table—like bacon, which appeared with breakfast. A young lady in our group told us bacon was from a bird that lived in Europe and Australia. The strips, she said, came from the wings. We believed her.

The bacon was crisp and delicious. Near the end of our voyage, after we had enjoyed many servings of bacon, the two Muslims at our table became horrified. They learned from others on the boat that they had been eating pork.

A few days into our journey, I forgot all about the Hindu injunction against beef and ate the forbidden beef curry. Saha was appalled. One week later, he uttered a Sanskrit verse and joined me. He had become equally sick of the limited menu.

One afternoon Ravi introduced me to Mrs. Robinson, a middle-aged English lady, who was a Quaker. Quakers, also called Friends, belonged to a liberal religious sect that began in the mid-seventeenth century as a reaction against Puritanism. Over time, Quakers established a worldwide network of Friends Societies, known for their charitable good works. Mrs. Robinson, in keeping with her Quaker tradition, had helped Ravi and his friends get their apprenticeships and admission to night classes so they could earn money while they studied. She also helped them with their travel expenses to England.

Mrs. Robinson was a school superintendent in England. But her passion was painting, nature studies in particular, and her passion brought her repeatedly to India to see her brother in Bombay, who had recently passed away. She had inherited his property and foundation for higher education for Indian Students. I enjoyed her company during the trip.

Saha was not as friendly with Mrs. Robinson. He doubted she could be such a fine charitable person because she drank—every single evening in the lounge. He was convinced drinking alcohol made people irrational—turned them into drunks.

Since leaving India, I had begun to see Saha in a different light. Foreign ideas and opinions made him suspicious and narrow-minded. He also tended to stay away from foreigners. But he was still a good man, and I continued to like him.

Soon our ship passed through the Red Sea, and we reached the Suez Canal, where we waited our turn to pass through the narrow waterway to the Mediterranean Sea. Our ship cruised to the port of Marseilles crowded with cargo ships and passenger boats. We took a bus tour, my first bus tour of the famous Riviera. In the sunny afternoon, graceful sailing boats moved along the azure sea; but most men on our bus stared at the scantily clad young ladies on the beach. We drove through Cannes and stopped for lunch at a restaurant in Nice, where the price of a meal exceeded our budget. All we could afford was a cup of delicious French coffee.

As our ship moved on to Gibraltar, Mrs. Robinson invited us to the opulent first-class deck. For a moment, I was envious, but I told myself that I would travel by first class when I became an established surgeon. Beyond Gibraltar, the weather turned nasty. The Atlantic Ocean was cold and turbulent. When we dared go out on the deck, we wore our winter clothes.

Finally, our journey ended when we docked at England's Tilbury port. After we went through the formalities, we took the train to London. There, standing beyond the gate at the far end of the platform, I saw Rachel with her cousin Miriam. What a joy to see her after such a long time!

~ 35 ~

LONDON

RACHEL'S LARGE BROWN EYES WERE smiling when I stood before her. But Miriam stared at me through cold eyes as she announced that she and Rachel had to leave right away. She pulled Rachel by the hand, but Rachel refused to go with her. Before Miriam walked away, she told Rachel to remember her father's stern letter.

Rachel and I took a taxi to the Indian YMCA on Woburn Square, a neighborhood devastated by the war. Rachael left, and I joined the other new students in the warden's office as he allotted a room to everyone but me.

"There's a problem," he said. He explained that my name had arrived after all the rooms were taken. But he promised not to send me into the street. "There's a small room in the basement. It lacks heating and water, but I could use the common washroom on the ground floor."

The warden led me to a tiny, ugly basement room that had a strange odor and so little natural light that I was unaware that it was raining outside. But I felt the damp, cold late February weather.

My spirits sank lower than the floor. I left my suitcase and books and rushed back up to the comfortable common lounge with its warm gas fireplace.

I thought about this awful mess and then I called Rachel. I hoped she would come to see me in the morning before she went to work at the hospital. By the time I finished dinner in the dining room, the chatter of students followed by an enjoyable lecture delivered by a professor lifted my spirits. I was determined to carry on and do well in my course at the Royal College of Surgeons, which started in two weeks. I had to pass the primary fellowship before my meager amount of money ran out.

I thought about Rachel. She told me that she had very little free time. I wondered when I would get to see her. I remembered Miriam's cold eyes at the train station. I assumed that she would try to keep Rachel away from me. I wondered what Mr. Bekhor had written to Miriam or Rachel.

I walked back down to the cold basement. The corridor was freezing, and I was shivering when I entered my ugly room. I put on my overcoat and sat in the single chair. It was so uncomfortable in this squalid space that I went to bed, fully clothed. When I awoke, I had no idea of the time since no natural light entered the room. I went upstairs in my rumpled clothing, where the clock told me that it was morning.

Once I was presentable, I joined the other students, and we walked to the Royal College of Surgeons where I met a secretary who went through my file with me. I was relieved when she said that everything was in order for the course.

We explored our new neighborhood walking by numerous restaurants and shops. We found the nearby entrance to the underground railway. I saw a branch of the Lloyds Bank and the Indian

High Commission office. Everything I needed was within walking distance of the Indian YMCA and our college. I could limit my travel expenses and save money. We had lunch at Lyon's Cafeteria where I was delighted to discover the food was inexpensive and tasty. For two and a half shillings, I enjoyed soup, fish and chips, apple pie, and a cup of tea.

When I returned to the Indian YMCA, I hung out in the common room. Rachel hadn't called. Saha invited me to see his room, which he shared with a roommate. The room was unremarkable, but its gas fireplace seemed a gift from God. I wondered when the warden would move me out of the basement. I could not study in that gloomy, cold room. But then I had nothing to study yet. I was also afraid to complain; the warden had a famous short fuse.

Later in the day, Rachel called. She couldn't see me. She had to take one of Miriam's daughters to the doctor before she went to work at the hospital. I said I understood. I was grateful that she had met me at the railway station.

The next few days I walked to the Royal College after breakfast and spent all day reading in the library and examining the specimens in the museum. I only left the college to have lunch at Lyon's Cafeteria.

On Saturday afternoon, when the library was closed, I was reading the newspaper in the common room when the warden's secretary approached me. She asked if I could change one thing, what would it be?

I said I would love a room with a fireplace.

She smiled and said I was lucky. She had a room for me on the second floor with a good fireplace.

The secretary showed me the wonderful room, which I would be sharing with an older student from Madras. She said that it was one of the best rooms in the Indian YMCA, but she reminded me that each room was given to students for only three months. The management assumed that during these three months, students would find accommodations called "digs," which were more spacious and less expensive and often provided tastier food.

I quickly transferred my belongings to my new room; and when Saha came to visit me, he immediately wanted to arrange to become my roommate. Saha said that both of our roommates were from Madras, so the switch made sense. The two Madras men agreed to the exchange and Saha and I became roommates. We both planned to study hard and appear for our primary FRCS exams in about eight months.

When our course began at the college, we attended lectures and demonstrations with professors and assistants who made certain we understood the material. They spoke to us at our level, unlike our professors back in Calcutta, who forced us to turn to books to grasp what they were saying. An assistant professor told us to be tenacious. He reminded us that only twenty percent of the students passed the exam the first time. I had heard about this pass rate, but I thought it was a joke since most of the students in our course had been at the top of their class in their home country. Somehow, I had to be in this twenty percent.

One night Saha told me he worried about his age, his wife, and his son. He felt gloomy. I told him to stop brooding and focus on his studies so that he could pass the exam. But the prospect of the twenty percent success rate gnawed at him. I couldn't cheer him up.

Rachel called and said she would come visit me on Saturday before she went to Miriam's home. Since no women, except relatives, were permitted in our private rooms, Rachel and I met in the common room. We went for lunch in a café near the YMCA; then we strolled around the university and the college hospitals. Rachel invited me to go to Miriam's place with her. I decided it would be polite to say hello to Miriam and her family. More importantly, I wanted to see how the couple would react when I arrived with Rachel.

We took the underground to Miriam's apartment, which was built by the Jewish community for European refugees. The impoverished neighborhood was depressing. Chunks of ice clung to the building exterior and the stairwell was cold. The small apartment barely accommodated Miriam's family. She and her husband Jonathan slept in the one bedroom and their two girls, Renee and Sarah, slept in the living room. They had a sitting area at one end of the kitchen. I wondered how they managed in this place after living in their spacious Calcutta house.

Miriam said she wished they could move, but at least the rent was low. Her husband had never finished his secondary education, so he couldn't get a decent job. He was a messenger carrying files between offices. They were lucky she had a good clerical job, so they were able to cover their expenses.

Miriam blamed her husband's parents for causing this mess. He wasn't their favorite son, and they received no financial help from them.

I saw the embarrassment in Rachel's eyes as the couple continually complained.

While we sat in Miriam's apartment, Rachel said very little; but I felt her presence, and this made me happy. At one point, she opened her handbag and took out some small gifts for the children. Miriam protested, but the two girls had come to expect little presents from Rachel, so Miriam's protest was fleeting. She appreciated that Rachel was a good aunt looking after her two children's needs and pleasures.

When it was time for me to leave, Rachel insisted on walking me to the tube station. We held hands and she said that she was glad I was here in London. I told her that I hoped she realized that I always enjoyed her company. She pressed my hand and looked at me with her smiling brown eyes. As I headed back to the YMCA, I saw myself in the future: I was qualifying as a Fellow of the Royal College of Surgeons; I was proposing to Rachel. I imagined her liquid brown eyes smiling back at me as she said yes. Good things could really happen.

~ 36 ~

GETTING SETTLED

ONCE OUR COURSES BEGAN, I met classmates from all over the world. I figured that students from the Subcontinent, the Middle East, and Africa would find common ground when we discussed the ongoing political changes that began after World War II. However, I discovered that skin color heavily influenced the attitudes of the Middle Eastern students. They resented the elitism of the British and the Americans. Since Arabs had an older civilization and shared the same skin color, they expected to be treated as equals in discussions governing Middle Eastern politics and economics. However, the British and Americans hated Arab nationalism and feared Arab supremacy. They were only interested in the Middle East's oil and gas reserves.

I had heard about the advent of Arab nationalism, but I was unaware that this movement was spreading through the educated middle class. These students longed for their rightful place in the world.

As I settled into my new courses, the British tutor who instructed the small group of students in my tutorial class, rarely asked me questions or answered any of my questions. I thought that this was because I was physically smaller than most of the other students, but I soon discovered that he ignored most non-white students.

One day an Egyptian student remained standing with his hand raised until the instructor acknowledged him. He berated the student before he let him ask his question. So, the skin color problem existed, but this Egyptian had compounded the problem for himself. All the teachers ignored him.

After two months of living in the YMCA, Saha and I moved into a dig, which was close to a tube station, which made it convenient for me to see Rachel. She and I loved talking together as we strolled in nearby parks where the spring flowers had started to bloom, and birds flitted on leafy branches. Occasionally, Rachel and I went to the movies in Leicester Square. We discovered that we could see two films for the price of one in some London theaters.

When I began preparing for my Primary FRCS exam, Rachel was about to receive her State Certified Midwife degree. She planned to become a staff midwife in the maternity hospital. I decided the time had come for us to discuss our relationship.

I knew that Rachel liked my company. I knew that she trusted me. I also knew she was lonely. She had no close friends at the maternity hospital. Rachel longed for intellectual conversations, which never occurred between her and Miriam, and she began spending more of her free time with me. I worried about our growing friendship. Rachel would face insurmountable obstacles from her family if she decided to marry a non-Jewish man.

On Saturday Rachel and I walked through Hyde Park and visited the Royal Albert Art Museum. After we had high tea in a café, Rachel left for Miriam's apartment where I planned to see her the next day when I watched over Miriam's youngest daughter while the family went out.

When I arrived at Miriam's apartment on Sunday, Rachel flashed me a smile, which annoyed her cousin. The family left me with their little girl Sarah in the cold unfriendly apartment where we tried to play together until Miriam returned to feed her daughter lunch.

Miriam said she wanted me to care for Sarah because she wanted to talk to me alone. Mr. Bekhor had written to her and told her that I had evil intentions. I had come to England to pursue his daughter. Rachel was too impressionable and too young. He didn't want me near her. He admitted that I had been good to the family, but he told Miriam to keep me away from Rachel.

Miriam glared at me. She told me that I had to respect the will of the family. I was not to have any more contact with Rachel. She also told me to keep quiet about this conversation. I should tell no one, not even Rachel.

I refused to make such a promise. I said goodbye and left.

I ignored Miriam and a few days later called Rachel who had just become a midwife. She was on duty, so I left a message.

Rachel called me that night and asked me why I had left Miriam's apartment before they had returned from their outing. She said Miriam had insisted that I had hurried back to my place to study. She also claimed that I wanted Rachel to leave me alone and not waste my time. Rachel asked me if I had said this to Miriam.

I heard the sadness in Rachel's voice. I wanted to talk to her face-to-face. We couldn't meet until Friday afternoon. As we sat eating sandwiches and tea in a café, I told Rachel about Miriam's rant. She wasn't surprised. Her face turned red with anger. She said she had never agreed to an arranged marriage and reminded me that she and Naomi had decided to become nurses so that they could be financially independent and create their own lives.

I loved Rachel's spunk. I saw why her family said that she was stubborn. She was a rebel with a mind of her own.

Rachel told me that she spent her free time at Miriam's apartment so that she could help her two nieces. She felt sorry for them. She was saving money from her salary to buy a coat for her older daughter. She wanted her to be warm when she went to school.

I told Rachel that she needed to save her money for her own emergencies. She had no one to help her in this foreign land.

Rachel laughed. "What about you? Can't I depend on you?"

I laughed and said that I would be there for her. But it would be a few years before I could ever help her financially.

"I know that," she said.

Rachel had to leave, or she would miss dinner at her nurses' residence. I convinced her to go with me to an inexpensive Indian restaurant. The food was lousy. But it tasted like comfort food and left us both in good spirits.

I had to continually watch my finances. Saha and I discovered that the cost of our dig could jump up dramatically because we had to put coins into a slot machine to pay for the gas that we used in our gas fireplace and for our baths. To have a hot bath, we needed to feed a hungry slot machine. The dirty color of our bath water never surprised us. We bathed once a week. In the cold weather, our rooms were also chilly. We huddled near the fireplace fully dressed and armed with a blanket for extra warmth.

On holidays and weekends, we made lunch in our room from a ready supply of apples, cans of sardines, loaves of bread, and packets of processed Swiss cheese and butter. These meals were cheaper than anything we could buy in a restaurant, and we never felt deprived. I kept reminding myself that my hardship was temporary; one day I would have money. But I never invited Rachel to my room. I didn't want to embarrass her. I always met her in the hall, and we would go out together. Nonetheless, the dig seemed fine. Life felt good.

~ 37 ~

MOVING FORWARD

TIME WENT ON. OUR TEACHERS moved quickly through the material so that we could complete our course in time. Saha became depressed and complained about everything from our meals to the distance from our room to the bathroom. He said that he wasted so much time just to pee.

One evening I found him sitting with tears in his eyes. "What's wrong?" I asked.

"What isn't wrong?" He said his brothers were right. He had made a big mistake. He wasn't going to pass the course. He was terrified of failing.

I told Saha that he had to believe he would succeed.

Saha sighed. He started talking about the wealthy Arab students. They had wives back home, but they had sex regularly with women here. Even if they failed the course, their futures were secure because they had lucrative appointments waiting for them back home.

Saha said that some Indian students were also having sex

here. Two Punjabi boys continually discussed their sexual exploits with Punjabi women who lived in London. Saha insisted that every man needed a woman. He looked at me. "You have a girlfriend. You know about this."

I told him that Rachel had been my friend for years. We were not in a sexual relationship.

Saha apologized. He said that he felt sad and confused.

In six weeks, Saha and I would face our course examiners. We tried to answer questions from earlier exams, but we never felt adequately prepared, especially when we reviewed the oral questions that accompanied the examination.

A few weeks before our exam, I went to Lloyds Bank for my monthly remittance from Calcutta. The assistant manager apologized, but the Calcutta bank had failed to transfer my money into my London account. He advised me to contact the bank manager in Calcutta and ask him to resolve the problem.

It was Friday. I had to pay the landlady by Monday for next week's room and board. It would take two weeks to get this problem sorted out with the Calcutta bank. I didn't know what to do. I was in a mess, and I struggled to sleep that night.

Rachel came to visit me on Saturday. After a few minutes, she asked me what was wrong.

I lied and said that everything was fine, but Rachel knew me too well.

"Something is wrong," she insisted. She asked me if I would want to know if she had a problem.

I said, "Of course."

"Then you should understand that I want to know what's bothering you." Rachel suggested that we go out for coffee. "Her treat," she said.

When we were sitting in a café, Rachel asked if my problem was related to a girlfriend.

I told her that she knew full well I didn't have a new girlfriend.

Rachel gave me one of her naughty smiles. She said that she would not leave until I told her what was wrong.

I gave up and told her what happened at the bank.

Rachel told me not to worry.

After Rachel left the café, I sent an airmail letter to the Calcutta bank asking the officials to resolve the problem. I could do nothing more but worry.

On Monday when I returned to the dig from college, the landlady smiled and told me that my girlfriend had left me an envelope in the letter rack.

Rachel had left a note that said she had come by after I had left for college. The envelope included some pounds. Rachel hoped that it would get me through my crisis.

Rachel's generosity and kindness overwhelmed me. She had loaned me enough money to cover my lodging for a month. I sat in the lounge and thought quietly for a long time as I tried to crystallize my thoughts about this wonderful girl.

I knew that I cared deeply for Rachel. I realized that while she was reluctant to show her feelings, her actions expressed more than she could say. I had to be successful when I took my exams. I had to succeed as a surgeon so that I could take care of Rachel and look after her despite all the odds. We had to overcome the obstacles put in place by her family and my family to a lesser degree. Unlike Rachel, I wasn't close to my family. My dear mother was gone, and I couldn't forget my brother's refusal to give me my share of our family inheritance.

I called Rachel, but she was at work. The next night when we finally spoke, she was nonchalant about the money. She said that it was important for me to focus hard on my exam.

That Friday I heard from the manager of Lloyds Bank. He discovered that a local branch of the bank was in error. My money was quickly transferred into my account. I could concentrate on my upcoming exams.

Finally, Saha and I suffered through two days of written exams in the mornings and oral exams in the afternoons. Ninety minutes after we finished our exams, we students waited nervously for the secretary to announce the names of the successful candidates. When I heard "Ray," I was so excited that I asked if he had really said my name. The secretary smiled at me. "Yes, good chap, if your name is still Ray."

I was so happy, but I found no one who could celebrate with me. The rumor was true: only twenty percent of the students had passed the exam, and Saha was not one of them.

An older student Neil Gupta, who was an eye surgeon, stepped forward and congratulated me. He had also passed the exam. Neil said that he was good friends with Amjad who was finally coming to London. His uncle had gotten him a scholarship from Pakistan to start the course. I was thrilled.

Neil invited me to his residence, which was nearly as lavish as a hotel. We sat in the lounge, and he ordered two beers, and we celebrated. Then we had dinner together. I enjoyed my evening with Neil. He behaved like a loving elder brother, and he asked me to stay in touch with him.

I was eager to tell Rachel that I passed the exam, but she was on a two-week holiday with staff midwives at a seaside resort in Folkstone. I called her. She was so happy to hear my news. She invited me to come see her.

The next morning, I took a short train ride to the seaside resort. As I walked to the hotel, I saw Rachel in her summer clothes. She looked healthy, tanned, and so beautiful standing in the sun. She ran to me with her smiling large eyes. We hugged for the first time. She said that she knew I would pass.

"How did you know?" I asked.

"Because I know you are smart."

We strolled for a while on the beach before we enjoyed a leisurely delicious meal in a nearby fish restaurant. I took the next train back to the city. I was such a happy man.

~ 38 ~

EAST LONDON

SAHA'S BEHAVIOR TURNED WORRISOME. I was his good friend, and I wanted to help him, but he avoided me. I called Mrs. Robinson, who occasionally invited us to dinner, and told her about Saha. She contacted Saha and took him to see a psychologist who was a member of the Friend's Society. A few days later Saha thanked me for talking to Mrs. Robinson, but he doubted that she and the psychologist could help him because he did not want to disclose his deepest secrets.

Tears welled in Saha's eyes as he admitted that he had been avoiding me because he felt guilty. He knew that he had sinned.

I assured him that I would never judge him, nor would the psychologist who was trained to help him through any difficulty.

He told me that he and his two Punjabi friends had been visiting women to have sex. He didn't know why he indulged in this behavior. He didn't enjoy the company of these coarse women, but he had sex with them, willingly. As Saha discussed his transgressions, his remorse became so intense that he couldn't shake away his guilt. He begged me not to share this information with anyone.

I consoled Saha until he agreed to discuss his sexual encounters with the psychologist. I was so relieved. I hoped that Saha would eventually overcome his depression.

The next day, I met with Neil, who wanted to discuss a possible job working for a Bengali, doctor S. B. Lahiri in the East End of London. Lahiri, who had failed to get his fellowship in medicine, had become a registered general practitioner and had purchased a well-established practice from an elderly doctor with an enormous number of patients. Dr. Lahiri worked hard and ended up with the most successful medical practice in the country, an accomplishment helped in part by the introduction of the National Health Scheme, which ensured the payment of all his services. His income exploded and he had decided to slow down and enjoy life.

Dr. Lahiri had asked Neil if he would like to work for him. Neil wanted me to take on part of the job. I would cover nighttime house calls and help run the clinic from 6:00 p.m. until 7:30 a.m. and Neil would handle the practice over the weekend. We would be given free accommodation and a stipend to cover our personal expenses. We received nothing more.

Neil and I met Dr. Lahiri at his practice, which was on the ground floor of a house in East London. We would live in the two rooms on the upper floor. One room served as a sitting room; the other room was a bedroom with an adjoining half-bathroom. We were also given a small kitchen and a full bathroom on the ground floor behind Dr. Lahiri's office.

Neil and I knew that Dr. Lahiri was taking advantage of us. We were both professionally qualified, registered medical practitioners recognized by the National Medical Registration Board. Still, we decided that the set-up was adequate for our needs, and we agreed to take the job for one year.

Two weeks later, Neil and I moved into our new accommodations. We quickly discovered that our workload was exhausting. I rarely made it through a night without making oneor two-house calls. We also realized that the small stipend that Dr. Lahiri paid us hardly covered the cost of our food, and then only if we ate at home. But my weekdays were free, which gave me time to take my preparatory courses for the next exams.

I signed up for a seven-week course in surgery at the postgraduate school of medicine in Hammersmith. On the first day, I was required to attend a welcoming party to meet the professors. After the party, I hurried to the clinic and arrived twenty minutes late.

Dr. Lahiri was furious. He said that I had to be at work at six o'clock, not five minutes later. He marched to the door and left.

I told Neil that Lahiri's behavior made me wonder if he resented Indian students who were trying to succeed where he had failed.

Neil said to forget about Dr. Lahiri's motives. We would never change him. But Neil was lucky, he rarely saw the doctor. I faced him daily.

One day I arrived at the clinic early. Dr. Lahiri asked me to watch him examine a patient. Then he asked me to examine his last patient of the day. I took a teenage girl into the examination room and examined her, modestly.

Lahiri told me to stop being so timid. He told the girl to take off her clothes and lie down on the table. He put a white sheet over the girl and carefully moved it around to examine her entire body. When Dr. Lahiri finished his examination, he told the girl to dress.

Dr. Lahiri told me that it was good that I worked for him. I would finally learn the basics of clinical medicine, which were never taught in hospital surgical wards. This, he said, was why he offered the job to Indian students. They needed to learn how to examine patients. Dr. Lahiri was right: I had been too shy to expose that young lady. But I also knew that he would have to offer a decent salary if he hired a non-Indian doctor.

~ 39 ~

WORKING FOR LAHIRI

ONCE I STARTED THE COURSE in surgery I realized my theoretical knowledge, though deficient in some ways, measured up to the level of most of my classmates at the Postgraduate School of Medicine. But I had to catch up to their clinical approach to surgery and their analysis. The students easily outranked me.

During the duration of this course, I also fulfilled my responsibilities at Dr. Lahiri's clinic. Neil and I had established a good working arrangement. He was so generous and kind that he even tried to accommodate my love of the British Museum by occasionally arriving early at the clinic. This gave me many opportunities to visit the museum on my way home from the hospital. I loved wandering, wonderfully lost, and reading material from the collection of writings or studying the marvelous exhibitions of sculpture from India, Egypt, and Greece.

I knew that many of these artifacts were stolen or plundered, but I could never decide if these artifacts should have been left in their countries of origin or if they were better off in the museum. So many important artifacts had been destroyed because of improper handling and the curse of religious bigotry, which led iconoclasts to destroy temples, shrines, and churches. During wars and regime changes, conquerors also had the right to remove plundered artifacts from the conquered country. It seemed plausible to conclude that these treasures were better preserved in this country, where a stable government could protect them.

A couple of weeks before I finished the course in surgery, I knew I had to take other advanced courses that would adequately prepare me for the final FRCS exam. I also needed to work for one year in the surgical ward of a hospital recognized by the Royal College of Surgeons. Neil and I decided that we would stop working for Lahiri once we completed our commitment. Neil said that he would talk to his friends who could help me find work in a hospital.

Around this time Amjad arrived in London and moved into Neil's old hotel. On Sunday, I prepared a nice dinner for the three of us at our flat. While we ate together, Amjad told us that his uncle Fazlul Huq had become the new governor of East Pakistan. Amjad was fortunate. He had received a four-year government scholarship, which he could extend for an additional year. He would have no financial worries while he studied for his fellowship.

As soon as Amjad registered for his preliminary courses at the Royal College office, he met with Saha. Our friend was so depressed that Amjad called me.

When I discussed Saha's behavior with Neil, we agreed that I should wait until I completed my course before I went to see our friend. A week later, the course ended and I had a few free hours before I needed to report to the clinic. I visited with Saha at our old room in the dig. Before I left him, he told me that his life was useless. He insisted the end was near and it was far from bright.

Neil, Amjad, and I were so worried that we arranged to meet with Mrs. Robinson and the psychologist. The psychologist concluded that Saha had become utterly depressed after he had failed his exam. He worried that a second failure could be disastrous for him. The psychologist also admitted in private to me that Saha also suffered from massive guilt over his sexual behavior.

In December Rachel was offered a staff midwife position at the Jewish Maternity Hospital in Northwest London. She packed a suitcase for me to carry to her new residence. Later that afternoon when we headed back to her old residence, we walked among flowering trees and shrubs in a lovely nearby park. After we stopped to sit on a bench near a lake, we walked over to the water. Rachel slipped. As she started to fall, I caught her in my arms. I don't know what possessed me, but I kissed her. Without speaking a word, we returned to the bench and sat down.

I looked at Rachel as she gazed into the lake. I studied her beautiful face, with her lips still moist. I asked her what she was thinking.

Rachel said that she felt like nothing would be the same again.

When we returned to her old residence, I said goodbye and I walked slowly to the tube station to return home.

Later that night when I was in bed, I saw Rachel with her large liquid brown eyes and her long light brown hair. She was smiling. Sentences carved in stone appeared before me as if I were taking an oath in a Sanctum Sanctorum. I heard myself saying aloud the words that I read: Rachel would be my soul mate for the rest of my life and it was my duty to love and care for her always and shield her from all problems and adversities.

As I lay in my dreamlike sleep, I knew that if Rachel agreed to marry me she would face strong opposition. I had to become a successful surgeon. I had to pass the FRCS exam.

I was so happy in the morning. I asked Neil if he had heard about any hospital appointments. Our year in the clinic was coming to an end. Neil told me not to worry. He looked at me carefully and asked if something else had motivated my question. Without letting me answer, he said that I needed to take time before I made any decisions about my long-term future.

That afternoon I finished helping Rachel move to her new residence. She told me that she had trouble sleeping that night. She had paced up and down in the bedroom until finally, she studied her face in the mirror to see if she looked different after what had happened between us. She said that the receptionist at her old residence had told her that she was lucky to have a handsome gentleman friend. But she had added that she hoped I was responsible and reliable.

I told Rachel that I hoped she believed that I was worthy of her friendship.

When I returned to the flat, Neil surprised me with good news. He said that a doctor friend had told him that a senior house surgeon's post would be available in two months at the Tottenham General Hospital in North London. Neil added that the doctor who currently held the job was willing to recommend me for the post.

I thanked Neil. It was the perfect job for me.

A few days later I had an interview with the Tottenham interview board. The board president said that he hoped that I would work hard and become as popular as the doctor who currently held the position. I promised him that I would do my best if the board selected me.

After waiting 30 minutes with three other candidates, the board president took me aside and offered me the job for six months, with a possible extension. He also said that I would be given the post of junior registrar since I had already passed the primary FRCS exam and I had already spent two years as a house surgeon in Calcutta.

I was thrilled. Training jobs always paid poorly, but a junior registrar was paid more than a house surgeon. My new job also provided accommodations in the doctors' residence and free meals in the dining room.

I hurried back to the flat and shared my good news with Neil. I also decided to ask Rachel to be my partner in life. I believed that I could have a good career as a surgeon anywhere in the world as long as Rachel was my wife. How could I propose to her and how could I get her consent? Would she go against the wishes of her family?

That evening, when I had dinner with Neil, I told him that I wanted to marry Rachel. I said that I didn't care that my brother would object to my marriage, but Rachel came from a large family of fair-skinned orthodox Jews who had emigrated from Iraq. They considered themselves European and disapproved of marriages to dark-skinned Jews from Cochin or Ben Israel Jews of Bombay, who were considered inferior to the Iraqi Jews. I was a dark-skinned Asian Hindu. It would be difficult for Rachel to defy her family and agree to marry me.

Neil thought a moment before he said that I owed it to Rachel to hear her opinion about this. She needed to speak for herself.

~ 40 ~

THE MOMENT

I TOLD DR. LAHIRI THAT I had accepted a surgical position in a hospital so that I could get back into surgery and prepare for my fellowship exam. I was leaving at the end of my contract.

Dr. Lahiri said that I should forget about the fellowship. He insisted that principals in family practice earned as much as specialists in the National Health Scheme. He also said that I might never become a consultant. He reminded me that many older English doctors were still waiting for their promotion to this position. If I stayed with him, he promised that I could take over his practice when he retired.

I thanked Dr. Lahiri. But I was insistent. I would leave the clinic in six weeks.

The time had come to propose to Rachel. I went to the sitting room and left a message at her residence for her to call me. I tried to read something, but I couldn't concentrate. As soon as Rachel called, I hurried to see her. I told her we were taking a subway to the Strand, a popular commercial street in central London. We were eating in a good Italian restaurant.

"What's the occasion?" asked Rachel.

I told Rachel I had good news. The board of Tottenham General Hospital had hired me and had given me a great job. I would be a junior registrar.

When the waiter asked for our order, I told him to get us the best chicken breast dish they prepared in the kitchen.

Once the waiter left our table, Rachel smiled as she studied me with her large eyes. "I knew that you would get the job. You are chalak."

I laughed. Rachel had said the Bengali word for smart.

As we ate our dinner, I asked Rachel if she ever thought about getting married.

Rachel said that every girl thinks of getting married. Why was I asking?

I asked Rachel if her parents had discussed with her the kind of man that she should marry.

Rachel said to forget her parents. Their idea of an arranged marriage would lead to disaster. Just look at Miriam. She was an intelligent girl married to a stupid man who diminished her in every way.

I summoned my courage. "What if I told you that I love you very much, what would you say?"

"I am fond of you, too. But there are so many obstacles. My family will never agree. My father told Miriam to stop any relationship between us."

I was relieved that Rachel had said that she was fond of me. I told her to think carefully, not only with her mind but also with her heart. I promised her that if she married me, I would be fully responsible for her for the rest of my life. I assured her that I would replace the safety net created by her family and their society with all my love and care. I promised her that we would be well off so that financial hardships would never disturb our love and happiness.

Rachel said that she had great confidence in me and that she had always looked to me for help or advice. She saw how good I was to her brother Jacob. But she worried about her mother, who was so emotional. She was afraid that this marriage proposal would lead her to do something drastic. If this happened, Rachel said that she would never forgive herself.

I told her that we needed to discuss these difficulties again, and soon. I walked Rachel to her residence and the two of us agreed to meet the next evening.

The next day I brought Rachel long-stemmed red roses. Her lovely eyes were shining when she took them, and her face was flushed. She thanked me and put the roses in her room.

We went for a stroll around Serpentine Lake in Hyde Park. I asked her if she thought more about our conversation. Rachel said that she had done all her thinking about my proposal long ago. But she still worried about her family's reaction.

I told her that I hoped that we could get married before I started my new job in four weeks, but I didn't have enough money to buy her a diamond engagement ring.

I knelt in front of her. "I would be so honored, Rachel, if you agreed to marry me?"

Rachel said softly, "Yes. I agree." She added that she didn't care about a diamond ring. It wasn't important.

I told Rachel that we had to tell Miriam, and we had to write to our families and ask for their blessings, which I doubted would come our way. But we should get on with our decision to get married and we should get on with our lives.

Rachel wanted to talk to Miriam alone. But I insisted on going with her.

On Saturday morning when Miriam opened her apartment door and saw me standing with Rachel, she showed her disapproval. Miriam spoke to Rachel: "You read your father's letter. You promised not to see K.D. anymore."

Rachel said that she never made any promises. She told Miriam that I had proposed to her, and she had said yes.

Miriam called Rachel a coward. She lacked the courage to come alone to the apartment. Instead, she brought her "laurels" with her. Did Rachel really think that Miriam would be impressed because I was a doctor?

Miriam began to shout at me. She accused me of betraying the family's trust by stealing the daughter of a respectable Jewish family from Iraq.

Miriam turned back to Rachel and said that she had looked after her cousin for two years so that she would never feel lonely in this country. In return, Rachel had insulted them. She asked Rachel what she saw in me. Miriam predicted that her family would disown her, and I would desert her. She would be forced to beg for food.

We tried to change Miriam's heart, but it was impossible.

Rachel and I left the apartment. When we returned to the underground station, Rachel said that she had to go back and talk to her cousin alone. "You never know," she said. "She might change her mind."

Minutes after I returned to the clinic, Rachel called. She was in tears. Miriam's husband Jonathan had heard everything. He said that there was nothing more to discuss. If she continued to see that Indian boy, she wasn't welcome in his house anymore. He told her to go and never come back.

I told Rachel to come to our flat and I went to the underground station entrance and waited for her. As soon as I saw her, I hugged her. We said very little even when we sat together in the sitting room. Neil appeared with a tray of tea and biscuits. He said a cup of tea would feel good to us. He excused himself and went into the bedroom.

After Rachel and I had tea, I asked her if she would like to go see a movie. I thought it would make us both feel better.

The movie improved our spirits. We walked through a park, and I bought ice cream for us. After a while, I told Rachel that I was sorry that she had to suffer so much hostility, but we would face it sooner or later. She understood, but she said that her encounter with Miriam was just the beginning. More anger would arrive with each letter we received from our families back in India.

I waited and waited for Rachel to call me with her family's reaction to our plans. I worried that her mother, in particular, would have the ability to change Rachel's mind. The days crawled by.

~ 41 ~

OUR BIG DAY

RACHEL FINALLY RECEIVED A LETTER from her father. He said that he and her mother were extremely upset. Her mother didn't wish to live if her favorite daughter brought such shame to the family. She had fasted for a day, prayed at the synagogue, and she cried all the time. Rachel was so worried that she thought we should call off the engagement.

I showed Rachel a copy of a letter that I had written Jacob and his reply to me in which he said that their mother was distraught, but she was calming down. He and Naomi had no objections to our marriage, and they wished us the best. He believed that all the wounds would heal in time, and we would have a good relationship with his family.

That evening Neil asked me about our wedding plans. I told him that we needed to do something simple and inexpensive. He suggested that we go to the local borough hall and plan for a simple civilian ceremony. He also thought that he could arrange for us to have an inexpensive reception at the newly constructed Indian

YMCA.

The next morning Rachel and I went to the borough hall and met separately with the officer who issued marriage certificates. My meeting with the gentleman was brief; he only asked a few formal questions. But he spent a long time with Rachel because he thought that she was European and that I was a Muslim. He warned her that marriages often failed between Europeans and Muslims. After all, her future husband was legally allowed to have more than one wife. As he recited other cultural and social differences, Rachel shut him up. She said that we were both from India and I was a Hindu.

Later that week, Neil, Rachel, and I were enjoying a meal at an Indian restaurant, when he told us that he had made arrangements for us to hold our wedding dinner at the Indian YMCA. We were overjoyed, but I said that I hoped the dinner party would not be expensive. I had so little money in the bank.

When our wedding was only four days away, Neil broke out with chicken pox. My best friend in London, who had worked so hard to create a successful event, could not attend. Still, Neil continued to make plans by telephone. He even arranged for a photographer to take pictures after the ceremony.

Rachel and I were married at the borough hall and nearly everyone we invited was there. None of Rachel's relatives, including her brother Daniel, who had recently arrived in London and promised to attend our wedding, shared in our joy. Miriam had said to cancel the stupid wedding and warned Rachel that her brother Joseph had vowed to break every bone in my body when he came to London.

When Rachel and I arrived at the YMCA as husband and wife, we had many more guests than we expected. Neil had invited everyone I knew, including the landlady and her husband from the dig where I had lived with Saha before I moved into the flat with Neil.

The dinner party was wonderful. Dr. Lahiri made a funny speech that everyone enjoyed. Rachel stood up and thanked everyone, and so did I. Mrs. Robinson stood up and thanked everyone for attending our memorable celebration. She counted herself lucky to be our friend and said that we were a wonderful couple. She wished us happiness and success for the rest of our lives. She asked everyone to make a toast to us. Cheers reverberated through the hall. For the rest of the evening, everyone enjoyed themselves and the lovely dinner.

Before Rachel and I left the YMCA, I called Neil to tell him about the reception. He was delighted that he had succeeded in his mission. When Rachel and I were ready to leave, the YMCA warden surprised us and said that Neil had paid for everything. Amjad offered to take all our presents to our flat so that we could spend the night in a nice hotel. I thanked him profusely; then Rachel and I said our goodbyes to everyone.

When we arrived at our hotel, we registered as husband and wife. We went to the movies, but we couldn't concentrate and went back to the hotel. Rachel's company was enough for me. There was no space for anything else in my heart and mind. I felt blessed. Everything Rachel said sounded like music to me and I loved her angelic looks. When we finally went to bed, I felt energized knowing that it was my duty to keep Rachel comfortable and protect her from trouble. I loved her so much. I had been given the best reward of my life. I had Rachel by my side as my loving wife.

~ 42 ~

NEW HOSPITAL, NEW FRIENDS

THE NEXT DAY RACHEL AND I went to Brighton for a weekend honeymoon. Our hotel room overlooked the sea and a Victorian boardwalk where people could hire a boat. Sadly, I had too little money to give Rachel such a nice treat. Instead, we strolled on the pier and found a stall with a fortune-teller who offered to predict Rachel's future. I told her to have some fun.

The astrologer correctly said that Rachel was a new bride married to a man with darker skin. After an initial rough period, she would have a happy and prosperous married life with me. Rachel was pleased. The astrologer had earned her fee.

We walked along the boardwalk and watched all the sailboats and motorboats bobbing in the sea. That evening we soaked in the sights before we chose a restaurant and enjoyed a delicious dinner of Dover sole. Nighttime was wonderful and once again Rachel and I talked nearly until dawn. On the final evening of our brief honeymoon, we had a delightful Indian dinner where the aroma of the dishes floated through the air.

The next morning when we returned to London, we registered for two nights in a small family hotel near our hospital. Rachel had three more days of holiday, but I had to report to the hospital to meet the nursing staff and some of the doctors and familiarize myself with the hospital wards. The office secretary at the doctors' residence told me that since I would be on call at night, Rachel could stay in my room whenever it suited her. Once I received my keys, I called her to come to see the room, which had a double bed, along with a hot and cold washbasin. The bathroom was down the hall.

We also found a large furnished room in an old rooming house where tenants on each floor shared one bathroom and had access to a large kitchen. The landlady insisted that she always chose quiet tenants who were generally married, middle-class workers. She said we fit in and offered us a room immediately, on a monthly basis.

It took about a week for me to get accustomed to the medical facilities in the hospital. The operating room was modern, with unfamiliar equipment. On the ward, I needed to learn advanced procedures in biochemistry. Day and night I stayed in the hospital compound, but Rachel often had dinner with me and the other doctors. Everyone got along well, and we had lively conversations as well as good meals.

When I worked at the clinic for Lahiri, the pay was terrible, but I had time to take courses to prepare for my exam. At the hospital, the pay was still inadequate, but the work was rewarding and improved my skills as a surgeon. Overall, I was happy, and the hospital staff and patients complimented me for my hard work and good manners.

When I finished my fourth month at Tottenham Hospital, only two months remained on my original work agreement. I hoped that the management would renew my contract for six more months.

I needed more time and experience before I would be ready for a promotion to middle registrar.

At Tottenham, I worked under the guidance of the current middle registrar, who handled emergencies and assumed responsibility for all the patients after two p.m. when the chief surgeon left for the day. The middle registrar seemed to appreciate the quality of my work, but he never let me operate.

One day a senior doctor finally asked me to perform an inguinal hernia operation. He assisted me as he assessed my capabilities as a surgeon. I was delighted and did the surgery as fast as I could. It went well and the doctor congratulated me, but he reminded me that technique and thoroughness make for a good surgeon; speed was unimportant.

That night I discussed the operation with the middle registrar. I hoped he would be motivated to let me do some operations. Instead, he said that I would only get to operate when he thought that I was ready.

Time passed. Finally, the management invited me to stay for another six months, but I did not get a pay raise or a promotion.

One evening the registrar was sick and I had to cover the nightshift. He told me to call the senior registrar if there were any emergencies. Within an hour, a boy with acute appendicitis was admitted to the hospital. The senior registrar agreed that the boy needed immediate surgical intervention. He let me operate. The anesthetist telephoned the senior registrar before I finished working on the boy and said that the operation went smoothly. The operating room nurse also complimented me and boosted my morale.

Our registrar was sick for the next two days. By the time he returned to the hospital, I had performed another appendectomy, and I had operated on a patient with a strangulated hernia. The registrar complained to the visiting surgeon. He didn't want me operating on emergency patients without supervision. The visiting surgeon told him that he had been with me when I performed the hernia operation and that my technique was perfect. He asked the registrar to let me perform more operations under his supervision since this was part of the official training program.

The visiting surgeon told me to be careful. It would be unfortunate if I alienated the middle registrar. I knew this advice was important. But I resented the registrar's attempt to control me. He accepted me as his assistant, but he never gave me any genuine responsibility. I knew that I could never advance to middle registrar without performing an impressive list of operations as a junior registrar.

Six months raced by. I finally performed operations, and all my cases recovered without complications. I believed that I had proved myself and I thought that I was now entitled to the full privileges of an experienced junior registrar. I also gained the confidence of the general surgeon and the orthopedic surgeon. I believed their respect would help me get my next job.

~ **43** ~

NEXT STEP

LIFE FELT GOOD—AS SWEET as the delicious fruit that I tasted on the mulberry tree in the Tottenham Hospital compound. By now Neil worked part-time at an eye hospital and Amjad had passed his preliminary exam on his first attempt at Edinburgh. Unfortunately, Saha failed the exam once again.

One night Neil invited Rachel and me to have dinner with him and Amjad. I called Saha and asked him to join us, but he declined. The despondent tone in his voice disturbed me. On the night of the dinner, I asked Rachel to stay at home so that I could go see Saha and try to get him to change his mind.

Saha was desperate. He wanted to kill himself. He saw no other solution to his problems. I told him that such an act would be unfair to his son and Joya. He said that since he had been unfaithful to her, he doubted that he could face them again.

Somehow, I convinced him to go with me to have dinner with Amjad and Neil. After we said goodnight to Saha, we discussed our concerns about our friend. We decided that I should write to his older brother and ask him to convince Joya to come to London to be with her husband. We knew that she was a stable influence on him.

A week later I received a reply from Saha's brother. Joya was coming to London as soon as possible, but her young son would stay in Calcutta to continue his schooling. Joya planned to write to Saha that she was coming here because she was too lonely without him.

Naomi, who had been offered a nursing job in a London hospital, arrived in England a few days later. We were thrilled to see her. Rachel, who had always been close to her older sister, stared at her for the longest time before the two of them broke into smiles and embraced. After we enjoyed a fine meal together, I went back to my hospital residence so that the two sisters could have a private evening to catch up on their lost years.

Two weeks later Joya arrived in London. Her presence re-energized Saha. By the end of the month, the two of them shifted to Scotland where Saha planned to take an easier version of the primary exam at the Royal College of Surgeons in Glasgow. I promised them that Rachel and I would come visit in two months when he passed the exam.

Soon, winter arrived bringing miserable smog and cold temperatures. Every evening Londoners lit coal-burning fireplaces and added an ugly layer of soot to the smog. Each night when I got home from work, I was so filthy from the pollution that when I washed my face and hands, the water in the basin turned black.

In time Amjad, Neil, and I received great news! Saha had finally passed his primary exam. I kept my promise to him, and Rachel and I took a train to Scotland on our first free Saturday and spent the night in Glasgow. It was wonderful to see Saha looking happy and confident. I told Saha that Joya had brought him good luck. As we all walked to our hotel, Saha, ever worried, took me

aside and told me to keep my mouth shut about his earlier esca-
pades. I laughed to myself. Why would I share this information with
anyone?

When Rachel and I were back in London, I started planning
my next career move. My post at Tottenham Hospital was ending.
The three consultant surgeons at the hospital agreed to provide me
with good references and I began my search for a position as a middle registrar at a London-based hospital. I applied to four regional
hospital boards. Two of them asked for my references and requested an interview.

My first interview was at St. George's Hospital, which was
near Dr. Lahiri's clinic. I wasn't eager to work in East London again.
However, this hospital had excellent staff consultants, and I would
perform numerous operations. I would have an invaluable learning
experience.

At the interview, two surgeons and four members of the hospital board questioned me. The chief surgeon, Sir John Nicholson,
who asked most of the questions, seemed pleased with my answers.
After the interview, the secretary of the board asked me to wait
while they met with four other candidates.

When the secretary returned, he called out my name and led
me back into the room. Sir John told me that the board had selected
me. He said that once I completed six months as the middle registrar, the board would extend my position an additional six months
if the surgeons were satisfied with my work.

I was thrilled. I was moving closer to my goal to become a
fellow at the Royal College of Surgeons. Rachel and I went out and
enjoyed a delicious dinner that evening. We had something wonderful to celebrate.

~ ~ ~ ~ ~

On my last day at Tottenham Hospital, I handed my cases over to the newly appointed junior registrar. That afternoon the nurses threw a small party for me, and I said goodbye to everyone. They all wished me well and warned me that the consultants at St. George's Hospital would work me to death. I finally walked out of the hospital and took a long look at the spacious compound in the waning daylight before I walked through the gate and left Tottenham Hospital.

The next day Rachel and I cooked a special dinner for Naomi. When she arrived at our room in the rooming house, I started to fix a drink for myself. Naomi surprised me and asked for a gin and tonic. I had never seen her drink before. She told us that she had met a man at a dance hall. I asked her about the gentleman, but she quickly switched the subject.

That Monday I started my new job at St. George's Hospital. I was taken to the surgeons' room, where Sir John greeted me and introduced me to another middle-aged doctor, Mr. Bingham, who was a urological surgeon. Friends since their student days, the two men came from similar upper-class families. However, Mr. Bingham did not hold a title because he was the second-born son in his family.

I also met Sister Kelly, the senior nursing sister, who took us on ward rounds with the house surgeon. She stunned me with her knowledge of each patient. Even Sir John relied on her. She also knew every consultant and member of the managerial staff at St. George's. Sister Kelly was the rock at this hospital.

When the former registrar handed over his cases to me, he offered me some honest advice about Sister Kelly. He said that she not only gave Sir John information about every patient, but she also passed on the latest hospital gossip and volunteered her opinion of each doctor. He was convinced that she had kept him from getting a yearlong extension. The former registrar advised me to remain on Sister Kelly's good side.

I vowed to work hard, and I told myself to be pleasant with everyone and keep my opinions to myself. If Sister Kelly ever gossiped about me, I wanted her comments to be favorable.

When I performed my first operation at St. George's, Sir John watched for a while and then he left. Sister Kelly smiled. She said that I had passed the test. If Sir John had any issues with my technique, he would have stayed until I finished. I was so relieved. I gave quiet thanks to my chief at Tottenham who had trained me.

As the weeks passed, I enjoyed working with Sir John, Mr. Bingham, and Sister Kelly. Usually, Sir John performed one or two major operations each day and I performed the remaining scheduled operations. During this time, I received excellent training in the science and technique of surgery, but I worked extraordinarily long hours.

Every morning when Sir John arrived at the hospital, I was expected to have all the patient information ready for his review. Three times a week we did ward rounds. We completed scheduled operations, took care of surgical outpatients, and visited each postoperative case. I also worked at the clinic for three additional hours each day. By the time I finished the evening round of our ward, prepared patient reviews for Sir John, and handled emergencies, I was exhausted.

If I ever needed assistance at the hospital, I could contact the senior surgical registrar, but he was responsible for two entire hospitals and he also taught the students who visited St. George's. Instead, I relied on Sister Kelly who willingly introduced me to all her helpful friends in each department. They helped me do my work.

Once I was familiar with my long routine at the hospital, I understood why new registrars never had time to prepare for their exams. My nights went late, and my work was grueling. I wanted to appear for the final exam in six months, but I hardly had time to sleep.

One Saturday night Rachel and I had dinner with Naomi. She finally talked about her new friend, Harry Newman. She said that Harry, a middle-aged divorcee without children, was of Polish Hebrew ancestry. He had come to England as a child, and he had taken over his father's successful business. Harry, who was wealthy, considered himself British and behaved like a British man.

I asked Naomi if she knew why Harry had divorced his wife.

Naomi said that it was too early in their relationship to ask such a personal question.

That night as I lay in bed, I wrestled with a new dilemma involving Sir John. He had asked me to assist him with his private cases. His request signaled his trust in my work and increased my income, but this additional work came at a price. I would have no time to study for my exam. Rachel told me not to worry. She was certain that I would become a fellow of the Royal College of Surgeons. But I did worry, and sleep eluded me. I needed to pass this final test.

~ 44 ~

EARNING ANGER AND RESPECT

WORK CONTINUED TO EAT UP most of my time, but I forced myself to study whenever I could. When I was in the surgeon's room, I frequently asked surgeons questions about procedures and techniques. I knew that their answers were more valuable than anything I could learn from books.

One evening when I fell asleep as I tried to study, the phone rang. I was half-awake when I picked up the receiver. A shrill Indian woman said that her name was Esther, and she was a friend of Rachel's mother. Esther claimed that she had met me at the Bekhor's apartment. Esther was in London and needed to meet Rachel. She had to give her an important message from her mother.

I told Esther that I would pass on her message to Rachel.

Esther said that she would not talk to a disgusting man like me who had betrayed Rachel's family. In the eyes of God, our marriage did not exist. She told me to rot in Hell.

I calmly asked Esther for her telephone number and said that Rachel would contact her if she felt like it. Then I foolishly called

Rachel and imitated Esther's voice as I repeated everything that the woman had said to me. I told Rachel that she should leave me. I was a wicked man.

I could almost hear Rachel fuming on the line. She told "the lady" to mind her own business and slammed down the phone.

I knew that the conversation had rattled Rachel. I hurried to the other registrar's room. I told him that I had an emergency at home, and I asked him to cover for me. I took the underground train to our rooming house.

Rachel was surprised to see me. She told me a stupid woman named Esther had called her. She repeated the terrible things that the woman had said about our marriage.

I sat down on the bed and told her that the woman had called me earlier. She had said awful things to me, too. She had asked for Rachel's telephone number.

Rachel was outraged. "Why did you give our telephone number to her?"

I put my arm around her and said that I didn't give the number to the woman.

She looked confused. Then her face flashed with anger. "I see," she said. "You called me. You wanted to see how I would react to this woman." She told me to go back to work. She didn't want to talk to me.

I felt stupid. I promised her that I would never again be so thoughtless.

Rachel remained quiet for a long time before she finally forgave me. We never discussed this episode again.

When I started my sixth month at St. George's Hospital, Sir John told Sister Kelly and me that he was going on a holiday for a week. He had informed the hospital secretary that I would be in charge of all his patients and carry out his duties while he was away. Sir John also wanted me to manage two operating sessions and two outpatient clinics. He assured me that this valuable experience would compensate for the heavy workload. If I needed help, he advised me to turn to Mr. Bingham or the hospital secretary.

I knew that this was a great opportunity to act as a consultant surgeon for seven days, which would be an asset when I applied for my next position.

When Sir John left for his vacation, Sister Kelly warned me that he was so powerful that other consultants were jealous of him. They would probably sniff around this week and try to find fault with me. Sister Kelly promised to keep me up to date with each patient. She would also inform me about any new hospital gossip. Every night that week I stayed in the hospital. I wanted nothing to go wrong in Sir John's absence.

When Sir John returned from his brief vacation, I gave him a comprehensive review of everything that had occurred in the hospital. He said that he felt refreshed, and he was ready to start work. Before he began his hospital rounds, I asked him if I could have the next weekend off and complete freedom from any hospital telephone calls. He smiled and said that I had earned the free time. I had two days to be with Rachel.

~ ~ ~ ~ ~

That Saturday, Naomi had dinner with us. She was happy and talked about her special friend Harry. She said that he was so British that he preferred to socialize with British businessmen and officers of the British and continental commercial houses. He spent time with very few Jewish families. He also disliked authentic Jewish cuisine.

As Naomi talked about Harry, we learned that this wasn't the only Jewish thing he disliked. Naomi said that while Harry respected Moses' Ten Commandments, he didn't care for Jewish noses, and he considered her nose a typical aquiline specimen. It identified her as a member of the Hebrew race. He wanted her to undergo plastic surgery to fix it. She insisted that Harry liked everything else about her.

Naomi asked me what I thought about this request. Before I could respond, Rachel said that she would never cut her nose for anyone. I agreed and told Naomi that her nose was fine.

She said that Harry was willing to pay for the cost of this procedure, which proved that he cared for her.

I knew Naomi felt vulnerable. She worried about finding the right life partner. But I didn't think that she should agree to the operation. Who knew if her future with Harry would ever lead to a marriage?

After Naomi left the rooming house, Rachel told me that she was afraid that Naomi was too trusting. She thought that her sister would undergo the operation to please this man.

When I returned to the hospital on Monday, I knew that I had to find a way to work late at night so that I could take important courses during the daytime to prepare for the exam. Once I was able to implement my new strategy, I began smoking a pipe when I tried to study late, after work. The pipe helped me stay awake.

Days later Rachel told me that Naomi had decided to have her nose reconstructed. The reconstruction was a success, and she said that Harry went to visit Naomi in the hospital every day.

Rachel thought that maybe Harry really loved her sister. Why else would he spend so much money on her and treat her with such good care?

I wasn't convinced.

One month after Naomi's operation, we finally met Harry when he invited us to dinner at a fine French restaurant. He was in his late 30s, slightly overweight, and had a receding hairline, but he was well-dressed and well-behaved. He was also overbearing.

Harry asked us if we liked Naomi's beautiful new nose. Before we could answer, he said that it complemented her face. He bragged about his successful business importing curios from Russia and other Eastern European countries. He bragged about his plans to take Naomi on a holiday in Europe to visit his old haunts. He was convinced that she would have the time of her life.

~ ~ ~ ~ ~

Finally, I took my critically important exam. I thought that I did well on the clinical and written sections of this difficult test, but I was upset with my performance during the orals. My examiner, who had conducted extensive research on cirrhosis of the liver, had placed numerous liver specimens on the table. He asked me to determine which specimen exhibited signs of the disease.

I had never treated anyone for this illness. None of the surgeons at St. George's Hospital focused on the liver, nor did any of my courses, which covered only standard surgical procedures. Everything I knew about the disease I learned from books and most of these books were dated.

My examiner's unfortunate choice of subject caught me off-guard. I had no idea if my answers made sense to any of the distinguished professors. They were masters of the inscrutable expressionless face.

After I finished my exam, I joined Neil and Rachel who were waiting for me. We waited in the hall for an anxious long hour while the examiners compared notes. Finally, the clerk appeared and read out a few names. My name was not on his list.

I had hoped that I had done well enough on the written and clinical sections so that I could squeak through the entire exam, but I obviously did poorly on the pathology oral exam. Cirrhosis of the liver defeated me.

I knew that these exams were difficult. I also knew that I was lucky to have passed the primary exam on my first attempt. But I was devastated. This was the first time in my life that I had failed an important exam. Neil had also failed. Amjad would face the oral examiners tomorrow. When Rachel reached out to hold my hand, I saw the tears in her eyes.

We went to Neil's hotel and joined a few other examinees. Only a few people had passed the test. Most of us would face this rigorous exam another time. I had a glass of beer and then ordered another. I noticed a registrar from another hospital, an Indian chap, who had failed the exam a few months ago. I remembered my attempts to console him as he drowned his sorrow with glass after glass of beer. He was so sure that he had passed the exam that he insisted the examiners had discriminated against him. He said that so many local boys, who were ill-prepared, had passed.

The Indian chap came over and told me that he had finally passed the exam. He asked me how I did. I said that I was not so lucky. I had to try again.

The next morning, I hugged Rachel and returned to the hospital. Everyone knew that I had failed the exam, but Sir John told me not to worry. He failed his first attempt at this test.

Mr. Bingham also comforted me. He advised me to forget

studying old textbooks. He said that I would be better prepared if I studied pathology specimens and read newly published articles about diseases in periodicals that were available at the Royal College. He also thought that I should take another course before I took the fellowship exam. All this goodwill from two fine surgeons boosted my spirits. But my future success was no guarantee.

~ 45 ~

MISUNDERSTANDINGS

ST. GEORGE'S HOSPITAL APPOINTED A new registrar, which made me the senior registrar and increased my responsibilities. I spent so much time at the hospital, and I couldn't wait to spend time with Rachel in the rooming house, where I also developed a nice relationship with Nellie, our landlady.

When I arrived at the rooming house one evening, Nellie looked alarmingly different. She had lost weight, and her eyes were unusually prominent. I asked her if she was okay.

She said that she had trouble sleeping. Her family physician gave her a two-week prescription for sleeping pills. Once she started sleeping, he said that she would be fine.

I went to my room, but I kept thinking about Nellie. I thought that she suffered from more than a lack of sleep. The strange look in her eyes made me wonder if she had an over-active thyroid gland. I told Rachel that I felt it was my duty to speak candidly with Nellie.

When I knocked on her door, Nellie was surprised to see me. I told her that I worried about her thyroid gland. She laughed. She said that she trusted her experienced doctor. Nothing was wrong with her.

As I explained the disease in detail and urged Nellie to make an appointment with a consultant physician, she started to sweat, and her eyes looked terrible. She shook with rage and said that if she wanted my medical advice, she would have asked for it.

Sunday night I went back to the hospital, and I forgot all about Nellie as I immersed myself in my work. That Thursday Rachel called. Nellie had confronted her in the hall and said that she was furious with me. She had seen her doctor who reassured her that she was only suffering from anxiety and depression. He said that she needed kind reassurance and sympathy, along with sedatives, that would calm her down and let her sleep. He told her to avoid any more unsolicited, incorrect advice.

Rachel said that Nellie no longer wanted me to spend nights in the rooming house. I could only come to the rooming house to visit, nothing more.

I was surprised. I had tried to help her, but my help had back-fired.

Rachel and I decided that I should stay at the hospital and study.

A few days later, Naomi returned from her trip with Harry to the Continent. She raved about the food, the good wines, and all the beautiful places that they had visited. She expected a proposal from him.

I still thought that this man was an insincere phony. I asked Naomi if he had taken her to meet his mother. Naomi said that Harry believed his mother would not understand their relationship.

When she left our room, I asked Rachel what there was to understand.

~~~~~

The Christmas season filled the hospital with joy and transformed our middle-class neighborhood. Most of the simple houses, gaily adorned with lights, looked joyful, and so did our hospital, which was decorated for the season. Doctors discharged most of their recovering patients so that they could spend the holiday at home. Only a few extremely ill people remained on the wards. Non-emergency surgical operations were reduced to a minimum so that doctors and nurses had time to celebrate.

On Christmas day, the nurses invited us to come to their decorated ward for food and a drink. Rachel and I slowly toured each ward where I enjoyed more and more Scotch. By the time we reached the surgeons' ward, Sister Kelly was waiting for us. She said that she had a special drink for me from her home country of Ireland. The Irish whisky was strong. I was already tipsy. The world around me started to move.

Rachel, who never drank, guided me back to my room and got me into bed. Three hours later I woke up groggy with a pounding headache. I was relieved that we could stay in the room all day. I needed to recover!

After the holidays, Rachel and I spent an evening with Naomi. When she talked about Harry, she still thought that he would propose to her, but Naomi admitted that whenever she discussed their relationship, he became irritated. He insisted everything was fine. Why complain?

Rachel kept quiet about Harry. She wanted her sister to make her own decision about this man.

~ ~ ~ ~ ~

Once the New Year began at the hospital, work resumed, and I still had very little time to study. The exam was a couple of months away. I had never worked in the orthopedic surgery department, so I decided to attend preparatory classes and demonstrations covering this technique. I also received permission from Sir John to take a course in general surgery but in return for my hospital absences, he insisted that I could have no days off. My workload became so heavy that I only slept four hours a day.

One evening Rachel called to tell me that Nellie's condition had deteriorated. She told Rachel that she regretted being so rude to me. She wanted to talk to me before she saw another doctor.

The next day I received an urgent message from Nellie. She was frantic when I spoke to her and quickly apologized for her behavior. She said that she was still losing weight, and her hands had begun to tremble. Her family physician had finally sent her to a specialist who said that she was suffering from a toxic thyroid. He told her that she had to begin treatment, which included surgery. Nellie asked me to visit her.

I took the evening off from work and went to see her. She asked me to talk to her new doctor before she started her treatment. I agreed to call him, but I told her that it was important to begin her treatment without delay. Before I left, she apologized again and said that I should feel free to stay in our room whenever I wished, day or night.

I hurried back to the hospital and made certain that everything was in order before Sir John arrived in the morning. After I finished my morning rounds, I called Nellie's consultant physician who promised to keep me posted about Nellie's treatment.

Within a month Nellie had undergone successful surgery and completed her initial treatment. She felt so much better that she had a small cocktail party in her room. Rachel glowed when Nellie sang my praises calling me the "smart doctor" who first diagnosed her problem.

In one month, I had to take my exam. But I had so many responsibilities at the hospital that I still struggled to study. One morning after making rounds with Sir John, I found the courage to ask him if I could have a few days' leave from work so that I could read my textbook and notes at least once.

"Alright," he said. "You can have one week off. But your leave is unofficial. I'm personally helping you. Don't forget this."

I thanked him profusely.

Once Sir John left the room, Sister Kelly said that I was lucky. He had never done this for any other registrar.

I called Nellie and asked her if I could rent a small room for one month so that I could study for my exam. She offered to rent me her office and said that she would put a bed in for my use. Nellie's offer was perfect. I could study without disturbing Rachel.

I arranged for the other surgical registrar to look after my workload until I took the exam. I promised to repay the favor when he needed some time in the future. When I finally began my week-long preparation for the exam, I quickly forgot about the hospital and its problems. Every thought in my head revolved around my long-neglected books and notes.

I worked hard these few days and nights. I rarely ate and I smoked a lot to stay awake. Every morning, I marked up the day's pages that I planned to study, and I never went to bed until I reached that day's goal. When Rachel came to see me in the morning before she left for work, she opened the window and the door to freshen the air. After I washed and ate a small breakfast with a large cup of coffee, I repeated my study routine.

On the day that I took my exam, I hoped that I would remember everything that I had read. When the examiners announced the results, Rachel took the day off, but she was too nervous to wait with me at the Royal College. She stayed in the rooming house.

Unfortunately for Neil, he failed the exam on his second attempt. But my dear friend kept me company in between my oral and written exams.

I thought my exams went reasonably well, but I didn't think that I had done exceptionally well. I knew that I made an incorrect diagnosis of one case. I had tried to explain my answer to the examiner, but his face remained inscrutable. I couldn't tell if he accepted my rationale.

Neil and I joined the other anxious examinees in the hall, and we waited. Finally, after 90 minutes, the secretary stepped into the hall and announced the name of the first successful candidate. The rest of us waited until he appeared again to announce the second name. A third time he appeared. He called my name. A thrill traveled like lightning from my head down my backbone. I felt numb as I followed the secretary into a room where seven examiners shook my hand and congratulated me.

When I left the room, Neil ran toward me. He gestured with his hands that he had telephoned Rachel. She was on her way to the college.

My remarkable friend was so happy. That he had failed the exam just a few days ago did not dampen his happiness for me. We waited on the sidewalk in front of the college. After twenty minutes Rachel ran through the crowd and fell into my arms. Her body was shaking, and she radiated her love for me.

We thought of going to Neil's place, but we decided against it. Amjad was studying. He would take his exam next week. Instead, I called Amjad and gave him my good news. I also called Sir John and Sister Kelly. She told me to be ready for a big hug the next morning. Rachel called Naomi who was delighted for me, but Rachel said that Naomi seemed unhappy. She hoped that her sister was okay.

Neil, Rachel, and I went out to dinner. Suddenly, my fatigue, which had been building all week, washed over me. I was glad that no one expected to have a long evening. Neil reminded me that from the moment he met me, I was determined to get my British Fellowship. I had reached my goal. It was a great achievement. I reminded Neil how many friends thought my determination was foolish.

When Rachel and I returned to our room at the rooming house, Nora and Nellie came to congratulate me. Nellie said that she wanted to arrange a small party for me. Her goodwill pleased me. I was also happy to see that she was feeling much better.

It had been quite a day for me: first the exam and then the celebration. I realized how much I loved sharing this important moment with Rachel. I was so grateful that she was by my side. She was always my inspiration.

When I returned to the hospital the next morning, everything felt different to me. Sir John shook my hand. Sister Kelly hugged me, and all the nurses congratulated me. When I saw Mr. Bingham in the surgeon's room, he addressed me as Mr. Ray. I had passed the prestigious exam and earned a new title. I was no longer called doctor.

In Britain, male surgeons are addressed as Mr., a tradition that goes back to the eighteenth century when physicians were typically "gentlemen" with a formal medical degree, while surgeons often took apprenticeships instead. Everyone addressed me as Mr. Ray, which occasionally confused me, and I failed to respond. I needed more time to accept my hard-won transformation.

~ 46 ~

PAINFUL DECEIT

SIR JOHN HAD PROMISED ME the post of senior registrar when it became available, but this was not a certainty. Our current senior registrar was waiting to become a consultant, and his promotion would only occur when a consultant retired or died. He was already in his forties. He had been waiting a long time.

I decided that I should explore my options back in India with an officer at the India High Commission. But right now, I wanted to enjoy life with Rachel. Good times had eluded us during these last few years.

One day Naomi called me at the hospital. She said that she needed to talk to me. I invited her to come on Saturday and spend the night with us. She could sleep in our small study room, which we continued to rent.

Friday night Nellie had a small cocktail party in the rooming house. She had invited a few friends, and the evening was wonderful. Rachel and I were happy and so relaxed. We had crossed a major hurdle in our lives, and we believed that all our goals were within reach.

Naomi was tired when she arrived on Saturday. As we sat together enjoying a drink and hors d'oeuvres, she told us that she no longer trusted Harry. He spent less time with her, and he was always moody and demanding. Then a nurse at her hospital told Naomi that she saw Harry with another lady at an expensive restaurant. Naomi was devastated. She began to wonder why Harry never told her where he worked and why he never gave her his telephone number.

Naomi had stolen one of Harry's business cards from his overcoat. She gave me the card, which included his work address and phone number. I told her I would investigate Harry for her. I promised her that he would never know.

I called the number on the card. A gentleman, who said he was a salesman, answered the phone. He explained that the company was an import and export house started by David Chaimovitch, a Russian Jew. He volunteered that the son, Moshe Chaimovich, had taken over the business after the father's death.

Posing as a prospective buyer, I asked if I could look at the merchandise. The salesman agreed as long as I presented a valid business card.

I suddenly remembered that Nellie's father was a businessman who had come from Central Europe. I called her. She said that her father knew David Chaimovitch and considered him an honorable importer. Nellie didn't personally know the son Moshe, but she had heard that he had made a fortune after the war by trafficking in illegal antiquities from Russia and Central Europe. She also heard that Moshe was a womanizer.

Nellie offered to get me a business card so that I could visit the warehouse. She told me to take someone strong with me. The business manager at the hospital, who was a hefty Irishman, agreed to accompany me as the chief buying agent for our merchant house.

I called the salesman at Harry's company and said that I would like to look at their merchandise with our company's buying agent. He said that his company's general manager was in Poland and Czechoslovakia, but he could walk us through the warehouse.

The business manager and I paid a visit the next afternoon. While the salesman showed us stunning Christian and Jewish gold antiquities, I wondered how the company could acquire these articles from churches and old palaces without local collaboration. I also wondered if the British authorities knew about these imports.

At one point I saw a photograph of a man with a woman and two children on a table. The man was Harry. I mentioned the lovely people in the picture to the salesman. He said that I was looking at Mr. Chaimovitch and his family. They would return to London next week.

When we left the warehouse, I thanked the business manager for his help and returned to the rooming house. I told Rachel the results of my investigation. She was saddened to discover that her sister had been the victim of a deceitful predator.

Days later when Naomi came for dinner, I asked her about Harry. She said that she had not heard from him in two weeks. She thought that he was out of the country or maybe he was sick. I said that her first guess was correct, and I told her about my trip to the warehouse.

Naomi's face went white. She sighed, then announced, "So that was that!"

I took her hand and said that Harry had a big ego. He probably wanted to hold on to his conquests. I reminded her that he was also rich and powerful and his connections with the mafia made

him dangerous. I told her that she needed to forget about this relationship, but she also had to leave her job at the hospital before
Harry returned from the Continent. She had to disappear and work
somewhere else. I advised her to use my name and my hospital as
her forwarding address. Finally, I told Naomi not to talk to him or
see him if he contacted her.

When we ate dinner together, we all felt close. After supper,
Naomi went to my former study room and stayed there for the
night. She left on Sunday morning.

On Monday Naomi talked with the matron at her hospital who
listened sympathetically to the abbreviated account of her troubles.
She called the matron of another hospital outside London and asked
her if she needed a well-qualified staff nurse.

The matron had a vacancy. Naomi was given a new job.

The next morning, I took the day off from work and accompanied her to the new hospital. I also helped her get settled into the
nurses' quarters.

I returned to London with a heavy heart. Naomi was no longer
in Harry's awful clutches, but he had left indelible marks on her
body and soul. Every time she looked into a mirror and stared at her
reconstructed nose she would remember this unpleasant episode of
deceit. It would come back to haunt and hurt her.

~ 47 ~

UNEXPECTED HONOR

ONCE I BECAME A FELLOW of the Royal College, people at St. George's Hospital behaved differently toward me. Lab and X-ray technicians worked more quickly on my requests. Sir John gave me more operations to perform on my own. Then one day he invited Rachel and me to an afternoon gathering at his house on the Thames River to watch the annual boat race between Oxford and Cambridge Universities.

Sir John's home was a gorgeous mansion that once belonged to a courtier of Queen Elizabeth I. On the day of the race, we sat at tables and chairs on the spacious verandah where we enjoyed wine, beer, and sandwiches. Rachel and I also met Lady Nicholson, who was Sir John's wife.

Soon boats from both schools, with oarsmen rowing in perfect order, passed close by us on the Thames. The Oxford boat took the lead as the boats moved on. When Sir John's alma mater won the race, he served us victory champagne. It was a delightful afternoon.

Rachel and I called Naomi from time to time. Her sister said that she liked her new hospital and her surrounding neighborhood with its lovely parks. Naomi told us that she was doing well, and she looked forward to seeing us. We promised to visit her soon.

One afternoon I received a call from Miriam. She was furious. She had been unable to contact Naomi for weeks. She had finally called Naomi's hospital, where an administrator directed her to call me.

I told Miriam that Naomi was fine. She would contact Miriam when she was ready.

Miriam said that I had no right to keep Naomi from her family. She said that some man had called her husband and had important information for her. I told Miriam that I would be happy to give the information to her cousin. She hung up on me.

I worried for days that Harry would call me next. But he never did.

But one morning after I made the rounds with Sir John, my free time vanished. Sir John told me that he had accepted an invitation to give lectures in South Africa for a month. He planned to tell the Regional Board that he wanted all his duties delegated to me in his absence. Since I was a qualified surgeon and a Fellow of the Royal College, he believed that I had the skills to cover for him. He hoped that the board would compensate me for the extra work that I did during these weeks.

A few days later I appeared before the hospital board. Sir John was at the meeting when the president said that he had agreed to let me assume the duties of the consultant surgeon while Sir John was away. But I would also be responsible for my normal hospital duties. He said that if I felt uncomfortable with these additional obligations, I had the right to refuse the offer. He also informed me that the board would not give me additional compensation for the extra work. The president asked if this additional information would change my decision.

I said that I never considered the remuneration as an entitlement. It made no difference to me. Sir John told everyone in the room that the matter was settled. I was allowed to leave.

Later I learned from Mr. Bingham that the board had argued with Sir John over his plan, but Sir John had prevailed. Mr. Bingham asked me to alert him if I had any problems in the hospital while Sir John was away.

When I saw Sir John, he told me that some people were petty for not authorizing extra payment, but he assured me that he would find ways to compensate me when he returned.

Once Sir John left for South Africa, I discovered that I also had to attend some staff meetings and make myself available for conferences with the management. Still, the unending work was exhilarating.

As I finished the hectic month. I was so eager for Sir John to come back to St. George's. But my spirits soared when I received a letter from the president of the Royal College of Surgeons that congratulated me for becoming a formally elected Fellow of the Royal College. The letter gave a boost to my sagging spirits.

Sir John finally returned from South Africa. He was pleased that the hospital had experienced no real problems in his absence.

Once again, I had some leisure time, and I spent every minute of it with Rachel. We went to see Naomi. She told us some delightful news. The London office of Jacob's company had finally confirmed his job transfer. He would leave Calcutta in a few weeks. She also said that her brothers planned to move their parents to England once the boys were settled at their jobs.

~ ~ ~ ~ ~

A few days later, I received a letter from Dolly. She told me that she had given birth to a healthy baby boy with lovely brown eyes that reminded her of me. She hoped that he would grow up to be kind and clever. That night, hours after I had mailed a congratulatory letter to Dolly and her husband, I had trouble sleeping. I kept reliving that day many years ago when I had first met her. I hoped that she would be happy and feel fulfilled with the unconditional love of her baby boy. I hoped that she would be able to enjoy all his smiles and every one of his milestones as he grew up.

A couple of days later the senior surgical registrar, Dr. Hues told me in confidence that he was leaving his job in six months to take a position as a full-time consultant surgeon at a hospital in Kent. Dr. Hues asked me not to discuss his departure with anyone, except Sir John, whom he thought might be able to help me get appointed to this position in the hospital. Four days later I finally summoned the courage to talk to this great man. He promised to help me.

Finally, the news about Dr. Hues' resignation became official. Sir John encouraged me to apply for the position. He admitted that I would probably face stiff competition, but he believed that I was as qualified as any other good applicant.

One month later the Regional Board asked me to appear for an interview at the regional teaching hospital. On that day, when I stood before the professor of surgery and other distinguished surgeons, including Sir John, and some of the board members, they asked me about everything but my qualifications as a surgeon. They were particularly interested in knowing why I wanted to stay in England.

When a board member reminded me that India had a dire need for qualified surgeons, I explained that my family had lost its ancestral properties during the Partition and that I couldn't support my wife on a modest salary while I built up a surgical practice in India. Sir John finally intervened when an interviewer informed me that I wouldn't be guaranteed a future appointment as a surgical consultant in England. Sir John told him that I was well aware of this. Before I left the room my interviewers assured me that they were only trying to point out the potential difficulties that could affect my long-term career. They weren't trying to steer me away from considering this position at St. George's Hospital.

For the next few hours, the board and the other interviewers grilled three more candidates. At the end of the day, they came into the room and told us that they hadn't reached a decision. We would be notified in due course.

The next morning, I didn't discuss the interview while I did rounds with Sir John. Since he said nothing to me about the job, I feared the worst. But when I saw Mr. Bingham, he told me that I was in the final running with one other candidate who was currently the middle registrar at the teaching hospital. The professor of surgery at the teaching hospital tried to claim that the registrar's teaching background would make him a superior teacher.

Sir John then pointed out that the middle registrar had never done any teaching even though he worked at the teaching hospital. He explained that I had repeatedly observed the consultants when they taught at St. George's Hospital. I had also performed a greater number of operations, and I had assumed all his duties for a month while he was on vacation.

Mr. Bingham said that the interviewers planned to meet in three days to make their final decision. After speaking with Mr.

Bingham, I was deeply grateful to Sir John who had spoken so highly of my qualifications.

After a few more days of agony, the Regional Board told me that I had received the appointment. I was thrilled. This was such a big promotion. But I had to wait five more months before I started this important new job.

~ 48 ~

NEW LIFE INTERVENES

A FEW WEEKS LATER RACHEL and I spent a quiet weekend with each other, but she seemed oddly absent. I asked her if she was annoyed that I had not invited her sister or brother to be with us. She said that she was happy to spend the weekend with me. She didn't want any company. I asked her if I had annoyed her somehow. She told me not to worry about her.

That evening we went to dinner at a good Indian restaurant. Rachel said that she didn't want spicy food, so we decided to have tandoori chicken and vegetable pilaf. She ate slowly, which was so unlike her. She also ate a lot less food than she normally enjoyed. I asked her if she was feeling all right.

That night when we slipped into bed, Rachel said that she was sorry if she had spoiled our dinner. Her lovely brown eyes were moist, and her face was flushed. I asked her what was wrong.

Rachel said that I wouldn't like her news, but she had under-gone a pregnancy test at her hospital, and she was pregnant. She asked me if I was disappointed. She knew that this was the wrong time for us to have a baby.

I said that we were not always careful, especially after I had passed my exam. But I told her that we still should be happy even if we had to change our plans.

Rachel said that she hoped that I wouldn't accept Dr. Lahiri's offer. She would feel so guilty.

I assured Rachel that Dr. Lahiri's offer was not under consideration. I told her not to worry, and I promised that in a few days, I would figure out our best options so that we could make the correct decision for the two of us. I asked her to make an appointment right away with an obstetrician so that we could start visiting a prenatal clinic. We also agreed that she should give up her full-time work. She said that she would talk to the matron at her hospital and arrange for a part-time position.

The next morning when I returned to work, Rachel's revelation changed everything for me. I couldn't stop worrying about our financial situation. Rachel's income would soon be cut in half and my income would remain the same for four more months. Once I became the senior surgical registrar, I would still have a modest salary. We would need extra funds to move to a flat and live comfortably with the new baby and I would need to buy a car since I would be the senior surgical registrar at two hospitals.

My thoughts and anxieties jumped from the short term to the long term. How long would I end up working as a senior surgical registrar? Even with Sir John's help, I might never receive the post of consultant. This dear man was getting older. He might retire before he could help me get this coveted position. I might have no choice but to find a family physician who would bring me into his practice as an associate. I could waste years, and my financial position would be terrible.

I remembered that I had promised myself that I would protect Rachel, and we would be financially well off. I also remembered Miriam's prediction that Rachel would be poverty-stricken and desperate if she married me. As I worked at the hospital, all these worries and fears followed me from ward to ward.

I waited until Sir John left for the day before I talked to Dr. O'Connell, who was one of our consultant obstetricians. He was understanding and said that he would be available to Rachel and me if we needed his help.

I called Rachel. She assured me that she had registered with the antenatal clinic at her maternity hospital. She had also made an appointment to talk with the matron the next day. When she said that she couldn't arrange an appointment with her hospital's consultant obstetrician without a referral from her family physician, I told her that I would make an appointment for her with Dr. O'Connell at our hospital.

When Rachel met with the matron at her hospital, she was accommodating. She asked her to work full-time for one more week before she switched to part-time. She also went to the antenatal clinic, which again confirmed the pregnancy. They gave her a prescription for prenatal vitamins and other items for would-be mothers and their babies. We were getting prepared for her pregnancy.

When Dr. O'Connell examined Rachel, he was concerned about a thick scar that she had on her right lower abdomen. He asked her if she had suffered from an appendicular abscess that was drained during an appendectomy.

Rachel said that she was only four-years-old when she got the scar. She was told that she had a large abscess that was drained by a retired Scottish army surgeon in Calcutta.

I wondered if this so-called surgeon was qualified and if he knew what he was doing. Some British army doctors, who stayed in India after their retirement, continued working in government hospitals and no one questioned their qualifications.

When Dr. O'Connell examined Rachel, he determined that the scar, unfortunately, was attached to the uterus. He said that this could become a problem as the uterus enlarged during her pregnancy. We would have to wait and see.

From the time that I learned about Rachel's pregnancy, I felt as if some external force had pushed me into an undefined and unpredictable territory. I continued to do my work at the hospital, and I assumed that I was behaving normally. But one morning after Sir John left the hospital, Sister Kelly asked me if something was wrong. She said that I was acting as if I had lost the joy of my life.

I hadn't planned to talk about Rachel's pregnancy with anyone. But I opened up to Sister Kelly. I told her all my concerns, including my fear of being unable to support a baby in just a few months.

Sister Kelly brought me a glass of sherry. As I slowly sipped my drink, she told me that I had a heavy load to carry. She said that Sir John was also worried about me.

I felt better after Sister Kelly said that she and Sir John would help me. I felt as though I had become a member of a small family with Sir John as the father figure. We all cared deeply about each other.

Sister Kelly said that the best person to advise me would be Dr. Hues, the senior surgical registrar. She promised to have a word with him and get back to me. She also thought that I should wait before I discussed my changed circumstances with Sir John.

I went back to work at the surgical outpatient department. While I was tending to a patient, Dr. Hues came and asked me to meet him in the surgeons' room after I finished my work. When the two of us were alone, he listened patiently to my concerns. He said that it was so strange that just when everything fell into place something like this happened. He thought that Sister Kelly should break the news to Sir John. He also wanted to speak to Sir John before I finally approached him. He doubted that I would ever become a specialist surgeon in England. Perhaps, Sir John could help me get a posting as a lone resident surgeon in a rural hospital, but the job would take up all my time.

Dr. Hues thought that I should become a member of the British Colonial Service. Unfortunately, jobs were shrinking in this sphere since so many British colonies were becoming independent. But even if I only worked a few years for the service, I could save money. Most likely, I would also be compensated for my career loss if the political status changed in the country where I was posted.

Dr. Hues knew a Colonial Service doctor, Dr. Walsh, who was currently visiting London. He thought that his friend would agree to meet me and talk to me about the service. He also told me that I shouldn't despair over such good news. I was becoming a father. I would find the appropriate direction for my career.

Dr. Hues and I decided that I should notify the regional authorities to let them know that I could no longer accept the position of senior surgical registrar. They could accept the runner-up and create a smooth transition.

I asked Dr. Hues to try to arrange a meeting with his doctor friend who was visiting London. I needed to know more about the Colonial Service. I also needed to discuss everything with Sir John.

Once I left the hospital, I called Neil. I always valued the advice of this caring friend. When we met later in the day, he also believed that I had no future in the United Kingdom or in India, where I could never make enough money. He thought that the Colonial Service was my best option. Dr. Hues made an appointment for me to meet his friend Dr. Walsh. As soon as Dr. Walsh offered me a glass of beer, I sensed the gentleman sizing me up. He asked me repeatedly why I wanted to join the Colonial Service. None of my replies seemed to satisfy him.

Dr. Walsh asked me if I liked to hunt. He said that other than hunting and playing cards, there was little else to do in the colonies, such as Northern Nigeria. He also said that the working conditions were better in Northern Nigeria than in any other colony because the local leaders appreciated the work of the British officers. He said that the work was hard, but the officers usually lived in homes with servants in expatriate neighborhoods. There were also good shops, which were managed by Europeans who catered to the needs of foreigners.

He explained that ninety percent of the senior officers posted in Northern Nigeria came from Britain, Australia, and New Zealand. Some officers were also white South Africans. A few Germans and Dutch were also hired on a contract basis, but they were not part of the permanent service. He didn't know if the Colonial Service would allow me to become a British officer. No Indians were presently serving in Northern Nigeria.

I thanked Dr. Walsh for helping me. When I left his house that cold drizzly afternoon, everything felt dismal to me. The doctor's words were not encouraging.

I hurried back to meet Rachel at the rooming house. I told her about my meeting. I asked her if she would consider going to live in a British colony if I could become a British Colonial Service officer.

Rachel said that she would go anywhere with me if it was good for my career and offered good medical facilities.

I called Dr. Hues and told him about my meeting. He said that Dr. Walsh's prejudices probably colored some of the things that he had said to me. He also told me that he had talked to Sir John, who would speak to me soon.

After our ward rounds on Tuesday morning, Sir John and I were alone in the surgeons' room. He thought that I could be successful in the United Kingdom and was convinced that I had the right material. If I wanted to stay in England, he would try to help me. He chuckled as he reminded himself and me that he was getting older. The new powers-that-be no longer listened to him the way that they did in past years.

Sir John said that if I preferred to join the Colonial Service, he didn't think that it would be difficult for me to secure an appointment. He knew the Colonial Service Secretary. He would write a personal letter to him on my behalf. He also agreed that if I wanted to join the service, I should be gracious and quickly recuse myself from the job of senior surgical registrar before it was time for me to step into that position.

I was dumbfounded as I listened to Sir John. I was certain that this dear man would be upset with me. He had pushed so hard for me to get my new appointment at the hospital.

~ 49 ~

BRITAIN'S COLONIAL SERVICE

DAYS LATER I CALLED THE Colonial Service office and made an appointment to meet Dr. Buchanan, who was the medical advisor. As a career-long member of the service, he could answer all my questions.

After I told him why I wanted to join the organization, he said that the British colony of Nigeria would be the best place for me to work, but he was not involved in recruitment. He also didn't know if I was qualified to apply since I was not a British subject. I reminded him that India was a member of the Commonwealth.

Dr. Buchanan called someone to discuss my eligibility. He smiled and nodded to me as he asked the person on the phone to prepare the application forms.

I thanked him and went to the recruitment department, where a young lady gave me a packet of forms. When I returned to St. George's Hospital, Mr. Bingham helped me pour through the Colonial Service application. He laughed and asked me how my love affair was progressing with this organization. I said that there was no love affair yet. I still needed to learn the rules of our courtship.

He encouraged me to apply. He doubted that many other candidates could match my qualifications and superior references. He also pointed out the provision that allowed for the employment of Commonwealth citizens, so my nationality was not a problem. Mr. Bingham thought that a personal letter from Sir John to the Colonial Secretary would crush any resistance from minor bureaucrats. He also offered to serve as a referee.

I filled out the application forms and waited until Sir John gave me the signal to hand deliver my application to the Colonial Service office. The secretary in the recruitment department told me that the review process would take time.

Days later Sir John told me that his friend Dr. Leonard Johns, who was the Colonial Service Secretary, had acknowledged his letter and had wished him and his prodigy the best. I was relieved.

A few days later the registrar from the teaching hospital came to see me at work. He thanked me for recusing myself from my new job. He had heard from the current senior registrar that I was leaving the hospital as soon as I received a job offer from abroad. I was relieved that the senior registrar had not mentioned the Colonial Service.

Everything proceeded smoothly at St. George's. The registrar from the teaching hospital helped me repeatedly when I needed time to spend time with Rachel at the rooming house. Nellie also visited with Rachel, and so did Naomi whenever she had free time. But Jacob rarely came to see his sister. He seemed to prefer to spend his time socializing, often with his brother Joseph, who still would not come to see us.

I hoped that everything would go well with Rachel's pregnancy. She was a healthy young woman, who ate sensibly, and she did not smoke or drink. But I continued to worry about our future. I was afraid that the Colonial Service would turn me down.

After a month I called the secretary. I asked her about the status of my application. She said that my application was still under review, which she claimed was a good sign.

Nellie called a couple of evenings later. She asked me to come quickly to the rooming house. Rachel was not well. I alerted the registrar at the teaching hospital and hurried home.

Rachel was curled up in bed, with Nellie sitting by her side. She had pain in her lower abdomen. She had been bleeding and wanted to see an obstetrician.

I called Dr. O'Connell and told him that I was taking Rachel to the hospital. I asked Nellie to telephone Sister Kelly and then I called for a taxi.

When we arrived at St. George's, Sister Kelly had arranged for Rachel to be admitted into a private room.

Dr. O'Connell arrived and examined her. He told us that bleeding during the first three months of pregnancy was common, and it normally stopped without causing any damage to the fetus. He also said that while he was still concerned about the adhesion of the uterus to the abdominal wall, he did not think that the adhesion had caused the bleeding.

But Dr. O'Connell ordered Rachel to stay at the hospital for a few days until everything settled down. He also prescribed a hormone preparation that would arrest the bleeding. He hoped that the adhesion would soften and that everything would be fine.

When everyone left the room, Rachel finally relaxed and felt that her pregnancy would proceed normally. I went to my room to rest.

Naomi came to see Rachel the next morning and stayed with her sister the entire day. The next day she returned with all her brothers and Miriam. They had decided to bury the hatchet and show their goodwill and support for Rachel.

Still, Miriam took a shot at me. She asked me if I was happy now that Rachel's tummy would soon reach her chin.

I kept a straight face and said that I was very happy. I was also pleased that her family had come to see her and that everyone had decided to help her during her pregnancy. I could see that their visit had boosted Rachel's morale.

Rachel had many other visitors, including Sir John, and thanks to Sister Kelly, she received plenty of fresh fruit and chocolates. After six days Rachel left the hospital. Her bleeding had stopped.

When she returned to the rooming house, Naomi took leave from work for another week to stay with her sister. I also visited her whenever I could get away from the hospital. These days were important to us in surprising ways. The advent of the baby had introduced something very tender into our relationship. An unspoken strong bond brought us even closer together.

While work went smoothly at the hospital, I waited another month before I received a phone call from the Colonial Service. I was asked to appear for an interview one week later at ten o'clock. On that morning, I entered a room at the Colonial House where formally dressed men, with stiff collars, sat around a table. For once, I was not intimidated.

The interviewers asked me many questions, especially about my general knowledge of Africa and Nigeria. I was prepared, and I think my answers satisfied them. But everyone, including the medical advisor Dr. Buchanan, asked me absolutely nothing about my knowledge or skills as a doctor. They were more interested in knowing why I wanted to join the Colonial Service when my home country of India had such an acute shortage of doctors.

I said that I was choosing to offer my services to a country that was less developed than India.

The interview took a long time, and I was relieved when it finally ended.

When I got back to St. George's, Sir John and Mr. Bingham were sitting in the surgeon's room. I told them about my interview. They said that the machinery in the Colonial House moved slowly, but the recruiting office was thorough. They asked me if I had noticed any other applicants. I said that no other doctor was waiting for an interview. They smiled. They thought that I would hear good news very soon.

~ 50 ~

THE LONG WAIT

DR. BUCHANAN INVITED ME TO his office. When I arrived for my appointment, I gathered from his talk that I had been accepted into the Colonial Service. He told me about his experiences in Africa. He said that living there could be difficult for me because I would be the only senior civil servant from the subcontinent. He added that I should not expect well-equipped hospitals in Nigeria. The colony only had one qualified anesthetist. All the other anesthesiologists were local nurses trained by British doctors. Some were good at their work; some were not.

He suggested that I might find my position untenable since the British officers would be on one side and the locals would be on the other side. I would lack any real support. He also didn't know if my job would last long. Most British colonies were clamoring for Independence. But he said that the situation in Nigeria was better than anywhere else. He reminded me that most Nigerians living in Northern Nigeria were Muslim. As a Hindu, I might consider this an additional problem.

I told Dr. Buchanan that I was aware of these issues, but I fully expected people to appreciate my work since the colony had a shortage of doctors. I also reminded him that I had always worked well with British doctors in England. They had been very kind to me.

He said that he just wanted me to understand the conditions in Nigeria. At last, he told me that I would probably be offered a position, but not as a specialist. He said that no one was initially accepted at such a high rank. But, given my surgical qualifications and experience, I could expect to get the best available offer as a medical officer, special grade. He also explained that I would only receive a three-year contract, which was subject to renewal on the recommendation of the director of medical services in the colony.

I told him that I didn't object to starting as a special grade officer if this was the customary procedure with all new appointments. But I wanted to be assured that I could be promoted in due course to the rank of specialist. I also couldn't accept a position on a contract basis. Contract hires rarely received promotions. I also knew that they weren't entitled to any privileges that weren't specified in their contracts.

He said he understood my concerns, but he doubted that the Colonial Service office would change its policy for me. I had to understand that no one was offered permanent service unless the person was filling a job specifically requested by the colonial administration in the host country. He asked me to be patient. I would soon receive a written offer from the Colonial Service office.

I went back to the hospital. Sir John had left for the day, but I saw Mr. Bingham and I told him about my disappointing offer from the medical advisor at the Colonial Service office.

Mr. Bingham didn't look happy. He said that he would never

advise me to go to any British colony without an offer of permanent service. He worried that Nigeria could receive its independence. I needed the assurance of permanent service so that I qualified for compensation if I lost my job when Nigeria became an independent country.

He said he would talk to Sir John. He thought that my excellent qualifications would be invaluable in Nigeria or any other developing country.

Days later Sir John and Mr. Bingham had successfully worked out a good compromise with the Colonial Service. Sir John had wanted to get me a specialist post, but this was impossible. I had to accept a special grade but with a good starting salary. He did succeed in getting me accepted as a member of the permanent service with full privileges; however, I had to agree that my first three years were probationary and subject to review. He said that this was normal procedure, so I was prepared to accept the revised offer. I was so surprised that this entire application process had taken six months.

I made an appointment to see Dr. O'Connell. I told him about my appointment in Northern Nigeria. I asked him if he thought that Rachel could make the journey and deliver our baby in this British colony. Dr. O'Connell said that Rachel was doing well. As long as she had reasonably good obstetric care in the colony, he thought that she could complete her pregnancy in Africa.

I met with Dr. Buchanan. He congratulated me for getting the job on my terms. He laughed and asked me how I had earned the protection of so many guardian angels.

Then he asked if he could give me some personal advice. He reminded me that I had been in England for five years. He thought a British passport could help me if I wanted to stay in the service for a long period or if I wanted to settle in England.

I told him that I hadn't made my plans beyond a few years. I preferred to keep things the way they were right now. I also knew that an existing provision allowed commonwealth citizens to join the Colonial Service. Once I was confirmed I believed that I could change my nationality, if it was necessary.

Dr. Buchanan said that this was technically true. But I wouldn't meet anyone else in the service from the subcontinent. He asked me to be careful and to make a few friends among my fellow officers. He wished me all the best and a very good voyage to Nigeria.

The next day Rachel and I met Mr. Atta, a medical student from Nigeria, and his wife. He assured me that his country would require the skills of expatriate doctors even after the country won its independence. He also admitted that working conditions would be dramatically different for me in Nigeria. But he thought that we could expect good medical care.

Rachel and I finally agreed that we would go to Nigeria. I studied the different grades of service for Colonial Service officers. I realized that I would make more money in Africa than I would make if we stayed in England.

Miriam wanted Rachel to stay in London until the baby was born. She and her family had recently moved to a new rent-subsidized house, which was built by the city council. She said that she could easily accommodate Rachel and look after her until the baby's birth. Miriam insisted that none of us knew the real conditions in that Godforsaken African colony.

Rachel stopped the discussion. She told everyone that she was going with me to Nigeria.

~ **51** ~

PREPARATIONS

I NOTIFIED THE COLONIAL SERVICE's travel agency, Crown Agents that Rachel and I wanted to go by sea to Nigeria. We looked forward to a first-class, two-week, leisurely holiday on a boat. While we waited to hear back from the agency, Dr. Martin Reed, who was the newly appointed senior surgical registrar, officially joined St. George's. He repeatedly told me that I could take time off to prepare for my move.

The Colonial Service provided Rachel and me with a list of clothing that we needed to take with us from England to Nigeria. The clothing cost us a lot of money, which Neil was kind enough to loan us. He was such a fine friend!

In a matter of days, I learned the details of my first posting in the Colonial Service. I would work in Gusau, a remote Northern Nigerian town with a good hospital. Because of my medical qualifications and status, I would only stay there for three months, while Dr. Curry, the Colonial Service officer, went on his home leave. This was great news. Most new officers received an initial 18-month assignment in a small town before they were posted in a city.

Then Crown Agents contacted us. The passenger boat going to Nigeria was small, with a limited number of first-class cabins. All the double occupancy cabins were reserved. The agency had to book me in a single-occupancy cabin in Lagos, the capital and chief seaport of Nigeria. Rachel would fly to Nigeria. We were so disappointed. We had wanted to travel together. But we had no choice but to meet in the British colony.

Mrs. Robinson arranged a farewell dinner for us. After dinner, Mrs. Robinson asked me to choose one of her paintings as a gift. I selected a beautiful watercolor of the Land's End in Cornwall, which also appealed to Rachel. I said that I hoped that we would meet again during my first leave from Nigeria. Then we said goodbye.

Everyone at St. George's Hospital was so happy for me when I was accepted into the Colonial Service. The hospital doctors and nurses arranged a farewell party for Rachel and me, and Sir John gave us a sherry party. By now, the hospital had a new house surgeon since Dr. Patel decided not to renew his position at the hospital. He preferred to take six months to prepare for his primary exam. I wished the best for the doctor. I told him that he would easily get a job once he passed his exam.

Before the new registrar assumed my old position at the hospital, I had to perform a difficult operation. A nineteen-year-old young man, who was working in a nearby factory, got his right hand caught in an industrial machine. The supervisor stopped the machine, but it had nearly lopped off the boy's entire hand just above the wrist, and the bleeding was profuse.

I was shocked when I examined the young man in the emergency room. Nearly every structure in his hand was severed except for the median nerve and the radial artery, which, thankfully, continued to pulse. The ambulance attendant applied a tourniquet to stop the bleeding, but he warned me that the patient had lost a lot of blood.

The surgery that the boy and I faced was daunting. I called Sir John, but his secretary said that he was not arriving at the hospital until the evening. I contemplated sending the patient to another hospital, but any delay in surgery could irreversibly damage the tissues of the right hand because of the lack of blood supply.

I ordered blood work, started the IV fluids for blood replacement, and arranged for emergency surgery. The anesthetist arrived; and as soon as we received the blood work report, he anesthetized the patient, and I started a blood transfusion.

It took seven hours to repair all the severed tendons, nerves, and one of the two main arteries. I was so lucky that my patient was an otherwise healthy young man. But still, I worried and prayed for the recovery of his hand. Almost immediately, its color improved, and the repaired artery stopped bleeding.

I felt uncomfortable leaving the patient under the care of the house surgeon, so I stayed overnight in the hospital. I slept very little since I repeatedly returned to the patient's bedside to examine his hand. I hoped that the antibiotics would prevent any infection.

In the morning the color of the patient's hand was normal. I also felt a strong pulse. Still, I stayed at the hospital, so that I could keep a good eye on him. When I saw Dr. Reed, I told him about the complicated operation. He agreed that I should stay the rest of the weekend since the patient remained in danger. He told me that while the unexpected accident came at a bad time for me, the hospital staff and the community would always remember me for this incredible surgery. We decided that if the hand remained healthy for 48 hours, I could feel good about the outcome and apply a plaster of Paris casing.

On Sunday night I applied the plaster of Paris cast. Dr. Reed felt that the hand had been preserved, but I still chose to stay at the hospital until Monday morning when I planned to hand over my cases to the new registrar and say goodbye to Sir John, Mr. Bingham, Sister Kelly, and all the other doctors and nurses. Finally, I walked out of the hospital one last time. I stared for a couple of minutes at the old building before I walked quietly to the tube station.

Before I left for Nigeria, I wanted to have one long last look at London, a great city that I had come to love these last five years. During my time here, I learned so much about the heart and science of surgery, and also about human relations. I had met people from all over the world who had come to this great city for personal reasons. I loved learning about all of them, and I discovered so many similarities within our diversity.

I had also fallen in love with London's culture and architecture. Through these years I took great pleasure in walking along the banks of the Thames and wandering through her great parks. I would carry memories of all these places for the rest of my life. I spent many of my final hours in London taking one last tour of this great city.

The day arrived for my departure. Rachel and I took a taxi to the railway station. A gentleman from Crown Agents received us at the station and for the first time since my appointment, he addressed me as sir. I was startled. He smiled and said that I would soon get accustomed to my new title.

After the agent paid the taxi driver and managed my luggage, he ushered me to my seat in the first-class compartment of the train that would take me to Liverpool. He handed me my relevant papers and assured me that he would see that my wife was safely transported back to her rooming house.

The agent also promised me that he would take good care of Rachel when it was time for her to leave London. She would be comfortable and safely transported to her plane.

I struggled to say goodbye to Rachel, even though we would only be apart for three weeks. I watched her until she disappeared from the station platform before I went and sat down.

I loved traveling first class. But all the time that I spent on this train I wished Rachel was sitting next to me and going with me on the boat to Nigeria.

It was late afternoon when I reached Liverpool. The sky was grey, and so were all the city buildings. Yet again, another courteous gentleman from Crown Agents received me. I wondered if these employees represented the old England that was fast disappearing.

I slowly walked up the ramp to a glossy white boat surrounded by other men, women, and children. Most of the men were officers of Her Majesty's Overseas Civil Service. They were going to distant British colonies to carry out their duties for their country. I was traveling with them—a new member of this distinguished organization.

PHOTOS

K.D. and Rachel in London when they were students

K.D. and Rachel's wedding

K.D. and Rachel in London

Rachel and K.D. with friends in London

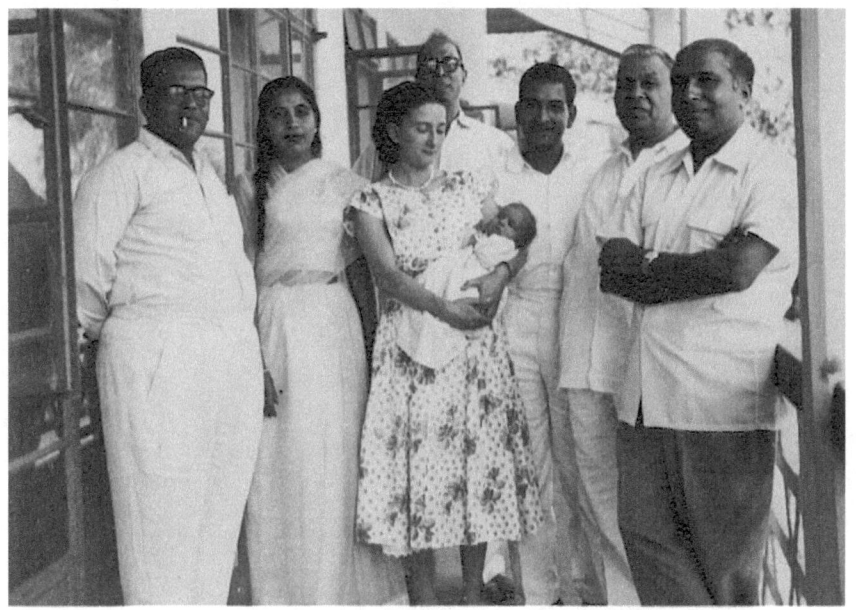

Rachel and K.D. with friends in Nigeria

K.D. with daughters Monica and Sheila

Rachel's parents Yehuda and Georgina Bekhor

K.D.'s parents Charulata and Atul Chandra Ray

~ Part 3 ~

NIGERIA

~ 52 ~

ON THE BOAT

I WAS THIRTY-THREE-YEARS-OLD and traveling as a first-class passenger on a beautiful British ship. An orchestra played on the front deck, and I watched people standing on a receding quay as they bid farewell to their friends and relatives who, like me, were sailing from Liverpool to Africa. It was 1956. I was a senior Colonial Service officer setting off to work in Northern Nigeria.

When the harbor lights finally faded in the distance, I joined other passengers as they filed down the stairs from the deck. I located my first-class cabin with its attached bathroom and looked around. My accommodations bore no resemblance to the four-bunk cabin that I had shared on my journey from India to England.

I explored the ship's lounges and entertainment rooms and drifted into a bar where passengers were drinking with old friends. They were all returning to Africa after home leave. I sat down in a lovely, upholstered chair, and a waiter, addressing me as sir, asked if I wanted to order something. Moments later he returned with my drink.

When it was time for dinner, I found my assigned seat at a table with two couples and a middle-aged man. The two husbands, who were permanent Colonial Service officers, were engineers for the Public Works Department in the Gold Coast (presently Ghana). Their wives were teachers. The single gentleman, Dr. Dunn, was the head of the medical department in Northern Nigeria. He told me that he was in charge of all the British medical officers and nurses. He was also in charge of the health department. He said that he was so busy with his duties that he rarely practiced medicine.

When I told Dr. Dunn, I was a special grade officer, he said that my designation didn't matter. I would be taking orders from a senior medical officer. I sensed the doctor's hostility and tried to enjoy the food placed before me.

After we finished our dinner, I excused myself and walked around the ship. I heard a band playing dance music, and as I approached a lounge, I saw couples dancing and laughing together. I suddenly felt tired and lonely. I returned to my cabin, took a long hot bath, and went to bed wishing Rachel were on this voyage with me.

I suddenly imagined Rachel slipping into the room. As I moved over in my bed to make some space for her, she smiled and asked me if I had really expected to leave her behind and go alone to Nigeria. I fell asleep only to wake up later. The lights were on inside the cabin. I was alone. I heard footsteps in the corridor, and I listened as deckhands swabbed down the deck on the far side of my cabin window.

The next morning as I strolled on the deck after breakfast, Dr. Dunn caught up with me. We talked about Northern Nigeria, and he reminded me once again that as a medical officer, I would work under the direction of a senior officer. He also voiced his doubts that I would ever get promoted to the rank of specialist. I was happy when the doctor hurried away. He seemed determined to diminish my qualifications and my rank.

As I resumed my walk along the deck a young African man joined me. While we chatted together, he told me that he had just received his medical degree in England. He was returning to the Gold Coast to practice medicine. The young doctor added that he was traveling with another African doctor who had just been appointed the new director of medical services for the Gold Coast.

The young doctor told me that only a few privileged African men and women ever traveled first class. Most Africans traveled third class in awful conditions. Third-class passengers lacked cabins; they were forced to sleep under tarpaulin covers on the open deck where they only had access to a few latrines and cold water taps. Their food was generally lousy: usually, soups made from octopus, okra, and boiled guinea corn.

I said that I hoped that things would change once the Gold Coast gained its freedom in 1957. Maybe new boats would provide better accommodation for West Africa's emerging middle class.

As we journeyed on the sea, I enjoyed reading the boat's library books, magazines, and newspapers on the deck. I particularly enjoyed reading about the world's religions.

One day while I was studying some verses from the Bible, I noticed a middle-aged Anglican priest was watching me. I assumed that he was a missionary who was on his way to Nigeria to try to convert the unconverted.

The priest sat down next to me. He said that he was happy to see that l always read the Good Book. His face lit up when I told him that I had read the New Testament and the Old Testament several times. He said that the Holy Ghost must have entered my soul. He asked if I believed that Jesus was the Son of God who had died for our sins. Before I could answer he asked if I believed that everything in the Bible was the infallible truth. I said that I didn't know. The light went out of his eyes. He asked if I had found something in the New Testament that I couldn't believe.

I told the priest that I wasn't a theologian. I couldn't decipher the inner meanings of Jesus's actions or speeches. As an example, I cited the parable of the fig tree. I asked the priest why the poor fig tree had to wither and die due to no fault of its own. Since the tree was unable to bear fruit out of season, how could it always satisfy Jesus's hunger? Yet the fig tree was punished. I was baffled.

The priest said that the only way to salvation was through Him. He called me a disbeliever who was forever condemned before he hurried away.

While I sat on the deck, I occasionally saw three elegantly robed African gentlemen taking an afternoon stroll. One day the gentlemen decided to sit down near me. I greeted them politely and they greeted me back. I asked them where they were from and why they had been in England.

One of the men said that they were traditional chiefs from Gambia. The British government had invited them to England where they had met different politicians and city councilors. They exchanged ideas about local governance. They had also engaged in discussions with the British government about its plans to introduce freedom, in stages, to Gambia. The traditional chiefs said that they would assume an important role in this gradual transfer of power and the creation of their new country's constitution.

I assumed that Gambia had only a few well-educated people and limited economic resources, so I asked one of the chiefs if his people were ready to administer their country.

The three chiefs seemed insulted. One of them said that the British government obviously didn't agree with my supposition since it was fully committed to transferring power to the country. He reminded me that Gambia's poverty stemmed from the slave trade, which had moved through the colony. The chief added that if the British and Americans paid reparations for their past activities, Gambia could easily build a modern infrastructure and carry out modern trade with new products that crossed the ocean and reached lucrative markets.

I was embarrassed that my question had antagonized these three distinguished men. I quickly changed the subject and asked them if they were enjoying their voyage. One of the chiefs said that the accommodations were fine, but they didn't like the food provided to first-class passengers. If these ships expected to carry Africans, they had to provide good African meals. The chief was relieved that only a few Gambians were traveling in third class, but they were grateful that they were able to get some of these passengers to bring them food from their kitchen. The food wasn't very good, but at least it had an African flavor.

When I told the chiefs that they couldn't expect the same quality of food prepared by their servants, one of them corrected me. He said that their wives cooked their food back home. I couldn't carry on this conversation, so I excused myself. Despite all my best efforts, I always seemed to insult the people who traveled with me on this boat. But when we docked at the port of Bathurst in Gambia, the three chiefs surprised me. They asked me to accompany them on the short trip to their capital city.

When one of the chiefs pointed out the city center, he told me that Gambia wasn't as impoverished as the British portrayed in their newspapers. As I looked around the city, I could see with my eyes that it had roads and buildings, but it had nothing more. When the chief added that things would improve in Gambia once his country received its independence, I kept quiet. By now I had relearned an old personal lesson: "Don't express any opinion unless you are pressed into speaking."

A couple of days later while I was on the deck and enjoying the afternoon sun and sea breezes with some other passengers, a middle-aged lady asked a group of younger women why they were going to Africa. One of the young women said that they were married. They were accompanying their husbands to the cities or towns where they worked. One of the young women asked the middle-aged lady where she was going. The older woman looked uppity and said that she didn't have a destination. She planned to travel and visit some good old British colonies.

A young British man, whom I later learned was a journalist, told the woman that she had better hurry. If she took her time, the colonies would vanish before she arrived.

The lady scoffed and said with a straight face that the journalist was too young to understand the consequences of this 'independence' wind that was blowing across Africa. The poor Africans who were enjoying peace and prosperity under British rule would be stuck in anarchy and become impoverished. The journalist smiled at the upper-class lady and said that he would be glad to see the end of all this African peace and prosperity.

Everyone felt so uncomfortable that we left, one by one. The young journalist caught up with me and said that he was making his first trip to Nigeria. He expected to write about Nigeria's preparedness for independence. He told me about Dr. Nnamdi Azikwe who was an Ibo from Nigeria's Eastern region. He was an experienced, able leader with many followers who wanted him to lead their country. But he was also anti-British.

The journalist said that the British had filed numerous court cases against Dr. Azikwe that claimed the man had embezzled funds. They wanted the court to convict him so that he would be barred from holding administrative or ministerial posts. He hoped to find out if these claims against the doctor were true during his visit to Nigeria.

I had heard of him. I knew that his followers called him Zik. I excused myself and searched for the young doctor from the Gold Coast. When I asked him about Dr. Azikwe, he introduced me to a companion who was a young engineer from Eastern Nigeria and an ardent Zik follower. The engineer said that the British didn't want Zik in power because he would ignore the will of the British and do what he thought was best for his own people. The engineer was also convinced that the British government was motivated by its need to control rich oil resources in Eastern Nigeria. The British knew that they would lose control of these oil fields if Zik were in the government. The British also had the backing of the Northern Nigerians, who didn't trust Zik.

The next morning, I saw the journalist again. He told me about an unpleasant incident that had occurred last night on the boat. He said that some of the British passengers often swapped wives after the dancing ended in the lounge. The swap was intended to be a one-night affair, but last night a bachelor had picked up one of the wives. Since the man was obviously single, the lady's husband was left without a partner. The two men ended up in a fistfight and the husband lost.

The journalist said that this morning the wife, who didn't have children, said that she didn't want to return to her husband. Since the bachelor worked for a commercial firm in Nigeria, the senior government officers on board the boat had no control over him. They also knew that if they initiated an inquiry, they would expose their scandalous wife-swapping game. I had no idea that such crazy things took place on this boat.

When the ship docked on the Gold Coast the young doctor introduced me to the new director of medical services. The director said that his new country, which they planned to call Ghana, would need good physicians and surgeons to build an efficient healthcare system. He hoped that I would be happy working in Northern Nigeria, but he invited me to write to him if I ever wanted to practice surgery in his country. He gave me his card.

A couple of days before we reached Nigeria, Dr. Dunn introduced me to a malaria specialist. Dr. Cable led a team of malaria field specialists and lab technicians who worked for Northern Nigeria. He said that living standards in Nigeria would never improve unless an American or European discovered a malaria vaccine. Many Nigerians were vulnerable to a particularly virulent strain called cerebral malaria that led to a loss of consciousness commonly followed by death unless intravenous chloroquine was administered immediately. Dr. Cable advised me to take the anti-malarial drugs regularly so that I wouldn't get a fatal infection.

The night before we docked in Nigeria Dr. Cable and Dr. Dunn invited me to have a drink. As always, Dr. Dunn talked to me about working in Nigeria. He told me that I would quickly discover that some Colonial Service officers were rednecks. But if I remained humble and stayed loyal to the crown and my fellow officers, I would have no problems. He also told me not to socialize with the locals. Such fraternization would lower my status with the Europeans.

When I asked the doctors about Rachel and her pregnancy Dr. Cable said that Kaduna, which was the regional capital in Northern Nigeria, had an excellent nursing home for expatriates and a fine obstetrician, Dr. Adkins. Dr. Cable offered to contact his good friend Dr. Doyle who was Kaduna's senior medical officer. Dr. Doyle could make arrangements for Rachel at the nursing home. He also thought that this doctor and his wife would invite Rachel to stay with them a few days before and after the delivery. I thanked Dr. Cable for this good news. The next morning our boat docked in Lagos. I was ready to start my new life in Nigeria. I just needed dear Rachel.

~ 53 ~

NEXT STOP GUSAU

AFTER BRITISH GOVERNMENT AGENTS AND transporters handled our immigration and customs formalities, they took us to the Lagos government rest house. Mosquito nets hung from all the doors and windows. Everything looked so tidy and inviting. I was so tired that I stayed in my room and went to bed.

The next day I was driven to the railroad station. After my travel agent assured me that my baggage was safely placed in the luggage van, he steered me to my reserved seat in the first-class compartment. He saluted and left.

That night I struggled to sleep as my mind raced along with the train. By daybreak, the landscape had changed. The lush green rainforest had given way to scrubby trees and bushes and sandy soil. Occasionally, I disembarked at train stations where other passengers, laden with baggage, rushed from the crowded third-class compartments. While vendors tried to sell food to the Nigerian passengers, they only offered me curios.

By late afternoon the train reached the northern city of Zaria, which was the headquarters for the surrounding district. I stepped onto the platform where a man from the Department of Health greeted me. He picked up my luggage and drove me to the government rest house.

After I settled into my room, the senior medical officer Dr. Turner, who would be my new boss, came to see me. He gave me an advance of my salary to get me through my first month and told me that a driver would take me tomorrow morning to the Kano airport hotel to meet Rachel.

Dr. Turner apologized that I wouldn't have time to rest in Zaria, but I had to get to Gusau. Dr. Curry, whom I was replacing for three months, had to transfer the hospital over to me before he and his wife hurried to Lagos to board their boat to England.

He said that my wife and I were lucky. We were moving into the doctor's fully furnished house where his servants and cook would take care of us. He told me that after I finished my three months in Gusau, I would shift to the city of Kano, where I would serve under the specialist surgeon. If the surgeon thought that I worked well with him, I would get to stay in Kano for a while. Dr. Turner clarified that while I would be doing surgeries in the Kano hospital, I didn't have the rank of a specialist. I was a medical officer, special grade.

He invited me to have dinner at his house. I apologized to his wife for arriving without flowers or a suitable gift. Mrs. Turner assured me that everyone had been in this same boat at some point. When she regretted that she wouldn't get to meet my wife, I took the opportunity to ask her if I could possibly contact Rachel in Kano. I knew that she was lonely.

Dr. Turner called the Airport Hotel, but no one named Rachel was on the guest list. He called Kano's senior medical officer Dr.

Diko, who explained that Rachel was detained at immigration because her last name was misspelled on her passport. By the time he sorted out the problem, the hotel was full. Rachel was staying at the government rest house.

He called the rest house, and I finally spoke to Rachel. I told her that I would reach Kano the next day. She should get a good night's sleep.

The next morning after I completed my paperwork with Dr. Turner, the driver took me on a long, uncomfortable ride to the Kano rest house. I was overjoyed when I saw Rachel waiting for me in her room.

Before sunrise the next morning we quickly ate breakfast and started our journey to Gusau on a partially paved road. We crossed numerous skinny bridges that lacked railings and endured four hours of hazardous driving. When we reached Gusau's rest house, Dr. Curry was waiting for us. He escorted us to our suite and apologized to me that he had to leave in the evening for Lagos. After he told Rachel that everything was ready for us at his house, he led me to another room where he launched into an unending talk about the hospital and the expatriates who lived in Gusau.

Two hours dragged by as Dr. Curry rattled on about the hospital and each member of the staff. He said that I had to control the Nigerian fellows who were Ibos (former name for Igbos) from the eastern region with an iron hand or they would ignore me. The pharmacist, who was also an Ibo, could do his job, under supervision; but he was a slippery character. He reminded me, repeatedly, that he was the only medical officer in Gusau, and he also ran the health department. He paused briefly to praise his superintendent of health Mr. Swift, whom he called a competent Irishman.

At the end of the third hour of this lecture, he said that it didn't matter if I was bored. He had to complete the handover. Finally, he decided it was time for me to see the hospital. I told Rachel to have lunch without me and followed Dr. Curry who stopped at the dining hall to order two cups of tea and a sandwich for each of us. I was starving.

When we reached the hospital, he introduced me to the chief clerk Mr. Okafor. As Dr. Curry pulled out file after file to familiarize me with the administration of the hospital, he told the chief clerk that he better not take advantage of me during his absence, or that he would make the clerk's life miserable when he returned.

When we left his office, he told me that the clerks had to be kept in order, like children. Once we entered the hospital ward, he started describing the case details of each patient and bragged about his excellent cure rate.

Dr. Curry introduced me to his senior surgical nurse, Nurse Akapo. He said that the anesthetist stationed in Kano had trained the nurse, so he knew how to anesthetize patients. He told him that I was a qualified surgeon. I would demand high standards of work from him. Nurse Akapo smiled and said that he would do his best.

He finally took me to the health department, where I met the superintendent of health, Mr. Swift. Then we went next door to the Native Authority, where I met the Wakelin who was the Northern Nigerian representative overseeing the entire medical department for the local Emir.

Dr. Curry said that the British government had overall control of the colony, but traditional rulers, who were called Emirs, governed certain regions of Nigeria. He reminded me that a similar division of power existed in India's native states before my country's Independence.

It was nearly five o'clock. I was exhausted. My mind was

about to explode. But he was relentless. Once we returned to the rest house, he led me to a room and ordered two cups of tea and some cookies. As we sipped the tea, he launched into a lengthy description of the European residential area and expressed his disgust with the British government for letting a few Lebanese and Greek Cypriot merchants build houses in this area. He figured the Nigerians would start living here next. I was so tired that I hardly listened to the man as he told me about everyone's medical problems and disclosed every shred of gossip.

Dr. Curry's wife finally arrived at eight o'clock. She told her husband that they had to leave, or they would miss their train. He was devastated. He said that he had failed to tell me everything. He shrugged and left.

~ 54 ~

GETTING SETTLED

DURING MY FIRST DAYS AT the Gusau hospital, I had so much work that I stayed from 7 am to 5 pm and only took a lunch break. I was so relieved that the nurses were eager to familiarize me with the hospital and their routines. I also appreciated the efficiency of the chief clerk Mr. Okafor. He told me that he had been stuck in the same position for six years. Dr. Curry and his predecessors had refused to promote him because of his politics.

Mr. Okafor and most members of the nursing staff were Christian Ibos from Eastern Nigeria. They were educated as missionaries and had received technical training that gave them an advantage over Northern Nigerian Muslims, who were under Arab influence. Muslim Nigerians, who fiercely disliked and mistrusted the Ibos and the Christian Yorubas from Western Nigeria, forced them to live outside Gusau in an area called "sabongari," which meant the abode for strangers. Similar sabongaris existed throughout Northern Nigeria.

That weekend four servants greeted us when Rachel and I

moved into Dr. Curry's rambling old bungalow. The chief steward, who saluted, informed us that the other steward who normally worked for Dr. Curry had gone home. He would return to his master's house when he returned. He introduced his younger brother Audu and said that he would be our steward. Audu handed us typewritten papers from his previous masters who described him as hardworking and reliable. (I soon learned that I had to accept the use of the word master in reference to me. The term meant employer.) Our cook Ojoh, who was an Ibo, was upset that a Muslim Hausa from the north would be working in the house. He shook his head and mumbled, "Trouble coming."

I went outside to inspect the spacious backyard. After the gardener pointed out some cashew trees and other Nigerian trees and bushes, I headed back toward the house and noticed a large water tank on the roof over the bathroom. I had heard that prison inmates filled these tanks with water from the river. I made a detour and wandered into the kitchen and pantry, which were connected by a corrugated tin walkway to the bungalow. I knew that Rachel would be horrified when she saw these smelly, dingy rooms.

When I went inside, Rachel asked me if I had seen any snakes. I reminded her that Dr. Curry had told me that snakes were uncommon in this area. Rachel disagreed. She said snakes were out there, somewhere.

Early the next evening when I returned from work, a driver arrived with our new Opel Capitan, which I had bought in Lagos. Rachel wished that I had purchased a standard sedan. She thought that the fancy Opel was too slick for our roads. I knew she was right, but I liked the stylish car.

A few days later when I came home from work our cook Ojoh lamented and prayed loudly for the master (me!) and God to come to his rescue. Rachel had entered his kitchen. The chicken carcasses that hung from the roof so appalled her that she ordered him to remove them against his strong objections.

Ojoh, who always reminded us that he had learned to cook at a Christian mission, complained that he needed a chicken carcass to remake the wonderful soup that he had served us last night. He failed to understand the Madam's anger. Kitchens always smelled of food. I told him that I was confident that he could make an excellent soup from fresh chicken, which we would enjoy with our evening meal.

That weekend four car accident victims were brought to the hospital. I saw each patient, but Nurse Akapo, our surgical nurse, cleaned and sutured their wounds. I told him that I'd be pleased if he treated all future trauma cases as long as he promised to ask me for help when he needed it.

The next day Rachel saw Ojoh pour water directly from the tap onto green beans that he had boiled for our supper. She was furious. He told Madam that she was no lady. Ladies never went into the kitchen. Besides, he was following instructions that he had learned from his Mother Superior.

Rachel was disgusted. She told me that Ojoh never used filtered water because no filter existed in the kitchen. I promised her that we would hire a good cook once we moved to Kano. I also purchased a filter from the government store.

I told Ojoh that Madam was the daughter of a Bishop. She had supervised the kitchen during important functions at a cathedral. She knew everything about kitchen cleanliness. I handed Ojoh the new filter and told him that he had to use it and soak every vegetable for his salads in a permanganate solution before he washed them in filtered water.

Finally, Rachel and I had established a reasonably good household routine. Since we had no electricity, we used kerosene lamps, which was Audu's responsibility. He also did the washing, cleaning, and other household chores with his brother. Ojoh bought our vegetables, fish, and fowl from the local market. We purchased everything else from Lebanese or European shops.

One night Gusau's senior administrative official Mr. Smith called me at midnight. A young officer and his wife needed urgent medical assistance. Their steward had found them unconscious inside their home.

I was shaken. I had never dealt with this kind of emergency. I remembered that the malaria specialist Dr. Cable had told me that cerebral malaria could lead to unconsciousness and death. I called Nurse Akapo and told him to hurry to the couple's house with IV sets, injections of chloroquine for malaria, and an emergency kit.

When I reached the couple's house, Mr. Smith told me that he doubted that the couple had contracted malaria since neither of them was hot to the touch. He wondered if they had taken poison and committed suicide. Anything was possible in those days.

I asked the couple's steward if his master or madam had said anything to him before they went to bed. He reported that the young couple said that they felt feverish and shivery. He had brought them some water and the couple went to bed. When he came back to extinguish the lanterns, he discovered them, unmoving, with their eyes closed.

Once Nurse Akapo arrived, we started an intravenous infusion of Ringer's Lactate in the young officer who had extremely low blood pressure and I drew blood from each of them and made smears for analysis of blood counts and malarial parasites. I started administering chloroquine intravenously and told Nurse Akapo to spend the night by their bedside to see that the medication flowed properly. I also asked him to check their pulse and blood pressure hourly. Two neighborhood ladies agreed to stay with the nurse.

I went home, but I was too worried to sleep. My first difficult case involved British officers. I wondered if I would be blamed if the couple failed to recover. When I returned to the couple's house in the morning, the ladies thought that my treatment was working. I hurried into the bedroom as the young woman tried to open her eyes. She and her husband were slowly regaining consciousness.

Soon the house swarmed with people. I told the young officer and his wife that they had cerebral malaria. They were fortunate. We treated them early.

I went home and thanked my lucky stars.

That morning, I learned that the wife's father was the British Resident of the Emirate of Sokoto, which was a Northern Nigeria province under dual administration. Mr. Smith called the Resident and told him about his daughter's miraculous recovery.

The next day expatriate officers came to the hospital and showered me with praise. I told each of them to take their anti-malarial pills. No one wanted to experience this deadly illness.

The Resident and his wife also came to see me. They invited Rachel and me to dinner that evening at the senior administrator's house, where the Resident and his wife praised me again and invited us to Sokoto. He said that I would make the customary goodwill visit to meet the Emir and his Majlis (or council). I would probably also meet the Nigerian Premier Sir Ahmadu Bello who was the most powerful man in Nigeria.

As Rachel and I bathed in all this attention, we hoped that the respect would continue. I was fully aware that I had been fortunate to meet a malaria specialist on the boat. His valuable information helped me make an excellent judgment call. Then I simply followed my common sense.

~ 55 ~

BUMPS IN THE ROAD

WHILE I WAS COVERING FOR Dr. Curry, I had so much work at the hospital that I had no time to oversee the health department. Fortunately, the health superintendent Mr. Swift didn't need my oversight. But one morning he came to visit me at my office. He said that he knew that I was a Fellow of the Royal College of Surgeons, but I was posted in this district as a medical officer, not as a surgeon. He wanted me to stop doing all the difficult operations. Complicated surgical cases were sent to surgeons working in better-equipped hospitals.

I asked Mr. Swift how Dr. Curry knew what I was doing in the hospital.

He smiled and said that he had many British friends in Gusau in high places. He hoped that I would listen to his friendly advice.

This warning surprised me. I had eight more weeks left in Gusau. I would undoubtedly face more difficult cases. I wondered what Dr. Curry would do if I performed any more major surgeries.

The chief clerk Mr. Okafor saw that the health superintendent had upset me. He told me that everyone in Gusau was happy with my work. But he told me to be careful. Mr. Swift was Dr. Curry's friend.

I thanked Mr. Okafor and told him not to worry about me. I called our district's senior medical officer Dr. Turner and asked him if I had permission to perform surgical operations. He said that I could perform operations as long as I believed the hospital and the staff could properly care for the patient.

The next day Mr. Smith asked to tend to a sick officer who had consumed too much alcohol. He had serious abdominal pain. I examined the young officer who had low blood pressure and a rapid pulse. His abdomen was rigid, and I failed to hear any peristaltic sounds through the stethoscope. The young man needed an operation for a perforated peptic ulcer.

I told Mr. Smith and the young man that I needed to begin IV fluids, including IV morphine for pain. As I inserted a gastric tube into his stomach, I assured him that I had successfully performed this operation many times in England. Still, I wondered to myself if this hospital could give him appropriate post-operative care.

The morphine made the young patient feel better, but I noticed that when he aspirated, bright red blood oozed from his stomach into his tubes. His ulcer was bleeding. I discussed the young man's condition with Dr. Turner. Since the officer was suffering from a perforated ulcer, we knew that he needed an immediate operative intervention, or he would bleed to death. But Dr. Turner worried that the young officer would never survive the long journey to the better-equipped hospital in Kano. He also knew that if the young officer traveled to the hospital in Zaria, no doctor would be able to perform this surgery. He decided that I had to operate on the officer in Gusau. He sent a telegram to the hospital that authorized me to perform this emergency operation.

I sent specimens of the young officer's blood for analysis to the lab in Zaria. I also arranged for blood donors who provided four pints of blood so that I was prepared to do the difficult operation. When I repaired the bleeding vessel, the young officer's life remained in danger because of his perforated duodenum.

After I transfused the first unit of blood, the officer's condition slowly improved. By the end of the operation, the young man had used all four units. His blood pressure slowly returned to normal, and we sighed with relief. A few days later the officer had sufficiently recovered. I let him leave the hospital.

Soon, Rachel had to leave for Dr. Doyle's house in Kaduna where she would stay until she went into labor. The Wakelin asked to travel with us. He needed to meet with a government official and he wanted to return with me to Gusau.

Once we reached Kaduna, I took Rachel to meet Mrs. Doyle who helped her get settled in her room. After the Wakelin returned from his meeting, I said a difficult goodbye to her. The Wakelin and I started back to Gusau. As I drove my car, my mind wandered. I hit a tree that had fallen on the road. I flew into the air and when I landed, I felt great pain in my neck, left shoulder, and left arm. Luckily the Wakelin was unhurt. He jumped from the car, removed a prayer rug from the trunk, and gave thanks to Allah.

There were no homes anywhere near our battered car, but the Wakelin saw a Land Rover approaching from the distance. The driver took us to a government rest house where I called Dr. Turner who rushed to see me with a medical officer. I was bruised, but I needed X-rays to determine the extent of my injuries.

Once I was alone, I called Rachel. I always felt better after I spoke with her. She knew that I couldn't be back at the house so quickly, so she asked me where I was. I didn't want to tell Rachel about the accident, so I told her that I had stopped to discuss something with Dr. Turner. I asked her how she was feeling.

Rachel said that everything was fine. She planned to visit the nursing home tomorrow with Mrs. Doyle. We hung up and I had a stiff drink of scotch and ordered supper from room service.

By the end of the next day, I had met with the police and the insurance company agent who approved the purchase of a new car. I also talked with the medical officer who had arranged for X-rays. When I was alone in the room the Wakelin stopped by and requested permission to return to Gusau. I asked him to wait until I learned the extent of my injuries. I wanted to go back with him.

Within an hour Dr. Turner came to see me at the rest house. He said that I was the Wakelin's boss. I should never ask a favor of a subordinate, especially when the subordinate is an African. He told me that the Wakelin had every right to go home immediately. His family and his people were worried about him. As Dr. Turner spoke to me, I realized once again that I had much to learn about my new position as an officer in the British Colonial Service.

When the Wakelin came back to see me, I told him that he could return to Gusau. He never mentioned that he had complained to the senior medical officer. The episode was over for him. He was going home.

The next day I had my X-rays, and the medical officer detected no serious bone injuries. But he asked me to stay another day while he had an X-ray specialist in Kano review the films. Later in the afternoon Rachel called and asked me if I was okay. She had gone to a fundraising event with Mrs. Doyle and saw the Nigerian premier. He said that he was relieved that neither the Wakelin nor I had been injured during our car accident.

I told Rachel that I was fine. I only suffered minor bruises. I told her that I had bought a Vauxhall, which was a medium-sized, well-built British car. It would arrive in Gusau in a week.

The next morning, I received the X-ray report from the Kano specialist. I had no bone injuries and only a couple of minor cracks in two cervical discs. That afternoon Dr. Turner arranged for a car with a chauffeur to drive me back to Gusau. When I arrived at the house the gardener said that Ojoh and Audu had fought while I was away. My life in Gusau had resumed.

~ 56 ~

SHEILA

THAT EVENING, I CALLED RACHEL to hear about her visit to the nursing home. She said that she had felt comfortable with Dr. Adkins who would deliver our baby. She also told me that Dr. Cable, the malarial specialist, had stopped by to visit her.

Our house was so lonely and joyless without Rachel that I spent most of my time at the hospital. One morning I forgot to bring my flask of boiled and filtered water to work. When I was thirsty the caretaker offered me some of the water from his big bottle. He said that it was safe to drink. The clear water tasted so good.

The next day Nurse Akapo saw me drinking some water. He asked me if it had come from my flask. Before I could respond, the caretaker said that the water came from a well. Nurse Akapo told me that well water often contained guinea worm eggs. I was horrified. I was well aware that many people came to the outpatient department because this disgusting white worm had broken through the skin on their foot or lower leg. They were waiting for a nurse to carefully twist the worm's head and neck around a tiny stick. Each day the nurse would rotate the stick a bit more until the worm was finally extracted. If a segment broke off inside the infected body, the worm grew a new head, and the nurse had to start the slow process all over again.

A clerk interrupted my thoughts to tell me that the Emir of Zunguru was waiting to see me in my office. While I chatted with the Emir, he told me that Premier Ahmadu Bello was his good friend. He said that the two of them believed that the demand for independence frightened the Northerners. While the Eastern and Western regions of their country had already adopted the British proposal for provincial autonomy, this change had little impact in Northern Nigeria where expatriate officers continued to run the government.

As a result, Northerners were unprepared to take control of the British bureaucracy. The Emir worried that Nigeria's southern leaders also wanted the British to leave quickly so that educated Southerners could occupy all the senior positions in the new Nigerian government and army. Once they were in power the Southerners would be able to exploit the less educated Northern Nigerians. He suddenly shifted the conversation to his medical problem, which, he said, many doctors had attempted to cure but with no success. I examined him and suggested a new treatment.

After he left my office, the Wakelin, who was waiting to see me, showed his respect to his leader. He said that I was lucky to have such an important friend. He also told me that the Emir had sent a nice turkey to my house as his gift.

That evening, I received a call from Dr. Doyle. Rachel was in the early stage of labor at the nursing home. He said that Dr. Adkins would call me as soon as the baby was born. Moments later I heard shouting, then someone banged on my bedroom door. I opened the door to find Ojoh standing there with blood trickling down his face.

He said that Audu had assaulted him for no reason. Audu yelled from the verandah that Ojoh had insulted him. When I asked them if they could forgive each other, Audu refused to apologize and Ojoh said that the Muslim steward had to go to jail. I called Mr. Smith, who told me to ask the police to come and separate the two men to avoid further violence. Once the police took Audu away, I sat down on the sofa and poured myself a drink. I knew that this would be a long night. I was so worried about Rachel and our baby.

Dr. Doyle called me in the morning. He said that Rachel's labor was slow, but the baby was not in distress, so he doubted that Dr. Adkins would need to perform a Caesarian section. I was concerned, but I knew that I had to be patient. When I went into the dining room for breakfast, an unfamiliar young man saluted me. Ojoh said that this fine young Christian boy from his area was a steward. He wasn't wild like Audu.

I didn't know the protocol for this delicate situation, so I told Ojoh that I needed to wait for the madam to return before I made a decision about our help.

I ate breakfast and went to the hospital. As I walked to my office, Audu's brother and some other stewards, who were dressed in their conventional uniforms, stood near the door. They all said, "Good morning, sir." Audu's brother wanted to talk to me. I summoned Mr. Okafor and asked him why these stewards wanted to see me.

My clerk, who was intelligent and loyal, said that the stewards had come to my office to vouch for Audu. They understood that Audu shouldn't have assaulted my cook, but Audu had waited for the police to arrive. He had accepted his punishment. He didn't run away. Mr. Okafor said that the stewards wanted me to ask the police to release Audu. They knew that Audu would behave properly once he was released from jail.

Mr. Okafor stayed with me while I asked all the stewards to come into my office and promise in writing that Audu wouldn't be violent again. Once they wrote out their promise, I called the police station and asked them to release Audu.

I performed only one operation that morning. I couldn't concentrate. Instead, I completed all my pending office work. When I went home Audu was waiting for me. He apologized and said that the nice turkey had caused the conflict. Ojoh had wanted to kill the turkey, but Audu objected because Madam wasn't home. Audu had told Ojoh that the turkey should be sacrificed after the baby's birth, not before.

That evening the nursing sister in Kaduna called and said that Rachel was in her second stage of labor. She was holding on and the baby's heartbeats were fine. They expected the birth would occur during the night. Hours later the telephone rang and woke me up. Dr. Adkins congratulated me. I had a healthy, beautiful baby girl, and Rachel had experienced no problems with the delivery. Our baby had simply decided to make everyone wait a long time. Our daughter continued to show her forceful personality by crying and sucking her lips alternately, presumably for food.

I got up from the bed, walked around for a while, lit a cigarette, and had a drink of Scotch. When I finally relaxed and went back to sleep, I dreamt of beautiful Rachel and our baby. Rachel was happy and her large eyes were shining. She asked me to hold our daughter. I took the baby girl into my arms and imagined the wonderful new life that awaited the three of us.

That next morning my new car arrived. I was delighted. I would be able to drive to Kaduna to see Rachel and the baby and bring them home. But when I called Dr. Doyle, he said that Dr. Adkins wanted to keep Rachel under his care for a couple more days. He promised to call me when Rachel could come home.

While I waited to hear from Dr. Doyle, I completed all my work at the hospital, so that I could spend a little time with Rachel and the baby when we were all together in our home. Finally, Dr. Doyle called and told me to come get my wife and new daughter. When I reached his house, I was overjoyed to see Rachel in the living room. Her days of rest had done her so much good, and just as I had dreamt, Rachel gently carried over our little girl to meet me.

We named our daughter Sheila, which was a sweet Sanskrit name that was easy for foreigners to pronounce. Sheila had inherited her mother's liquid brown eyes. They were beautiful and so expressive. When I picked her up a strange emotion engulfed me. Sheila seemed the fulfillment of life itself. I felt a bond of unlimited proportions develop between the two of us.

~ 57 ~

OFF TO KANO

DURING OUR LAST MONTH IN Gusau Rachel and I held a delightful party to honor Sheila's birth. We invited all our expatriate friends and some of our Nigerian friends, including the Emir of Zunguru. But to our surprise, none of our Lebanese friends came to the party. The next morning a good Lebanese friend came to my office and explained that he and his friends didn't attend our celebration because they never celebrated the birth of a girl who was the first-born in a family. This unfortunate attitude was so inappropriate in our modern age.

Days before we moved to Kano, someone circled an article in the local newspaper and left it on my desk in the hospital. The article reported that many people were so upset with my transfer that they planned to set up a blockade to keep me from leaving Gusau. When Mr. Okafor confirmed the article's information, I called Dr. Turner who had heard about the planned protests. He had already arranged for a Land Rover to take Rachel and Sheila to a government rest house in Kano tomorrow night. He also told me to shift to

Gusau's government rest house until Dr. Curry returned.

When he came back from home leave, we met at the government rest house. He had heard about the protests. He didn't want me to go with him to the hospital. When I left for Kano, I knew that these demonstrations would create problems for me with the British officers.

The next morning, I reported to the senior medical officer Dr. Taylor who said that my tour in Kano was on an experimental basis. The head of surgery, Dr. Baddock, wanted to see if a second surgeon would ease his workload. Dr. Taylor said that I would also assist Dr. Thomas Hinds who was the principal of Kano's new medical school. I would teach students once the school opened, and I would also help Dr. Hinds create the new school curriculum.

The following day, I went to City Hospital, which was built by the Emir of Kano under the auspices of his Native Authority. This hospital, which was Northern Nigeria's largest medical facility, was managed by the British government and staffed with British doctors, including specialists in general surgery, anesthesiology, medicine, obstetrics-gynecology, and orthopedic surgery. Several full-time and part-time British nurses as well as Nigerian nurses also worked at the hospital under the guidance of the British nursing superintendent.

I met with Dr. Baddock and Dr. Clinton who was the medical officer in charge of the hospital. Dr. Baddock pointed out that even though I had a fellowship in surgery, he was in charge of the hospital's surgery department. Dr. Clinton added that he expected me to perform all the duties of a medical officer. I sat there and wondered if either of these British doctors really wanted to work with me.

I also met Dr. Hinds at the new medical school. As we talked together the burly Dutchman told me that he was angry with the

British officers because they hadn't appointed him the director of medical services at headquarters, despite his superior resume. They gave the position to a British officer who had worked in East Africa. They didn't choose him because he was Dutch. Dr. Hinds told me to be careful. Many of the British doctors at City Hospital were jealous of my resume.

One afternoon I received a call from Mr. Okafor, the chief clerk in Gusau. He said that Dr. Curry, who was still furious with people for protesting my transfer to Kano, had launched an investigation into my private practice in Gusau. He was convinced I had broken some rules.

This unsettling information disturbed me. I didn't need trouble at the start of my career with the Colonial Service. I contacted Dr. Turner and asked him if he would write a letter that assessed my performance as Dr. Curry's temporary replacement.

The next evening when Malam, who was the son of the Emir of Zunguru, came to my house to thank me for curing his father's medical problem, I told him about the chief clerk's disturbing phone call. Malam said the doctor in Gusau couldn't harm me. Because of provincial autonomy, the Nigerian Minister of Health had the right to overrule the British. The British might become a nuisance for me, but the Minister would protect me. All my Nigerian friends, including the Prime Minister, wanted me to stay indefinitely in Northern Nigeria.

Days later I received Dr. Turner's official letter in which he expressed his appreciation and gratitude for my work in Gusau. He said that I had left a good name behind me. I knew that this letter could help me if Dr. Curry tried to sully my reputation. I only wished that my colleagues at the hospital showed the same appreciation for my hard work.

One day Dr. Hinds and his wife invited my family to afternoon tea at their house. After we chatted a while, Dr. Hinds took me aside and said that some British officers insisted that I was crafty and ambitious. He told me to remember that the British were still the masters in Nigeria. If these officers turned against me, Dr. Taylor, who decided my fate, could send me to a punishment station or make certain that my confirmation only occurred in my dreams. I wondered if Dr. Hinds had delivered this warning out of his concern for me or because his British friends had told him to make me nervous.

Weeks passed. My fears slowly faded away. My private practice grew as Lebanese businessmen, who heard that I was a good doctor, came to me for medical treatment. I was always careful. I never once treated a private patient at the hospital or during hospital hours. When Dr. Baddock went on his three-month home leave Dr. Clinton asked me to perform all the surgeries in the hospital. I was extremely busy, but I enjoyed all my work.

A few months after my transfer to Kano, the Emir of Zunguru and his friend Alhaji Abdullah who was the senior member of the Northern Nigerian Public Service Commission came to see me for medical treatment. While I talked with the Emir, he mentioned that it was customary for every senior Colonial Service doctor to pay a courtesy call to the Emir of Kano. He asked me to make an appointment to see this important gentleman.

The next morning when I asked Dr. Taylor for permission to visit the Emir, he was surprised that Dr. Clinton had failed to arrange my visit. He called the doctor and told him to make an appointment for me. When I returned to the hospital Dr. Clinton was angry. He told me never to go over his head again. He was convinced that I had complained about his lapse in protocol to Dr. Turner.

Once Dr. Clinton arranged my visit to the Emir, I went to

his palace, which was a collection of mud dwellings, inside a big compound near Kano. I was ushered into the largest mud dwelling, where the middle-aged Emir who wore a snow-white turban and gown sat in a chair surrounded by his councilors, including the Emir's brother who was called the vizir.

The Emir was happy to see me. He said that he had heard many good things about me from his friends and some of my patients. He hoped that I would have a good stay in Kano. If I ever needed his help, he asked me to contact him.

Rachel and I enjoyed our time in Kano despite my issues with my colleagues. Sheila, who was already a few months old, always knew what she wanted, especially when it came to her food. Rachel boiled and strained mashed vegetables and mashed up chicken for her. She even made fresh tomato juice for Sheila, whose loud cry always announced when she was hungry. Sheila also raised her alarm when she was wet, and she wouldn't stop crying until she was changed. Whenever Sheila suffered from colic, I always picked her up and walked her around or we all went for a drive, which usually put Sheila to sleep.

Audu continued to work for us, but we had a new Ibo cook Lawrence, who had been raised in a Catholic mission in eastern Nigeria. Like Ojoh, he also swelled with pride whenever he said that the Mother Superior had taught him to cook. Unfortunately, we soon discovered that a wide gap existed between our memory of delicious dishes and Lawrence's versions that landed on our table.

After Dr. Baddock returned from his home leave, I assumed that I would continue my work as the second surgeon. However, Dr. Baddock began to handle cases that he had previously assigned to me. He also put me on call most weeknights and weekends. When I asked why he had made these changes, he said that he decided that he didn't need another surgeon. He only needed an assistant. His decision was unfair, but I continued to follow his orders.

A few days later Dr. Hinds told me that I had wounded Dr. Baddock in his sensitive spot. When the doctor came back to Kano, he was furious when he discovered that many of the expatriates in his private practice preferred to see me. Three weeks later Dr. Taylor informed me that I had been transferred to Ilorin, a provincial town near the southern edge of Northern Nigeria. I would be the medical officer in charge of a small hospital; another medical officer would work under me.

When British colleagues congratulated me for receiving a coveted position so early in my career, I knew better. I would no longer be working in a huge hospital in an important Nigerian city. In remote Ilorin, I doubted that I would get to handle many serious surgical cases. This awful transfer had robbed me of the opportunity to make use of my surgical skills.

~ 58 ~

TRANSFER TO ILORIN

AFTER THE ATTENDANTS LOADED OUR luggage into a truck, Lawrence and Audu hopped on board. Soon the truck was following our car through the countryside of Nigeria, where the landscape slowly changed from scrubland to lush green trees and shrubbery. When we reached the Niger River, we boarded a narrow ferryboat powered by men pushing long poles against the banks as we journeyed to the other side.

I continued driving into the evening until we finally reached the government rest house in Ilorin. The caretaker beamed when we praised the clear tap water and electricity. He said that Ilorin had the best tap water in Nigeria. That evening the medical officer in charge of the hospital came to see me. As Dr. Patmore and I talked over a beer, he told me that Ilorin's hospital served many surrounding villages and towns. The doctors and the staff worked hard treating all the patients. He said he knew that I was an excellent surgeon but told me not to overextend myself by scheduling too many surgeries. He also told me that the other medical officer Dr.

Azopardy, who had expected to be put in charge of the hospital, was upset with my appointment.

Dr. Patmore shifted the conversation and talked about Ilorin's health department. He said that I had to inspect numerous government pharmacies throughout the district, where many of the dispensers cooked their books and sold medicine to corrupt agents. He also described Sandra Jones who was the district's health superintendent. He said that she frequently started projects without approval from her superiors, which forced the district's senior medical officer to explain her unapproved projects to medical headquarters in Kaduna. Since I was in charge of the Department of Health, he advised me to visit her regularly and monitor her projects.

The next morning, I met the district's senior medical officer Dr. Robinson who assured me that he wouldn't interfere with my work at the hospital. He was too busy overseeing the medical department and inspecting the district's health centers. He told me that most Nigerians living in the district were Christians and culturally similar to the Yorubas of the south. The rest of the people were Muslim and aligned with the Northern Nigerian ruling party.

Their local leader was the Emir of Ilorin who ruled with the assistance of his ministers. Dr. Robinson told me not to form any close friendships with the local people. Socializing with Nigerians went against the customary behavior of British officers. He brought up the trouble I experienced in Gusau after local Nigerians wanted me to be their doctor instead of Dr. Curry.

I kept quiet. I didn't want to discuss my trouble with this British doctor. Before I left his office, Dr. Robinson called the British Resident Mr. Callaghan who wanted to meet me right away.

When I sat with the British Resident, he delighted in telling me fantastic tales about India that he had heard from friends who were former members of the Indian Civil Service. Before the avuncular Irishman finally let me leave his office, he told me that Her Majesty Queen Elizabeth was going to stop in Ilorin when she toured Nigeria. Since I was the officer in charge of the hospital, my wife and I would be invited to have lunch with her. He laughed as he said that this was one of the perks of serving in a small town. I would never receive an invitation if I were back in Kano.

When Rachel and I moved into our house Lawrence and Audu, who liked their new quarters, were in good spirits. By the end of the day, they had unpacked everything and had started to organize our house. The next morning, I reported to the hospital and started to take over from Dr. Patmore. After he introduced me to the senior clerk Mr. Oladapo and other administrative personnel, he told me that these educated Yorubas never worked hard, and they lacked ambition. I also met Dr. Azopardy who clearly resented me. I would need to find a way for him to feel comfortable working with me in the hospital.

The next day before Dr. Patmore took me to meet the health superintendent Sandra Jones, he told me that despite all the good work she did for local people, many expatriates didn't like her. When we arrived at her office, Miss Jones greeted him and introduced herself to me. Once we began to talk together, I realized that Miss Jones was straightforward and frank. I liked her immediately.

During our visit, she asked Dr. Patmore to get someone to repair her refrigerator before all her valuable vaccines were ruined. When the doctor said that no money was left in the Health Office budget, I volunteered that I would do everything in my capacity to get her a new refrigerator. On our way back to the hospital Dr. Patmore rebuked me. He said that the Welsh lady's refrigerator was working fine. I should ignore her.

The next day when Dr. Patmore and I did our final rounds together he brought up a case that involved a Nigerian woman named Amina who was the favorite daughter of the Emir of Ilorin and the senior wife of the eldest son of an emir in a distant emirate. He said that a few weeks after Amina learned that she was pregnant she had started to bleed. When a senior medical officer examined Amina, he discovered a large fibroid and advised her to have a hysterectomy so that she wouldn't bleed to death.

Amina was devastated. She was also so afraid that her husband's other wives would use this diagnosis against her that she told the doctor not to mention her condition to anyone, not even her husband. Instead, Amina told her husband that she wanted to go back to her father's palace in Ilorin to have her baby.

The doctor who originally examined Amina decided to discuss her condition with Dr. Patmore who was currently treating her in Ilorin. He told me Amina's bleeding had intensified. As he discussed this important case, I realized that successfully treating the Emir's daughter would be my first challenge in Ilorin.

I finally signed my papers and officially assumed control of the hospital. As Dr. Patmore started to leave his office, he turned and said that he needed to caution me. He said that I needed to jump over two hurdles before I would become successful in Ilorin. I had to get Dr. Azopardy to work harmoniously with me and I had to accept that Nigerians who lived in this district were more sophisticated than the people who lived in Kano and Gusau. Nigerians who lived here accepted the superiority of the British; but they might need time to accept me, an Indian. They might think I wasn't a good doctor or a superior officer.

As Dr. Patmore and I finally walked out of the hospital, he gave me one more piece of advice. He told me not to treat people who were in car accidents unless they were expatriates or very important Nigerians. If I treated everyone who entered the hospital, my staff and I would be overwhelmed with work.

I thanked him for his advice and waited until he got into his car and drove away. At last, I was in charge of the hospital, and I knew that I would do things my way.

~ 59 ~

AN IMPORTANT BIRTH

MY FIRST OFFICIAL ACTION IN the Ilorin hospital involved the senior clerk Mr. Oladapo. I asked him to sit with me in my office and tell me about himself, his family, and his work. When he finished speaking, I asked him if I could do anything that would make his work more efficient and more pleasant.

Mr. Oladapo said that the clerks weren't as smart as doctors, but they didn't like to be called stupid or useless. It made them angry and filled them with self-doubt. I invited all the other hospital clerks into my office and promised them that I would treat them with respect. But I expected them to work hard, and I also expected them to be loyal and honest.

Next, I asked the senior nurse Mr. Abiola to come into my office and tell me about himself. He said that he had completed two courses in the administration of anesthesia, so he felt confident when he used the skills that he had learned from his training. However, he had very few opportunities to administer anesthesia because the doctors in the hospital rarely performed surgeries.

After I told the senior nurse that I hoped he would work more often in the operating room, I asked him to feel free to tell me about any problems he encountered in the hospital. I said I was new to his country. I had many things to learn.

After a similar discussion with the senior surgical nurse, I told him that I had heard that automobile accident victims often came to the hospital. I asked him to tell me when anyone with severe injuries needed treatment.

Finally, I made a round of the wards and visited the outpatient department where I talked to more staff and patients. I encountered no insurmountable problems, and everyone was cooperative. I believed that I was off to a good start at the hospital.

When I went home Sheila raised her tiny hands, which was her signal to pick her up. I played with her for a while before I went outside to study the unfamiliar shrubs and trees in the compound. I noticed Lawrence staring intently at a bush. As I walked over to him, a chameleon perched on a branch changed its color and blended into a leaf. I picked up a twig, lifted the chameleon, and placed it on another leaf. As the chameleon changed color again, I heard a shriek and turned around.

Lawrence had fallen to his knees with his hands folded in prayer. He looked at me and said that moving a chameleon would cause an injury or even kill someone in our household.

Our cook's superstitious attitude surprised me. I asked him why he believed in Voodoo. Lawrence assured me that he was a good Christian, but he was also an African. He knew that when people disturbed or harmed a chameleon, they suffered grave consequences. Every African priest would confirm this.

The next morning when I returned to the hospital an African gentleman greeted me. He said that he was the eldest son of the

Emir of Ilorin. His father had sent him to seek my advice about his pregnant sister Amina. She was bleeding. I asked the Emir's son to bring his sister to my office. Then I told a female nurse to prepare the private examination room so that I could do a pelvic examination. I was aware that this room, which was attached to my office, was reserved for expatriates.

When the Emir's daughter Amina arrived with her brother Dr. Azopardy was with me in my office. I told him that I planned to treat the Emir's daughter in our examining room. He scowled before he went to do his rounds.

The Emir's daughter, who spoke English, told me her medical history and admitted that the ladies in her family normally never consulted a doctor for childbirth. A local midwife delivered their babies at home. But when she had started to bleed, she had gone to see the senior doctor in her husband's district. He had told her she had a big tumor in her uterus. He wanted her to have surgery.

Amina said that her husband, who would probably become the next emir, was a good man with modern ideas. She proceeded to contradict Dr. Patmore's information and told me that she was her husband's only wife. But if she couldn't bear children, her husband would be forced to marry again so that he had an heir.

I told Amina not to worry. We would talk after I examined her. I told the nurse to prepare the Emir's daughter for her examination, and as I waited in my office I thought about the difficulties of women in underdeveloped countries. So often tradition and ignorance interfered with the quality of their lives.

After a few minutes, the nurse announced that she was unable to feel a baby's head or detect a baby's heartbeat. The Emir's daughter couldn't be pregnant. When I went into the small room Amina had on most of her clothing. Only her lower abdomen was exposed. I asked the nurse how I could possibly examine the patient if I didn't have access to her body.

The nurse said that this was how doctors always examined ladies from the Emir's family. When I asked Amina if she had been wearing her clothes during the other doctor's examination, she nodded. I promised Amine that I respected her as my sister, but I had to examine her properly so that I could diagnose her medical condition and give her the correct advice. Amina agreed to disrobe.

I went back to my office and waited until the nurse said that Amina was ready for her examination. When I returned to the small room the Emir's daughter had disrobed and the stirrups were in place. I soon discovered that her baby was in a breech presentation. I told Amina that I heard a faint fetal heartbeat, and I also explained to her that she was bleeding because the placenta partially covered her cervix.

My diagnosis surprised the nurse. She was certain that Amina was not pregnant.

When Amina was dressed and sat before me in my office, I told her that if she agreed to stay in bed for a week, I could deliver her baby by Cesarean section. I asked her to have a midwife examine her daily and report back to me. I said that I might have to operate immediately if her bleeding turned severe, and an early operation could pose a risk.

Amina said that she accepted the risk as long as she left behind a son who would eventually become the Emir. She smiled and said that from this day forward I was not her brother; I was like her father. I had given her such good news.

While the nurse drew some blood so that I would have matching units available for a possible transfusion, Amina told me that no one, not even her husband, knew about the tumor in her uterus. She made the nurse and I promise that we wouldn't discuss the mistaken diagnosis with anyone. After I told the nurse not to utter a word, Amina warned her that her father would cause her harm if she betrayed his daughter.

I called her brother into my office. When I told him that I needed to deliver his sister's baby by Cesarean section he said that he would send for Amina's husband.

Two days later when her husband arrived, he thanked me for taking good care of his wife. But he admitted that he was worried about her operation.

Once our hospital had the matching units of blood, I admitted Amina and performed the Caesarian section. She suffered from excessive bleeding and needed a blood transfusion, but she gave birth to a healthy baby boy.

Well-wishers, who soon crowded the hospital verandah and lawn, beat drums, sang, and danced in celebration of this important birth. Amina's husband was so thankful that his wife had decided to return to Ilorin for the birth of their child. His town didn't have a surgeon who could perform difficult operations. I told him that God was good. He should be happy. His wife had blessed him with a beautiful son.

When the Emir of Ilorin came to my office to thank me personally, I was exhausted from the long operation. But I was relieved for Amina and myself. I prayed that the gratitude of the Nigerians would extend to the British staff and continue for the duration of my tour in Ilorin. I would be so happy if I finally worked in a supportive environment.

The following day the senior medical officer Dr. Robinson asked me to come to his office. He said that he had heard that a Nigerian woman had used the private examination room reserved

346

for expatriates. When he made this remark, I was so disappointed. I wanted to tell him that many Nigerian senior civil servants and ministers who worked in Kano and Kaduna were allowed to use the nursing homes that had once been reserved for expatriates. But I knew the wisdom of prudence and kept my criticism to myself. I promised the doctor that I would obey his instructions since he was my superior.

~ 60 ~

TOURING THE COUNTRYSIDE

I SOON LEARNED FROM THE senior clerk Mr. Oladapo that Dr. Azopardy told Dr. Robinson that I had examined the Emir's daughter in our private examination room. I needed to improve my relationship with Dr. Azopardy, so Rachel and I invited him and his wife as well as Sandra Jones to our house for dinner. That evening, I told the doctor that neither of us got to choose our assignments in Nigeria, but I promised him that I would take his preferences into account each time I determined our work schedule.

He immediately told me that he disliked inspecting the district's dispensaries. He also said that he wanted time off to go hunting during the fall when the forests were filled with game. After listing more preferences, all of which sounded like demands, I realized that he and I would never be good friends.

But Rachel and Sandra Jones got along so well that evening she started dropping by our house to visit Rachel and to play with Sheila. She also took Rachel shopping or on enjoyable rides through the countryside that often ended up at her house, where I joined them after work. Sandra, who knew that I was fond of Scotch, always offered me a drink. She also passed on important station gossip to me. Rachel shunned this kind of talk.

One day Sandra brought us some grapefruit, which she said she had purchased from the Department of Agriculture's experimental gardens. She said this garden also sold other fruit and vegetables. So, one afternoon Rachel and I visited the garden and met the Nigerian agricultural superintendent Mr. Gambari. As the superintendent gave us a tour of his gardens, he said that British officers had brought many of the original seedlings from different countries, such as the West Indies, India, and Ceylon (now Sri Lanka). He illustrated his point by showing us rows and rows of English vegetables, including sweat peas, cabbage, and carrots.

Mr. Gambari ended the tour at his chicken house. He said that most expatriates came here to buy their eggs because they were far superior to any eggs available in the market. He also occasionally sold them table birds when male chickens were large enough for roasting and when a hen produced too few eggs. Mr. Gambari offered to sell me a chicken since I was new to Ilorin and such a fine doctor. Rachel and I ended up buying a dozen eggs, one plump chicken, and some lovely vegetables. We promised Mr. Gambari that we would be back.

After a few months, I planned a long trip to a dispensary which was near the Niger River. The administrative officer Jim Wade invited me to stay in his guesthouse so that he and his wife could enjoy my company in the evening.

I left Ilorin early in the morning and drove straight through the countryside until I reached the dispensary just before lunchtime. A long line of people stood outside the dispensary waiting for me to treat them in my afternoon medical clinic. I quickly ate the sandwiches that Rachel had prepared for me and informed the pharmacist and his assistant that I wanted to examine the children first. The pharmacist said that I should first see the important people. I promised him that I would treat everyone who wanted to see me, but I insisted on starting with the children.

I didn't finish my last examination until four o'clock when I finally began to inspect the dispensary. By the time I pulled into Jim Wade's property the setting sun was casting long shadows across his front lawn. Jim and his wife ushered me to their guesthouse, which reminded me of a pleasant country cottage. Their steward brought me a bottle of beer and a bowl of groundnuts. A young boy filled the bathtub with hot and cold water pumped from tube wells.

The forestry officer and his wife were also visiting the Wades that evening. We sat together enjoying our drinks and hors d'oeuvres as we chatted about the history of Nigeria and the changes that were destined to occur after Independence. We agreed that Nigeria's impending freedom had nothing to do with British altruism. The British colonies were too expensive for England to maintain.

Jim Wade and the forestry officer, who were unlike all the other British officers I had met in Nigeria, shared my belief that the government should provide reasonable wages to its Nigerian teachers and pharmacists. They also supported my belief that the government should purchase medicines and books for Nigerians instead of allocating most of its limited resources to the construction of expensive new buildings.

I asked Jim if he would endorse a request that I had recently made to Dr. Robinson for the purchase of water purification tablets for the dispensaries. I was certain that pharmacists used impure water to create their medicines. Both men promised to lend their support to this idea in their next letter to the district's senior medical officer.

That evening, I especially enjoyed our dinner of local fish. Its delicate flavor reminded me of my favorite Calcutta fish, bhetki. When Jim told me this fish was rarely available in the market, I said that I wished that I could bring some home to Rachel. She would find it so tasty.

The next morning Jim took me in his Land Rover over bumpy roads to the Emir's palace. We entered a compound where colorfully dressed bodyguards who carried long spears stood at attention in front of a collection of mud dwellings. One of the guards took us to see the Emir who sat in a large room with his ministers and his Vizir.

Jim introduced me to the Emir who addressed us in his native language while his Vizir served as his interpreter. The Emir said that I had an excellent reputation in his country and God willing I would stay in Nigeria after independence. His country needed good doctors.

The Emir invited us into his private quarters, where he immediately began to speak in English since he was no longer conducting official business. After he told us that his family had ruled this area for more than 200 years, he showed me a signet ring that he wore on his right index finger. He said that the great British navigator Mungo Park had presented this ring to one of his ancestors.

Jim told me more about Mungo Park once we left the Emir's compound. He said that this Scotsman had led an expedition from Gambia into Nigeria in the late 1700s. When he reached the Niger River, he was forced to turn back. In 1805 Mungo Park tried once again to explore Nigeria, but according to local lore, the Emir's people killed Mungo Park and ate him and his companion. The ring on the Emir's finger served as their evidence.

While Jim doubted that much cannibalism occurred in Nigeria's Muslim north, he did believe that it had been common in this part of Nigeria. He had seen huge cauldrons used for boiling human beings, especially the early missionaries who first attempted to introduce Christianity into southern Nigeria. Cannibalism didn't end when Nigerians began to convert to this foreign religion. The practice continued until the colonial government finally passed a law that required shopkeepers to display the part of the animal skin that was originally attached to each piece of meat.

When Jim and I headed back to his house we stopped at a local market. Jim steered me toward a meat shop where a piece of goatskin or lambskin was displayed next to each slab of meat. As I stared at the odd display, I found it hard to believe that this strange requirement had ended the practice of cannibalism and the sale of human meat.

It was nearly midday when we arrived at Jim's house. His wife had kindly packed sandwiches and prepared a flask of cool water for my return trip to Ilorin. I got home just before sunset. When I went inside Rachel was in Sheila's bedroom putting our daughter to bed. I ran over and hugged them. It felt so good to be together again.

~ **61** ~

ROYAL VISITS

THE NEXT MORNING THE BRITISH Resident Mr. Callaghan called me to his office. He told me that Her Majesty the Queen, who was traveling through Nigeria in her Royal Train, was visiting Ilorin tomorrow. She would stay here for three hours. The Resident invited Rachel and me to the royal reception and the luncheon that he was holding at his residence. He said that a huge tent was already set up on the grounds of his compound and catered food from Lagos would arrive in the morning. He was thankful that Her Majesty's meals were flown in each day from London.

Mr. Callaghan personally informed each guest. No one would receive a printed invitation until a couple of hours before the Queen's train pulled into Ilorin. The Resident needed to alert the Native Authority, but he worried that the Nigerians who worked in this department wouldn't keep the plans for the Queen's visit secret.

He asked me to empty one wing of the hospital. He also wanted me to tell the doctors and staff to be prepared for emergencies and remain on duty until late tomorrow afternoon. He thought that the Queen might visit the hospital as a social courtesy, but he doubted that she would have enough time.

Two hours before the scheduled arrival of the Royal Train I told the entire staff to stay at the hospital until four o'clock. I put Dr. Azopardy in charge of the hospital and told him and the nursing administrator Mrs. Stewart that the Queen was visiting Ilorin. An hour later I received my official invitation. I called Rachel and said that we had to arrive at the Residency at noon.

Once Rachel and I were formally dressed for this remarkable occasion we started out for the Residency. Soldiers at road barriers positioned about a half mile from the Residency stopped our car and inspected our official invitation before they let us enter the protected area. When we walked into the Residency compound, I noticed the Emir of Ilorin and Amina's father-in-law chatting with some other distinguished African gentlemen. I also saw the son of the Emir of Zunguru who joined me with his friend who was the Minister of Health.

While we talked together British officers moved nervously around the compound waiting for instructions. Finally, the army brass band that stood near the Residency entrance began to play "God Save Our Gracious Queen." Her Majesty entered the tented area accompanied by the district's Governor and the Nigerian Premier, her Aide-de-Camp, and other important British and Nigerian officials.

After each guest bowed before the Queen and shook her hand, the Governor and the Premier made short welcoming speeches that thanked Her Majesty for her visit to this colony. She spoke for five brief minutes and said she was pleased to be among her people. The brass band resumed playing and the Queen and the dignitaries disappeared inside the chancery. This was the end of our grand reception.

Only a few guests were invited into the official residence for champagne and fancy hors d'oeuvres. All of us knew that we would never get to speak with Her Majesty who was always surrounded by the so-called high and mighty and her Aide-de-Camp and three army officers. Even the Resident Mr. Callaghan couldn't get near her. As Rachel and I prepared to leave the Residency, Malam said that he wanted to see me in the morning at the hospital.

When I arrived, I asked him about his father the Emir of Zunguru. He said his father had passed away the previous month. He missed him dearly, but he accepted the will of God. Malam told me that he had recently been appointed the new Emir. And since he was also the Minister of Public Works, he was extremely busy overseeing provincial construction projects and helping with the formation of the new Nigerian government that would take power at Independence.

Malam asked to speak to me in confidence about his health. I ignored Dr. Robinson's warning and took him into the examining room. The young new Emir told me that some British construction firms had invited him and a few other Northern Nigerian ministers to an Ivory Coast resort where they met some pretty girls at a party. Things happened. He had acquired a disease.

I examined the Emir and told him that he had gonorrhea. While I assured him that this disease was easy to cure, I told him it was also easy to infect someone else. The Emir assured me that he hadn't been with any of his wives since that weekend. He promised to refrain from sex until I told him he was cured.

I wrote out a prescription and asked the orderly to get the medicine from the nearby pharmacy. I told the Emir to come back and see me in two weeks.

Over time, as I expanded the range of operations I performed at our hospital, I discovered that the senior nurses were extremely knowledgeable. One morning while I was operating on an elderly man who had been diagnosed with a simple inguinal hernia, I discovered the diagnosis was incorrect. With a simple hernia, the bowel slips out of the abdomen and can be safely resected. But in this case, the elderly man's entire bladder had slipped out of his abdomen. I carefully dissected the bladder and pushed it back in place before I repaired the gap to prevent any future recurrence.

Nurse Abiola who had administered the anesthesia said, "Thank God! Finally, a doctor has not amputated a man's bladder in this hospital. This patient will be saved and cured."

Nurse Abiola explained to me that he had watched British doctors repeatedly misdiagnose a hernia and remove the bladder. The patient usually died from kidney failure a couple of weeks later, but not one doctor ever realized the error that had caused the death of each man.

When I asked if he had ever talked to these doctors about their mistake, he said that he had spoken to a British doctor years ago. The doctor disciplined him and denied him a raise for three years. He reminded me of the misdiagnosis that involved the Emir's daughter. If the British doctor who had claimed the Emir's daughter had a fibroid had actually removed her uterus, her baby would have been tossed in the municipal dump.

All day long I kept thinking about this disturbing conversation. Many elderly people living in Nigeria suffer from hernias. The realization that some patients had died because their doctors had failed to distinguish the bladder from a true hernia horrified me. I was equally upset to learn that knowledgeable nurses who were aware of this mistake were punished for daring to speak up. I wished

I could discuss this costly medical mistake with Headquarters, but I knew that if I ever questioned the work of British doctors, I would also pay a heavy price.

~ **62** ~

ILORIN

DAYS LATER THE MALARIA SPECIALIST Dr. Cable called me at my office in the hospital. He asked me to get a copy of his plans for a new malaria control project that he had sent to our health department. He wanted to discuss it with me when he came to Ilorin. After I told Dr. Cable that I had heard about his project from Miss. Jones, he asked me how I got along with the tiger lady. I said that Miss. Jones and I worked well together. I considered her a family friend.

When Dr. Cable arrived in our city, I invited him and Sandra to dinner at our house. That evening when we discussed his malaria control project, he brought up my treatment of the two cerebral malarial cases in Gusau. He said my success was remarkable since I had just arrived in the country. I reminded him that I had merely followed the wonderful advice he gave me when we met on the boat from Liverpool to Lagos.

He talked about Dr. Curry's attempt to discredit my work in Gusau. When he reminded me that he had warned me that I would encounter problems with British officers and local Nigerian officers because I was from India, Sandra told him that the Nigerians worshipped me. The narrow-minded British were my problem. They were trying to cause trouble for me in Ilorin. He assured me that I would find a way to survive because I had to care for two lovely ladies. He pointed at Rachel and Sheila.

While we lived in Ilorin, Lawrence, and Audu began to have endless spats with one another. Each time they fought Lawrence would tell us that Audu was unfit to be the steward of the Master's house. Poor Audu was at a disadvantage. We were stationed in the southern part of Northern Nigeria near Lawrence's home and family. Very few Hausa stewards worked in this part of Nigeria. Audu felt like a foreigner. When I asked him what he would like to do, he said that he preferred to stay with us until the end of my tour. He would decide once he learned about my next posting.

One day I received a letter from Neil who told me that he had passed his fellowship exam. He was a Fellow of the Royal College of Surgeons. Unfortunately, Saha failed his exam a second time. He and Joya were distraught. Neil said that Amjad had also passed his fellowship exam, but in Edinburgh, and now he was determined to join our ranks and retake the fellowship exam at the Royal College of Surgeons. But his scholarship from Pakistan had ended. Neil said that Amjad had asked him for a loan so that he could study for six months before he retook the exam in London. Neil, who was always so generous, said that he was inclined to help our friend.

A few days after I received Neil's letter I was invited to a surgical conference at the Ibadan University in Western Nigeria. In 1948 the British government and the University of London built this lovely university and its fine medical school and hospital to offer deserving Nigerian students a world-class education. When I attended the three-day conference, I was in the company of medical professionals from nearly all the commonwealth nations. We sat in a spacious hall, and I marveled at the idea that Nigeria had created such a fine university. Even the delicious cafeteria food was far superior to any food available in British hospital cafeterias.

For three wonderful days, I listened to informative papers and discussions that enhanced my knowledge and stimulated my mind. I took extensive notes and collected valuable reference materials from other medical professionals, including the delightful Dr. Ram who served as a moderator during the opening session. Dr. Ram, who had trained in London, was under a three-year contract as a professor of surgery at Ibadan University. I also met his wife Dr. Asha Krishnan who was a resident in medicine and their young baby girl Meena. I invited them to come visit Rachel and me in Ilorin. I knew that she would like them.

Once I went back to work, I called the district's senior medical officer Dr. Robinson to tell him about the conference. He asked me why the British had even bothered to establish this white elephant of a university in such an underdeveloped country. I told him that Ibadan University would be the finest British legacy of the British administration. It would educate members of the Nigerian middle class who would become the backbone of the young country. Dr. Robinson disagreed. He said unworthy Nigerians, who would take over the government and the management of this university after Independence, would run the school into the ground.

One morning the Vizir of the Emir of Ilorin visited me at the hospital. He said that the Emir was so pleased with my service to his people that he wanted to honor me at my house. When the Emir arrived at my home the next afternoon he was on official business, so he spoke in his native language with his Vizir acting as his interpreter. The Emir thanked me for being so good to all the Nigerians and he wished me and my family good health and happiness. At the end of his brief tribute to me, we walked outside where a newspaper reporter and photographer were waiting for us. After the reporter interviewed the Emir and the photographer took some photos, the Emir presented me with four camel leather ottomans. He instructed his driver to give a big turkey to Lawrence before he and his entourage left our house.

The next morning Dr. Robinson called me into his office. He had read about the Emir's tribute to me in the local newspaper. When he said that officers were not allowed to entertain local dignitaries in their homes I tried to explain to him that I had performed a successful caesarean section on the Emir's daughter, and she had given birth to an important grandson. Dr. Robinson said that the birth of the baby didn't alter British protocol. Colonial Service officers were not supposed to cultivate friendships with local dignitaries.

A few weeks later when Jim Wade came to Ilorin to present his annual report to the Resident, I invited him and his wife to have dinner at our house. He arrived with an icebox packed with some of the delicious local fish that he had served me in his home. I was so grateful to this thoughtful man. I knew that he had spent days collecting ice from his refrigerator. Ice wasn't sold in his small town.

The next week I was working in the outpatient department when a British officer rushed in to see me. His 10-year-old daughter had severe abdominal pain, and she was vomiting. When I went to the officer's house, his wife said that their daughter hadn't moved her bowels all day. She had given her daughter an ounce of Milk of Magnesia, but she continued to vomit, and her pain had intensified.

When I examined the young girl, I was certain that she was suffering from acute appendicitis. She needed an appendectomy.

She also needed IV fluids. She was severely dehydrated. When the Resident Mr. Callaghan arrived at the officer's house I told him my diagnosis. He asked me if I could safely operate on the young girl in Ilorin. I said that I thought this was her best option since the 10hour road trip to Kano could lead to complications. As I spoke with the Resident, I realized that he was in charge of this girl, not her parents. He told me to start the IV fluids and to get the girl's blood count.

I called the nursing administrator Mrs. Stewart and asked her to hurry to the house with the lab technician. I had the girl's mother collect some urine from her daughter while I drew blood and started the IV. Once we were able to admit the young girl into the hospital I removed her acutely inflamed appendix. The next day she was ready to go home. Five days later I removed her stitches. The officer's daughter had made a remarkable recovery.

My tour in Ilorin was soon coming to an end and my thoughts were turning toward home leave. Rachel and I were looking forward to our delightful ocean voyage to England and our stay at Jacob's house, which was near London. We looked forward to catching up with dear family and friends. We even imagined going on a short holiday in Europe.

~ 63 ~

HOME LEAVE

BEFORE I FINISHED MY TOUR in Ilorin, I purchased two bank drafts and repaid my loans from Uncle Hem Ray and Uncle Bidhan. I was so grateful to these two fine men. Their unexpected generosity enabled me to become a Fellow in England.

On my last day at the hospital, the staff organized a big party for Rachel and me. They made speeches, presented regional dances and songs, and gave us some memorable photographs and gifts, including a formal Yoruba dress and wooden carvings. Their affection moved me. I was delighted that my tour in Ilorin had been so successful.

Crown Agents confirmed our boat passage to Liverpool and our train ride to London. The Public Works Department stored all our possessions. Rachel and I retained Lawrence and Audu for our next tour and gave them their full salary for the duration of our holiday. They would meet us at our new post once we returned.

After we said our goodbyes to everyone we drove to Lagos and boarded the passenger ship that took us to Liverpool. Days later we were traveling first class on the train to London. Jacob met us at the station and drove us to his small townhouse in Hampstead where we met his German girlfriend, Hilda.

While Rachel and I were in London we saw our friends Neil and Amjad. I repaid Neil and said that I owed him much more than money. He was an irreplaceable friend. His eyes filled with tears. He told us that he planned to go back to India after Rachel and I left again for Nigeria. He wondered when we would meet again.

When I met Amjad he said that he had borrowed some money from Neil so that he could take the London exam. As he told me about this loan, I knew that our friend had emptied his savings account to soothe Amjad's pride.

I also called Saha who ranted on the phone over his failure to pass the dammed exam. He said that he was stupid to continue this wild goose chase. But he would suffer so much shame if he gave up and went back to India. His prospects in England were equally bleak. He would need to work under a general practitioner before he could ever start a family practice. I couldn't discuss these emotionally charged subjects with him on the telephone. I promised Saha that we would get together and figure out a sensible solution for him.

Rachel and I went to the Indian High Commission and had her name fixed on her passport so that we would no longer have any problems at immigration in Nigerian airports. From the High Commission, we walked through Convent Garden, which had always been one of our favorite places in London. But only a few of its many stalls that had once sold imported vegetables remained in the garden, and they were scheduled for demolition to make room for cafes and shops. Convent Garden had lost its soul.

One Sunday we visited with Mrs. Robinson who had also invited Amal and Glenda and their baby to her house. We were delighted to learn that Amal had received an important promotion in his company. When I told Mrs. Robinson that I thought Saha should try to join the Colonial Service she liked my idea. But she advised me to adequately describe the working and living conditions in Nigeria so that he and his wife wouldn't blame me for any unexpected hardships.

When Naomi came to visit us at Jacob's house, she told Rachel that their father had experienced a mini stroke. She said that their mother had looked after the coffee shop during his recovery. Jacob hoped that he would be able to buy a bigger house in a couple of years so that his parents would have a place to stay if they shifted to England.

Naomi also told us that she hoped to go on a vacation in Israel. She said that when she told her mother about her plans, she quickly lined up two Israeli relatives whom she said would be appropriate for her daughter. Naomi said that both relatives were uneducated. She would never marry anyone who reminded her of Miriam's husband.

I went to St. George's Hospital and visited with Sister Kelly, Sir John, and Mr. Bingham. Sister Kelly surprised me with the news that Dr. Mary Naidu and Dr. Patel had a baby. When Sister Kelly said that they had left the hospital I was relieved. I didn't want to face them.

I asked Sir John if he could possibly arrange for me to observe some gynecological operations that would help me perform a wider range of surgeries in Nigeria. He called the chief of gynecology who agreed to let me assist him in the operating theater. For the next couple of weeks, I worked with him and had a valuable opportunity to learn some new surgical procedures.

Rachel's cousin Miriam also invited us to spend a Sunday with her family. She paraded her daughters before us and bragged that her eldest girl had the mental capacity of Einstein. She added that her younger girl was also smart, but she suffered from asthma, which interfered with her education and well-being. I worried that Miriam's oldest daughter would develop a superiority complex if she kept hearing such high praise. I also felt sorry for the younger daughter who seemed so quiet and lonely.

When Rachel and I finally spent a few days with Saha and Joya, he said that his brothers were urging him to return to Calcutta. They had offered to finance a small pharmacy for him so that he could generate an adequate income while he established a medical practice in Calcutta. Joya said that she thought Saha should make his own decision about his future, but she admitted that she worried about their son back in Calcutta. He was so far away from his parents.

I told Saha that he should consider applying for an appointment in the Colonial Service and living in Nigeria for a few years. If he came to Nigeria, I assured him that he would get a good starting salary and make enough money to educate his son properly. But I told him that he needed to apply soon if the idea appealed to him. In six months, the service would stop recruiting doctors because Nigeria would no longer be a British colony. I gave Saha the contact information for the London office and told him to speak to the recruitment officer. Saha promised to call me before we went back to Nigeria.

Once Rachel and I had visited most of our family and friends in London, I decided that our family should have a nice holiday in Europe. A few days later we boarded a boat and crossed the English Channel, where we took a train to the French Riviera. We spent some wonderful days visiting the local sights, including Monte Carlo with its lovely, terraced buildings and gardens.

Our next stop was Rome, where we stayed at a hotel on the famous Via Veneto. We took a city tour and visited many historic buildings, ruins and fountains. We also enjoyed every single meal and our time relaxing with little Sheila who was speaking her first words.

When we returned to England the secretary at St George's Hospital had arranged a reception for me. She told me to bring Rachel. When we arrived at the hospital, she guided us into the party room where we saw so many old friends and acquaintances, including Sir John and almost everyone else I had known at the hospital.

The crowd quieted as the director of a reputable engineering company stepped forward to introduce the young man who had been in the industrial accident at the end of my tenure at St. George's Hospital. I didn't recognize him. After a year of extensive physiotherapy the young man, who continued to work for the company, had made a near-total recovery. I felt wonderful as the young man shook my hand and thanked me for performing the miraculous operation. Rachel and I were so touched as people made speeches in my honor and a company director handed me a letter of appreciation. Tears fell down my cheeks. I felt blessed. It wasn't just this wonderful party that had me feeling emotional and blessed. Rachel was now pregnant again.

The next day I received a letter from the Medical Headquarters in Nigeria. Officials told me that my next post would be in Kano. I was very aware that my Colonial Service three-year probation would conclude with this next assignment. At that time, I dearly hoped to receive my promotion to the rank of permanent officer, but I knew that many of the doctors at the Kano hospital and some senior officers resented me because I was from India. I wondered how medical headquarters would handle this matter. Would they purposely ignore the rules? I hoped for a fair outcome based on merit, but I didn't know if this would happen. That same day Crown Agents informed us that we would fly back to the city from London. Our home leave was over. It was time to return to Nigeria and face the next challenge.

~ 64 ~

FALSE CLAIMS

A FEW BRITISH COLLEAGUES AT City Hospital were civil towards me when I reported to work, but most of the doctors showed their resentment as soon as I entered the lounge. My country of origin fueled some of this resentment, but the fact that I, an Indian officer, was also a fellow at the Royal College of Surgeons and I had entered the service with a superior rank simply galled them. I believed my achievements were easily more annoying to them than any of my friendships with important Nigerians.

Even Dr. Hinds agreed with this assessment. He told me that from day one some British officers were determined to find proof of my incompetence as a surgeon or as a senior officer. He reminded me that fully qualified Indian doctors had been forced to accept posts as assistant surgeons working under British doctors when India was part of the British Empire. That memory left most British officers in Nigeria, who had once served in India, nostalgic for the good old days of the British Raj.

But despite my problems at City Hospital, I built a thriving private practice in Kano. Lebanese traders who had known me in Gusau or Ilorin insisted on seeing me whenever they had medical problems. The Emir of Zunguru and his brother also introduced me to many other Northern Nigerian ministers and civil servants who were waiting to take over senior positions from British officers. All these distinguished Nigerians, who considered me their friend, genuinely trusted my medical expertise and wanted me to look after them. Whenever I saw any private patient, I was always careful to abide by every single government rule and regulation. Even still my successful practice soon became the topic of conversation in the doctors' lounge, and this always stopped once I walked into the room.

Around this time Dr. Hinds invited Rachel and me to afternoon tea at his house. When he asked me to go outside to see his rose garden, I soon realized that he didn't bring me outside to admire his flowers. He told me that I had only been posted to Kano because he had insisted that I teach anatomy to the medical school students. He said that I shouldn't be surprised if I were suddenly transferred.

Two weeks later officials informed our hospital staff that a newly appointed special grade medical officer was joining the hospital. Within days Dr. Maruti, who was a qualified Indian surgeon, arrived in Kano with his British-born wife. He knew the protocol and quickly visited every important British officer in the city. He was an enthusiastic supporter of the Colonial Service and all the doctors at the hospital seemed to like him. Dr. Maruti fit right in.

Every day after I finished my work in the hospital, I rushed to the medical school to prepare my lectures in the school library, which had become my sanctuary. But I still felt obliged to spend time helping Dr. Hinds with his work for the school or just keeping him company. One day he told me that he was convinced that my situation in Kano had deteriorated with the arrival of another Indian Colonial Service officer. The other doctors realized that they could easily complain about me as long as headquarters treated the new Indian surgeon fairly. He was already popular with the British doctors and enjoyed socializing with them. Dr. Hinds said that everything would become clear to me at the end of the school semester.

The next morning the Wakelin came to see me at the hospital as I was completing my ward rounds. I went with him to his office. He closed the door and said that he was disturbed to learn that my fellow countryman, an Indian doctor, was plotting against me. He told me that several doctors had agreed to submit personal letters to Dr. Taylor that claimed they couldn't get along with me because I was arrogant. They also told him I was neglecting my official hospital duties to see more patients in my private practice. He said that Dr. Maruti had specifically asserted that my absence in the hospital repeatedly forced him to perform most of the scheduled surgeries.

I told the Wakelin that I had never treated private patients during my official hospital working hours.

The Wakelin said that the hospital gatekeepers kept a register that recorded each doctor's arrival and departure. He knew every time I arrived at City Hospital and every time I departed each day. He was aware that I worked more hours than any other doctor at City Hospital. A similar register at the medical school kept track of the hours I spent there. The Wakelin said that the Vizir had installed the hospital register three years ago when the British Resident had complained to the Emir of Kano that the expatriate doctors were overworked. He had also installed the register at the medical school. He doubted that any British officer knew about these logs.

I thanked the Wakelin for his helpful information. Later when I passed through the gate at the medical school, I thought about these registers. The British officers didn't understand the Nigerians in the Native Authority were so smart.

After I presented my lecture to the students, Dr. Hinds asked to talk to me. I told him that I had to get home. As I started to leave, he reminded me that I always had his support.

When I got home, I hugged Rachel and Sheila. I didn't tell Rachel anything about my new troubles. Instead, I told her that I wanted the medical officer at the Kano nursing home to examine her. I wanted us to both know that her pregnancy was fine. She didn't like the idea but agreed when I insisted that I would feel better if a competent physician gave her at least one full examination. I didn't let on that I was worried that we wouldn't stay much longer in Kano. I didn't want to upset her.

I worked hard at City Hospital, and I never let on to my colleagues that I knew about their conspiracy. I even felt secure since the Native Authority registers proved that I worked more hours than any other doctor.

Two weeks later Dr. Taylor called me to his office. He said he heard that I was building up my private practice instead of concentrating on my duties at the hospital and the medical school. When I responded that I only spent time in my private practice once I completed all my official work, he removed a letter from a file and gave it to me.

The letter was from Dr. Maruti who asserted that I spent most of my time working in my private practice. Dr. Taylor said Dr. Clinton, who ran the hospital, was aware that other doctors were prepared to file additional complaints against me. He added that I shouldn't try to register a claim of racial prejudice with British officials at the Ministry of Health. My accuser was also an Indian. Dr. Taylor gave me a copy of the letter and told me that I had 24 hours to explain myself. He said that our meeting was over.

I was enraged and went to talk to the Wakelin. When he read Dr. Maruti's letter, he smiled. He said that the original plan of the doctors must have changed. Only one complaint had been sent to Dr. Taylor. The Wakelin called his clerk into his office and told him to make a list of my arrival and departure times at the hospital. He also requested the same information from the medical school clerk. The Wakelin assured me that important Nigerians would protect me. He told me not to worry. He knew that the Emir of Zunguru would deal with the senior British officers.

Within an hour I had the lists that would allow me to prepare my defense. When I went to the medical school I hurried to the library and prepared my lecture. After I taught my anatomy class Dr. Hinds said that he was aware that a complaint had been registered against me. He promised to put in some favorable words about me to lessen the impact of my punishment.

I told him that I didn't need his help. The people who falsely accused me had problems, not me.

At home, I didn't discuss my problem with Rachel. Instead, I excused myself and wrote a long letter to Dr. Taylor that refuted the allegations in the complaint. I included my chart of hours from the two registers.

The next morning after the Wakelin's clerk typed up my letter, I delivered it to Dr. Taylor before I returned to the hospital and went to work as if nothing were wrong. A couple hours later Dr. Taylor asked me to come to his office to meet with him and Dr. Clinton. He announced that he was giving me one more chance to admit my culpability and ask for leniency because I was new to Nigeria.

I told Dr. Taylor that I didn't have anything to admit. I had done nothing wrong.

Dr. Taylor said no official record supported my claim that I had worked all these hours at the hospital and the school. He asked Dr. Clinton how many hours I spent in the hospital. Dr. Clinton said that normally when he looked for me in the hospital I wasn't there. Dr. Taylor called Dr. Hinds. He asked him if he could remember the number of hours I spent teaching. Dr. Hinds assured the doctor that I was normally there most afternoons.

Dr. Taylor glared at me. He accused me of trying to pull a fast one.

I insisted my list of hours was correct. My hospital hours and medical school hours were recorded in Native Authority logbooks kept by the clerks who manned the gates at each building.

When Dr. Clinton said that I was digging my grave with these lies Dr. Taylor called the Wakelin. He asked him if the Native Authority kept logbooks at the hospital gate. The Wakelin obviously said yes because Dr. Taylor demanded to know who had authorized these logs. He told the Wakelin to bring the logbooks to his office. He put down the phone and told Dr. Clinton that the Wakelin said that he couldn't bring the logbooks without a formal order from the Health Councilor.

Dr. Taylor said that he would talk to me again after he verified the authenticity of these books. Before he dismissed me, he reminded me that the British government was still the sovereign power in Nigeria.

I returned to the hospital and finished my work before I went to the medical school. When I arrived at the gate the guard handed me a note from the Wakelin. He wanted me to meet him at the Emir's rest house later in the afternoon.

Dr. Hinds found me in the library and asked me why Dr. Taylor wanted to know how many hours I had spent at the school. When he said there was no record of this information, I told him he was wrong. The Native Authority wasn't dumb. It kept a record of our hours.

When I met the Wakelin at the Emir's rest house, he told me that the Health Councilor and the Emir knew about this episode. The Emir would sort out everything at the Ministry of Health.

After two suspenseful days, Dr. Baddock told me that Dr. Taylor had summoned both of us to Dr. Clinton's office. Dr. Taylor said that he had great reservations about the sudden appearance of the so-called "logbooks," but he had decided to overlook my delinquent behavior. Nonetheless, I had to promise to obey the rules and regulations from this day forward.

When Dr. Baddock, who was in charge of the surgery department, asked Dr. Taylor why no one had told him about Dr. Maruti's complaint, the doctor said that I was posted here as a medical officer. I reported to Dr. Clinton since he was the officer running the hospital. The complaint against me didn't involve surgical incompetence.

I left the office with Dr. Baddock. I knew that the senior officers were furious with me because of my friendships with important Nigerians. But I also knew the real reasons behind their latest attempt to punish me. Dr. Baddock looked at me. His face was a study of bemusement as he welcomed me to the shape of things to come. He said that he was glad that he was leaving Nigeria at the end of his tour.

~ 65 ~

BANISHED

WHEN I RETURNED TO THE medical school, Dr. Hinds asked me if everything had been settled in my favor. I told him that I was unaware that anything had to be settled. I excused myself and went to the library.

That evening, I tried to behave normally at home, but Rachel knew that something was wrong. She asked me if we could go for a drive in the car. The clouds always disappeared when we all took a ride together.

A few days later I met with the Minister of Health at the Emir's rest house. He said that he planned to go to Zunguru and tell the council to authorize Nigerian control of the British Health Department, including Medical Headquarters. While the British Permanent Secretary would get to appoint a medical advisor and continue to run the medical department, the secretary would have to report to the Nigerian Minister of Health.

The council knew that some British doctors would object to this new Nigerian authorization, and they would choose to leave the country. But if they resigned from their posts, the Ministry would recruit more doctors from the United Kingdom and other Commonwealth countries. The Minister of Health assured me that the Nigerian leaders intended to protect me. He seemed sincere.

The next afternoon Dr. Hinds said that he was happy the storm had blown over. When he asked me how I knew that the Native Authority kept a logbook at each gate, I figured my response would get back to Dr. Turner. I said that long ago when I had returned an umbrella to the guardroom, I saw the logbook on the table. The clerk had told me that the guards always kept a record of our presence in the school and the hospital so that they could keep us safe.

I was still angry with Dr. Maruti who had been so greedy for his career advancement. Early the next morning I waited for him in the doctors' lounge. Dr. Baddock, who knew that I wasn't performing any morning surgeries, asked me why I was already at the hospital. After I told him that I wanted to talk to Dr. Maruti, he smiled and said that he would leave before the thunder.

The minute Dr. Maruti entered the lounge I told him that I wanted to have a word with him. When he said that he had to prepare for his operations I told him to sit down and listen to me or I would confront him in an official meeting in front of witnesses. I asked if he knew that he was the only doctor who had falsely accused me. No other doctor had filed a complaint with Dr. Taylor.

Dr. Maruti said that I was wrong. He was told that every doctor had registered a complaint against me.

I told him the British officers had made a fool of him. I had every right to ask headquarters to discipline him for making false charges. I could also hire a lawyer and take legal action against him. After I told Dr. Maruti to think about his deceitful behavior I left the lounge.

I went to the outpatient department and took care of some surgical patients who had arrived in the morning. When I returned to the doctors' lounge Dr. Clinton was waiting for me. He said that Dr. Maruti had told him about his morning encounter with me. He warned me that I would be starting a case against all the doctors if I took legal action. They were fond of Dr. Maruti. They would protect him, not me.

When I told Dr. Clinton that I wasn't worried, he changed his tone and insisted no one on the medical staff wanted to harm me. Everyone was willing to forget about this incident and start afresh with me.

When I headed home, I saw Dr. Maruti's car pulling out of our driveway. Rachel said that he and his wife had come to the house to apologize. Mrs. Maruti had insisted wily Dr. Clinton had forced her husband to write the complaint. Her husband begged for forgiveness.

After I finally related the entire sorry saga to Rachel, I told her that Dr. Maruti needed to learn a lesson. But Rachel thought that he had suffered enough. I sat down with a glass of Scotch and agreed to put aside my anger with the doctor. But I wondered what my colleagues would do next.

For two weeks the doctors treated me decently and I wondered if my problems were over. I made time to go shopping with Rachel who hated to shop by herself. I caught up with my correspondence and wrote to Neil who was a consultant in Calcutta. I told him that I planned to take the family to India once I was confirmed and promoted to the rank of specialist. I also wrote to Saha who had applied for a job in Northern Nigeria. I told him that I thought he would be happy here. The country's upcoming independence wouldn't interfere with his work because the Nigerian leaders appreciated good doctors. They had been very kind to me.

At the hospital, many new surgical patients came to me with their medical problems. I finally realized that the Native Authority had told local chiefs to send their unhealthy villagers to me. So many of them knew my name when they entered the hospital.

One afternoon Dr. Hinds said that he thought that I would be better off working somewhere else. When I said that I liked Kano, the old fox clammed up.

A few days later the Wakelin met me at the hospital gate. He had bad news. Dr. Taylor had informed the Native Authority that Medical Headquarters was making me the medical officer in charge of the Maiduguri General Hospital in the district of Maiduguri. The current doctor who ran the hospital was completing his second tour. I was the most suitable replacement. The Wakelin said that he didn't want me to leave Kano. But if the Nigerians intervened in this transfer, they would create bad blood with Native Authority officials in the Maiduguri district who were thrilled with my appointment.

Finally, Dr. Taylor called me to his office. He complimented my good work at the school and in the hospital before he announced that I had received an important post as the medical officer in charge of Maiduguri General Hospital and the district. Since the district was far from Kano, I would get to make many decisions on my own. I would also be busy since the hospital only had a couple of doctors. But the medical officer in charge of the health department would also assist me.

Dr. Taylor had played his cards brilliantly. He had succeeded in getting me far from City Hospital, where I had finally been posted as a surgeon.

Dr. Taylor said that I needed to be in Maiduguri in two weeks so I could become acquainted with the hospital and the hinterland dispensaries before the current doctor left for home leave. Dr. Taylor handed me the order sheet. Our meeting was over.

I was miserable. A friendly administrative officer had already told me that the post in Maiduguri often destroyed the reputations of medical officers.

Rachel was unhappy when I gave her the news. She liked her obstetrician at the well-equipped Kano nursing home where she had hoped to deliver our baby. I also regretted that I would soon be living quite a distance from my important Northern Nigerian friends. I would also lose the income from my busy private practice. I doubted that I could establish much of a practice in Maiduguri. When I said goodbye to the Emir of Kano, he expressed his disappointment that he couldn't keep me in the city to take care of his people. But he smiled and promised that one day I would be back in Kano.

~ 66 ~

NEXT STOP: MAIDUGURI

RACHEL AND I PACKED OUR BAGS and began our early morning journey to Maiduguri with Lawrence and Audu who traveled with our luggage in a truck. Around midday our car stalled, and I steered it to the roadside. While Rachel, Sheila, and I waited under a shady tree on the dusty ground, Lawrence went to find a mechanic in the next town. Two men suddenly arrived and spread out a comfortable woven bedspread and gave us an earthen jar full of water. We didn't know who they were, but we appreciated their kindness.

When Lawrence returned with a mechanic who fixed our car, he told us that the head of a nearby village had sent the two men to look after us. We thanked the men and gave them some money before we continued our journey.

We reached Maiduguri late that night. Early the next morning I strolled through the grounds of the rest house. Lush flowering shrubs were such a lovely contrast to the scrubby bushes in Kano. Mid-morning I received a telephone call from Maiduguri's chief medical officer Dr. Wilson who asked if he could come to meet me.

I told him to come right away.

He was in his early forties, a confirmed bachelor, and a connoisseur of food and drinks. He said that I would like the Nigerians who lived in the district. Many of them were well-educated and worked for the provincial government. He advised me to keep the elderly Emir and his Vizir on my side. They could be helpful to me in the future. He also told me to maintain good relations with the Wakelin and other Nigerians who worked for the Native Authority.

When Dr. Wilson discussed my job, he said that senior officers posted in Maiduguri usually made most decisions on their own. Headquarters only showed up when there were serious complaints from an administrative officer or someone in the Native Authority.

He invited my entire family to dinner at his house where we could meet a few of his friends. We met the medical officer in charge of the health department, Dr. Allen and his wife, who ran the forestry department, and Paula Cook who was the hospital matron in charge of all the nurses. Our lively discussion about the future of the colony continued during a delicious dinner that Dr. Wilson had prepared for us. He also served a tasty red wine that he said we could purchase in the neighboring French territory of Chad.

While we stayed at the rest house, I was informed that a Nigerian gentleman had come to see me. When I opened the door, I recognized Malam Abdul Lawan immediately. I had met him one evening when I was visiting with the Emir of Zunguru. He presently served under the Director of Agriculture in Kaduna, but he was poised to become the Permanent Secretary in the Ministry of Agriculture.

Malan Lawan had come home to Maiduguri for a one-week holiday. He hoped that we would become good friends. Through the course of our conversation, his intelligence and knowledge impressed me. His understanding of history and current affairs extended well beyond Nigeria and the African continent. He also talked about several distinguished Nigerian men who lived near Maiduguri. When I finally walked him to his car, I knew that I really liked this man.

Before Malam Lawan returned to Kaduna, he took Rachel and me to see his orchard, which was just beyond the city limits. When I noticed some mango trees, he said they were Alfonso mangoes. He had also tried unsuccessfully to grow a litchi tree that he had personally brought from India. Malam Lawan pointed to several rows of papaya trees and said that these trees were like Africans. Only one male papaya tree grew in each row, the rest were females. This arrangement worked very well.

That same week I introduced myself to the middle-aged British Resident Mr. Brandon. He was genuinely friendly and asked me about my medical qualifications and my earlier experiences in England. We also chatted about India and its current politics and economy. He hoped that I would find enough intellectual stimulation in Maiduguri. He said that he had established good relationships with some highly educated Nigerians who lived in the area. He hoped that I would also enjoy their friendship.

I left Mr. Brandon's office with a very good opinion of this representative of the Queen. He was unlike any other top administrative officer that I had met in Nigeria. He was an intellectual and he seemed to genuinely like the people in this country.

Finally, Rachel and I moved to our house and Lawrence and Audu shifted into their quarters. When I reported to Dr. Wilson at the hospital he asked if I wanted to perform some operations. He had a backlog of cases. Of course, I agreed. Every day I performed several surgeries. This was the way that Dr. Wilson and I slowly began the transfer of duties that would ultimately leave me in charge of the hospital. I did several operations daily until I had treated everyone on Dr. Wilson's waiting list.

One morning an elderly man suffering from acute retention of urine was brought to the emergency room. The last time Dr. Wilson had seen someone with these symptoms he was unable to insert a catheter, and the patient had died from renal failure. He asked me to care for this new patient.

The elderly man had an enlarged prostrate with urinary obstruction. I couldn't insert a catheter, so I performed a suprapubic cystostomy and left the suprapubic catheter in situ. The operation successfully relieved the man's urinary obstruction, and he said that he felt better. But he didn't want to go home with the catheter inside his body.

I told him that I could remove the catheter, but I would have to remove a large gland that was compressing his urethra and obstructing his flow of urine. At his elderly age, he might not survive such a risky procedure. When I asked the senior surgical nurse to repeat everything to the elderly man in his own language, the man seemed to understand the risk. He told me to operate. He said that only Allah could determine the time of his death. Until then, he wanted to live normally.

I talked to Dr. Wilson who advised me to discuss the life-threatening operation with the senior members of the medical staff and the Health Councilor at the Native Authority. They needed to understand that no one had ever performed this operation in this hospital. He doubted that anyone had ever performed this prostrate surgery in all of Nigeria.

When we conferred with our staff almost everyone agreed that I should operate on the patient. The outcome would also determine if I should ever repeat the procedure in Maiduguri. Only the other medical officer Dr. Sandhurst objected. He believed our hospital had inadequate lab and technical facilities. But Dr. Sandhurst was wrong. We had a lab technician who could do the required tests, and we had available blood donors from the nearby army base. The results of the blood work, including kidney function tests, also fell within acceptable limits, so we planned to operate the next week.

During this time the Health Councilor at the Native Authority contacted me. The Emir wanted to meet me and see Dr. Wilson. The Health Councilor, who met us at the palace compound gate, took us to see the Emir. The Vizir and his councilors spoke on behalf of the Emir who was mentally and physically impaired. They expressed thanks to Dr. Wilson for his good services and hoped that I would be equally worthy.

The Vizir smiled at me and said that although I didn't know them, they all knew about me. Maiduguri lacked a good telephone service, but their "bush telegraph" kept them well informed.

The next morning Dr. Wilson asked me to go with him to two dispensaries so that I could get a general idea of their quality and see the countryside. When we reached the first dispensary a long line of patients waiting for treatment. Dr. Wilson first checked the pharmacy and showed the pharmacist some errors in his records, including his failure to account for the total dispensation of medications. The pharmacist apologized and insisted his errors were a result of his busy dispensary. He lacked the time to record everything. He wasn't trying to cheat the government.

Dr. Wilson and I addressed the needs of the patients. We divided them into two groups and treated everyone before we left for the government rest house where we would spend the night. During our drive, Dr. Wilson told me that we were going to have dinner with the wife of one of the expatriate officers who lived in this small station. She was lonely when her husband, who was the forest officer, went on a trip.

The rest house caretaker had prepared our rooms and hot water for our baths. Dr. Wilson told the caretaker that we wouldn't have supper, but he wanted the cook to prepare us a hearty breakfast. When we reached his friend's house he gave our attractive hostess Rona a nice gift and quickly hugged and kissed her.

After ushering us into her sitting room, Rona asked Dr. Wilson to come into the kitchen to help her prepare our drinks. While I sat in the sitting room, I noticed a painting of Windsor Castle hanging on a wall next to a photograph of Queen Victoria. When I walked over to examine them, I passed the entrance to the kitchen. I saw Rona and Dr. Wilson locked in a deep embrace. I hurried back to my chair as Dr. Wilson returned with the drinks.

While Dr. Wilson and I enjoyed our cocktails, Rona went into the kitchen to supervise our dinner. When she returned, she turned on some classical music that created a lovely mood as we talked together and enjoyed our tasty fish and a lovely salad. I felt relaxed after such a long day.

After dinner, Dr. Wilson asked me if I wanted him to take me back to the rest house. I sensed that he wanted me to leave so I said yes. Hours after I slipped into bed the noise of a car woke me up. I glanced at my watch when I heard the door open to the next room. It was just after midnight. Dr. Wilson had returned.

The next morning, we visited the second dispensary before we headed for home. I was so happy when I finally saw Rachel and Sheila. I loved them so much.

When Dr. Wilson and I returned to the hospital, our lab technician had grouped and cross-matched the elderly man's blood. He had also arranged for several units of blood for a possible transfusion. The next morning Dr. Wilson asked if he could observe when I performed the prostatectomy. Once the patient was prepped, I carefully demonstrated each step of the procedure to him, and many hours later I completed the surgery. It was successful.

A couple days later he asked me to examine a Nigerian woman who had been in labor for over 24 hours. She had a marginal pelvis, so everyone had expected her to deliver the baby naturally. But her labor was not progressing, and the baby was in distress. She needed a Cesarean section.

Fortunately, I had spent time with the obstetrician-gynecologist in London who had taught me how to perform the more modern lower segment Cesarean section and total hysterectomy. But in Northern Nigeria, doctors, including surgeons, performed classical Cesarean sections and subtotal hysterectomies. They only performed total hysterectomies when benign tumors caused bleeding.

Dr. Wilson observed as I performed the lower segment Cesarean section on the patient. I was so relieved and happy when we removed the healthy baby. But Dr. Wilson looked depressed. I asked him what was wrong. He said that he wondered if he was wise to assist me in operations. He worried that the nurses might lower their opinion of him. I told him not to worry. He had successfully treated so many patients during his two tours in Maiduguri.

But I understood why Dr. Wilson was concerned. I knew that every British officer needed to believe that no one could match his skill and reach his lofty position. By assisting me while I performed these operations, he had jeopardized his supremacy.

~ 67 ~

DR. WILSON

I TOOK CHARGE OF THE hospital and district's medical department a few days before Dr. Wilson left for home leave. During this time, he encouraged me to contact him at his home if I had any questions about a patient or a hospital file. One morning when I was reviewing the employment records of various members of the hospital staff, a file stated that a staff nurse was blacklisted and denied promotion for dishonesty and insubordination. However, the file didn't reveal any evidence that substantiated these claims.

After my early morning walk along the river, I went to see Dr. Wilson. I smelled the aroma of coffee before I rang his doorbell. Paula Cook, who was wearing a chiffon nightgown, opened the door. She smiled and invited me into the living room before she disappeared into another room.

Moments later Dr. Wilson stepped into the room with Paula, who had slipped a robe over her nightgown. He offered me a cup of coffee and asked what brought me to his house so early in the morning.

I apologized and said that I should have called first. He said "Nonsense!" I could visit him anytime. After I asked him about the file, he promised to discuss the matter with me at the rest house where he planned to spend his last night in Maiduguri. I had a delicious cup of coffee and left.

When I went to see him at the rest house, he told me about the file as we drank scotch together in his suite. He also told me his predecessor had this nurse blackballed many years ago for insubordinate behavior. Dr. Wilson had planned to remove the nurse from the list, but then the nurse refused to carry out Paula's orders. He told me to watch the nurse's behavior and suggested that I should upgrade his file if he changed his attitude toward his work.

Dr. Wilson changed the subject and said that he had his own reason for wanting to see me. He said that he was grateful that I hadn't talked to anyone about our dinner with Rona. He appreciated my discretion. He was quiet for a moment before he discussed Paula, whom he had known for many years. He said that headquarters had promised to promote him to the rank of senior medical officer. When Nigeria gained independence, he and Paula would receive their pensions and their loss-of-career compensation. The two of them planned to get married and they both hoped to secure appointments in the West Indies.

I enjoyed talking with Dr. Wilson. He treated me as his equal. So it was easy to say yes when he asked if I would do him a special favor. He said that Paula was an excellent nurse, but she was unpopular with Nigerians because she was strict and rarely diplomatic. Many important Nigerians had registered complaints against her and wanted her transferred from Maiduguri.

He asked me to look after Paula. She wanted Maiduguri to be her final tour in Nigeria. But if the Director General of Nursing in

Kaduna or his deputy wanted to post her somewhere else, he said I needed to convince Paula to accept the transfer so that she protected her Colonial Service record.

Dr. Wilson sipped his drink before he finally told me that headquarters was watching me. When he asked me about my earlier problems, I recounted my problems in Kano. I said that I thought my troubles were over because the senior officers had discovered that the accusations made against me were false.

Dr. Wilson said I was wrong. My future with the service remained in doubt. Officials in Kaduna didn't want me to be a senior officer in the Colonial Service. They thought I was anti-British. Headquarters had told him to spy on me and submit a confidential report before he left Maiduguri. He handed me a copy of his report and told me to read it.

His account of my service in Maiduguri was completely favorable. But Dr. Wilson said that his report wouldn't end my troubles. He told me not to trust Dr. Sandhurst. He was racist and the Nigerian nursing staff and many Nigerian patients disliked him. Unfortunately, this narrow-minded doctor had connections with influential officers at headquarters. I remained vulnerable because I wasn't confirmed. Dr. Wilson encouraged me to become good friends with the Resident, Mr. Brandon. He was the only British officer in Maiduguri who had enough power to stand up to headquarters.

After Dr. Wilson and I said good night and headed home, I knew that I had to heed his advice. I had to work on my friendship with the Resident and establish strong allies among influential Nigerians in Maiduguri. I expressed my concerns in letters that I wrote to Malam Lawan and my friend the Emir of Zunguru. They both informed me that they already knew that more trouble was brewing for me at headquarters. They were sorry that the Nigerian

Minister of Health had not forced the removal of every complaint against me from my file.

On the day that I discharged my prostatectomy patient, the Vizir was waiting near the ward. He said that my patient was his uncle. He had come to take him home. The Vizir was grateful that I had performed such a difficult surgery on his dear uncle who had cared for him since the death of his father. As they left together, I was happy for them.

One day Dr. Allen, who was in charge of the Health Department, told me that he had been transferred and headquarters wasn't sending a replacement officer. I would assume all his duties. Before he left my office, he said that Dr. Sandhurst was a deep-water fish. I should watch out for him.

Two weeks later I received an official letter from headquarters that confirmed everything I had heard from Dr. Allen. Headquarters claimed that my additional assignment was a result of an unfortunate shortage of doctors in Nigeria. I wasn't happy.

The Health Superintendent, who had two inspectors working for him, promised to handle the fieldwork; but I had to assume responsibility for the department's budget and administration. Since I had a small private practice in Maiduguri, I hoped that I could handle these additional official responsibilities. The increased workload would be intense.

~ 68 ~

SETTLING IN

BEFORE DR. WILSON LEFT MAIDUGURI, I had asked him to examine Rachel. He assured me that she and the baby seemed fine. We had also sent all her medical records to Dr. Clark, who ran the nursing home in Jos, which was a distant hill station, where Rachel would deliver our baby. He notified us that he wanted her to come to Jos a few days before her due date. When we were stationed in Ilorin, we visited Jos. During our brief holiday, we stayed with a local Indian businessman Mr. Vishnuram, and his family. He invited Rachel to stay with them again until she was admitted into the nursing home. He assured me that she would be in good hands.

I wished that I could stay in Jos with Rachel and Sheila during this important time, but my responsibilities in Maiduguri overwhelmed me. Once the two of them were settled in Jos I also knew that we had no reliable long-distance phone service in our remote city. I would not be able to communicate with her doctor. Rachel's delivery date was still weeks away, but already I was worried. I didn't like knowing that once she was in the nursing home I would be kept in the dark most of the time.

Once Dr. Wilson left Maiduguri his friend Paula warmed up to me. She was grateful that I hadn't talked about her relationship with Dr. Wilson to anyone else. She was also impressed with the way that I handled my additional responsibilities. She insisted that everyone in Maiduguri appreciated my work.

Soon I was faced with another prostatectomy when an elderly Nigerian who suffered from urinary retention came to the hospital. I discussed my reservations about repeating this surgery with the Health Councilor at the Native Authority. He reminded me that Muslims believed that their time of departure was always in Allah's hands.

I performed the surgery, and the elderly man went home after a prolonged post-operative recovery. However, I still felt uneasy about doing this operation in our remote hospital.

Days later I had an opportunity to spend some extra time with my family. Sheila was walking and talking, and every smile melted my heart. Rachel had also developed a calm maturity during her second pregnancy. She looked more beautiful than ever. While I regretted that many of their wonderful moments occurred without me, I consoled myself by remembering that my first duty was to provide support for my family. I had to take care of their financial needs.

During the next week, two elderly Nigerian gentlemen from the hinterlands who suffered from prostrate complications came to our hospital. By now I had successfully treated many people in Nigeria who had suffered from urinary obstructions related to chronic gonococci infections. However, these two men suffered from enlarged prostates that caused their urinary obstructions. Usually, this rare condition was untreated due to the patient's advanced age.

He generally died over time from renal failure.

The possible complications from this surgery were so grave that I didn't want to operate on either of the men. But both men refused to let me insert a permanent catheter so that they could go back home. I was forced to admit the men into the hospital and insert temporary catheters that would drain their bladders. My treatment helped one patient, but the other patient required an operation.

Many influential Nigerians, including the Health Councilor, urged me to do the difficult surgery on this man who was a village chief. No one would blame me if he died. His grown-up children, who cultivated the man's large tract of farmland, wanted their father to enjoy the remainder of his life while he also performed his religious duties.

The sons told me that their father's condition kept him from going to Mecca to perform the Hajj, which was the sacred obligation of every Muslim. They thought that Allah was testing his will. If I cured their father, he would get to go to Mecca. If he died from the operation, it was God's will that he would fail to perform his sacred duty.

I could never argue with someone's faith, so I operated.

I took every precaution, but the man didn't survive. I felt terrible and wondered about the wisdom of the surgery. But none of the local Nigerians blamed me. They said that Allah didn't want him to make the pilgrimage. The old man had been a greedy rich farmer.

Fortunately, this sad outcome was quickly followed by many successes that occurred when I fulfilled a final request from Dr. Wilson. Before he left Maiduguri, he had asked me to operate on some patients who risked gangrene from their strangulated hernias. No doctor had ever performed this difficult operation in Maiduguri, but all the patients survived.

I received numerous congratulations from the Vizir and some of the Emir's councilors. Malam Lawan, who was visiting the city, brought me a basket of Indian mangoes from his orchard. He said that the news about my successful operations had reached all the way to Kaduna. Because of the bush telegraph, which was very active during this pre-independence period, he said that I had earned the support of more influential Nigerians. Somehow, I was successfully managing all my official duties in Maiduguri. I was so relieved and pleased. I had never worked so hard during all my time in Nigeria.

~ 69 ~

TROUBLE

ONE NIGHT MR. BRANDON, THE Resident awakened me at three o'clock and asked me to hurry to his house. He greeted me at the door and rushed me into his teenage daughter's room where she lay, unconscious, in her bed.

Mrs. Brandon showed me an empty prescription bottle and said that her daughter had swallowed 20 sleeping pills. After I failed to get the young girl to vomit, I called Paula and told her to hurry over to the Resident's house with an IV set, an oxygen cylinder with a mask, and a lavage set to wash out her stomach.

Once Paula arrived at the house, I started the IV while she emptied the contents of the girl's stomach. Finally, the young girl inhaled a long breath and started to whimper. We stayed until she had recovered enough to cry.

It was morning. I hurried home and dressed for work. On my way to the hospital, I stopped at the Residency to see Mr. Brandon's daughter. She was sleeping and her vital signs were fine. Mrs. Brandon said that their 17-year-old daughter, who had been a good high school student, had just started college in England. She had met a much older boy and had announced her engagement to her parents. But Mrs. Brandon had hated the boy. She had told their daughter that she had to continue her education. She had thought her daughter would forget the boy. She looked forlorn as she said that I had witnessed the outcome.

When I finally left for the hospital, Paula asked me to have a cup of coffee with her. She told me that she had suffered a long time from Mrs. Brandon's unkind gossip. She had wanted to confront the woman, but Dr. Wilson had begged her not to antagonize the Resident. Paula continued to believe that she had the right to defend her name.

I remembered that Dr. Wilson had said that Paula's stubborn streak often led to conflicts with prominent Nigerians, including the Native Authority Health Councilor. I told her that she would suffer if she went after the Resident's wife. I also asked her to keep quiet about the daughter's suicide attempt. It was a private matter involving a young girl.

The next week a Nigerian Deputy Permanent Secretary came to the hospital with his huge entourage to visit his father who was a patient in a ward. He arrived fifteen minutes before the official visiting time, so Paula flew into a rage and ordered all the men from the ward.

The next day the Deputy Permanent Secretary arrived with some food for his father. When Paula shouted at him for once again violating the visiting hours, he complained to me and the Native Authority Health Councilor. The Health Council notified the Vizir who requested a meeting with me to discuss the matron's unacceptable behavior.

Dr. Sandhurst said that the matron's outbursts against Nigerians were always creating trouble for the hospital. He raged against Dr. Wilson who had repeatedly told him to keep quiet about the matron because of their personal relationship. Dr. Sandhurst was tired of keeping quiet. He didn't care if Paula was valuable to the hospital.

When I met with the Native Authority Health Councilor, he said that I had to get Paula transferred. The Nigerian officer whom Paula had offended also wanted me to get rid of her. I told each of them that postings and transfers were beyond my control. But I promised to pass on their complaints to the proper authorities.

Before I contacted my superior officers, I received a letter from headquarters announcing a highly irregular inspection of our hospital and health department that would begin in one week. Hospitals normally receive two weeks' notice. Headquarters said that Dr. Dunn, who was the senior medical officer in a neighboring district, would supervise the inspection. The Director General of Nursing from headquarters would assist the doctor.

I remembered Dr. Dunn from my ship voyage to Nigeria. I didn't look forward to meeting this snooty, unpleasant man again.

This would be the first inspection at the Maiduguri General Hospital in four years. It would be thorough. Paula worked feverishly to get the wards cleaned. My office clerks organized all my files and papers. Just before the inspection team was scheduled to arrive in Maiduguri, Dr. Sandhurst and a British nurse asked for a private meeting with me. They said that they planned to ask the Director General of Nursing to transfer Paula to another station.

After the inspection team arrived at the rest house in Maiduguri, everyone assumed that they would only discipline the Nigerian staff members who had received complaints. We also assumed that the inspection team would sit with the expatriate officers and discuss any work problems.

I followed standard protocol and invited the team along with Paula and Dr. and Mrs. Sandhurst to dinner at our house. No one engaged in controversial discussions during cocktails or around the dining table. Conversations focused on Nigeria's independence and our future plans. When everyone left our house Rachel, and I assumed that our guests had enjoyed the evening.

The next morning Dr. Dunn and the Director General began their inspection, pulled out random office files, and scrutinized their contents. They made ward rounds, checked the laundry room, and examined the kitchen before they went for lunch at the rest house.

When Dr. Dunn and the Director General returned to the hospital, they took over my office so that they could conduct private interviews with the Nigerian clerks and nurses. I noticed that these two officials seemed to single out Southern nurses and clerks. I also thought that their interviews sounded like interrogations.

Some Southern staff members who were in tears came to see me. They thought that they would lose their jobs. They were upset that the powerful Northerners who could fight back with help from their relatives and friends were treated with kid gloves.

The inspection stopped at four o'clock and resumed at eight o'clock the next morning. Again, they took over my office to meet individually with the hospital's two nursing sisters before they interviewed Dr. Sandhurst. I grew uneasy, but I stayed committed to my work and did my rounds in the ward. Finally, Dr. Sandhurst informed me that the inspectors wanted to talk to me.

I said good morning to the inspectors as I sat down in the chair in front of my desk. When Dr. Dunn asked me about my work plans once Nigeria gained independence, I said that everything depended on my future opportunities with the Colonial Service. Dr. Dunn said that unless I was confirmed I would become a contract officer. My service would end with the termination of the colonial government.

Next, Dr. Dunn and the Director General asked my opinions of the Nigerian nurses. They wrote down my answers and added them to their growing stack of paper. They asked me about each expatriate sister and finally questioned me about Paula.

I said that Paula was an excellent nurse and administrative officer, but I admitted that many important Nigerians complained about her inconsiderate behavior. I said that she was neither popular nor well-liked.

When Dr. Dunn asked me to suggest an appropriate remedy, I said that Paula should probably be transferred to another station in Nigeria. Any transfer wouldn't hurt her career. I said that the Native Authority councilor had asked me to convey this request to my superiors, but I had received his request just before I was notified about the hospital inspection, so I had decided to pass on their request in person.

Dr. Dunn turned hostile. He said my answer made no sense. He asked me who came up with the idea to do prostatectomies and other difficult operations at this hospital.

I said that it was my idea.

Dr. Dunn said that the British officers in out-stations were only authorized to repair hernias, remove painful lumps, and treat people for injuries. No one was posted here to show off his surgical skills.

Dr. Dunn said that they would finish the rest of the inspection without me. Before they left my office, they said that they wouldn't meet with me again. They were leaving early in the morning.

The senior clerk came into my office and told me that Dr. Dunn had made appointments to visit the Native Authority Health Councilor and the Vizir later in the afternoon. He said that my absence from these meetings was unusual. I sat at my desk and reviewed this entire episode before I headed home. I was upset, but I decided not to share my thoughts with Rachel. I didn't want to burden her with any unsettling news. She would soon give birth to our second child. I wanted her to remain calm during this important time in our life.

~ 70 ~

BAD NEWS

THE INSPECTORS WERE FINALLY GONE, but I struggled to get back to my work. Dr. Dunn had rattled me. When I saw Paula, she told me that the inspectors said I wasn't giving her enough administrative support. The Health Superintendent told me that Dr. Dunn said that he was doing the work that I was supposed to when I was put in charge of his department. Finally, the Native Authority Health Councilor told me that he wished I had accompanied Dr. Dunn and the Director General of Nursing to the meeting. He and the Vizir told the inspector they thought the matron was a good administrator and teacher, but her behavior offended important people in Maiduguri. They wanted headquarters to transfer her. They also told Dr. Dunn that everyone liked me and hoped that I would remain in Maiduguri for a long time.

I assumed that Dr. Dunn was trying to block my confirmation as a permanent officer. I wished that I could pick up the phone and get advice from a friend in Kano or Kaduna, but the long-distance phone service in Maiduguri was horrible. A clerk knocked on my door and handed me an envelope that had arrived in the mail. A letter from headquarters announced that the Ministry of Health had implemented a series of administrative changes. Dr. Bryon had been appointed to the new position of medical advisor. He would report to the newly designated British Permanent Secretary.

The letter also announced the formation of a committee of Nigerian politicians and British officers that would select the permanent officers who would be invited to join Nigeria's Civil Service after the British transfer of power. The remaining permanent officers and all contract workers would be dismissed from their jobs.

I knew that headquarters would make its decision about my confirmation in two months. I had to become a permanent officer. But the inspection had proved that I had enemies who were determined to end my Colonial Service career. I had to protect myself.

I made an appointment to see the Vizir. I also called Mr. Brandon who agreed to see me right away. As soon as I entered his office the Resident told me that he had just heard that the Premier and the Vizir were going to be knighted by Her Majesty, the Queen. He was certain that one day the Vizir would become the governor of the northern districts. Mr. Brandon brought up the committee that would choose the officers who would work in Nigeria after its independence. He was confident my name would be on this critical list.

When I said to Mr. Brandon that this would only happen if I became a permanent officer, he asked me why I doubted my confirmation. I told him that I realized the inspectors had come to Maiduguri to make trouble for me with the senior officers at headquarters. I asked for his help.

Mr. Brandon said my opinion of the inspection confirmed his strange suspicion. Dr. Dunn and the Director General of Nursing had broken protocol by not seeing him during their inspection. The

Resident promised to help me, and so did the Vizir when I met him the next day. I also wrote to the Emir of Zunguru, Malam Lawan, and a few Nigerian Permanent Secretaries. I asked them all for their help and advice. Each one of them wrote back quickly and promised to assist me.

One morning I received an envelope from the Ministry of Health that was stamped private and confidential. The new medical advisor, Dr. Bryon regretted to inform me that the Ministry of Health had received numerous complaints about my inappropriate work behavior as the medical officer in charge of the district of Maiduguri. Dr. Bryon stated that I had undermined the capable matron of Maiduguri Hospital with false claims that the Native Authority and other Nigerians wanted her transferred.

Dr. Bryon went on to enumerate a list of unnecessary surgeries, such as prostatectomies, that I had recklessly performed at the ill-equipped hospital in Maiduguri. He said that these dangerous procedures, which had resulted in unjustifiable patient deaths, consumed too much of my time and led me to neglect the medical needs of Nigerians who lived in this remote area. Lastly, Dr. Bryon accused me of ignoring my duties at the health department. He cited my rejection of a loan application from the newly appointed Nigerian Health Inspector. He said that my inappropriate decision ultimately kept the inspector from fulfilling his responsibilities.

As a result of all these complaints about me, Dr. Bryon stated that he had submitted the following two recommendations to the Permanent Secretary:

1. Because of my irresponsible behavior, I was unfit to be the medical officer in charge of any large station.

2. I deserved to be severely reprimanded and posted to another station.

The Permanent Secretary had granted me two weeks to respond in writing to these charges. Once he evaluated my written response he intended to interview me in Kaduna. After I met with the Permanent Secretary, I would learn if my unacceptable behavior had jeopardized my Colonial Service career.

I put the awful letter down on my desk. I put my head in my hands and felt my body sink deep into my chair as my mind became freighted with a series of terrifying new fears. I wondered how I could ever fight so many unfair accusations and so many misinterpretations of the facts.

~ 71 ~

DECEPTION

THE TIME HAD COME TO take Rachel and Sheila to Jos where they would stay with the Vishnuram family until she went into labor. Headquarters would only give me permission to stay one night with my family, so Rachel and I saw her doctor at the Jos nursing home right after we arrived. After examining her, Dr. Clark assured us that she and the baby were fine. That next morning, I struggled to say goodbye to Rachel and Sheila.

When I returned home Lawrence handed me a letter. Dr. Dunn informed me that he was posting Dr. Sandhurst to Banuchi for a month to help the doctor who was stationed there. This was laughable. Banuchi was small compared to Maiduguri. Without Dr. Sandhurst, I would be the sole doctor responsible for the entire hospital and the health department.

I was so tired from the day's long journey I had a hot bath and sat down in the drawing room with a glass of Scotch and a plate of groundnuts. I wondered why my goal to become a permanent officer seemed so unattainable. Maybe even Sandhurst was involved in this campaign to destroy me.

I longed to talk to Rachel and hear her comforting voice, but long-distance calls to Jos were impossible. I also wished I could talk to one of my good Nigerian friends in Kano or Kaduna, but they were also beyond my reach. I picked up the phone and called Malam Lawan's residence, but he wasn't in Maiduguri. I called Mr. Brandon and told him that I had taken Rachel to Jos, but I had no way of learning about her condition at this delicate stage of her pregnancy. He promised that he would send messages to Jos from time to time so that I would be informed.

Mr. Brandon also said that he had heard from the Permanent Secretary who had told him that he wouldn't make any decision about the allegations against me until he had interviewed me in Kaduna. The Resident said that this gave us more time to fight their charges.

A few days later I received a telegram from Mr. Vishnuram. Its short message said: "Baby girl born. Other news to follow." I suddenly worried about Rachel, and I raced to Mr. Brandon's office. He sent a radiotelephone message to the Resident stationed in Jos. A short while later, we heard that Rachel had received a transfusion. She had lost a lot of blood.

Dr. Brandon sent a telegram to Dr. Dunn requesting permission for me to go to Jos to see my wife. He denied the request. He wouldn't let me leave Maiduguri until Dr. Sandhurst returned from Banuchi. I was outraged. My wife had suffered, but Dr. Dunn wouldn't let me be with her. The next afternoon I received a telegram from Mr. Vishnuram that said that Rachel was recovering. She and the baby would be fine.

The Vizir heard about Rachel's difficult delivery and came to see me at my house. When I told him that Rachel was getting better, he promised to bring us a ram to honor the birth of our second daughter. The Vizir said that he was going to Kaduna to talk to the Premier. He promised that he wouldn't allow the British officers to discipline me. He was also going to get the Medical Advisor's letter removed from my file.

The ministry "suddenly" found a suitable medical officer who could be posted to Banuchi, so Dr. Sandhurst returned to Maiduguri. I hurried to Jos and stayed for two nights. Dr. Clark told me that Rachel had suffered from precipitate labor and our baby had been born with caul. While he was removing the caul from the baby's head, Rachel started to bleed. She lost so much blood that she needed five units of blood. The donors, who were at the officer's club, were evidently drunk. Rachel, who never touched liquor, fell asleep from the high alcohol content in her blood.

As I looked at Rachel, Sheila, and our new baby Monica, I knew that I was blessed. We thanked the Vishnuram family for their help and left for Maiduguri. When we got back home, Lawrence gave me a letter from the Emir of Zunguru who told me that the Vizir and the Premier were in London where they would be knighted by the Queen. The Emir was certain that they would discuss my problem during their trip.

A few days later Malam Lawan came to visit me. He told me in confidence that the Premier and the Vizir had come up with a plan to help me. They would agree to my transfer from Maiduguri if the British dismissed the charges against me and made me a permanent Colonial Service officer.

A month later I received a letter from headquarters that stated I was officially transferred to the town of Makurdi. The letter told me to hand over all my official duties to Dr. Sandhurst and go to Kaduna for my interview with the Permanent Secretary before I reported to my new post. I wondered if this transfer meant that the Vizir and the Premier had succeeded with their new plan.

But the next day Paula told me that the Director General of Nursing had called her after dinner last evening. He told her that I was going to be transferred because I had mistreated her. The Permanent Secretary was going to interrogate me at headquarters. When Paula told the Director General that she had written a letter to me that stated I had always supported her work, the Director General insisted that her letter was written under duress. He remembered everything that Paula had told him and Dr. Dunn during their inspection in Maiduguri.

Paula's account of this telephone conversation unnerved me. I went to see Mr. Brandon who assured me that he would help me defeat these people. The Vizir also pledged his support and said that the little men at medical headquarters would soon realize that they had to leave me alone. I wrote more letters to my Nigerian friends. I became so involved with my problem and the preparations connected to my transfer that I asked the senior surgical nurse to treat everyone in the hospital's outpatient department.

That evening before I could tell Rachel that we were leaving Maiduguri, she asked me if we had been transferred. I sat down beside her and said that I had just received my new orders. As I finally told her about the new problems that had come to a head after the inspection, I felt Rachel's anxiety course through her.

Three days later I received official notification from the Permanent Secretary that my interview with him would be at the Ministry of Health at 10 A.M. on Wednesday. Before I left Maiduguri with my family, the Vizir told me that Premier Sir Ahmadu Bello wanted to see me in Kaduna. The Vizir handed me a letter that he asked me to give to this important man. When I met the Premier in Kaduna, he read the Vizir's letter and told me not to worry. My problem was now on his shoulders. I was moved with gratitude and thanked him.

Before my appointment with the Permanent Secretary, I had to meet with the Medical Advisor Dr. Bryon, and the Deputy Permanent Secretary. Dr. Bryon said that he had rejected my written responses to his allegations against me because I was essentially claiming that the highly competent medical officers who had accused me were liars. The Medical Advisor said that he had no choice but to recommend severe disciplinary action. The Deputy Permanent Secretary leaned forward and added that I must have hired a lawyer to cook up all this rubbish.

I told him that I didn't have a lawyer. I had done nothing wrong.

When the three of us finally went to the Permanent Secretary's office I noticed that his Nigerian clerk was waiting to take the minutes of the meeting. The Permanent Secretary invited me to make a statement in my defense. After I refuted the charges, I asked the officer to review the letters that I had attached to my written response. I also brought up my conversation with the two British nurses who worked at the hospital. I informed the secretary that these two nurses had told me that they planned to tell the inspectors that they wanted the matron posted to another station. They had said that she repeatedly interfered with their work.

The Permanent Secretary didn't believe me. He said that the two British nurses from Maiduguri were in Kaduna. They had just submitted written dispositions in which they claimed that they never wanted the matron transferred from the hospital. After the Permanent Secretary reminded me that earlier complaints already existed in my file, he announced that he would consider all the accusations. He would make his decision based on the facts. He adjourned the meeting and dismissed me from his office.

~ 72 ~

TRANSFERRED, AGAIN!

AFTER MY DISHEARTENING MEETING, THE Emir of Zunguru called me to the Kaduna government rest house. He was sending a car to bring me to his residence. When I met my friend, he said that the Nigerian Premier and the British Governor had decided to convene a commission of inquiry if Dr. Dunn and the Medical Advisor didn't withdraw their allegations and remove every complaint from my record. The conclusion of their commission would be binding. My spirits brightened as I listened to the Emir. I was so indebted to my Nigerian friends and Mr. Brandon who had considerable sway with the Governor.

The next morning Rachel and I left for Makurdi, which was in a neglected part of Northern Nigeria. After traveling for hours on neglected roads we reached the Makurdi government rest house. The facility lacked filtered water, but we were grateful for the electrical power.

That evening none of the district medical officers came to welcome us, so I finally called the senior medical officer Dr. Goldberg, who said that he would see me late the next day. Next, I called the medical officer who ran the hospital, Dr. McGuire. The Irishman was in no rush to meet me. He said to call him after we were settled.

I went into the bedroom where Rachel was spoon-feeding Monica and giving her a bottle. I felt miserable about my new assignment until I glanced out the window and saw our friend Sandra walking toward the rest house. Once she was sitting with us Sandra asked how I got myself posted in this godforsaken place. She said that Makurdi was considered a "punishment station" for renegades. The floodgates opened up for the three of us. We talked nonstop. Rachel and I were so pleased to see our good friend.

The next afternoon I met Dr. Goldberg who was a middle-aged Jewish refugee who had fled to England before the Second World War. He said that headquarters disliked him, and he had only received his promotion to senior medical officer because of his seniority.Dr. Goldberg said that Dr. McGuire would assign me my duties in the hospital. I needed to understand that I would do more than surgeries.

Once our family moved into our home, I went to the hospital to meet Dr. McGuire. He said it was about time I showed up. The doctor oozed self-importance as he explained that Makurdi was a large hospital with a small staff of doctors. Everyone was equal and pulled his weight. If I also looked forward to a big private practice in this outpost, I should forget about it. Few expatriates lived in Makurdi.

When I started work at the hospital Dr. McGuire assigned me to the outpatient department. He told me that whenever a patient needed surgery, I had to talk to the nursing sister in the operating room to see if she could make space for me in the schedule.

I decided to introduce myself. Nurse Dawson said that she

knew all about me from her good friend Sandra. My spirits lifted. I had possibly met an ally.

Nurse Dawson agreed that Makurdi was a punishment station, but this didn't mean that Makurdi was a fool's station. Many officers had done nothing more than criticize their superiors at headquarters for implementing some stupid new rule.

One day a Nigerian employee in the hospital told me that he had heard about me from friends who had worked with me in other Nigerian cities. He said that the people who lived in this area were fortunate that I worked here. By the third week, more surgical patients began to come to the outpatient department. I was so overwhelmed with work that I couldn't perform all my scheduled surgeries.

One morning I realized that the Nigerian senior surgical nurse was caring for people in the outpatient department while I was busy in the operating room. He said that Nurse Dawson had permitted him to treat patients without me. Because of his fine skills, I realized that I could safely devote almost two full days each week to surgeries.

One day I received a letter from Malam Lawan who thought that I would appreciate reading the detailed notes of meetings that the Permanent Secretary had held after his interrogation with me. He described a meeting where the chief secretaries of the Premier and the Governor had warned the Permanent Secretary that they would initiate a commission of inquiry against him if he didn't drop the allegations against Dr. Ray.

The clerk wrote that the Permanent Secretary quickly met with the Medical Advisor and the Deputy Permanent Secretary and told them to summon Dr. Dunn to the Ministry of Health. When Dr. Dunn arrived in Kaduna, the Permanent Secretary told the doctor about the ultimatum offered by the Premier and the Governor.

The clerk wrote that Dr. Dunn announced that he would resign from the service before he would stand in front of any Nigerian commission. He said that the British government was transferring power to a bunch of ignorant Nigerians and their megalomaniacal Premier. He wondered aloud how the Nigerian Premier could support an Indian doctor against the words of responsible senior British officers. Their foolish demand, which would harm him personally, would also hurt the Nigerians because every British doctor would leave the country.

The Nigerian clerk informed Malam Lawan that the Medical Advisor suddenly noticed that the clerk was furiously transcribing notes. He asked the clerk what he was doing. The clerk wrote that he told the advisor that he was doing his job. He was taking notes so that he could correctly transcribe the proceedings of the meeting. The Premier received the clerk's transcript of the meeting with Dr. Dunn one hour after the British officers left the Permanent Secretary's office. The Executive Council of Ministers immediately accepted the doctor's resignation.

Malam Lawan also told me that by the time people in Kaduna were buzzing with the news that Dr. Dunn was no longer a permanent officer, the Permanent Secretary had registered his displeasure with the Governor. The Governor reminded the Permanent Secretary that the provincial government was autonomous. The decision of the Executive Council prevailed. He told him that Dr. Dunn and the Director General of Nursing had mishandled this unfortunate episode. They were foolish to ignore the British Resident in Maiduguri and the Native Authority officials who supported me.

Malam Lawan said that the Nigerians had taught the British officers a good lesson. He hoped that I was pleased with the outcome. I was more than pleased. I had tasted some sweet revenge.

~ 73 ~

MORE SHENANIGANS

LATER IN THE WEEK LOUD knocking on our front door woke us up. The Resident of Makurdi and his wife were frantic. His brother had been drinking at the Makurdi Expatriates Club when he suddenly grabbed his stomach and fell to the floor. A doctor at the hospital thought that the Resident's brother had a perforated gastric ulcer. He acknowledged that his brother had a history of ulcers.

Makurdi was so far from Kano that I knew that the brother would need to undergo a life-threatening daylong journey in a Land Rover. The doctors at the hospital who knew that I was a successful surgeon wanted me to operate on him. I asked the Resident to get Dr. Goldberg and Dr. McGuire to authorize the operation. When I received the authorization, I hurried to the hospital, examined the brother, and agreed that the earlier diagnosis was correct.

When I had operated on the young Colonial Service officer in Gusau who had also suffered from a perforated peptic ulcer, his successful recovery had helped establish my reputation during my first Northern Nigeria tour. Maybe the brother was another good omen for me.

The operation was successful, but the Resident's brother also suffered from a respiratory infection that prolonged his recovery. After a few days, he finally went home. Once again, this difficult operation had worked in my favor. The doctors at the hospital stopped grumbling about me and yet more surgical patients came to see me in the outpatient department.

Just when Rachel and I assumed that our social life in Makurdi would be limited to get-togethers with Sandra, we received our first formal invitation. The Resident invited us to dinner where he introduced me to his other guests as the doctor who had saved his brother. Several of the people who met Rachel and me that evening sent us invitations to their own dinner parties. Rachel and I suddenly had an active social life in Makurdi.

One day Dr. Goldberg called me at the hospital and asked me to come to his office. He asked me to sit down before he handed me an envelope with a letter from the Permanent Secretary. It stated that the officer had completed the investigation initiated by Dr. Dunn and Dr. Bryon. The Permanent Secretary was pleased to inform me that the Ministry of Health had withdrawn all the complaints against me. They were unproven and unsubstantiated.

Dr. Goldberg said that I must have angels working for me. In his twenty years of service, he had never seen headquarters back down. He added that the Medical Advisor had actually called him before I had arrived in Makurdi to say that he should watch out for me. I was a troublemaker. The advisor had also told him that I was under investigation and that I would probably face disciplinary action.

When he asked me about my ordeal, I described Dr. Dunn's unfair accusations that had led to the investigation conducted by the senior officers at headquarters. I also told him about the help that I had received from Maiduguri's British Resident and the Emir's Vizir. Dr. Goldberg was convinced that the Vizir Sir Ali Ibrahim would soon become the governor of Northern Nigeria. As he talked about this important Nigerian, I sensed that he was changing his opinion of me. Dr. Goldberg seemed to be offering me his respect.

Before I left Dr. Goldberg, he said that my victory had to rankle the Medical Advisor and the Permanent Secretary. Since they probably considered me a greenhorn, he thought that they would try again to block my confirmation.

I went home and showed Rachel the letter of vindication from the Permanent Secretary. We decided to celebrate my victory. We sent Lawrence to get us a nice fish from the market and invited Sandra to join us for dinner. We had such a lovely evening together, and on this happy night, we let Sheila stay up late while her favorite friend Sandra was visiting us.

Dr. Goldberg, who was single, rarely received invitations to dinner parties in Makurdi, but we always invited him to our parties. He also frequently joined Sandra, Rachel, and me for an informal dinner at our house. Rachel and I discovered that the three of us had many things in common, including mutually favorite haunts in London.

One evening when Dr. Goldberg came to our house, he said that the Colonial Service official gazette reported that Dr. Dunn had resigned and gone home. When he asked me if I knew what led to the resignation, I reminded him that Dr. Dunn had helped engineer the false complaints against me. Dr. Goldberg said that he felt bad for Dr. Dunn even though he had never liked the doctor. He had forfeited a lot of money by resigning from the service.

~ ~ ~ ~ ~

I enjoyed my work in the Makurdi Hospital since I often had the opportunity to operate on interesting surgical cases. I also enjoyed our happy family life. I was able to spend time with Rachel and our two wonderful girls. We were also comfortable with our servants Lawrence and Audu.

But one day Lawrence, who was a Christian Ibo from this area, called Audu, who was a Muslim from the north, a foreigner. Audu abruptly packed and left us for his part of Northern Nigeria. Lawrence seized this opportunity to introduce us to a nice young Ibo named Simon who spoke good English. Simon showed us testimonials from his previous masters that said he was honest, well-behaved, intelligent, and industrious. Lawrence vouched for this glowing praise and said that Simon was an excellent steward. Once we hired Simon, we discovered that he immediately understood everything we asked him to do for us. He was also very good with Sheila and Monica.

One afternoon Sandra unexpectedly arrived at our house while I was having lunch with Rachel. Sandra looked exhausted. She asked me for a Scotch. Sandra was furious, but she needed to settle down before she could explain that she had just received official notification from the senior officers at the Ministry of Health that they had decided not to renew her contract. The senior officers didn't offer Sandra any job in any other colony.

Sandra was devastated. She liked working in Nigeria and the Nigerians liked her. She only had trouble with British officers, especially the senior officers at headquarters. Sandra had wanted to complete two more tours in Nigeria. She asked me if I could help her.

I promised Sandra that I would talk to Dr. Goldberg in the morning. I also said that she could probably get a job with the Northern Nigerian government, but she would lose her Colonial Service benefits and her protection as a British employee.

When I met with Dr. Goldberg, he was sympathetic to Sandra's situation. But he said that headquarters didn't like him, so any help from him would backfire. He thought that Sandra should resubmit her application and ask the senior officers to reconsider their decision because she wouldn't be able to find a job at her age if she went back home. She would face serious financial hardship.

While I sat with Dr. Goldberg, I asked him if he had heard anything about my confirmation. He hadn't heard any bad news, so he figured my file was slowly moving from desk to desk up the bureaucratic chain. He assumed that I would eventually be confirmed. But I wasn't so sure.

I also talked with Dr. McGuire about Sandra. He said that he and the health superintendent considered Sandra to be an invaluable asset in Makurdi. The doctor promised to write a favorable letter about her and ask headquarters to extend her contract. There was nothing else he could do for her.

Around this time, I received a letter from Saha who said that the London recruitment officer at the Colonial Service had interviewed him. He thought that the office would accept him. I was happy for Saha. If he became a member of the service, he could practice medicine and finally earn a decent income. Rachel agreed with me, but she was afraid that if Saha came to Nigeria, he would become dependent on me. She had grounds to worry. But I still hoped the best for my friend.

~ ~ ~ ~ ~

Two weeks passed. I still hadn't heard anything about my confirmation. I tried to reassure myself by thinking headquarters would have notified me if my confirmation had run into trouble. That next Sunday Dr. Goldberg called to tell me that he wasn't feeling well. He would be unable to join us for dinner.

I decided to go see him. As his steward ushered me into his front room, I noticed Dr. Goldberg rushing up the stairs to his second floor. I followed him up to his bedroom. He told me that he was running a fever, but he would be better in a couple of days. His behavior puzzled me. Something else was going on. That evening Lawrence told me that his friend who was Dr. Goldberg's steward said that his master wasn't sick.

When I went to work on Monday, Dr. Goldberg asked me to come see him in his office. He handed me a letter from the Medical Advisor that he had received on Friday. The Medical Advisor informed me that my confirmation had been delayed because of a new complaint from the divisional manager of an important British mercantile company. I read the complaint, which was attached to the letter.

The divisional manager Gordon Long stated that a medical officer had sent repeated bills for services tendered to an employee to his district manager of UAC in Makurdi. Mr. Long wondered if the medical authorities had changed its policy because normally the company never paid for the treatment of any Nigerian employee. He enclosed a copy of the bill, which I had signed for medical services on behalf of David Inwenu.

I told Dr. Goldberg that I remembered Mr. Inwenu. When I first arrived in Makuri the district manager of UAC had asked me to treat this employee and send him the bill. After I originally examined him at the hospital, I told him to return the next day when

I would receive his lab reports. I didn't send a bill to Mr. Inwenu's employer for this hospital visit.

But that evening when I was at home, Simon informed me that a man named David Inwenu had come to see me. He was feeling bad and needed his prescription. He handed me a letter from his manager that said that UAC would pay for the visit. I was annoyed. But rather than argue with Mr. Inwenu, I decided to teach him a lesson. I sent a bill for this visit to my home to his company. I figured his company manager would ask his employee why he had come to my house for treatment.

Dr. Goldberg said some people were trying to entrap me. He promised to meet with Mr. Inwenu and the district manager of UAC. After his inquiry, he would send his report to headquarters.

When I went home that evening, I asked Simon if he knew David Inwenu. He said that he often spent holidays with him. I asked Simon to bring the young man to the house so that I could ask him a few questions. When Simon returned with Inwenu, the employee acknowledged that he remembered coming to see me at my house. I asked him if he was aware that he wasn't supposed to seek treatment at my home. He said his district manager, Mr. Armstrong had told him that the company would pay for his medical treatment, so he had come to see me.

Simon was our witness when Inwenu said that he would give these same answers to anyone else who posed these questions. But I still worried. I had done nothing wrong, but I needed Dr. Goldberg's inquiry to reach the same conclusion. I waited a week before Dr. Goldberg finally advised me that he had scheduled a meeting with the local district manager Mr. Armstrong and the divisional manager Gordon Long on Saturday. He asked me to wait in the hall outside his office that morning in case he needed me to testify.

I arrived early Saturday morning and waited in the corridor while Dr. Goldberg waited in his office with his chief clerk. An hour passed before the UAC district manager Mr. Armstrong finally appeared. He greeted me and entered Dr. Goldberg's office. A few minutes later he reappeared with Dr. Goldberg. Mr. Armstrong said that he was sorry that someone had made a mountain out of a molehill. He volunteered that he had recently learned that his employee David Inwenu had come to my house for treatment. He said that he gave Dr. Goldberg a detailed account that would resolve this unfortunate incident.

When I asked Mr. Armstrong why he had asked me repeatedly to send him a bill for Mr. Inwenu's medical treatment, the manager insisted I had received these requests from a clerk. They meant nothing. As Mr. Armstrong excused himself and hurried down the hall, I knew that he had personally signed each request for a bill. Something strange was going on.

Dr. Goldberg told me that once he completed his inquiry, he wanted me to hand deliver it to the Permanent Secretary and the Medical Advisor in Kaduna. He also wanted to allow me to defend myself against this latest unjustified attempt to block my confirmation.

When I told Rachel about the meeting, she was relieved that the UAC district manager had apologized and had submitted an honest account of the incident to Dr. Goldberg. But Rachel wondered whether my troubles would ever end. She was convinced these officers would come after me again. She didn't think they would ever give up.

~ 74 ~

CONFIRMATION

MONDAY AFTERNOON DR. GOLDBERG FINISHED writing up his inquiry in which he concluded that the new allegations against me were unwarranted. He contacted the Medical Advisor and told him that I would hand deliver the report and address the incident and its effect on my confirmation. When I went to his office, he handed me two sealed envelopes. One envelope contained his report; the other contained Mr. Armstrong's letter that absolved me of any wrongdoing involving the Nigerian employee Mr. Inwenu.

By the end of the next day, I arrived at the Kaduna government rest house. I called Malam Lawan and told him about this latest attempt to block my confirmation. He said that he would ask the clerks who worked in the Ministry of Health if they had read or overheard anything about the UAC allegation. He told me to call him after my meeting.

The next morning when I went to headquarters, I discovered that the Deputy Permanent Secretary was attending my meeting with the Medical Advisor. Dr. Bryon didn't conceal his displeasure for me when he accused me of charging the UAC employee who sought treatment at the hospital. When I told him that I never charged any Nigerian patient I treated at the hospital Dr. Bryon glared at me. He said that I had sent bills that I had personally signed to the UAC district manager. These bills proved the allegation against me.

I told him that I had brought him Dr. Goldberg's report which proved my innocence.

Dr. Bryon skimmed through the report and told me that Goldberg's assessment was worthless. He believed the UAC managers. I handed him the second envelope. The Medical Advisor withered as he read Mr. Armstrong's retraction. He said that it didn't matter if the company made a mistake. He still had to conduct his investigation.

After the Medical Advisor asked the Deputy Permanent Secretary to take the letters to the Permanent Secretary, I asked Dr. Bryon why he had taken action against me before he had even determined the merits of the complaint. He said that the ministry had merely delayed my confirmation. He insisted that headquarters would give me my signed confirmation papers before the end of the day. Dr. Bryon asked me to go with him to the Permanent Secretary's office.

The Permanent Secretary shook my hand and congratulated me for my confirmation. He told me that I could look forward to moving back to Kano. The medical school needed me to teach the students. I would also perform surgeries at the City Hospital.

I told the Permanent Secretary that I would be unhappy in Kano if I was appointed as the second surgeon under Dr. Baddock. I wanted my own surgical ward and operation time. The Permanent Secretary said that the ministry could honor my request.

The Deputy Permanent Secretary came into the office with

copies of my signed confirmation papers. After the Permanent Secretary handed me a copy for my records, I I said goodbye to him. As I started to leave the office, Dr. Bryon said that he would send the terms of my transfer to Kano and Makurdi.

I was overjoyed and exhausted when I finally left the building. I had defeated these superior powers who were so determined to destroy me. I was grateful to so many important people who had helped me in my long fight. In this particular skirmish, Dr. Goldberg and Mr. Inwenu had proven that they were honorable men. They had spoken the truth on my behalf.

I walked to my car and drove back to the government rest house where I repeatedly read the copy of my confirmation. I still struggled to believe that my battles had ended. I was finally a Colonial Service permanent officer.

When I called Rachel, I felt her relief and happiness in each of her words to me. We had survived a horrible ordeal. A short time after I left a brief message for Malam Lawan, I was thrilled to see him standing at the door to my room. I told him about my meetings with the Medical Advisor and Permanent Secretary as we enjoyed a pot of tea and biscuits. He relished every detail.

Malam Lawan said that a Nigerian clerk had informed him that the Medical Advisor and the District Manager of UAC Mr. Gordon Long were friends. They often spent time together at the Kaduna Club with their disgraced friend Dr. Dunn before he resigned and went back to England. The clerk reported that Dr. Bryon and Mr. Long had several phone conversations before Dr. Goldberg began his investigation of the UAC allegation. Malam Lawan didn't have definitive proof of a conspiracy, but we both assumed that when Dunn resigned Dr. Bryon decided to go after me with the help of Gordon Long.

I thanked my friend Malam Lawan for all his help and his trust in me. After he left me that evening I felt like rejoicing. I was a permanent officer. I dearly hoped that Rachel and I could look forward to a healthy and happy future in Nigeria.

~ 75 ~

BACK IN KANO

I RECEIVED THE OFFICIAL ORDER for my transfer to Kano two weeks after I returned to Makurdi. While the future seemed so promising for my family and me, Rachel and I worried about Sandra. We were fond of her and our children loved her. When I spoke again with Dr. Goldberg about Sandra's termination, he said we could never change the minds of the powerful officers at headquarters. Sandra told us she had rejected the sexual advances of an important officer in Kaduna. She was the victim of his revenge. He had made certain that her contract wasn't renewed.

I realized that Anglo-Saxons might have an advantage in the Colonial Service compared with non-British employees, but this advantage didn't protect Sandra. Personal loyalty and personal animosity were powerful forces that determined many careers. The British also had every right to terminate its relationship with Sandra. She had no legal recourse. She was on contract; she wasn't an employee.

When our family left Makurdi we stopped in Kaduna so that I

could visit the Nigerian officer that I knew in the Ministry of Health. I hoped to look at Sandra's file. He obliged me and I soon discovered that the Permanent Secretary had rejected the petition that several officers in Makuri had signed on Sandra's behalf. He had instructed the department to proceed with Miss Jones' termination. I left the Ministry of Health with a heavy heart.

We continued to Kano and arrived at the government rest house that evening. The next morning, I went to City Hospital and was pleased to see that the Permanent Secretary had kept his word. He had given me my own surgical ward and he had authorized my exclusive use of the operating room two days a week. But the attitude of many of the British doctors hadn't changed. They continued to clam up around me. Only the Wakelin seemed genuinely happy to see me back in Kano.

When I went to the medical school Dr. Hinds asked me why Dr. Dunn had quit the service and abruptly returned to England. Dr. Hinds couldn't imagine why any doctor would willingly forfeit so much money. When I didn't provide Dr. Hinds with any answer, he said that no one would talk about the doctor's departure.

The students gave me a rousing welcome when I arrived to deliver my first lecture. I loved the school, but I knew that it was shortlived. Nigeria was building a new university that would include a medical school in Zaria. The officials at the Ministry of Health were no longer accepting new students for the Kano Medical School. The government planned to demolish the building after the current batch of students successfully completed all their courses.

I worked hard to prepare my students for their preclinical exam. They would sit for their exam in a month and external examiners from the London University and Nigeria's University of Ibadan would determine the results. I delivered comprehensive lectures and held several tutorials to increase their knowledge. I wanted them all to succeed.

I became so busy at the City Hospital that I reduced my lunch hour to fifteen minutes so that I could care for two or three additional patients. Once I finished my official hospital duties I rushed to my private practice where I treated more patients. I also agreed to give free medical treatment to some wealthy Northern Nigerians and officials from the Native Authority. I needed their goodwill. All my work made me feel guilty because I spent so little time with Rachel and young Sheila and Monica. I had no choice but to accept that all this hard work was the price I had to pay to secure my family's financial future.

While I was working at City Hospital, every Colonial Service permanent officer received an official form from the Ministry of Health that asked each of us to indicate our preferred employment status once the British transferred power to the Nigerians. I hoped that the Nigerian government would include me on their Select List B. The permanent officers selected for this preferential list would receive their current salary and all current Colonial Service perks and privileges.

I was nervous after I submitted my application, but the senior medical officer Dr. Taylor assured me that the Nigerian government had already put me on its special list. But after enduring so many attempts to stop my career in Nigeria I feared that someone would find an obscure reason to exclude me. The atmosphere in the doctors' lounge was fraught with anxiety. Every doctor worried about his career prospects once Nigerians took over the government.

After a month of anxiety, the Nigerian government chose only a handful of doctors for its Special List B. I was lucky. My name was on the list. But Dr. Maruti was not so fortunate. I advised him to go ask Dr. Taylor to get him on the Nigerian government's second list of doctors who would be protected by the British government but paid by the Nigerian Ministry of Health. A few days later Dr. Maruti was smiling when he said that Dr. Taylor had honored his request. He was so relieved. He would get to stay in Nigeria under more reasonable terms.

~ 76 ~

COOKS

WHILE SIMON WORKED HARD AND became an excellent steward, Lawrence turned lazy. He showed no interest in learning to cook simple Indian food for us. He preferred to brag about his training in the Catholic Mission kitchen where he said that he had learned to cook every recipe in the cookbook. But few of his dishes were tasty and few of them appealed to our eyes.

Lawrence cared for a wife and three children, so he often pilfered money from us when he shopped in the market. He also stole provisions from our pantry. Finally, Rachel and I lost our patience with him. I asked Simon if he would be upset if Lawrence left our house. When Simon said that he didn't care I seized the opportunity. I asked him if he would like to learn how to cook. Simon loved the idea, but I told him not to discuss our conversation with anyone.

The next morning, I treated a Christian engineer from the Ministry of Works who told me that he had recently met our cook. Lawrence had told the engineer that he found it difficult to serve in a non-Christian home. I told the engineer that he would do us a favor if he hired our cook. My non-Christian compassion had prevented me from sacking Lawrence.

Late that afternoon when I came home unexpectedly Lawrence was leaving the pantry with a big bowl of powdered milk. He told me that he was borrowing the milk for his son. He promised to replace it. I knew that Rachel would be furious. Our pasteurized milk was precious. We paid dearly for each imported tin of powdered milk, which she reserved for Sheila and Monica. I gave Lawrence three weeks' severance pay and told him to leave. He left with his family the next morning. Hours later we hired an Ibo steward named Musa and Simon became our cook. Simon quickly mastered several European and Indian dishes. Rachel and I finally enjoyed eating our dinners, and at last, our entire staff, including the gardener, got along.

My medical students finally took their pre-clinical examina-tion. After the Kano newspapers reported that all my students had passed the test, the Minister of Health expressed his gratitude to me for the fine quality of my teaching. Some British doctors, however, claimed that the Nigerian students were unfit to become doctors. When a doctor asked me if I felt guilty for letting all my students pass their exams, I told him to pose his question to the external examiners from the University of Ibadan and the London University. They determined the results.

One day when the Emir's driver was showing Rachel and me some of Kano's countryside he pointed to a nearby stream and said that it turned into a mighty river after heavy rains. He said that the surrounding farmers used the river water to irrigate their vegeta-bles and cotton fields. As we continued our drive the land beyond the stream quickly turned dry and sandy until the topography resembled a desert. While I studied the unproductive land, I told the driver that the forestry department was planting hundreds of neem trees to create a green barrier against the advancing desert.

The driver said that the village elders didn't like those foreign trees. They insisted the neem trees would damage their local flora and fauna. They also believed that they could cause huge fires that would wipe out entire villages, so the forest department wasn't allowed to plant their foreign trees near any villages.

On this afternoon we were driving through land that was such a contrast to the lush rainforest that thrived south of Kano. Farmers in that part of Nigeria cultivated tropical fruit and vegetables and established productive rice paddies. I remembered my discussions of Northern Nigeria's water problem with officers in the Department of Agriculture. The officers were confident that the villagers who lived in this part of Nigeria could easily reduce their dependence on imported food from the south by implementing low-cost water conversation projects that would increase their agricultural production. I hoped such projects would become a reality.

The driver announced that he wanted to take us to meet an elderly village chief who had watched the nineteenth-century British soldier Lord Lugard enter Kano after his military victory. The driver stopped at a gate that led into a walled-in compound and informed two tall guards that I was a friend of the Emir of Zunguru. I had come to visit their chief.

As we entered the compound an elderly man sitting on a hand-woven spread welcomed us. I told him our driver had said that he had watched Lord Lugard enter Kano. I wanted to know about his impressions of the British. The elderly chief said that Lugard and his men had marched past his house after he defeated the Emir in 1903. His men had killed his father who was a commander in the Emir's army.

The chief insisted that Lugard had come to Nigeria to put an end to the slave trade. But Lugard had also taken away everyone's slaves and freed them. The elderly man said that this foolish decision nearly cost him all his cattle because he and his brothers needed their slaves to care for the livestock and cultivate their land. Their land was left fallow for years. The chief said that the freed slaves had fared no better. When they couldn't find work many of them became thieves. So Lugard who was appointed governor of the Nigerian colony had harmed his country.

The elderly chief popped a mildly narcotic red cola nut into his mouth and began to chew it before he started discussing Nigeria's upcoming independence, which would occur on the first of October. The chief still didn't understand why the British even bothered to take control of Nigeria. His country wasn't rich like South Africa. He said that they were finally leaving Nigeria because they didn't find diamonds or much gold. The Nigerian chiefs were the losers in this fiasco. They had lost their slaves and most of their cattle.

After we said goodbye to the elderly chief and started back to Kano I thought about the British presence in Nigeria. The British knew that they couldn't change the land's harsh climate, so they tried to improve the living conditions of the Nigerian people by constructing roads, schools, and hospitals. They wanted to create a middle class that wasn't dependent on the country's semi-feudal system. I believe this was the British objective in Nigeria.

Unfortunately, the landed aristocratic families that Lugard had defeated at the end of the 19th century still controlled the power. Some of these aristocrats understood the principles of democracy, but I doubted they believed that an elected government should be accountable to its constituents.

I worried that this colonial experiment would only leave behind the scars of occupation. Historically, the British were particularly adept at exacerbating ethnic and religious divisions that existed within each of its colonies. But I hoped that the British officers and missionaries who ran Nigeria's educational institutions had successfully planted the seeds of individualism and self-respect. But these seeds needed to multiply to form an irresistible social democratic force across the country that would lead to profound changes in this society. Nigeria would either go through a silent revolution or it would experience a bloody insurrection.

I remembered something that the Emir of Kano told me when he officially opened a new secondary school in Kano. He said that Nigerians hoped that this modern school, which was constructed with the assistance of British voluntary organizations, would become a model institute of learning. The Emir understood that the students who attended the school would ultimately cause the downfall of his Emirate. But he was enlightened: he believed that it was his duty as the Emir to educate his people.

~ 77 ~

NIGERIA'S INDEPENDENCE

ONE DAY DR. WILSON CALLED ME. I was so happy to hear that he had returned to Nigeria for his final tour. When he came to our house to have dinner with Rachel and me, he told us that he had secured a future job in the West Indies. He had hoped to have a senior post in Kaduna, but headquarters wanted him to go back to Maiduguri. He had to sort out a new mess.

My old friend explained that Native Authority officials and some local Nigerians had trouble with Dr. Sandhurst after I left Maiduguri. Headquarters agreed to transfer the man, but the senior officers thought that the complaint against Sandhurst was politically motivated. They believed that Sandhurst deserved a promotion because he helped Dr. Dunn go after me. They put him in charge of the Kaduna nursing home. Dr. Wilson said that he should have received this post, but headquarters wanted him back in his old job. After I described my protracted battle with Dr. Dunn I assured Dr. Wilson that he wouldn't have any trouble in Maiduguri. Everyone liked him.

A few days later I picked up Saha and Joya at the Kano airport. They spent a couple of days with us and purchased a Peugeot before they drove to his first posting in a remote Northern Nigerian town. Saha and Joya were full of hope about their new life in Nigeria.

A few days later, Rachel and I received an official invitation to have lunch with the British Governor at the Governor's House in Kaduna. When we sat down with his four other guests, we were all so reserved that we hardly spoke to each other as we ate our meal. I only remember His Excellency saying that he hoped for fine weather on Independence Day on October first. Later, when I asked Rachel if she had enjoyed the luncheon, she said that she wasn't impressed by the Governor's House or by the company at the table; but she appreciated the Governor's Indian chef. He had made a delicious chicken biryani.

After officials at City Hospital increased the number of surgeons at our hospital, I realized that our operating room was severely inadequate for our needs. During our next monthly staff meeting, I mentioned that the hospital needed to improve its operating room.

Dr. Clinton said that the Native Authority was responsible for building maintenance. He advised me to ask my friend the Emir of Kano to update the space or build us a new operating room. He assured me that our Public Works Department would offer technical advice, and our engineers would supervise the renovation or construction.

A few days later I laid out Dr. Clinton's proposal to the Emir and the Wakelin. After I convinced them that a good operating room was essential for my work, the Wakelin offered to renovate the existing facility. But he wouldn't authorize any other improvements at the hospital. The Native Authority lacked the funds.

A few weeks before Nigeria's Independence I received a formal invitation from the Office of the Nigerian Premier requesting my presence at the official ceremony in Kaduna's new sports stadium. Rachel and I were allocated two preferred seats in this stadium that was named for Premier Ahmadu Bello. Malam Lawan secured us a special room in Kaduna's new hotel that was opening in time for Nigeria's great day. Dr. Taylor was annoyed that I was the only foreign doctor in Kano invited to this historic event. But he gave me three day's leave from the hospital.

While the ceremony marking the transfer of power occurred in the federal capital of Lagos, the most glorious celebration occurred inside the Abmadu Bello Stadium. Balloons floated in the air, flags fluttered around us, and cannons boomed when Premier Sir Ahmadu Bello and the new Governor Sir Ali Ibrahim entered the arena.

As soldiers held their guns in parade position and police officers marched at attention, I wondered if all these armed soldiers and police were loyal to the new government. A few traitors could wipe out the new rulers gathered in this stadium and wrest control of the country.

The Governor and the Premier saluted. Nigerian students of all ages and Nigerian performers who represented the country's diverse cultures sang and danced. The Nigerians crowded into the stadium had never witnessed such a public display of their wonderful art and culture.

After Rachel and I left the stadium, we went to Malam Lawan's government party. He provided a delicious buffet of lamb, beef, and chicken roasts and stews and a wide array of beautiful vegetables that we enjoyed while we chatted with Nigerian friends and acquaintances. They were all upbeat as they discussed Nigeria's glorious future, which was made more exciting by the recent discovery of a vast amount of oil and gas in the eastern part of the country. While everyone seemed certain that Nigeria would remain a united country, I wasn't so sure. But today was the time to celebrate.

The next morning, I met with the Emir of Zunguru at his residence before Rachel and I returned to Kano. During our long talk, I asked my friend about the prospects of political fallout because of the oil and gas that was discovered in Ibo territory. The Emir said that he and his colleagues knew that the Ibos might try to separate from the rest of Nigeria and form their own country. But he insisted that the oil belonged to several tribes, not just the Ibos. While the Ibos would probably try to subjugate these tribes, the federal government could introduce countermeasures to stop them. I hoped that my friend's assessment and vision of a united Nigeria would hold true. I wanted the best for him and his newly free country.

~ 78 ~

VACATION

AS COLONIAL SERVICE OFFICERS STARTED to leave the country Nigerians filled some vacancies, but the Ministry of Health needed fresh recruitments from abroad. The Public Service Commissioner Alhaji Abdullah visited me several times to discuss foreign recruits. While he was willing to recruit non-Muslim foreigners, he said that he would have a difficult time convincing some of his colleagues that secular-based recruitment would benefit their country. Currently, they planned to send government recruiters to interview candidates in Egypt, Pakistan, India, and the United Kingdom.

As I listened to my thoughtful friend discuss the recruiters' mission, I sensed the hope that ran through him. Alhaji Abdullah was looking forward to a bright future in newly independent Nigeria.

Before our family left for home leave, we decided to take a brief trip to Lake Chad, which was on the border of the three French territories of Niger, Cameroon, and Chad and close to Maiduguri. We were in the midst of the month-long religious holiday of Ramadan, so Dr. Taylor and the officials in Kaduna approved our four-day trip.

The Wakelin provided us with a chauffeur who knew Lake Chad and spoke good English. When we reached Maiduguri, we had a lovely evening with Dr. Wilson and Paula Cook. They were looking forward to getting married in London and moving to the West Indies to begin their new life together. Dr. Wilson said that Dr. Sandhurst was leaving Nigeria in three months at the end of his tour. He had misdiagnosed a case at the Kaduna Nursing Home that involved a young British boy.

Dr. Wilson said that Dr. Sandhurst, who didn't think the child who had a headache and fever, was very sick. He told the parents to give him aspirin and bring him back to the nursing home if his condition didn't improve in two days. When the young boy failed to respond in the morning his parents rushed him to the nursing home. The boy died without regaining consciousness.

The grief-stricken parents were furious after a blood smear identified malaria parasites. They sued Dr. Sandhurst and the nursing home for negligence. Sandhurst and the parents eventually settled the suit, but Dr. Wilson assumed that the doctor had agreed to give them most of his Colonial Service compensation. He wished that he had been in charge of that nursing home. He could have prevented the young boy's death.

The next morning our family traveled to the southern end of Lake Chad. We stood near the marshy, flat shoreline, which was covered with papyrus reeds, and stared into water that extended to the horizon. Water lilies and flowering water hyacinths floated on the surface. It was a pretty sight.

After Rachel and I played with Sheila and Monica on the shoreline, we took a boat ride around part of the lake. We watched fishermen as they hauled their catch into their boats and cattlemen who grazed their herds along the fertile shoreline with its green grass and bushes that grew in the swampy soil. The boatman pointed into the distance where we just barely saw the outlines of tall sand dunes on the northern shoreline. Our open boat didn't offer us any shelter from the hot sun, so we returned early to our car. We returned to Kano happy but tired.

A week later we sailed to Liverpool, where we took the train to London. Jacob, who had recently married his German girlfriend, Hilda, met us at the railroad station and drove us to his new two-story house. They made us feel welcome in their home. Sometimes Rachel and I cooked dinner for everyone; other times we went out to eat because Hilda wasn't fond of cooking.

Rachel and I frequently visited Central London to explore our favorite sites, and I visited the hospitals where I had once worked, but I felt anonymous. Most of the doctors and nurses that I knew had moved on. I called Sir John, who had finally retired. He invited me to have dinner with him and his wife at their house, but he told me not to come alone. He really wanted to see Rachel. As the four of us reminisced on his verandah, I loved watching the evening's light and shadows flickering on the Thames River. Sir John's maid served us a lovely dinner and we stayed until darkness descended and a sea of stars flickered overhead.

While Rachel and I visited with Jacob and Hilda, we realized just how much World War II had scarred Hilda. The Russians had killed her father, and her brother had died when her family had to walk the long distance to their farm in northwestern Germany. By the time the war ended her family had lost most of its land. But Hilda wasn't destitute. She had recently learned that her father had set up a trust fund for each of his children and she was scheduled to receive the first of five installments.

When Hilda asked me if I agreed with Jacob who wanted her to transfer her money to England, I said that she was married and living in London, so his suggestion made good sense. I suggested that she deposit her money into an account in her own name. My advice annoyed Jacob. He wanted Hilda to deposit her money into an account under his name because she was a foreign national. As a British citizen, Jacob could get a better exchange rate when he transferred her money from German Marks into British Pounds. She agreed to deposit the first installment of money under Jacob's name. I hoped the arrangement would work for them. I didn't want a financial issue to cloud their relationship.

During our stay in London, Rachel and I met many old friends, including Amal and his family and Amjad who had finally received his English Fellowship in surgery. He was a resident at a London hospital. A few days after Rachel and I spent time with Amjad he asked me to meet him again at an Indian restaurant.

When Amjad and I had lunch together he said that he had just received an offer from a Pakistani doctor who asked him to become a partner and surgeon in a clinic that the doctor was building in Kuwait. The Pakistani doctor insisted that Amjad would earn enough money in five years to live in semi-retirement.

Amjad said that he only needed to pay his passage to Kuwait, cover the first month of his board and lodging, and give the investors 500 pounds to pay for his partnership fee. He was certain that working in a wealthy country that had a shortage of doctors provided an excellent opportunity for him. But while he had enough money to pay for his airfare and personal expenses in Kuwait, he didn't have an extra 500 pounds.

Amjad asked if I could help him. He promised to repay me

within a year. When I asked him if he had repaid Neil, Amjad said that Neil wasn't in a rush to get back his loan. He planned to repay him once the clinic was up and running. Amjad just needed my help so that he could take advantage of this excellent opportunity.

Loaning Amjad 500 pounds sterling at this stage of my life wouldn't be easy for me. I also knew that while I trusted his intentions, I doubted his judgment, especially after he wasted money pursuing a second fellowship in surgery. But I agreed to lend Amjad the money if he paid back 100 pounds at the end of one month. I told him to contact me after he had finalized all his contracts. Rachel was unhappy to hear that I had loaned money to Amjad, but she understood that I had to help him under these circumstances.

During the rest of our home leave Rachel and I saw several shows in London's West End. We also visited Miriam and her family who had moved to a better neighborhood. Naomi, who had been dating a Jewish teacher from Brighton for six months, also spent time with us at Jacob's house. She thought that her new acquaintance would ask her to marry him. She blushed and said that she would say yes.

On one of our last evenings with Jacob and Hilda, Rachel and I invited all her brothers and her sister to Jacob's house for dinner. Everyone accepted our invitation, and Rachel and I cooked a fine meal. Even Daniel joined us despite his troubled relationship with Jacob. Sheila charmed all Rachel's siblings with her smile and her cute ways. Everyone also adored Monica, but she only noticed her mother. The two girls were already so different. Sheila was an extrovert eager to impress everyone. Monica was introspective.

That evening Joseph discussed their parents. He reminded his brothers and sisters that Uncle David had arranged for his own immigration to England. He would probably leave Calcutta in the next two years. Joseph worried about their parents living alone in India. He wanted them to move to London. But he knew that even after they sold their coffee shop, they wouldn't have enough money to cover England's cost of living.

When Jacob said that he and Hilda would buy a bigger house to accommodate his parents I suggested that the children should agree to contribute to their parents' living expenses. Everyone seemed to accept the idea, but Joseph said that not all of them could afford to contribute much money. I told them that Rachel and I planned to go to India on our next home leave and would assess their parents' situation when we reached Calcutta.

~ 79 ~

FROM KANO TO KADUNA

I WAS POSTED ONCE AGAIN in Kano. Dr. Baddock was still the senior surgeon at City Hospital, but he was leaving the service in three months and moving back to England. Dr. Baddock had ignored my advice and filed a complaint against Dr. Maruti.

The surgeon was never popular with the Ministry of Health officers, but they couldn't ignore his complaint because of his senior position at the hospital. Since Dr. Maruti was on good terms with the Medical Advisor and the Permanent Secretary, they only slapped him on the wrist. He was transferred to the salubrious mountain city of Jos.

Dr. Baddock, who rarely talked with me, didn't invite Rachel and me to his party when he finished his tour. But I was told to arrange his official farewell party. When he finally shook my hand, he told me to watch out for Dr. Maruti.

Once he left the hospital I was the only general surgeon on the staff. I had far too many surgical patients. I also shared the operating room with the orthopedic surgeon, which created a backlog of operations. Meanwhile, the operating room renovation was painfully slow.

Dr. Clinton finally called a meeting of the officials from the Native Authority and officials from the Public Works Department, which was supervising the construction. He also invited the chief engineer who had redesigned the existing facility. The Public Works Department officials blamed the local workers for the delay. The Wakelin defended the Nigerian workers and blamed the supervisors from the Public Works Department. The Wakelin also said that the workers usually asked me what they had to do each day because I was the only one who showed up on the worksite.

A Public Works Department official pointed his finger at me. He said that I caused the delays. I gave the workers wrong instructions.

After Dr. Clinton told me to stop interfering with the engineer's orders, I told him that whenever I went to the construction site, I rarely saw a supervisor from the Public Works Department and I never saw the engineer. Their absences probably caused the construction delay because workers were always asking me what they were supposed to do. I always tried to answer them so that they weren't sitting around doing nothing. Everything I told them always conformed to the engineer's plan. I reminded Dr. Clinton that I had asked the Emir to finance the construction. I wanted the work done properly. The Public Works Department promised to finish the job in two weeks.

While I performed surgeries at the hospital and continued teaching the medical students, I also started treating expatriates in my private practice. Our hospital's British orthopedic surgeon had also built up a lucrative private practice, but he tended to treat officers from British firms. He was intelligent and took good care of his high-paying clients.

One afternoon I received a call from the manager of UAC who asked me to come to his house to look at his son's arm. I hesitated. I still had vivid memories of the UAC manager in Jos who had tried to prevent my confirmation. I also knew that the orthopedic surgeon normally treated the manager and his family. I didn't want to encroach on his private practice, but the orthopedic surgeon told me to go ahead and treat the young boy. The child was very sick. When I examined the boy, I noticed the telltale lesion of anthrax on his forearm. I had only seen one other anthrax case in my career. That patient had worked on a cattle and sheep farm.

I told the father that his son had anthrax. He needed to be isolated and treated without delay. I called the pathologist from City Hospital who came to the house and looked at the lesion. He agreed with my diagnosis and collected specimens for the lab. When I reported back to the orthopedic surgeon, I heard the reluctance in his voice as he asked me to treat the boy.

The child eventually recovered from this dangerous disease. But just as the orthopedic surgeon had feared this unexpected case established my reputation with expatriates and many of his former patients preferred to see me. The orthopedic surgeon became my sworn enemy.

One day the Minister of Health came and told me that the ministers wanted me to become the surgeon at the newly completed Kaduna hospital. How I longed to tell him that he should also promote me to the rank of surgeon before my transfer; but I was afraid that I would antagonize him.

My new assignment appealed to me because this new hospital would have a qualified anesthetist, gynecologist, and medical specialist. But I knew that I would have a small private practice. Kaduna had few foreign-owned commercial houses.

One evening the Emir of Zunguru called me to say that the Permanent Secretary would be sending me the official transfer order. When I asked him if I would be promoted to the post of surgeon, he said that the Minister of Health had proposed my promotion some time ago, but the Medical Advisor and the Permanent Secretary had opposed it. The Emir doubted that the British would accept a second request from the Minister, and unfortunately, the Nigerian and British officials had to jointly approve all promotions. He asked me to be patient. He promised me that my promotion would be approved before the end of my next tour.

Kaduna's Sir Ahmadu Bello Hospital observed the unwritten rule that stated every new building in the North had to be named after the Premier. Luckily, the building wasn't painted green, which was the color associated with Islam. A devout Muslim Sir Ahmadu insisted that all his personal and official effects had to be green. The ink in his inkwell was green, and so were his pens. His Rolls Royce, which was a gift from the manufacturer, was also this color.

At the official opening of the spiffy new hospital, the senior staff stood at attention as the Premier's green Rolls Royce and the other cars in his motorcade pulled to a stop at the main entrance. Sir Ahmadu Bello cut a green ribbon and entered the hospital with his entourage to visit each department. When they reached the operating room, I stepped forward and shook Sir Ahmadu's hand. I joked and said that this was my workshop. The Premier laughed and thanked me for coming to Kaduna. The Minister of Health grabbed my arm and drew me into the official group as it headed to another department.

When the Premier and the other officials finally left the hospital, I returned to the surgical ward. The officer in charge of the hospital and a Nigerian doctor accused me of joining the Premier's entourage. They said my behavior was most unbecoming. I belonged in the surgical ward. I told them that the Minister of Health had corralled me. There was nothing I could do. When the Nigerian doctor laughed in disbelief, I realized that I might not have a smooth transfer to Kaduna.

But our family enjoyed the city and its lush countryside and river that skirted the edge of the urban area. We also enjoyed our spacious new house. Since the hospital transferred most of the difficult orthopedic cases to Kano, I was also under far less pressure as a surgeon. In addition, I could rely on the assistance of the qualified anesthetist and the obstetrics and gynecology specialist who had joined our team. My private practice in Kaduna was limited, but Nigerian Permanent Secretaries and Ministers came to our house for treatment. I also treated the Premier and Deputy Premier in their private residences.

These Nigerian patients created a sensitive problem for me. Nearly every male Nigerian official complained of erectile dysfunction and demanded testosterone injections to improve their sexual performance. I always believed that their Islamic traditions had caused their problem. Most of them had four wives and concubines. I wondered if false machismo drove them to have so many sexual partners.

When I treated these men for their erectile dysfunction, I used a preparation that released testosterone slowly over a period of time. I wanted to limit the number of painful injections. But a few men had also developed strictures of the urethra from chronic gonorrhea. They needed regular dilations at the hospital to prevent urinary obstructions.

Once Nigeria achieved its independence the government initiated more construction projects that increased the number of foreign contractors and Nigerian bureaucrats in Kaduna. Expatriate advisors who represented various United Nations agencies and foreign governments came to the city, as did many new medical recruits from the United Kingdom, Ireland, India, Pakistan, and Egypt. Qualified northern Nigerian doctors, including Dr. Atta whom I had met in London, also returned to their homeland.

While Dr. Atta was establishing his private practice in Kaduna, I invited him and his British wife to dinner. As we chatted about their transition to Nigeria, Mrs. Atta said that she was pleased that her husband had hired servants who did all the cooking and housework. But she wished that he could rent a house in our neighborhood, which was restricted to expatriates and Nigerian government officers. I told Mrs. Atta that she and her husband could apply for an exemption. However, Dr. Atta said that his patients, who were generally Nigerian, would resent him for moving into our exclusive area. Mrs. Atta mentioned that she had met some British ladies who attended her church. She hated that they often said unkind things about her children's skin color and the texture of their hair. One woman had even told her daughter that her lips were too thick and told her son that his nose was too flat. She wished that they wouldn't say such awful things in front of her children.

Rachel and I had a lovely time with Dr. Atta and his young family. But once they left our house I kept thinking about these deplorable remarks. Unfortunately, I had to admit that the racist comments of the British ladies didn't surprise me.

~ 80 ~

BACK TO KANO, AGAIN!

I WAS HAPPY TO GET a letter from Saha that he had been accepted into the Colonial Service. One day he called to say that he and Joya were coming to Kaduna. He planned to meet the Medical Advisor and discuss the limited number of surgeries performed at his hospital. He said that even patients with simple hernias, hydroceles, and benign tumors were untreated and Nigerians with strangulated hernias and compound fractures often died.

I invited Saha and Joya to stay with us for the weekend. When they arrived at our house, they seemed to be enjoying their new life in Nigeria. They were comfortable with Saha's first assignment and pleased that he made enough money to send their son to a private school in Calcutta. Joya said that the Nigerian government had agreed to pay their child's travel expenses to Nigeria so that he could visit them during his next school vacation.

After Saha's meeting, I had lunch with him. He said that the Medical Advisor doubted that there was enough money in the budget to post another surgeon and a nurse who was trained in anesthetics to his remote hospital. I told Saha that he should have asked his district's senior medical officer to present his request to the senior officers who were authorized to make these special appointments. The Medical Advisor could only advise.

During our last evening together, Saha mentioned that the senior medical officer in his district had told him that I would already be a specialist if I hadn't played politics with my superiors. Saha wished that I would stop quarreling with the British officers. They had such a low opinion of me. As Saha sipped his cocktail, he said that he got along just fine with the British and they liked him in return.

I told Saha that I was happy that he had good relations with the British. I pointed out that I also had good relations with some highly placed British officers. But if I hadn't established good relationships with the Nigerian leaders, I would have been forced to leave the country long ago and Saha would never have been accepted into the service.

Joya piped up and said that my intransigence caused my troubles with headquarters and the long delay in Saha's application process. Saha agreed with his wife and said that it was his duty as my friend to warn me that the Nigerian politicians would never alienate the remaining British doctors. My political friends would turn against me.

I realized that Saha and Joya had sided with the British officers who disliked me. They were grateful to the Colonial Service for giving Saha his well-paying job.

One afternoon Dr. Hinds called me from the Kano medical school. He said that the students were staging a protest against their new teacher Dr. Maruti who had been reposted to Kano. When I asked Dr. Hinds why he was telling me about this protest he said that I was coming back to Kano.

A few days later I was told to report to Dr. Crowley who was the new medical officer in charge of transfers. Dr. Crowley had served most of his career as a medical officer in the British Indian Army. He was known for his rough demeanor. Many British officers wished that Dr. Crowley would pull in his fangs and trim his nails. When I went to see Dr. Crowley, he showed up ten minutes late for our meeting. He said that he was so busy that he wished he had eight arms and two heads like all our Hindu gods. Dr. Crowley announced that I had to go back to Kano to teach the students at the medical school. He said the buggers were lousy students. He also thought that Dr. Hinds was a pain in a place that matched his name.

I went home from my meeting with Dr. Crowley and told Rachel about our transfer. She accepted the news, but she hoped that we wouldn't abruptly leave Kano before the end of the tour. We both knew that I could easily improve our family's financial situation once we lived there. I would have a huge private practice.

When I told the Emir of Zunguru about my transfer he said that the students wanted me to teach at their school. He assured me that I would return to Kaduna after the students took their final examinations. The Emir also told me that the Minister of Health had forwarded his recommendation for my promotion to surgeon specialist to the Public Service Commission. They were waiting for the Permanent Secretary to approve the request.

Our family quickly settled back into our busy life in Kano. Dr. Baddock was no longer at City Hospital and the newly appointed surgeon specialist accepted me with cautious respect. He promised that he wouldn't lord over me or scrutinize my activities as a surgeon even though he was the head of the surgery department and responsible for our department's reputation in City Hospital. He emphasized that I was responsible for the students at the medical school. He wouldn't teach those Nigerians for a single minute. It was a futile exercise. I kept a straight face as I asked him to pity me. I said that I hoped I would survive my assignment.

~ 81 ~

TROUBLE IN CALCUTTA

BOTH OF OUR SWEET DAUGHTERS were distinctly different bundles of joy. Every day when I came home from work Sheila ran out to me as soon as I stepped from the car. She would jabber about her day in a language that only Rachel understood. Baby Monica was walking, saying a few words, and eating on her own. But she would only eat bananas, mashed chicken, and mashed potatoes; and Rachel had to force Monica to drink a cup of milk each day.

Life felt good for us in Kano. Then, one day we received a letter with bad news from Rachel's brother Joseph. Mr. Bekhor had been hospitalized after he had suffered a stroke. He was slowly recovering in his apartment, but he was partially paralyzed on his right side, and he struggled to speak.

Mr. Bekhor had also suffered a huge financial loss. Over the years he had always paid a coffee supplier for partly processed beans that the supplier bought from Mysore coffee plantations and sent to his warehouse in Calcutta. Joseph said that his father, who bought coffee once yearly during the harvest season, always paid cash on a verbal contract basis. The coffee was expensive, so he gave the supplier a significant amount of money that he always obtained through a bank loan.

This year the supplier shipped the coffee to Mr. Bekhor's warehouse with an invoice that demanded full payment within seven days. Their father was still in the hospital; and when their mother saw the supplier's demand for payment, she knew that he had already been paid in full. But they didn't have a receipt. Their business had been based on trust. Mr. Bekhor had been swindled.

The bank was unable to help the Bekhors. They had already overdrawn their account before they had assumed the new loan. They owed so much money that the bank auctioned off the contents of the warehouse. Their parents only received about 50 percent of the value of their goods. They were forced to live on the rental income from the small unit attached to their flat and the money that Mr. Bekhor had put aside for his final years when he hoped to live in Israel. Fortunately, their Uncle David would continue to live in their apartment for another eight months before he immigrated to England. Joseph hoped that we could help his parents when we visited Calcutta. He wanted us to stay in the small sublet.

Before the arrival of this letter, Rachel had begun to imagine her happy reunion with her parents. She had imagined their delight in meeting our children. She had imagined showing them that we were living good and honest lives and that we deserved their blessings and respect. Rachel had never imagined this upsetting turn of events.

I wrote to Joseph and said that we would certainly spend time with his parents when we reached Calcutta in January. We were also willing to stay in their small sublet and we would cover all his parents' expenses while we were there. Joseph wrote back that his parents had agreed to this plan.

Over the next two months, I cut back my private practice in Kano so that I could offer additional tutorial classes to my students to better prepare them for their upcoming exams. The pathologist, the anesthetist, and the orthopedic surgeon also offered tutorials to their students. I chose a professor of surgery from the prestigious University of London to serve as the external examiner for the surgery exam. The three other doctors agreed to serve as internal examiners for their clinical and pathology specimen exams. Our exams would be professional and beyond reproach. Most of our students passed their exams, and once again the doctors in the lounge openly questioned the ability of these Nigerian students to pass their surgery exam. But no one dared accuse me of feeding questions to my students in advance.

One week later the Minister of Health told me in confidence that I would soon be promoted to the rank of specialist. I received the official notification two days later from Dr. Taylor. I was overjoyed. I was finally a specialist surgeon. I remembered some advice that Sir John had given me years ago. He had told me to be gracious whenever I defeated an adversary who had been mean to me as otherwise, I was no better than my adversary. I made up my mind to be gracious and always walk the high road from that moment forward. I didn't want to stoop to the level of anyone who tried to harm me.

Saha called a few days after I received my promotion. He told me that Joya was teaching at the local Catholic missionary school. Since she lacked a Nigerian work permit, the missionary school was depositing her salary into his bank account in London. Receiving remunerations in London was illegal, but Saha didn't ask for my opinion or advice.

Saha said that he had heard from the other doctor at his station that the Permanent Secretary and the Medical Advisor had reprimanded me for manipulating the results of the medical exams in Kano. He asked me why I was so determined to make a bad name for myself. I stayed on the high road. I told him that it was true that I had recently heard from these two senior officers. They had congratulated me for my promotion to the rank of specialist. The phone went silent until Saha said he didn't believe me. I told him that he would read about my promotion in the next issue of the government gazette.

~ 82 ~

CROOKS

I STAYED ON THE HIGH road and continued to enjoy my life in Kano with Rachel until a new problem unexpectedly blindsided me. One evening a Northern Nigerian businessman brought the German manager of an international construction company to my house to talk to me about the planned renovation of the Kano airport. The Nigerian businessman said that the government preferred to give all future infrastructure contracts to foreign companies that had local partners, so he formed a partnership with Mr. Hunger. As I listened to these men discuss their business relationship, I wondered how I fit into their picture. Mr. Hunger brought up my friendship with the Minister of Works. He said that one good word from me would do the deed. He promised to reward me.

I concealed my anger as I informed Mr. Hammer and the Nigerian businessman that I needed a few days to think about their proposal. I had no intention of engaging in this illegal activity, which I knew sugarcoated nearly every Nigerian business transaction. But I couldn't afford to turn a powerful Nigerian businessman into my enemy. I was suddenly in a bind.

I needed to talk with someone who could properly advise me, but who? I worried that many of my Nigerian friends were also corrupt. Finally, I decided that I could trust Malam Lawan who was the Permanent Secretary in the Ministry of Agriculture.

The next morning when I worked in the hospital, I kept thinking people were staring at me. I wondered if anyone had heard about the two men who had tried to bribe me. When I finally met Malam Lawan, he said that so many government contracts were up for grabs that he suspected most politicians and senior bureaucrats engaged in this illegal activity.

He called the Wakelin and asked him to come see us. When the three of us were sitting together my friend told the officer about the businessman's attempt to bribe me. The Wakelin promised to take care of the problem. He said that no one in Kano would ever bring foreigners to see me again.

After the Wakelin had left us, Malam Lawan said that our friend as well as most senior politicians knew about every business transaction in Kano, and they may all swear that they were pious and moral, but they were tainted. While all these greedy people lined their pockets my friend knew that Nigeria would pay a steep price in the future. When we said goodbye, he assured me that Mr. Hunger would never approach me again.

A few weeks before my family went on home leave Dr. Hinds asked if I would do him a favor while I was in India. He described a delicate matter that involved his sex life. He said that he suffered from erectile dysfunction, so he used an Indian-made artificial penis attached to a belt that someone had purchased for him in Delhi. He asked if I would get him a new one in Calcutta.

I knew that I would never have the courage to look for this

ridiculous contraption. When I told him that I wasn't going to Delhi he said he knew that I could find it in Calcutta. I stared briefly at Dr. Hinds and wondered about his bizarre request.

A few nights later Rachel woke up around two o'clock in the morning. She was hungry. She wanted a snack. As Rachel walked toward the kitchen she stopped abruptly in the living room. She saw two men and the light of their flashlight aimed at our liquor cabinet. She raced back to the bedroom and said that two robbers were in the kitchen.

I tiptoed into the living room and saw two Nigerian men removing liquor from our liquor cabinet. Rachel brought me an iron rod that I kept in our bedroom. As I held it over my head and screamed at the intruders the rod bent in half. Rachel had picked up the wrong rod in the dark.

Rachel opened the window and shouted to Simon and Musa that thieves were in the house. She told them to hurry. By the time they ran into our kitchen, the thieves were gone.

The police inspector told us that we were fortunate. Many burglars who broke into homes these days were violent. He advised us to get a guard dog and a gun. The next day I applied for a permit and bought a gun, which a policeman taught me how to use. I also found a British officer who was leaving Nigeria and needed a new home for his one-year-old dog. We all fell in love with his big strong black Labrador when he brought him over to our house.

When I told the Emir about the attempted burglary, he sent one of his bodyguards to protect us. Every night his guard who wore a long colorful robe and a tall turban walked back and forth in front of our house banging a big stick on the pavement. His sword hung by his side. He only stopped pacing when it was time for him to unroll his prayer shawl and pray; even then he kept his stick and sword within reach.

Before we left on home leave Neil wrote to tell us that he would meet us at the airport. He warned us that Calcutta had changed since Independence and few of these changes were positive.

During our remaining time in Kano, I spent more time with Sheila and Monica. I wanted them to understand that I loved them dearly. I also spent time thinking about our return trip to India. We had been away for so long. I planned for us to stop in Bombay so that I could see Dolly and her young family before we headed on to Calcutta. But I received a letter from Dolly's husband Debu, which tore apart these plans. He had lost the love of his life. Dolly had died of encephalitis. Before she slipped into a coma, she asked him to contact me if anything happened to her. Debu was grateful to have their son who looked so much like his mother. The news shattered me, but I had to go through my grief alone. The loss of Dolly was so personal and so tender that I changed our itinerary. I couldn't bear to visit Bombay.

A few days later the Emir of Zunguru told me that I was going to be posted in Kaduna after my home leave. He said that once we lived in Kaduna, he and many prominent Nigerians would often come to visit me in our home. They would want to feel comfortable if they discussed confidential matters with me. They trusted their friendship with me, but they worried about my Ibo servants. He said that Ibo servants often worked as spies for their leaders who wanted to overthrow the government. He asked me to hire new help.

I told the Emir that I seriously doubted that Simon and Musa were spies, but I promised to honor his request. His friendship was more important to me than anything else. I called Malam Lawan who understood the Emir's concerns. He said that all the senior government officials had to be careful when they were in the presence of Ibos.

I had a painful talk with Simon and Musa. I explained to them that our future in Nigeria was uncertain. Most likely Madam and the children wouldn't return after our leave, and I wasn't certain how long I would stay here without them. Under these circumstances, I could no longer offer them future employment.

I gave each of them one month's salary for each year that they had worked for us. I also gave them extra money because of their loyalty. But I hated to let Simon and Musa go simply because they were Ibos, and they hated to say goodbye to us. They had been so happy, and we knew that we would really miss them.

~ 83 ~

BACK TO CALCUTTA

WE WERE FINALLY IN AN airplane and flying east to Calcutta. Late in the afternoon when we started our descent, I stared out the plane's window and saw the city's perpetually crowded Howrah Bridge that crossed the Hooghly River. Immigration was just as slow moving and getting through the arduous process exhausted us. But my fatigue vanished once I spotted my dear friend Neil. As he drove us from the airport we traveled along a fine new road until we reached the city where we inched our way through a crush of traffic that crawled past decrepit buildings that looked far worse than they did when Rachel and I had lived here.

Mr. and Mrs. Bekhor had aged beyond their years. Their sad faces briefly lit up at the sight of their daughter and their grandchildren, but Mrs. Bekhor quickly succumbed to her tears. She became so emotionally wrought that she struggled to regain her composure. Finally, she let us go unpack in the small next-door apartment. When we returned with a basket of fruit and a bottle of brandy that we had brought for them from Lebanon, Mrs. Bekhor reluctantly accepted our gifts.

Mr. Bekhor had lost weight. But we were relieved that he could walk without difficulty, and he talked clearly. When Uncle David came home from work that day, he told us that most of Calcutta's Jewish people had immigrated to Israel, Britain, or Australia. He said that Rachel's parents would be alone once he went to England in a few months. I told him not to worry. We would figure out a good plan for them before we returned to Nigeria.

For the rest of the evening, David kept talking about the changes that had hindered his lifestyle in Calcutta once India achieved its independence. The Indian government had put an end to all the special privileges and advantages that had once been reserved for Europeans, Armenians, and Jews during British rule. In post-independent India the government maintained that everyone was entitled to an equal quality of life. In David's view, this attitude had led to a diminished living standard for the entire city population. India was going to the dogs.

After a few days in Calcutta, I went to Alipore, which was a prosperous city neighborhood, and visited my brother Kumar, his wife Asha, and their two sons. When Asha asked me why I didn't bring Rachel and the children with me, Kumar insisted that I would never bring my family without a proper invitation. I ignored him and told Asha that my family would love to come for a visit. A few days later when I brought Rachel and the girls to their apartment, we enjoyed a nice dinner together and their two boys seemed happy to play with Sheila and Monica.

One evening Neil threw a party for Rachel and me so that we could see many of our old friends. He also gave me a tour of his teaching hospital where he was a successful ophthalmic surgeon. Later that day we visited a couple of other Calcutta hospitals where

I briefly met with some medical school friends from England. One of these friends happened to be a successful ENT surgeon. Sheila suffered from chronic infections in her tonsils and adenoids, but we had never been able to find a reliable ENT surgeon in Nigeria who could treat her. My friend in Calcutta agreed to remove Sheila's tonsils and adenoids and she quickly recovered. But Sheila never stopped asking us for her big dish of ice cream.

As we traveled around Calcutta, Rachel and I were appalled by the city's congestion. Old cars belched black fumes as they crawled on roads next to dilapidated buses and Indian-made cars that were inferior copies of an old British Austin Morris. Skinny men rode bikes or pulled rickshaws or led horse-driven carriages or bullock carts as they maneuvered around stray bulls and malnourished dogs and all the grungy vehicles.

I wondered how anyone got anywhere. No one obeyed the traffic lights or the traffic police. But everybody had to stop when demonstrators took over entire streets to protest the government or private industrial and commercial enterprises. Strikes and protests were so frequent in Calcutta that industrial houses had begun to move from West Bengal, which eliminated local jobs and much of Calcutta's tax revenue.

Garbage removal was also not a municipal government priority. Piles of rotting food and refuse blocked sidewalks. Refugee families lived in footpaths inhaling the smoke that poured from their crude stoves and polluted the city air. Small children bathed in roadside water taps. An entire generation that was born in poverty was forced to grow up in the streets. I wondered if the municipal government functioned at all.

Buildings that I had treasured during my college days were in frightening disrepair. No one fixed obvious structural damage or spruced up any exterior with a fresh coat of paint. Even grand historic buildings, colleges, and hospitals were ignored and faced ruin.

Friends in Calcutta said that their city suffered because the politicians who controlled West Bengal's Communist government understood that villagers represented the majority of the state's population. The politicians chose to pay attention to rural needs rather than the needs of fickle-minded elites living in Calcutta who could easily vote out the current state government. In the past, the British and the Congress Party had neglected everyone in the state except the people in Calcutta. Only the Communists decided to try to lift the state's rural population out of its miserable existence. Many of my Calcutta friends also blamed their problems on India's central government. They cited statistics that proved that the national government was siphoning off customs and tax revenues instead of returning these funds to West Bengal.

Since left-wing intellectuals propagated the dictum of "simple living and high thinking" and many scholars extolled the glory of poverty, many new graduates of Calcutta's universities shunned the pursuit of wealth. Anyone with a contrary point of view usually left West Bengal and headed to more welcoming Indian cities or they immigrated to other countries, such as America. The Bengalis who stayed behind in Calcutta lived in a decaying city that was barely surviving on a bewildering form of life-support.

~ 84 ~

CALLS FOR HELP

WHEN I SPENT ANOTHER EVENING with my brother Kumar, he told me about Uncle Hem Ray's harrowing escape from our family's ancestral home once it became part of East Pakistan. A gang of Muslim thugs who were assisted by Pakistani soldiers raided the village and began to slaughter all the Hindus. Hem Ray who had always looked after his Muslim neighbors thought that they would protect him and Auntie Vasanti. But the local police chief said that the gangs were also killing Muslims who tried to defend their Hindu friends.

A brave Muslim elder hid Hem Ray and Auntie Vasanti in the basement of a nearby mosque. Every night he brought them food and water once everyone had left the mosque after evening prayers. The Muslim elder said that he didn't want the blood of our family on his hands.

Uncle Hem Ray and Auntie Vasanti stayed in the basement for over a week where they often heard Muslims arriving for prayers and the shouts of "Allahu Akbar." The Muslim elder finally told them that the thugs had left their village. They could leave the mosque after nightfall.

Vasanti cried when she and Hem Ray saw the charred remains of our ancestral compound. Her husband told her to save her tears and her strength. She needed her energy to flee their village, which was no longer safe for them. Uncle Hem Ray had very few banknotes in his possession and all of his gold, silver, and diamonds lay buried under heaps of ash, brick, and charred timber. But the two of them discovered that the thugs hadn't destroyed Hem Ray's warehouse, and it was still filled with jute, paddy, and mustard seeds.

Uncle Hem Ray sold everything for a fraction of its value to the Muslim elder who agreed to help them leave the village. He gave them fresh clothing and took them by boat to the railroad station. They boarded a train to the East Pakistan border and walked into the Indian state of Tripura where they made their way to Calcutta. Uncle Hem Ray died two years later. I was grief-stricken.

Kumar said that Auntie Vasanti and her two elder sons lived on the outskirts of Calcutta. The two brothers couldn't get well-paying jobs because they had only completed their secondary education, so they took whatever menial work they could find. Auntie Vasanti's youngest son Manab lived alone in Calcutta. He received his bachelor's degree in economics and currently worked as an assistant accountant in a firm.

I called Manab and arranged to visit him. When we met together at his small flat, he told me about his father's two-year battle with inoperable stomach cancer. During his final painful days, Hem Ray could barely swallow, and he could only drink clear liquids. Manab said that his father had wished to see me before he died.

Manab hoped to get more education one day so that he could become an accountant for a big commercial or industrial company. I asked him why he didn't want to become a chartered accountant so that he could sit at the top of the professional ladder. He said that studying for four years in England to become a chartered accountant would be much too expensive for him and he would be grateful if I would loan him some money to become an accountant.

When I told Manab that I would consider loaning him money if he became a chartered accountant, he was speechless. He had never thought that I would be so generous to him. I told him I still needed to discuss this loan with Rachel and Kumar before I made any commitment to him. I also needed to discuss it with his mother. A few days later Manab called to say that he had arranged a meeting between his family and me and my brother at his mother's apartment.

Manab and I took the train to Belgharia, which was a displaced people's colony on the outskirts of Calcutta. My presence overwhelmed Auntie Vasanti who sobbed as she thought of her husband, their lost ancestral home, and her financial hardship. Once she regained her composure, she asked me if I would be willing to build a home for them. Her two elder sons said quietly that their mother's request should stir my conscience. Their father would have expected me to do the right thing.

Kumar said that the family was trying to embarrass me. Uncle Hem Ray had never made this request before his death. I told Auntie Vasanti that I couldn't afford to build them a home, but I would be willing to loan money to Manab so that he could study four or five years in England and become a chartered accountant. Once Manab received his degree, he would make a good salary, and he could help out the entire family.

Kumar interrupted and said that Manab would never become a chartered accountant. If I looked at the results of his final examination, I would see that any loan to him would be a waste of my money. I told Kumar that he was unfair. Manab had put himself through college under difficult circumstances. He was earning his living as an assistant accountant. But my offer continued to bother everyone but Manab. Auntie Vasanti and her other sons asked me repeatedly not to finance Manab's trip to England. They wanted me to finance their house or at least a part of it.

I discussed Auntie Vasanti's situation with Rachel. She thought that we should support Manab's studies in London. Building a house for them was beyond our means.

A few days later I told my aunt that I would help Manab with the money to become a chartered accountant. Before I left their small apartment, I asked everyone to keep quiet about Manab's plans to study in England. I wanted my loan to be a private affair. But almost immediately I received calls from numerous relatives who asked me for small loans. I told each of them that I wished I was rich enough to help everyone, but my limited savings were going into Manab's overseas education.

One morning someone knocked on the apartment door. My grandmother's nephew Amal who had once owned lots of property in our ancestral village stood on the threshold. He said that he had been driven out of East Pakistan. He was a refugee.

I first met Amal when our family had performed my father's final rites at our ancestral home. I had seen him again when I was a medical student. He was in Calcutta with his elder son who was a university student. He had told his son to look after me. Unfortunately, his son was killed during the 1946 Calcutta riots that were known as the "Great Calcutta Killings." When I invited Amal into the small apartment, he talked about the death of his son before he asked if my wife and I would come to visit his wife and two daughters. They wanted to see me.

The next day Rachel and I went to his rented house in south Calcutta. Amal and his wife cried when they talked about their son who had died at such a young age. When they insisted that their son talked about me each time he came home from Calcutta, I sensed that they were exaggerating our relationship. Still, I felt sad about their son's death and the family's unfortunate refugee status in India. Nonetheless, Amal and his family seemed much better off than my Auntie Vasanti.

Amal's wife offered us tea and Bengali sweetmeats as her husband described their escape from our ancestral village when they heard rumors that Muslim thugs were going to raid the village. His wife and daughters had worn all their jewelry and hid money inside their clothing. They walked to the railroad station without any suitcases and slipped onto a train that took them to Calcutta.

Amal had used all his cash and the money that he had received from the sale of the jewelry to get a loan from loan sharks to start a retail drapery business. He was able to support his family, but he was too poor to arrange suitable marriages for his two daughters. I felt sorry for Amal, but I also realized that he wanted my help. I asked him not to dwell on the past but to look to the future.

Amal brightened. He said that he believed that God had brought me to his house in Calcutta because only I could help them face his future without destitution. He assured me that he could pay off the loan sharks in two years with interest. But they wanted all their money right now or they would seize his business. His family would starve because he couldn't settle his debt. As Amal sobbed, his wife came and sat by him while their two daughters stood silently behind their parents.

Moments passed before I found the strength to ask Amal what he wanted me to do. Amal promised to pay me back my money in two years if I settled his loan with the loan sharks. His business was growing; he was gaining credibility with wholesalers. I told Amal that I hadn't brought much cash to Calcutta, and I needed to pay for my family's expenses while we were staying here. I reminded him that I had also promised to send Manab to England for his advanced studies.

Amal blessed me for my kindness. He asked God to reward me a hundredfold, but he begged me not to forget him. He promised again that he would pay back every cent in two years. He also said that he had a friend who could finance the loan for me if I didn't have the money here in India. I could repay his friend by sending money to the man's son who was studying in London. I asked Amal to meet me at my father-in-law's apartment in three days. When Rachel and I left his house the two of us were bewildered. Amal hailed a taxi for us, and we watched his entire family wave goodbye.

Amal's request bothered me. I couldn't afford to commit so much money to people at this stage of my career. I also wondered if Amal and his family were genuinely in trouble. We already doubted that Amjad would ever repay my loan to him. We worried about losing more money. But Rachel didn't want to tell me what to do.

That evening Mrs. Bekhor said that she had received a letter from Joseph and Jacob who wanted their parents to immigrate to England without delay. She knew that the Indian government restricted the transfer of money from the country. She said that this restriction had forced many people to use the black market, which charged exorbitant fees.

When Mrs. Bekhor asked me if I could transfer their money to England, I told her that as an Indian citizen, I faced the same restrictions. But I said that if her husband deposited their money into my Calcutta bank account, I could arrange for them to get the equivalent amount in sterling pounds when they arrived in England. Mr. Bekhor objected. He wanted Joseph to receive the pounds before he gave me any money. I told him that we couldn't complete the transaction with Joseph before I had to leave for Nigeria. But I would be willing to give him a check from my British bank account, which he could send to Joseph. When he rejected this idea, his wife shouted at him. She said that he was stupid. He had to trust his son-in-law, or he would never get his money to England.

Mrs. Bekhor trailed after her husband when he left the living room. Rachel asked me not to be upset with her father. He had suffered so many knocks in his life that he was suspicious of everyone. Mr. Bekhor finally returned and told me that I could send a check to Joseph when I got back to Nigeria. The next day he deposited his money into my Lloyd's Bank account, and I immediately sent a check to Jacob for the same amount of money.

The next day Amal brought me his documents that showed the amount of his loan from the loan sharks. He also showed me his receipts that proved that he had regularly paid the interest to the moneylenders. Amal needed more money than I had imagined. When I asked him if he could pay the loan sharks half of their loan, he said that my proposition would put him in the worst of two worlds. The loan sharks would jack up the interest rate on the remainder of his debt to them. He would end up serving two masters. Once again Amal promised to pay me back my money in two years. At that time, he would be debt-free. He could arrange marriages for his two daughters.

I was in an awkward spot. I wasn't sure that Amal would keep his word and pay me back. When I finally wrote him a check for the entire amount of his debt to the loan sharks, I prayed that I hadn't made a mistake.

~ 85 ~

BACK TO NIGERIA

BEFORE OUR FAMILY LEFT CALCUTTA, we finished making the arrangements for the Bekhor's immigration to London. We were unable to discuss the move with Rachel's father. He didn't want to leave Calcutta. But we had lengthy conversations with Rachel's mother and Uncle David who promised that he would get everything organized for her parents before he left for London.

I spent my last two days in Calcutta riding the tram and buses to see more of the city. The city's deteriorated roads and hideous traffic seemed to exist as extreme examples of organized anarchy governed by madness. Traffic police overlooked every infraction of the law committed by pedestrians and drivers who perpetually ignored the dysfunctional traffic lights. I anticipated insurmountable traffic jams and violent disturbances, but disorderly order always snapped back into place and traffic lurched forward again.

Building exteriors were old and filthy, yet friends' homes were scrupulously clean. I wondered what trick of magic made people clean the interior of their homes but left them indifferent to building facades, footpaths, and gutters. Hydro water was not potable. Most households filtered their water. Local shops offered a limited number of products, but everything was available in the black market. None of the authorities questioned this injustice.

I took a break from my depressing tour and visited a communist friend who reminded me that no straight line was ever straight in Calcutta. This seemed a strange explanation for all of Calcutta's problems, but my friend insisted that life was improving for everyone. My eyes must have gone bad. I saw no improvements anywhere.

During our visit to Calcutta, I also realized that the difference between a superiority complex and an inferiority complex was nearly indistinct. Sometimes I thought that I was seeing a trace of envy in the sons and the daughters of cultured and educated Bengalis whenever they stared at wealthy Bengalis. I wondered where I fell inside this strange equation.

By the time we left Calcutta, I accepted that I was a misfit everywhere. As an adult, my views never aligned with the majority no matter where I lived. Even the English I spoke was different from the English spoken in any other country. I spoke a mixture of British, Indian, and Nigerian accents. People understood me and I understood them. But I never spoke the real thing. I was not the real thing either.

When we landed at the Kano Airport crowds filled the immigration and customs halls. Any trace of former British orderliness had vanished. I assumed that we would spend hours getting through arrivals. A retired British officer saw my look of distress and welcomed me to independent Nigeria. He said that if I stayed long enough in this hall, I might end up in a melee.

We waited for our turn with the immigration officer, but Nigerian passengers kept jumping ahead of us. When I heard a fight, I asked a police officer if Mr. Mohammedu was on the premises. He was supposedly the new chief immigration officer at the airport. The police officer said that he would try to find the officer.

I soon heard Mr. Mohammedu welcoming me back to Nigeria. He asked a junior officer to get our luggage and escorted my family to his office. He offered us refreshing drinks of Coke while someone took care of our papers. Once we received our luggage, he summoned the transport clerk from the Senior Medical Office who said that officials had changed my assignment. I was going to remain in Kano for three more months so that I could prepare the last batch of medical students for their final exam. I would also resume my work at City Hospital.

I called Dr. Curry who was the new Senior Medical Officer in Kano. I had covered for him in Gusau. I hoped that he would become my ally. He said that he had to keep the officers happy. No one else wanted to teach those duds. He laughed and said that I behaved like Alice in Wonderland who failed to see the shape of things. His opinion of me hadn't changed.

Our family moved back into our old house and hired three northern servants, including a gardener. I went to see Dr. Curry who told me that many British medical officers had left Nigeria during my home leave. I would discover that many of the new medical recruits, especially the Nigerians, were poorly trained. I would see inefficiency all around me.

I visited my Greek friend who was the manager of an automobile dealership selling Mercedes and Opels. He urged me to buy a Mercedes. He said that all my influential Nigerian friends drove this fine car. When I said that I couldn't afford a luxury car he laughed. He said that he knew every officer's pay and compensation package.

But he told me to take my time. He wouldn't pressure me.

In truth, my old car had problems, but the Public Service Commission was currently reviewing the employment status of all the officers on Special List B. I didn't want to buy a car until I knew that the commission planned to keep me on this list.

After I left the dealership, I called my friend Alhaji Abdullah who was a member of the Public Service Commission. He told me that most officers would receive a five-year extension, but he believed that I would be invited to stay in Nigeria for another ten years.

I went back to see my Greek friend and took a Mercedes and an Opel Capitan for test drives. I preferred the Mercedes, but I told him that I should take the Opel. It was in my price range. My friend sold me the Mercedes for the price of the Opel. I knew that he expected to do all the maintenance and repairs on the car even when we shifted back to Kaduna where he was opening up a new showroom dealing exclusively with Mercedes.

Dr. Hinds was delighted when I returned to the medical school. He asked me if I had bought him his special gift. I said no. I had never gone to Delhi, and I had no idea where to find the thing in Calcutta. Dr. Hinds insisted the device was available in every Indian city. It was a fake, but it satisfied his wife. He shrugged and walked away. We never discussed his sexual problem again.

My stay in Kano was extended to six months. I became swamped with work at the hospital and the school. While I limited my private practice to surgeries, it also kept me busy. I wondered how much longer I could work at this pace.

One day a Swiss lady and her Lebanese husband came to see me at my house. She said that she was vomiting and had lower abdominal pain. Dr. Hakan, who was a Lebanese private practitioner, had told her to come see me. He thought that she was suffering from acute appendicitis. I called Dr. Hakan who said that initially he had thought that she had gastroenteritis, but she didn't respond to his treatment. He asked me to examine her and let him know my diagnosis before I performed any surgery.

The young lady was pale, her hair was disheveled, and she was in extreme pain. I told her husband to take her to the nursing home. I would meet them there. When I performed a pelvic examination, I felt the telltale lump of an ectopic pregnancy and it seemed that the lump was leaking because she had lost lots of blood.

I called Dr. Hakan and asked him to come to the nursing home and assist me during the surgery. When the lady recovered from her operation her mother called me from Switzerland. In broken English, she thanked me for saving the life of her only child.

~ 86 ~

CHANGING TIMES

SHEILA AND MONICA WERE BORN around the same time of year, so Rachel and I decided to hold a big birthday party for them while we lived in Kano. We invited friends from every community, including the Chief of Immigration Mr. Mohammedu, and lots of children. After most of our guests left the party, I walked into the front room and saw Mr. Mohammedu pick up Sheila and kiss her. She was an affectionate child and kissed him back. This exchange was probably innocent, but I shouted at Sheila and told her not to do that. I embarrassed him and he quickly put Sheila down on the sofa.

I felt terrible and I told him that my anger had nothing to do with him. My daughter had to learn proper behavior. I reminded him that we both belonged to conservative societies. We only wanted our daughters to hug and kiss their parents and, one day, their husbands. I had to teach Sheila and Monica proper behavior. If they misbehaved, I wouldn't be able to get good husbands for them.

He shook my hand and said that he didn't want his daughters to behave like European girls or like some of the girls from the south who were promiscuous. Northern girls were still virtuous. They obeyed Islamic laws regarding modesty and decency.

How I wished that I could tell Mr. Mohammedu that Islam should demand the same standards of men, but I kept quiet. Besides I had also objected to his kiss because gonorrhea and syphilis affected so many Northern Nigerian men. Their infections often led to lip and tongue lesions, while syphilis spirochetes could be detected in saliva. An innocent kiss to an innocent child could transfer an awful disease.

During my tour in Kano, I began to notice that the Northern mistrust of Ibos, which had forced us to dismiss Simon and Musa, had spread to every sphere of work or business in the city. Nigerians openly celebrated their independence and expressed high expectations for their country's prosperity; but privately, many expatriate businessmen began to tell foreigners to send their money to a safe country. This rosy façade would shatter.

I worried about the odd tension that existed in Nigeria and I wished that some of my educated Nigerian friends were more open with me, but they were suddenly cautious whenever they spoke with an expatriate officer. They assumed that many of the British officers who had once ruled over them wanted Nigeria to fail.

One day during a visit with the Wakelin at his office in City Hospital I noticed that someone had replaced his portrait of the Emir of Kano with a portrait of Nigeria's premier, which now hung next to an old portrait of Queen Elizabeth. When I asked him what happened to the nice portrait of the Emir, the Wakelin said that times had changed. He had to honor the new leaders of independent Nigeria. The Emir's portrait was on the back wall. The Wakelin confirmed the Emir's demotion when he said that the Premier Sir Ahmadu Bello was Kano's most important ruler.

Sir Ahmadu Bello's power was evident throughout post-independent Nigeria. Every new government building was named after him and every important person scrambled to get a seat on the chartered plane that took the Premier on his annual pilgrimage to Mecca. He was also generous with gifts. A Nigerian doctor who had recently returned from England to join the medical department told me that when he paid his respects to Sir Ahmadu Bello, the Premier blessed the doctor and gave him a card that entitled him to a free TV set and a refrigerator from any Nigerian department store. I wondered who paid the bills for the Premier's largesse.

One day while I was treating a Lebanese patient, he said that he worried about the troubles that were brewing between the Christian Ibos and the Northern Muslims. He knew that the Ibos insisted that the newly discovered offshore oil belonged to them because it was in their territory. They figured that the Northern Muslims, who were in power, would never give the Ibos their money from their oil.

My Lebanese friend also thought that the traditional rulers and the current federal government were jockeying for power. When the traditional rulers held a meeting during Independence celebrations, Premier Sir Ahmadu Bello approached the dais to speak before the gathering. Every important Nigerian and Emir stood up and welcomed him, except the Emir of Kano who stayed seated in his chair.

My friend said that the Premier used his power to make the legislature pass an act that demanded an audit of the accounting records of every regional office of the Native Authority. Everyone knew that the Premier intended to embarrass the Emir of Kano. The Native Authority under the Emir's control was riddled with corruption. The Premier hoped that the results of the audit would force the Emir to resign.

A few days after my patient related this story to me the Emir of Kano announced that he was relinquishing his throne to devote his time to religious studies in Mecca. If he ever returned to Nigeria, he said that he would arrive as a scholar and teacher and live far away from Kano.

People were stunned that their Emir had resigned from his position. But they knew that the Emirate would survive without him. The elders convened a meeting and eventually selected another male member from the same family that had ruled the Emirate for over 100 years. The new Emir who had been the police chief of the Kano Native Authority was presently a consul at the Nigerian Embassy in Switzerland. In my estimation, this man who was well-educated and sensible would make an excellent Emir. I hoped that he would be like fresh air blowing through the fossilized atmosphere of the Emir's old palace.

Mr. Jackson who was our district's chief administrative officer called a meeting to discuss the arrangements for the new Emir's coronation. He explained to us that the formalities would begin with the Emir's arrival at the airport. According to tradition, the Emir had to be dressed in his official royal attire, which included a heavy three-horned headdress, before his followers were allowed to see him or he would be cursed. From the airport, the Emir would travel in a motorcade to the city mosque where the chief mullah would anoint him before the Emir continued to the palace for his formal coronation. Tradition dictated that all these ceremonies had to conclude before sundown.

Everyone at the meeting sat in silence before I finally asked Mr. Jackson why the Emir had to wear his traditional attire. The headpiece had to weigh half a ton, and it would be uncomfortable in the hot weather. Besides, I added, the man had adopted a modern lifestyle in Switzerland. He would probably prefer to live the same way in Nigeria. Mr. Jackson wasn't amused. He said that the specifics of the coronation weren't up for discussion. Nigeria needed its traditions, or the country would fall apart. He looked pointedly at me when he said that none of us wanted something awful to happen.

~ 87 ~

TENSIONS

SOMEHOW THE NEW EMIR DEFIED the hideous heat and managed to hold his head high despite the heavy weight of his three-horned head-piece when he descended from the airplane. The former police chief behaved more royally than the previous Emir as he was led to a car and taken in a motorcade to the mosque and on to his coronation at the palace. Never once did the new Emir who had often visited my house ever acknowledge in my presence that he knew me. I was a foreigner in his dark eyes that drifted over a sea of adoring Nigerian faces.

But the next morning when I was at the hospital a clerk informed me that the Emir wanted to see me in his summer palace at four p.m. When I arrived at his residence I was ushered into a private room. He offered me a chair and told everyone else to leave the room.

He said he was relieved that I, his old friend, was stationed in Kano. He could trust so few people. When the former police chief confessed that it wasn't easy to be the Emir, I knew from my man years of living in Nigeria that I shouldn't offer unsolicited advice. I simply said that I was glad to meet him again and I wished him good health.

He announced that his health was precisely his problem. He had felt so lonely when he was living in Switzerland that he had occasionally reached out to some women. He had caught a disease. He handed me a note from his Swiss doctor that stated his patient, who had contracted syphilis, was taking a protracted course of penicillin. He wanted me to treat him until he was cured. He promised to abstain from sex and asked me not to speak about his condition to anyone.

Over the next few weeks, I treated the Emir at his summer palace. In return, he sent me presents, including a beautifully carved ivory walking stick. He also increased the number of bodyguards who watched over my house day and night.

One morning an attractive Nigerian nurse came to see me at my office. After we exchanged pleasantries, I detected that something was on her mind. She said that she knew that I often visited the Emir at his summer palace. She asked me if he had a medical problem. When I said that I couldn't betray doctor-patient confidentiality the nurse admitted that she had been in a long-term relationship with him. He had always lovingly treated her, but when she recently went to see him he told her that she had to stay away for a while. She was heartbroken.

The nurse said that she was aware that the tribal elders had told the Emir to end his marriage to his current wife so that he could marry a woman whom they had chosen to be his queen. So she understood that he would never marry her. She also never wanted to be his concubine. But she did assume that they would renew their relationship. I told the nurse that I had known the Emir for years.

I advised her to give him some time to sort out his new life. After a couple of months, she would probably discover that he still had warm feelings for her.

A few weeks later all the medical school students passed their difficult exam. My teaching job ended in Kano. By then I had started to become uneasy about Nigeria even though most of my Nigerian acquaintances seemed happy. I also never saw signs of discontent among Nigeria's poor, who probably never expected their lives to improve. Only my closest Northern friends, who were all Muslim, admitted that they were worried about their country's future, and their mistrust of the Christian Ibos fueled their anxiety.

Before we moved to Kaduna the Emir of Zunguru came to visit me one night in Kano. As we chatted in our front room, he said that by the time Nigeria became independent, the British had appointed too many well-educated Christian Ibos to senior civil service positions. The British had also elevated too many Ibos to important ranks in the police force and the army. The Emir was afraid that all these powerfully placed Christians, especially the Ibo army officers, would attempt to mount an insurrection. His concerns made me nervous about Nigeria's future.

When my family and I finally left for Kaduna, our journey had a promising start. I enjoyed driving our fancy Mercedes Benz on the resurfaced and newly improved highway, and we easily overlooked the huge portraits of the Premier that appeared on every billboard in every village and town. We planned to spend the night in Zaria, which was an attractive town with a comfortable government rest house. But after driving two splendid hours on this fine new road VIPs who always traveled in huge motorcades repeatedly forced every private car and truck to stop on the side of the road. It was late afternoon, and we were exhausted when we pulled into the government rest house in Zaria.

Late the next day we finally reached the Kaduna government rest house. A few days later we moved into our house, which had a spacious yard that was big enough for a vegetable garden. When I reported to work at the hospital, I met two newly hired Nigerian doctors and four recruits from India. Most of the British doctors who remained on the staff were leaving Nigeria at the end of their tours.

Once we were settled in Kaduna Rachel and I had dinner one evening with Dr. Atta and his British wife. In the span of a few years, Dr. Atta had established an extremely successful private practice in the city, but as we sat together in his elegant house, he said that he was worried because he and his Christian family lived in a Muslim-controlled city and region. He was grateful that his children had been accepted into the new English medium school, but he believed that they had only gained admittance because he was an influential doctor who knew important people in the government. The English medium school normally rejected the children of Christian businessmen.

He talked about the trouble that was brewing between the two religious communities. The mullahs and Muslim politicians kept reminding their community that the British had always favored the better-educated Christians. Once the Muslims took over the government, they decided that it was payback time.

I thought Dr. Atta was right. Since independence, most senior federal government positions, including the posts of permanent secretary, were reserved for Muslims. Christians were only offered middle and lower-ranked jobs in the civil service and government corporations.

When I invited my friend Malam Lawan to have dinner with

us, I asked him if the federal government had a Muslim hiring pref-erence. My friend, who was still the Permanent Secretary of Agri-culture, said that the government's preferential hiring policy, which turned Christians against Muslims, would eventually backfire. He was grateful that some higher-ranked Muslim civil servants were committed to boosting Christian morale. He had also heard that the Ministry of Health wanted to promote Dr. Tikko who was a Chris-tian to the post of Permanent Secretary once the current British of-ficer retired.

He reminded me that the Christian Ibos were also creating problems in Nigeria. They were actively playing the Christian card to create an alliance with the Americans and Europeans who shared their faith and wanted the oil in Ibo territory. The oil companies from these countries were willing to pay the Ibos an enormous sum of money for oil production rights. Malam Lawan said that this valuable asset could drive an irreparable wedge between Nigeria's religious communities.

~ 88 ~

THE BRITISH TRY AGAIN

AFTER SO MANY YEARS I finally worked with a few British doctors in Kaduna who genuinely seemed to like me. But I soon discovered that I was up against a new source of hostility. One day a Muslim nurse told me that the Nigerian doctors, who were all Christian, resented my friendships with the Premier and other important Muslim officials. These Nigerian doctors and other Christian doctors with private practices in Kaduna wanted to cut me down to size. Even my friend Dr. Atta had joined their campaign to make life so difficult for me that I would resign and leave Nigeria.

I refused to let this annoying news bother me. If these doctors started to mistreat me, I knew that the influential Muslims whom they hated were in power. They were my friends, and they would protect me. So for now I put the matter aside and took pleasure in my happy home life with Rachel and our two dear daughters. Sheila and Monica, who were growing up so quickly, were students at the English Medium School. They always made me proud, and I took great pleasure in watching them discover more about the world and this African country that had become their homeland.

Rachel and I also had an active and enjoyable social life with expatriates and my Northern friends who appreciated our Indian food, and hospitality, and our Muslim servants who came from the North. But our Labrador terrified them. Before they ever came to our house they always called and told me to tie up the dog. They were convinced that foreigners trained their dogs to attack Africans.

When my Greek friend finally opened up his large Mercedes Benz agency and repair shop in Kaduna he invited our family for dinner at his house. At last, we met his wife and two children. We also met some other Kaduna businessmen who told me in the course of long conversations that they appreciated the Nigerian government's pro-business attitude. It was good for their profit line and the country's development. When I asked their opinion of Nigeria's oligarchy one of the businessmen said that any country with high illiteracy ended up with this form of government. He reminded me that an oligarchic government was generally conservative and strictly enforced law and order. An absence of law and order was ruinous for business. He cited the example of the Mau Mau in Kenya.

All the businessmen shared the same predictable views about corruption, and we all agreed that it was rampant in Nigeria. The businessmen said if they refused to offer bribes to politicians and government bureaucrats, they would never get contracts. Worse, the government would scrutinize their financial records and create problems for them. Every business factored the cost of bribes into its bottom line.

One day the Medical Advisor from the Ministry of Health called me to discuss a problem. He had been unable to get a room in the Kaduna government rest house or any of the city hotels for an Indian recruit and his family who were scheduled to arrive in

Kaduna. He wondered if the doctor and his family could stay at our house until he was ready to take his family to his post in Jos. Headquarters would cover all their expenses. I discussed this unusual request with Rachel who agreed to let the Indian family stay in our guest wing.

Once Dr. Mitra and his family temporarily moved into our house Rachel and I liked them immediately. We quickly discovered that we shared more than our West Bengal heritage. We had numerous common interests, including our appreciation of fine Bengali cuisine. Our young girls also got along very well together. When it was time for the family to leave for Jos, Dr. Mitra took me aside one evening and said that he had met many of the other new Indian and Pakistani recruits. He was surprised to hear some of them say that they disliked me. They claimed that I was haughty, and I failed to show them any respect.

After Dr. Mitra said he hoped that I wasn't turning these doctors into my adversaries, I explained to him that I had actually helped many of them get acclimated to their new lives in Nigeria. I had even invited them to dinners at our house. But ultimately, I preferred to cultivate only a few good friendships. I didn't need to be popular with everyone.

A few days later a Nigerian medical officer called and asked me to come see him at the Ministry of Health. When I arrived at his office he closed the door. He said that he wanted to give me some privileged information; but if I shared it with anyone, he would get into serious trouble. The officer told me that the Permanent Secretary and the Medical Advisor wanted to promote Dr. Maruti to the position of specialist surgeon and they intended to backdate his promotion by two years.

The news startled me. I asked the officer when Dr. Maruti

would receive his promotion. He said not for a while. The Public Service Commission still had to meet and approve the request. He thought that the promotion could take a couple of months.

I wasn't upset that top officials wanted to promote Dr. Maruti. He was an extremely fine surgeon. I also knew that the Permanent Secretary and the Medical Advisor were resigning in six months and Nigerian Civil Servants were scheduled to take over these senior posts in the Ministry of Health. They would be disinclined to request the promotion of expatriate doctors, but the decision to backdate Dr. Maruti's promotion by two years infuriated me. This unfair action would make him senior to me.

I realized that Dr. Hinds had been prophetic. He had warned me long ago that the big shots at headquarters would eventually try to get even with me after I forced them to make me a permanent officer in the service. But when I left the Nigerian officer, I kept my mouth shut. I didn't want to get this innocent man into trouble. Still, I had to figure out a way to stop the vindictive Permanent Secretary and his Medical Advisor from using Dr. Maruti's promotion to humiliate me with an unwarranted demotion.

A week later luck intervened. My Nigerian friend Alhaji Abdullah who was a senior member of the Public Service Commission, came to my house to discuss Dr. Maruti's promotion. It annoyed him that the Permanent Secretary wanted to backdate the promotion and then Dr. Maruti would then outrank me and ultimately, he would become the chief surgeon in a couple of years.

I said that I agreed that the new Medical Advisor and the Permanent Secretary obviously wanted their candidate to be senior to the preferred candidate of the Minister of Health. Alhaji Abdullah said that he would make certain that the Public Service Commission rejected the request for Dr. Maruti's promotion. I was so relieved.

Over the next weeks, I heard nothing more about Dr. Maruti's promotion. I longed to know the outcome, so I finally went back to see the Nigerian officer in the Ministry of Health. He told me that the Public Service Commission not only overruled the Permanent Secretary's recommendation, but it asked the Permanent Secretary to wait until Dr. Maruti had completed three years of service in Nigeria before resubmitting the application.

He said that the commission's decision had shocked him. He had never thought that this commission would reject a request from British officers. When he told me that Dr. Maruti had come to his office to learn the status of his promotion, the officer asked if I had discussed this private matter with him. I assured him that I had never discussed the promotion with Dr. Maruti. In fact, I was annoyed that he knew anything about these internal deliberations. I realized Dr. Maruti must have been aware of this latest British plan to outflank me. It would explain his reluctance to contact me when he had come to Kaduna.

~ 89 ~

DIPLOMATS AND DIPLOMACY

ONE EVENING THE EMIR OF Zunguru came to our house to tell me that India's High Commissioner, who was based in the capital city of Lagos, planned a visit to Kaduna. I knew that Ambassador Haksar who was related to India's Prime Minister Nehru had provided considerable assistance to Nigeria's federal government. My friend said that Premier Sir Ahmadu Bello wanted me to look after the High Commissioner and his First Consul when they arrived in Kaduna.

After my family and some Nigerian officials received the two Indian dignitaries at the Kaduna railway station, we enjoyed a lovely lunch at the Premier's attractive guesthouse. For the next few days, I took Ambassador Haksar and his first consul Mr. Singh to meet important ministers and senior civil servants, including the members of the Public Service Commission. One evening Rachel and I also held a large party in their honor so they could meet Indians and Pakistanis who lived in Kaduna.

When we said goodbye to Ambassador Haksar, he asked Rachel and me to be his guests once he and his wife moved into their new residence, which was currently under construction in Lagos. I felt wonderful after spending such a memorable time with this important representative of my country.

The expatriate community in Kaduna began to include officials from foreign oil companies and many more representatives from the United States, Canada, and the United Kingdom who were advising the Nigerian government about its agricultural, mining, and industrial development. Everyone in the corridors of the government and at the major commercial houses talked about Nigeria's impending prosperity.

But I still had my doubts. The present Nigerian leaders seemed determined to follow the old British colonial system. They only offered an education to the aristocrats and the rich. I doubted that Nigeria would ever move forward unless its government pressed for the horizontal growth of education and better work ethics. Some friends who were Peace Corp teachers had also complained to me that the Nigerian government consistently failed to introduce critical new programs into their educational system.

At the hospital, a Russian doctor who was affiliated with the World Health Organization joined our hospital lab. He often sat with doctors in the lounge and drank coffee as he listened to our conversations, but he rarely talked to anyone. Some British doctors decided that he was a member of the KGB. They said that we should be discreet.

But whenever the Russian doctor was alone with me, he talked a lot about our two countries. One time he discussed the favorable relationship that existed between India and the Soviet Union. Another time he insisted that the Soviet troops, who had defeated the invading Nazis, were the true victors in World War II, not the Americans. He reminded me that thousands of Indian soldiers had fought in the war and many of them had sacrificed their lives for the Allies. He was upset that the Europeans and Americans had failed to recognize India's enormous contribution to the war. I wondered if he chose these topics of conversation because he thought that we were somehow allies in the hospital.

One day the Russian doctor stated that most British politicians, who always came from the aristocracy, asked their soldiers to die for God, their king, and their country. But the spoils of the wars always became the property of the rich and powerful. Nothing trickled down to the less fortunate soldiers. The poor remained poor. In contrast, he said that Russian soldiers fought a patriotic war. They fought for themselves and their country.

The doctor's comparison surprised me. I always thought that patriotism was a common human quality. When any soldier took his last breath, I assumed that he probably thought of God before he received eternal salvation in the next world. I wondered about the Soviet soldier's final thoughts when he faced his death. He didn't pray to God. He never imagined salvation in the next world. He thought that his body simply decayed once he stopped breathing.

One day a nurse told some doctors in the doctors' lounge that she had just seen the Russian doctor's wife purchasing a huge stack of nylon stockings and lingerie at a department store. When the nurse asked the wife why she needed so many pairs of stockings and so much lingerie, the woman said that none of these things were available in Russia. Yet all Russian women wanted stockings and nice lingerie. They were willing to pay an exorbitant price in the black market. The nurse told everyone that she had heard that the wives of all Russians who worked at their Embassy or the United Nations smuggled these things back into the Soviet Union. The nurse was convinced that the doctor's wife was going to sell these coveted stockings and lingerie to her friends and make a bundle of money.

Everyone on the staff soon gossiped about the Russian wife's illegal contraband. But I didn't want to pass judgment until I had talked to her husband. The Russian doctor brushed aside the rumors. He insisted his wife had bought all the stockings and lingerie for his mother and herself.

I took a break from work so that my family could have a brief holiday in Jos with the Mitras. We looked forward to the temperate climate of this lush green hill station. We also enjoyed seeing our friends. Mrs. Mitra, who was a lovely lady, cooked some delicious Bengali dishes for us. Sheila, who enjoyed her time with their daughter spent hours playing with her new friend, while Monica who was quiet and shy preferred to stay close to her mom.

One night Mrs. Mitra arranged a dinner party and invited many friends, including some employees of India's railway system who were on contract in Nigeria to upgrade the country's railroad. Rachel and I met a pleasant young man Manash who told me that he wanted to get an advanced degree in engineering. I encouraged him to save his money while he worked in Nigeria and go straight from here to England to pursue his goal. Manash said that he and the other Indian employees didn't have passports. Once their contract ended in Nigeria they had to return to India.

The idea that these Indian contract workers lacked passports baffled me. I told Manash to go ahead and apply to some engineering schools in England. If he heard good news, he would have time to get his passport. But as I was driving back to Kaduna I kept thinking about Manash's strange situation. It seemed obvious to me that when the Indian government denied these workers their passports it also denied these workers their liberty. I couldn't understand how any modern democratic country could implement such a bad policy.

When I returned to work the commanding officer at the near-by military hospital came to visit me. Colonel Oba asked if I would be willing to perform surgeries one day a week at his hospital. Since an excellent surgeon worked for me at our hospital, I knew that my occasional absence from the surgery department wouldn't cause any serious problems. I agreed to work one day at the military hospital.

After the Permanent Secretary authorized the change in my schedule I went to the military hospital. Two of my former medical school students who were now young doctors eagerly gave me a tour of the hospital's departments and wards. As I got to know Colonel Oba who was a well-educated Christian Yoruba from western Nigeria, he admitted to me that he wasn't happy at his post. He felt uneasy working with so many Muslim Northerners.

I quickly learned that I would have to perform most operations at the military hospital under local anesthesia. The nurse anesthetist had limited skills. But I enjoyed working there. In fact, I felt great satisfaction with all my medical work in Northern Nigeria. I imagined staying in this country for years to come.

A month later I received a call from Manash. He had been accepted into two good engineering schools in England. He needed a passport. I asked him to send his completed passport application to me along with copies of his contract to work in Nigeria and copies of his letters of acceptance from the engineering schools. I told him that Rachel and I planned to spend a weekend with the High Commissioner in Lagos after we attended a conference at the University Medical College in Ibadan. I promised Manesh that I would talk about his need for a passport with Ambassador Haksar.

After a pleasant drive to Ibadan Rachel and I attended the

conference at the medical college. We also visited our friends Ram and Asha. Sheila and Monica had fun with their daughter Meena. When the conference concluded on Friday afternoon we drove to Lagos. Soon after we arrived at Ambassador Haksar's house, I told him about Manash. The Ambassador reviewed Manash's papers and agreed that this young man should get a passport so that he could study in England.

Saturday evening Mrs. Haksar arranged a small party so that we could meet some of their friends. She had invited the passport officer, so Mr. Haksar told him about Manash. When the officer asked me to meet him in his office on Monday, I explained that I was leaving Lagos on Sunday morning.

Mr. Haksar overheard the passport officer when he said that he was sorry that he couldn't help me. The Ambassador told him that the Northern Nigerian people considered me an Emir while the Northern Nigerian government treated me like an ambassador. He asked the officer to take the papers and go through them on Monday morning. I was so pleased. Manash would be able to go to England and get his advanced degree.

Once we were back in Kaduna, Rachel and I started talking about our plan to send Sheila and Monica to high school at a boarding school in England. They were still much too young, but we knew that we had to apply years in advance to secure their placement in a good school. But we wondered how they would adjust to living abroad. Some British friends told us about a lady in Brighton who ran a small year-round residential school for young children. We arranged for Sheila and Monica to stay there during our next home leave. We would see how they responded to living at a boarding school that was far away from their parents and Nigeria.

~ 90 ~

BACK TO ENGLAND,
OFF TO THE CONTINENT

Soon we were back in London and staying at Jacob's spacious new house where Hilda's fine gardening skills were evident in her lovely rose garden, handsome seasonal flowers, and their healthy green lawn. We took Sheila and Monica to the residential school in Brighton where they would spend their holidays. The school had a nice playground and the lady who ran the school seemed quite kind as she introduced our daughters to the other students.

When Rachel and I returned to Jacob's house, we spent time with her parents who had failed to adjust to England. Conversations with Mr. Bekhor remained a struggle since he was hard of hearing and refused to wear a hearing aid. He also preferred to stay in his bedroom. Mrs. Bekhor remained angry with Jacob because he had defied her wishes and married a German woman. That Hilda was converting to Judaism and regularly attended the synagogue couldn't mitigate Mrs. Bekhor's rage over the holocaust and her hatred for the Germans. Hilda was also pregnant. But her mother-in-law found no joy in this pregnancy. The thought that her grandchild would have German blood coursing through its veins appalled her.

I had always admired Mrs. Bekhor's strength, but in London,only sadness existed in her eyes, and it usually gave way to a harsh stare directed toward the ceiling. I wondered if this deeply religious lady was begging God to give her relief from her endless misery.

Joseph and Daniel, who frequently came to visit their parents, rarely witnessed these day-to-day problems. Naomi visited her parents when she could, but she had married the Jewish teacher, and they lived with their two young children in Folk Stone, which was a distant town on the sea. Miriam also visited her aunt and uncle. But her visits triggered emotional outbursts that irritated Hilda, who didn't understand that older people generally spoke loudly, and Jacob's family rarely lowered their voices.

The unhappiness of Mr. and Mrs. Bekhor and their dislike of Hilda upset Jacob. Nothing he did for his parents ever tempered their dark moods. I thought that Jacob should take them sightseeing, so he asked his parents if they would like to see Buckingham Palace and the changing of the guards. His father reminded Jacob that he and his wife were only passing time in his house.

Rachel and I failed to improve this unhappy situation, so we decided to make a quick trip to Germany to pick up our new Mercedes, which our Greek friend had ordered for us. When Rachel and I took delivery of the car snow still covered the ground. As we headed toward France to take the ferry to England a cold blustery wind at the Hook of Holland buffeted the Mercedes. Luckily, our new car had efficient heaters. We stayed comfortable.

But on the ferry to London, we were so cold that we decided to wait until the weather changed before we toured parts of Europe. One day during our extended stay in London we met Amjad who looked much older to us. When we had last seen him in London he had agreed to practice medicine in Kuwait. But before he had left for the Middle East the Pakistani investor pressured Amjad into agreeing to marry his young sister.

Amjad stayed in London for an additional year and enjoyed the hospitality of the girl's conservative family. He couldn't date the investor's sister, but he could see her inside her house. Amjad admitted that she was good-looking. After he married the Pakistani girl, his brother-in-law asked Amjad to become a full partner in the new Kuwaiti clinic.

A few months later Amjad and his wife moved to Kuwait. By then his wife was six months pregnant and he learned that she had serious psychological problems that had existed long before their wedding. His wife's condition deteriorated after she gave birth to their baby boy. She became so unstable that a psychiatrist feared that the young mother could harm her child. Amjad never left his wife alone with their baby. But after a few months, Amjad decided that he had enough of this stressful relationship. He divorced his wife. When the court awarded him custody of their child, his brother-in-law was furious. He vowed to destroy Amjad for dishonoring his wife and her family.

Amjad's expenses mounted in Kuwait because he had to pay for a Filipino nanny who cared for his child. But after he hired this Christian nanny, his in-laws accused him of having sexual relations with her. They claimed that Amjad planned to marry her and convert to Christianity. They reported him to the Muslim authorities in Kuwait who accused Amjad of violating Islamic laws that forbade sexual relations between unmarried couples and barred Muslims from converting to Christianity.

During a court trial, no one could prove the charges that were leveled against Amjad, but the nanny was deported back to the Philippines and the bad publicity destroyed Amjad's career in Kuwait. He brought his son back to England and worked as a senior surgical registrar. He knew that he would never get a job as a consultant in England. He also knew that he couldn't return to East Pakistan. His brother had usurped all the family property, and his influential uncle had died. I felt sorry for Amjad, but I couldn't do anything to improve his situation.

Finally, Rachel and I left London and headed to Paris, which was the first stop on our European tour. Every day we enjoyed the city, especially the Left Bank with its rows of bookstalls. We ate at cafes and restaurants where we enjoyed the delicious French cuisine. We also took tours in Paris, including a nighttime tour of five nightclubs.

After four wonderful days in Paris, we drove into the beautiful French countryside and crossed into Germany. We spent lovely days driving through the famous Black Forest where we saw the stream that eventually turned into the grand River Rhine. We passed attractive homes nestled in beautiful valleys and inviting shops that spoke of prosperity. When we finally arrived in Munich the jarring contrast of its massive old buildings and dingy areas took us by surprise. We spent the night, but we left early in the morning and drove back into the appealing German countryside before we finally crossed into Austria and followed a winding road to Vienna.

Austria, which had been under Soviet occupation during the war, lacked the prosperity that we saw in Germany and France. We drove by so many bombed-out buildings and fresh reminders of poverty. Before we had left Nigeria Ambassador Haksar had notified his counterpart in Austria about our upcoming visit to Vienna. The Ambassador kindly invited Rachel and me to have dinner with him and his wife.

The next day Rachel and I took a tour through the beautiful Vienna woods to see some famous landmarks, such as the Opera House and the Burg Theatre. We ended up loving this beautiful city and took every opportunity to hear great music. Our week in Vienna sailed by.

From Vienna, we drove on an unfinished road toward Salzburg when an unexpected snowstorm turned into blinding sleet that obstructed my view. We were so grateful that we didn't end up in an accident. Luckily, we were able to continue driving to Innsbruck, where we stopped for the night at a hotel.

Once we reached Switzerland we drove through more beautiful countryside to the stunning Neufchatel Lake where we stayed with the parents of my Swiss patient back in Nigeria. We spent six wonderful days with Mr. and Mrs. Maurice who showed us numerous lovely villages in the French part of Switzerland.

After our delightful stay with this couple, we followed the picturesque Great Alpine route as we headed to the French Riviera. We toured Monaco, Nice, and Cannes and passed pebbly beaches crowded with scantily clad ladies and men, and we gazed dreamily at the boats that bobbed in the azure sea. We headed up Monaco's winding roads and drove to the magnificent royal palace where we stopped to watch the changing of the guards. We also peeked inside Monaco's famous casino before we returned to Nice and spent the night in a hotel near the beach.

The next day we drove through the pleasant French countryside to the ferry that took us back to England. We were anxious to see Sheila and Monica, so we immediately drove to the residential school in Brighton and picked up our daughters. They had enjoyed their stay in this caring place. But we were all happy to be together again.

When we returned to Jacob's house Mr. Bekhor told us that he wanted to spend his last days in Israel. He showed me his visa application and asked me to take him to the Israeli Embassy for his physical examination so that he would be granted the right to visit this young country.

I took him to the embassy and told the doctor that my father-in-law wanted to pray before the sacred Western Wall in Jerusalem before his death. I assured the doctor that my father-in-law was well enough to visit Jerusalem for a couple of weeks before he returned to his family in England. I asked him to honor this man's wish and grant him a visa. The doctor told my father-in-law to go home and take his medications regularly. He would receive his visa in two weeks.

Rachel's father was so happy. For the first time in all the years of my marriage to his daughter, he told me that he was glad that I was his son-in-law. He smiled and added: "May God shine his light on you." A moment later when Rachel's mother kissed me on my forehead, I was so happy to see tears of pleasure spilling from her eyes once again.

~ 91 ~

KHURSHID

SOON WE WERE BACK IN Nigeria and temporarily settled in a new hotel in Kaduna. Rachel and I were delighted to learn that we would be moving back into our old house once it was ready for us. When I returned to work at the hospital only two British officers remained on the staff, but they were leaving Nigeria at the end of their tours. The hospital still had many other foreign expatriates, including my Pakistani assistant. After a short time, I was back into my old routine of working one day a week at the military hospital and the rest of my time at the civilian hospital.

Once our family had settled back into our familiar house Rachel and I discovered that nearly every foreign dignitary who visited Kaduna was honored with an official party, which the two of us were obliged to attend. These frequent events were tiresome because we had to wear formal dress, and we had to arrive on time. In addition, people always drank too much, including so-called Muslim teetotalers who drank "minister colas," which were soft drinks spiked with alcohol.

Rachel and I preferred our own private dinner parties or a quiet dinner party at the home of a friend. One evening Rachel and I decided to skip one of these official functions. The next day the Permanent Secretary called to tell me that a Nigerian officer had spent the entire evening looking for me. He reminded me that senior officers were required to attend these events.

Days later Manash called me from Jos. He had a new problem to solve before he could study for his advanced degree in England. I invited him to our house for the weekend. During his visit, Manash said that he needed to deposit a financial guarantee of 3000 pounds in a British bank to cover the cost of his passage back to India. Alternatively, he could ask someone with sufficient British funds to serve as his guarantor for the duration of his three-year course.

Manash didn't have 3000 pounds, so he had discussed his problem with Dr. Mitra and other Indian friends, but no one agreed to serve as his guarantor. They enjoyed talking to him and sharing a good meal with him, but this was the extent of their generosity. Each one of these friends had told Manash to speak with me. They said that I was the one who would help him.

I felt sorry for Manash. I had a name for these so-called friends who offered "chicken curry and rice" friendships. I discovered that these limited friendships were common among expatriate Indians in Nigeria. Many of my own so-called Indian friends who lived here were quick to criticize my faults and just as quick to run to me whenever they needed advice or help. I looked over Manash's papers. After a short discussion with Rachel, I agreed to serve as his guarantee. He was so relieved when he headed back to Jos. He was finally ready to get his advanced degree in England.

When the last British surgeon left Nigeria, I was promoted to Chief Surgeon of Northern Nigeria. This new designation filled me with pride, but it also added to my workload. I had additional administrative work, and I also had to travel to inspect government hospitals in six different cities and meet with the surgeons in charge of each surgical department.

Northern Nigeria had a shortage of qualified surgeons, so I generally let every medical officer perform simple operations, such as inguinal hernias, easily accessible benign tumors, and uncomplicated trauma injuries from accidents or violence. However, a few doctors from India wanted my permission to perform more complicated operations that I believed were too risky. I denied their requests.

Some of these doctors complained to my superiors. They called me arrogant and claimed that I was biased against my fellow countrymen. They said that they knew how to perform difficult operations. Indian friends, including Saha, worried that I was making far too many new enemies. But I ignored all their grumbling. I was convinced that these Indian doctors were expecting undue favoritism because I was an Indian. They assumed that we had a shared birthright.

One day a senior officer in the Ministry of Health asked me to come to his office. I braced myself for more complaints, but instead, he asked for a favor. A newly qualified female recruit who had trained in Karachi was coming to Kaduna. He wanted her to be my assistant for the next six months.

A couple of weeks later I met the new Pakistani recruit. Khurshid Ali, who was in her mid-twenties, had moved from the Indian city of Lucknow to Pakistan's port city of Karachi during partitioning. Her mother had died, and her father had come with her to Kaduna. When I learned that they had moved into a house in our neighborhood I called Rachel, and we invited them to our place for dinner that evening. We had a lovely dinner together.

When I learned from Khurshid that she had performed very few operations by herself in Karachi I told her not to worry. Our staff would help her. Khurshid proved to be a fast learner. Within a month she could do standard operations that she would need to perform in any small Nigerian hospital. She was also writing up all the charts and my handwritten notes, which pleased me. My additional paperwork was taking too much of my time.

After a few months when Khurshid could handle a wide variety of surgical operations, she told me that she was grateful to me for all her training. She also said that she was grateful to Rachel for her friendship. The two of them spent many hours together. But her father didn't like Khurshid spending so much time in our house. Mr. Ali frequently called to ask if his daughter was visiting with us. Khurshid told Rachel to ignore her father's calls, but it was difficult to ignore Mr. Ali's strong rough voice. Sometimes he would even come to our house to take Khurshid home; but if he arrived at dinnertime, we always invited him to eat with us.

One evening when Mr. Ali was visiting us the Minister of Education came to our house to see me for some medical treatment. I knew that Mr. Ali, who had been a teacher in Karachi wanted to teach in Kaduna, but he was not allowed to work in this country. Out of courtesy, I introduced him to the Minister. When he left our house, Mr. Ali begged me to ask the Minister to give him a job. I told him I would get into serious trouble if I asked any government official for a favor. Mr. Ali was annoyed. He said that he knew that I was on friendly terms with most of the authorities. If I had wanted to help him, I would do so.

Khurshid told her father to be quiet. He didn't understand Nigeria's rules. Mr. Ali reminded his daughter that he had spent most of his life's savings to educate her. He glared at his daughter and told her to look at his reward; then he stormed out of our house.

Khurshid continued to come to our house to see us, and he continued his annoying pattern of endless phone calls. But I felt sorry for the old man. He had received very little government compensation for his land in India and he had earned very little money as a teacher in Pakistan. He was dependent on his daughter.

As the months passed, Rachel and I continued to enjoy our stay in Kaduna. We became friendly with several families from South Asia, including two Indian doctors who were posted in Kaduna. We occasionally had dinners together and we enjoyed our drinks and our wonderful conversations. Unfortunately, one of the Indian doctors always drank too much. When he became inebriated, he lost his inhibitions. One evening when all the ladies, including Khurshid, were in our kitchen he asked me why this doctor spent so much time at our house and with me at the hospital. He said that seeing the two of us together all the time was odd.

I told him that Khurshid was Rachel's good friend. She was also lonely. Naturally, she felt safe and happy in our house with us. The doctor said that Khurshid was definitely happy, but what about Rachel? He insisted that I was oblivious to all the talk about my unholy relationship with this unmarried woman. He wondered why her father wasn't mad at me.

The ladies, who were still in the kitchen, overheard the doctor. His wife hurried into the living room. She told her husband to stop saying such offensive things. They were guests in our house, and so was Khurshid. Khurshid also confronted the man. As tears filled her eyes, she told the doctor that he was drunk. He was talking nonsense.

A few days later the Minister of Education came to see me at the hospital. He was disappointed that my friend and countryman Mr. Ali had come to his house to ask him for a teaching job. The Minister knew that I hadn't sent Mr. Ali to his house, but his visit and request were highly irregular. He wanted me to make certain that Mr. Ali never again asked for a job.

I apologized to the Minister and said that I had already told Mr. Ali that his immigration permit didn't allow him to work in Nigeria. The Minister told me to tell him that he would face deportation if he tried to go around the law. His daughter could also suffer from his unacceptable behavior. Khurshid felt terrible when I told her about the minister's visit to my office.

One evening Saha called and said that he and his wife were coming to visit us. When they arrived at our house Joya stayed with Rachel while Saha went to a meeting at the Ministry of Health. He was still trying to get an additional surgeon posted to his hospital. He told us that he planned to meet with some Indian and Pakistani doctors in Kaduna after his meeting.

The next morning as Saha and I ate breakfast together, he said that he had heard many disturbing things about me from his Indian and Pakistani friends. He asked me what I was doing. I had a lovely wife and two lovely daughters. I should be a happily married man. Saha claimed that no one dared to confront me because of my senior position in the service and my close friendships with powerful Nigerian leaders. But everyone knew what I was doing with that unmarried doctor. His Muslim friends told him that the woman's father was telling everyone that I was taking his daughter as my second wife. Saha said that this scandal was bound to blow up.

Joya joined us in the kitchen. She asked me if I had talked to Rachel about my commitment to this other woman. I told Saha and Joya that Rachel knew that I was doing nothing wrong. She trusted me fully. Saha still insisted that whenever he found smoke, he always found fire. I told Saha that I was speaking the truth.

Once Rachel and I were alone again I asked her to tell me her feelings about this sordid rubbish. Rachel said that she knew better than everyone else. She trusted me. I was so lucky to have such a wonderful wife.

One day I heard that some Pakistanis had confronted Mr. Ali about his daughter's relationship with me. Mr. Ali insisted that I loved his daughter. He was ready to bless her marriage to me. A short time later Mr. Ibe who was a middle-aged Ibo nurse at the hospital asked me if I was taking a second wife. He understood that most Nigerian Muslims took many wives; but as a good Catholic, he was against polygamy. I told Mr. Ibe that these rumors were ridiculous.

One night Mr. Ali called to tell me that Khurshid was ill. She didn't want the male Pakistani doctor who worked at the nursing home to examine her. He asked me to come see her at their house. Rachel was busy with the children, so I went alone to see Khurshid. Mr. Ali ushered me into his daughter's bedroom where she was lying on her bed. Khurshid winced when I switched on the bright ceiling light. She asked me to turn it off and switch on the small table lamp. Its soft light made the room look lovely and fresh flowers in a vase filled the air with gentle fragrance.

I reminded Khurshid that I wasn't a general practitioner. I was seeing her at her father's request. Khurshid felt warm to the touch and her face was flushed. She complained of a sore throat and heaviness in her chest. I opened her doctor's bag and took out some instruments to examine her. Khurshid had developed pharyngitis, but she didn't have an ear infection.

Khurshid suddenly removed the cover that she had placed

over her body. She lay there nearly motionless as the soft light exposed her naked body. Her perfect breasts moved gently with each breath as I examined her chest and heart. As I tried hard to ignore her nakedness, I told Khurshid that I was prescribing some antibiotics that her father or a servant could get from the hospital pharmacy. She would feel fine in a couple of days.

Khurshid sat up and grabbed my hand. She said that she had never met a man like me. She couldn't believe that I wasn't tempted when a woman offered herself with affection. I told Khurshid that I wasn't made of stone. I was attracted to her. I was tempted. But I would never take advantage of her.

Khurshid did not attempt to move as I mechanically drew up the bed sheet and covered her body. She said that she knew that her father had told people that I planned to marry her. She knew very well that this wasn't true. I told Khurshid that she was right. This is why we should never discuss this matter again.

Khurshid had a strange look in her eyes as she asked me if I would ever consider having her for a short time if she promised to keep the affair secret forever. I took my hand from her and said that this would be a terrible thing to do. We would lose respect for each other.

I went to the front room and told her father that his daughter had a throat and chest infection. I handed him the prescription and said that Khurshid would be fine in a few days. I left their house.

As I headed back home, I thanked my stars that I hadn't given in to temptation. It would have put an ugly stain on my sweet and trusting relationship with dear, dear Rachel.

~ 92 ~

RELATIVE PEACE

AT THE END OF MY next tour, Sheila would have to leave Nigeria to continue her education in England. She had a good time with her sister at the residential school in Brighton, but Rachel still wondered if Sheila would fit into a British boarding school. She was so high-spirited. Rachel and I met with the governess at Sheila's school and one of her classroom teachers who said that Sheila was an excellent student, but she had a mind of her own. The governess was more specific. She said that Sheila had little use for rules and regulations.

The governess suggested that we encourage our daughter to stay at the Kaduna school for three months while we took our next home leave. Since her school in Kaduna followed a similar structure and program as the English boarding schools, we would get to see if she enjoyed her experience. We discussed this plan with Sheila. She surprised us. She liked her school and the friends who would be staying there during the three months that we were away.

Once again Rachel and I skipped one of the weekly official

cocktail parties. This time the Permanent Secretary at the Ministry of Health made me call and apologize to one of the Nigerian Ministers. The Minister said that Nigerian officials wanted me at these gatherings. I was their friend.

The Minister's words were no comfort to me. Yes, I was considered his good friend, but I had to honor his demands, or he suspected my loyalty. Every important Nigerian had relationships with civil servants that reflected the attitudes of the ruling class who continued to live by Nigeria's feudal system. Only some of my powerful Northern friends, such as the Emir of Zunguru, were genuinely friendly and treated me with respect. The Emir was a true friend. He had helped me long before he became the Minister of Works. While we often discussed his health problems, our conversations always veered into the political health of his country.

One evening the Emir came to visit me and said that he and the other Northern leaders knew that Ibos were holding secret meetings in every Nigerian city, including Kaduna. The Ibos were planning a violent overthrow of the government. They wanted to assassinate the Northern leaders to destabilize the North. The Emir assumed that Northern Christians were working with the Ibos. The Northern leaders needed to identify the ringleaders and stop them. He asked me if I had ever overheard any discussions between Ibos. I told my friend that I had often seen groups of Ibos talking among themselves at the hospital, but I never knew what they were discussing.

A few days later the Emir told me that the federal government planned to open a Nigerian Defense Academy in Kaduna. Some Indian military officers, including a brigadier, were coming to train an expanded Nigerian army and police force. The Emir said that India's High Commissioner was coming to Kaduna to attend the opening ceremony.

When Ambassador Haksar and his wife arrived in Kaduna, he introduced me to the Indian brigadier and other Indian officers. For three delightful days, Rachel and I visited with the High Commissioner and his wife. One evening Rachel prepared a special Indian sweet called sandesh, which was a favorite dish of the Ambassador. He insisted that Rachel made the best sandesh that he had ever tasted.

Days after the opening ceremony of the defense academy the Emir of Zunguru said that the Premier wanted me to come to his residence to attend a special meeting. I was honored. Few foreigners were accorded this privilege. The Emir and I were ushered into the Premier's impressive meeting room where Sir Ahmadu Bello sat on the dais surrounded by Northern Nigeria's most important officials. High-ranking military and police officers sat behind them. Other senior dignitaries from Nigeria and foreign countries sat nearby. Everyone else squatted on a crisp white cloth spread on the floor.

The Premier, who had recently returned from his pilgrimage to Mecca and Medina, offered me a bottle of sacred water from a holy spring, which I graciously accepted. He thanked me for my service to his country before he addressed the gathering. He expressed his regret that politicians, businessmen, and top bureaucrats were preoccupied with the acquisition of personal wealth. He said that they ignored the needs of the common man whose condition failed to improve in Nigeria.

Sir Ahmadu Bello wondered if he would have time to realize his dream of bringing prosperity and happiness to all the Northerners. He was aware that people were plotting to assassinate him. But he wasn't worried. Only Allah controlled the time of his life and death. But he did worry that Southerners, especially the Ibos, wanted to control all of Nigeria. He feared for the well-being of Northern Nigerians.

Everyone stood up. They promised the Premier that they would never let anyone harm him or Northern Nigeria. I sensed the alarm that coursed through the room. I disliked the corruption that thrived with the government's compliance, but I still supported these leaders. They kept Nigeria stable.

A few days later Mr. Ali came to our house to tell me that he had brought a gift of food to the Minister of Education at the end of Ramadan. This was a common courtesy in Islamic societies. When he arrived at the Minister's house, he was surprised that he had to join a long line of men bearing gifts for this Nigerian official. More Muslims stood at the gates of other ministers who also lived in the area. After a two-hour wait, a servant finally collected the gifts and bestowed Allah's blessings on all the well-wishers.

Mr. Ali was offended. He said that these ministers might be Muslims, but they lacked all of Islam's manners and courtesies. They didn't even pray properly. As I listened to Mr. Ali, I knew full well why he had wanted to meet the Minister. I told him that the Premier had given me something special that I wanted to pass on to him. He would feel blessed. I handed Mr. Ali the bottle of holy spring water from Medina. As he stared at the delicate vial, I knew that he was struggling to understand why the Premier had given me, a Hindu, holy water from Medina. He finally asked me for a prayer shawl. Mr. Ali prayed in our front room before he quietly left our home with his precious gift.

After Rachel and I decided to leave Sheila at her school while we were away, we prepared for our home leave. The Ministry assured me that I would return to my post in Kaduna when we returned to Nigeria. During our absence, a surgeon would cover for me at the hospital and live in our house.

Rachel, Monica, and I flew to London where we stayed with Jacob and Hilda in their house. Rachel's parents had gone to Israel and their children doubted that they would ever return to London. Rachel and I visited our favorite parks in London. We also saw some wonderful shows in the West End. We enjoyed tasty meals in London's restaurants. The two of us also had a delightful dinner with Sir John and his wife at their lovely house on the Thames.

One day Rachel and I went to visit Dr. Lahiri. He said that his health was deteriorating, and he still hoped to turn his practice over to me. He said I was foolish to stay in Nigeria. He was convinced that the country wouldn't survive without the British. He wondered why I would want to live with my family in such an unsafe place. Dr. Lahiri wanted me to seize the opportunity to buy his lucrative practice. He knew that I had enough money. I was at a loss for words. I had no plans to leave Nigeria.

Rachel and I also spent some time with Amjad who continued to work as a registrar in a hospital. He was extremely unhappy. His life as a single parent exhausted him, and he lacked the energy to start a family practice. He also thought that his son was lonely. The young boy had no contact with his mother's family. I truly believed that Amjad could make something of his life. But I knew that first, he had to stop feeling so defeated.

Before the three of us had to return to Nigeria, Rachel, Monica, and I joined a bus tour through Norway, Denmark, and Sweden. Our tour guide who was a retired schoolteacher with a strong voice and equally strong views handed us brochures about the important sites that we would visit over the next two weeks. I noticed that she had omitted glossy pamphlets about nightclubs and casinos. Our guide was a prude.

Rachel and I had already seen these countries on an earlier trip, but Monica enjoyed the bright lights and city sights of beautiful Copenhagen; and when our tour reached Stockholm, she loved the royal palace. But as we walked through this magnificent building, I noticed that our guide had forgotten to show us my favorite painting. When I asked her about her omission the guide said that National Day celebrated male chauvinism, not the country's national day. She took us to see the painting and pointed out that all the women were stuck way back in the crowd of onlookers. Only the men were allowed to stand in the front rows.

When we returned to London the three of us were eager to fly back to Nigeria. We all missed Sheila. We missed her even more once we landed at the Kaduna airport. We wanted to pick her up from her boarding school, but when I called the governess, she said that the school was closed for the day. She promised to have Sheila ready to go home first thing in the morning.

That evening when Rachel, Monica, and I were settled in the government rest house Monica asked me why her sister wasn't with us right now. I explained to her that the school was closed. We would get her sister in the morning. But Monica wanted to see Sheila right away. She cried and cried before we could quiet her down.

The next morning Monica was dressed and ready to get Sheila before Rachel and I were awake. Rachel told Monica that we had to wait until 9 o'clock when the school opened for the day.

After breakfast, we hurried to the school where the governess waited with Sheila. Our lovely daughter was a joy to behold as she ran to hug her mom. Sheila suddenly began to cry. She said that she was so relieved to be with us again.

I felt guilty and tears filled my eyes as I walked over to the governess and signed the release forms. I thanked her and all the teachers who had looked after Sheila. When I picked up Sheila's bag, I asked the governess if she thought that Sheila had enjoyed her time at the school. She said that Sheila had done well with her studies. She had also stayed healthy. But Sheila wasn't an ideal boarder. She paused before she said that Sheila was a handful. In fact, she was a fiend. Her words startled me.

The governess explained that Sheila could be pleasant and reasonable, but she could also be unusually difficult, and she ignored all the rules. She didn't think our daughter would be happy in a British boarding school, which would observe similar by-laws and regulations. The governess said that she shouldn't be telling me these things, but she knew that we had boarded Sheila to see how she would fare. She felt that we deserved to hear the truth. As I drove my family back to our house, I asked Sheila if she had enjoyed her stay in the hostel. She said that everything was well and good as long as she never had to stay there again.

~ 93 ~

AMASSING WEALTH

ONCE WE MOVED BACK INTO our house, our cook and other servants reported for work. The Indian surgeon who had covered for me at the hospital had taken good care of our property and our vegetable garden. We would soon be blessed with a reliable and productive kitchen garden.

When I saw him, he said that he was unhappy about his transfer to a small remote hospital. He would be unable to perform any major operations. He also assumed that the hospital would lack a properly trained anesthetist. I said that he was probably right, but I had worked under worse conditions when I first came to Nigeria. The doctor was convinced that I could get him a better assignment because I was the chief surgeon. I reminded him that I had no control over any appointment. He needed to speak with the appropriate administrative officer.

Over the next few days, I visited with Northern Nigerian leaders who flaunted their wealth as they praised the leadership of their Premier who brought peace and prosperity to Nigeria. They seemed oblivious to the needs of ordinary Nigerians who saw no improvement in their lives.

During this time, I heard a crazy story perfectly illustrating Nigeria's corruption depth. Chief Ekotie Eboh, who was the Nigerian Finance Minister, had his Rolls Royce flown from Lagos to Kaduna so that when he arrived in a later plane his chauffeur could drive him in his luxury car to a meeting with government officials. I also heard numerous rumors about government leaders who were supposedly siphoning billions of dollars from the treasury. Everyone said that they were transferring the stolen cash into numbered bank accounts in Switzerland.

Each time I heard these terrible stories I thought about Malam Lawan who had complained to me that the government kept cutting off funding that prevented him from completing projects intended to help Nigeria's poor farmers. He said that he often had to beg foreign governments and non-profit agencies for money to complete his agricultural projects. If my friend in his official capacity as the Permanent Secretary in the Ministry of Agriculture couldn't complete simple agrarian projects, the country would never approve complicated yet necessary future agrarian reforms.

One evening I chatted with my successful Greek friend who had an extraordinary sixth sense about Nigeria's political and commercial climate. Because of his uncanny intuition, he usually ended up backing political winners during conflicts and earning lucrative contracts. My Greek friend said that he was willing to grease the palms of Nigerians to keep his business wheels spinning. After ten years he planned to go back to Cyprus with his family and his wealth.

The Emir of Zunguru also acknowledged the problem of corruption in his country, but he insisted that anyone who thought that the Premier was corrupt was wrong. He admitted that most people who visited Sir Ahmadu Bello left him money or gifts as a token of their respect, but the Premier donated everything to the poor. Westerners who were unaware of the Premier's selfless charity would never believe that this important man shunned wealth. But the Emir said that his mentor had less than 100 pounds in his bank account.

The Emir continued to lavish praise on Sir Ahmadu Bello. He was convinced that the Premier was the only person in Nigeria with the ability, grace, and strength to hold together the country. As I listened to my good friend, I thought that his loyalty to his mentor blinded him. The Emir failed to see that the Premier lacked vision. Sir Ahmadu Bello had kept in place the same administrative policies that the old colonial government had introduced many years ago. He couldn't envision an intelligent new plan that would guide his country into a future that valued accountability and social growth. In truth, all the Northern leaders noticed only the people who lived with them inside their small elite world.

~ 94 ~

NEW REGIME, NEW RULES

AT THIS POINT IN MY life, I had no financial worries. My service compensation, which I invested through my London bank, was secure and increasing in value. In addition to my usual salary, the British government also awarded its officers extra pay as an incentive to stay in Nigeria. I also made substantial money in my private practice.

My career was also gratifying despite many new staff changes at the hospital and an undercurrent of ethnic tension. Five Nigerian medical officers had recently joined our staff. Dr. Adoba, who had graduated from the London University Medical College and subsequently trained in England, was the new medical officer in charge of the hospital. Northern Nigeria's first specialist from the Royal College of Physicians in Edinburgh was our new medical specialist. The three other Nigerian doctors were general-duty medical officers. Our hospital also recruited an excellent Egyptian doctor who became my assistant and helped me perform numerous physically and emotionally challenging surgeries.

The remaining British staff members and I thought that the hospital functioned reasonably well, but the British matron told me in private that all the Nigerian doctors, including Dr. Adoba, were "greenhorns." She said he made so many misguided decisions that she wished that a more experienced doctor would replace him. But she knew that the hospital administrators were convinced that this young doctor would learn on the job.

Our Irish anesthetist Dr. Brown and I had worked together for years, and we both sensed the increased antagonism between the Northern and Southern members of our staff. We knew that the Southerners' resentment of the Northerners also extended to me because of my friendships with so many Northern leaders. So while my career was fulfilling I realized that this tour in Kaduna could be difficult for me.

But I found solace at home with my children and Rachel who helped me maintain my sanity during this period of hard work when staff conflicts simmered below the surface. Sheila who was an active child usually invited her school friends to our house most weekends. Their joy and exuberance turned our home into a lively place. The sound of their laughter often reminded me that there was much more to life than work with its problems and difficulties. I also found great pleasure in watching sweet Monica build her confidence and assert her own fine personality. Unable to play with the other girls because of the age differences, Monica had turned to her mother who happily spent time with her youngest daughter. Over time Monica blossomed and built up her self-esteem.

At the hospital, I had started performing more difficult surgeries. Initially, Dr. Brown and the British matron worried about our ability to manage these operations, but they were usually successful. We were proud that we were finally treating cases that we had normally transferred to the hospital at Ibadan University. However, Dr. Adoba disapproved of these challenging procedures. He said that they consumed too much of our time, stretched hospital resources, and reduced our output. He told me to confer with him before I scheduled any more difficult surgeries. He was in charge of the hospital. He had to authorize every medical decision.

He also told me to stop sending orthopedic patients to the orthopedic hospital in Kano. He disputed my claim that Kano's orthopedic surgeon was superior to the doctors in our surgical department. He was certain that we could do these orthopedic surgeries right here in our hospital. He told me to start performing tonsillectomies, too. He disagreed with me when I said that these patients should see a specialist in the ear, nose, and throat department at Ibadan's hospital. I ignored him and his attempts to convince the rest of the staff that I had to answer to him. I continued to do my work as I saw fit.

Unfortunately, I learned that Dr. Adoba had found an ally in an old British officer who had disliked me for years. The regional pathologist Dr. McDonald was delighted when he asked for his help to cut me down to size. One fine morning I received a memo that ordered me to send all future requests for laboratory work to the regional pathologist for his prior authorization.

I was furious. This time-consuming order would inconvenience many of our patients who usually traveled great distances to get to our hospital. They would be forced to make an unnecessary second trip for their blood work. The order also increased each doctor's clerical work. Our present system, which had been in place for years, was efficient. I called the regional pathologist and told him that I wouldn't follow the new rule.

The next morning Dr. Adoba and Dr. McDonald came to see

me in my office. After the pathologist said that I had to observe the new order, Dr. Adoba informed me that he had written up my refusal to cooperate. He planned to send his complaint to the Medical Advisor at the Ministry of Health. Unexpectedly, his trial balloon burst before our eyes when Dr. McDonald said that he had already complained to the advisor. The medical officer had told the pathologist to resolve his problem without him. Dr. Adoba refused to back down. He was in charge of the hospital, and he had approved the new order. Once again, I ignored the doctor and this irresponsible new rule.

A few days later a nurse came to my office and told me that Dr. Adoba had just confronted the lab technician Hassan in a ward as he was drawing blood from a patient. When he asked Hassan if the pathologist had authorized these lab tests, the lab technician said that he had been a technician for ten years. He knew how to do his job. Hassan asked Dr. Adoba why he was questioning him.

He reminded Hassan who was in charge of this hospital. He had every right to question his subordinate. Hassan said that Dr. Adoba wasn't his superior. If the doctor didn't like the way he was doing his lab work, he should go talk to the pathologist. Dr. Adoba ordered Hassan from the ward and told him not to return until he had proper authorization from Dr. McDonald to draw blood from a patient. When Hassan ignored Dr. Adoba, the doctor swore at him and pushed him. Hassan slapped the doctor and told him not to touch him again.

The nurse told me that everyone in the hospital knew that Hassan was a good man. He had worked here for years, and he was usually well-mannered. The nurse was worried that Hassan would lose his job. I told her not to worry. I doubted that anyone at the Ministry of Health would take action without a proper inquiry.

Later that day when I was doing work in my office the chief surgical nurse asked to speak to me. When he repeated the account of the incident involving Hassan, I could tell that his sympathies lay with Hassan. He referred to the lab technician as a true Northerner and a Muslim. Dr. Adoba was a Christian. The chief surgical nurse also said that Hassan's brother was the Emir of Kaduna. The Emir would never let his brother suffer. The nurse hoped that I would help Hassan since I was a friend of the North. I told the chief surgical nurse to watch quietly. We would see how things unfolded.

After a few days, the Permanent Secretary summoned Dr. Mc-Donald and me to his office. When the Permanent Secretary asked me about the incident with our lab technician, I said that I wasn't on the ward, but some nurses who had witnessed the altercation had reported it to me. Dr. McDonald told the Permanent Secretary that he wasn't present either, but he had heard about the incident from Hassan and Dr. Adoba.

The Permanent Secretary appointed me the chairman of a committee of inquiry. He said that his deputy Malak Abdullahi and the medical officer Dr. Diko would serve on the committee with me. He expected our report in seven days. The Honorable Minister of Health wanted this case resolved quickly.

At the inquiry, Dr. Adoba admitted to our committee that he had told Hassan to leave the ward, but he denied swearing at the lab technician and shoving him into the corridor. During questioning, he finally admitted that he might have touched the lab technician, but he didn't hurt him.

Dr. McDonald conceded that he had forgotten to post an official notice in the lab or in the ward that announced the new procedure. He also said that neither he nor the chief surgeon nor the medical officer in charge of the hospital had finalized the new order.

He believed that it wasn't in effect at the time of the incident.

Hassan admitted that he had slapped Dr. Adoba, but only after the doctor verbally and physically abused him. He said that he had become so angry that he was unable to restrain himself. He apologized for his conduct. Two nurses and a patient also appeared before our committee. They said that they had witnessed Dr. Adoba shout at Hassan and shove him from the ward.

Before we came to a conclusion, I knew that our committee had to take into account that Hassan and the other Nigerian witnesses were Northern Muslims and Dr. Adoba was a Southern Christian who was friendly with the Ibos. The Northerners would naturally resent him.

I wanted our committee to reach a consensus, but Dr. Diko who was a Christian from Dr. Adoba's district insisted on submitting his own report. The Deputy Permanent Secretary and I wrote a factual analysis of the incident in which we concluded that each participant had behaved improperly. No official notice had been posted to announce the new order. Dr. Adoba's violent provocation of the technician was unjustified, but Mr. Hassan's violent overreaction was unacceptable. We recommended that the Ministry should take appropriate disciplinary action against both.

Dr. Diko stated in his report that the subordinate officer should be severely disciplined for his violent conduct. He also suggested that the medical officer in charge of the hospital should have full authority over the entire staff to maintain discipline; otherwise, the hospital would descend into chaos.

One week later the Ministry of Health reprimanded Dr. Adoba and sent him to a small station. Mr. Hassan received a mild reprimand that wouldn't affect his career.

Dr. Bonda who was the new Nigerian officer in charge of our

hospital never tried to be friendly with the expatriate doctors. He favored Dr. Diko and the other Nigerian doctors. They became an exclusive group unto themselves. Nothing would change at our hospital.

~ 95 ~

SURREPTITIOUS MEETINGS

AFTER DR. BONDA TOOK CHARGE of our hospital the senior surgical nurse who was a Northern Muslim came to talk to me in my office. I had known him for years and I always assumed that he passed on information to the Northern leaders. He told me that the Christian doctors were holding nighttime meetings at the hospital with Southerners who were either Ibo politicians or their agents. The nurse worried that they were plotting against the government.

After work, I went to see my Greek friend. He told me that he had heard that the Ibos were trying to get the Yorubas to join their conspiracy against the Northerners. He had heard that the Yorubas had refused to join them; they didn't trust the Ibos. He said that all these rumors were finally affecting his bottom line. My friend also advised me to stay away from the Ibos, or my Northern friends would become suspicious. As I started to leave his office, my friend reminded me that my car insurance was due in three months. While I wrote out a check to him, he said that maybe all these rumors were just rumors.

The next time I worked at the military hospital Colonel Oba who was a Yoruba from Western Nigeria said that he was worried that some Ibo officers were trying to get control of Nigeria's ammunition depot. The hostility of the Ibos who outnumbered the Northern and Western officers at the military hospital scared him. He wished that he would be transferred to the West. Colonel Oba stopped talking. An Ibo officer was watching us.

A few days later Mr. Hamidu who was an old acquaintance from Gusau unexpectedly showed up in my office. He thanked Allah for making Sir Ahmadu Bello the Premier of the North. This wonderful leader had helped him start a business in Gusau that had become so successful that he turned it over to his brother so that he could open up a bigger company in Kaduna.

Mr. Hamidu took me to see his new office. When he asked his servant to bring us some tea, I recognized the young man. He had worked for a British officer who had recently returned to England. The servant took me aside and said that he had struggled to find a good job, but all the decent masters were gone. Mr. Hamidu overheard the boy. He told him that he should be happy that he had a good-paying job with a Nigerian master. He should be grateful that he lived in a free country and no longer had to work for the British. I was surprised that Mr. Hamidu believed that this young boy's circumstances had improved because he was working for a Nigerian. Nigeria's independence hadn't helped him. He was still a second-class citizen. I also knew that many Nigerian masters mistreated their servants.

A few days later Mr. Walker who was a retired Colonial Service officer came to the hospital. He asked me to come to his house to see his Nigerian wife who was the daughter of the former Emir of Kano. I drove to their riverside bungalow and met Mrs. Walker who looked elegant in her flowing African dress. She was upset that her husband had asked me to come all the way from the city to treat her. She was just suffering from an abdominal pain. But when I examined Mrs. Walker, I discovered that she was bleeding from a large fibroid in her uterus. I told her that she needed to have a hysterectomy before she became weak from anemia. A few days later I successfully operated on her and she quickly recovered.

Rachel and I became good friends with this gracious couple. Mr. Walker, who currently ran an export and import business, believed that the government's exploitation of its natural resources had outpaced its creation of a viable judicial system, which was a necessary cornerstone in a democracy. Mr. Walker thought that Nigeria was beginning to unravel. He feared an insurrection. He and his wife had recently advised their son to stay in England and not come back home. They no longer believed that honest people could succeed in Nigeria. I saw their worried looks each time our conversation dwelled on present-day Nigeria. I only hoped that common sense would prevail, and this couple's fears wouldn't come true.

One day Mr. Ibe who was an Ibo nurse came to speak to me in my office. When I closed the door, he said that many ears would try to listen to our conversation. Mr. Ibe explained that he didn't belong to any political group, but he had heard from reliable sources that something was about to happen to the government and the country. Mr. Ibe said that he knew that I had been good to his people. But Ibos hated the Northern leaders and most of them were my friends, so the Ibos naturally assumed that I had turned against them. When I told Mr. Ibe that I wasn't involved with politics he said that no one would believe me. But Mr. Ibe promised to keep me informed. Before he left my office, we fabricated a story to cover his visit.

Minutes later two Northern nurses asked why the old Ibo nurse had come to see me. I told them that Mr. Ibe was worried about his nephew in Eastern Nigeria. The boy had an enlarged spleen and needed a splenectomy. Mr. Ibe had asked me if I would perform the operation here. The two nurses told me to watch out. Ibe the Ibo was a slippery old fox. They didn't trust him.

Days later I received an invitation to have tea with Sir Ali Ibramin who had helped me repeatedly when I was stationed in Maiduguri. My friend was currently the Governor and the chancellor of a newly created university. When we chatted together in the Governor's House I asked him about his daughter. A few years ago, she told me that she wanted to become a medical doctor. The Governor said she was happily married to a prosperous businessman. She was about to become a mother.

Sometime later I discovered that this businessman was neither well-educated nor sophisticated. He also had another wife. I felt heartsick for the Governor's lovely daughter and sad for her generation of women in Northern Nigeria. If this enlightened man was pleased with his daughter's arranged marriage, what could I expect from unenlightened fathers of other aspiring women in the country? My hopes for Nigeria consistently turned into a pipe dream.

One evening the Emir of Zunguru came to my house to take me to see Sir Ahmadu Bello. Once we reached the Premier's compound we were ushered into his lavish meeting room. Several other ministers and provincial and federal legislators were gathered in the large space.

The Premier announced that he had received many assassination threats, but he wasn't afraid. He would die when Allah was ready to receive him. The Premier admitted that assassins could probably kill him and other Northern leaders, including their beloved Prime Minister. He and the Prime Minister wanted everyone at the meeting to promise that they would never allow murderers from the South to conquer Northern Nigeria.

Everyone stood up and expressed their solemn belief that Allah would protect their great leaders. They pledged their allegiance and vowed to protect every inch of the North. They promised the Premier that they would defeat their Southern enemy.

After the meeting, the Premier asked me to examine him in his private study. The Premier was in good health, but I told him to watch his weight and his blood pressure. We talked for a few minutes before I bid him goodbye.

The Emir of Zunguru invited me back to his house where a sophisticated young lady from the American Embassy joined us for dinner. As we chatted together the Emir said that the Northern leaders needed to accelerate the training of new military recruits and police officers so they could stop any threat to the government.

Later, when my friend took me out to his car to tell his driver to take me home, he asked me not to talk about the American lady I had met at his house. The Premier didn't want any minister to get close to girls who worked for the American Embassy. His good friend had concluded that the Americans intended to align themselves with the Ibos to get control of Nigeria's oil and gas.

On my way home I worried that this American woman was seducing my friend because he was close to the Premier. She would try to extract important political information. For hours I kept thinking about this American woman and the threats against the life of the Premier. I began to wonder about my family's future in this country.

I was glad that I had recently spent time with the Canadian High Commissioner who had suggested that I immigrate with my family to Canada. Our friends Dr. Ram Krishnan and his wife Asha who worked at Ibadan University were moving to Nova Scotia in a few months. The thought of living in Canada suddenly seemed appealing to me, especially if this wonderful family settled there before us.

I spoke to the First Consul at the Canadian High Commission who explained his country's immigration process and the various restrictions governing the transfer of financial assets from Nigeria and England to his country. He said that once Canada approved our immigration, I would have ample time to get my finances in order. If conditions deteriorated in Nigeria, Canada seemed a plausible option for us. I needed to talk with Rachel.

~ 96 ~

COUP!

ONE DAY RACHEL AND I received a letter from Uncle Hem Ray's son Manab who was studying in England. He wrote to say that he planned to sit for his qualifying chartered accounting examination in three years. I was thrilled to receive his good news. Rachel and I also heard from Manash who said that he had a good job in a factory attached to his engineering school. His studies were going well, and he was enjoying England.

Every January our family held a huge celebration in honor of Rachel's birthday. Since we had a spacious property, we always held the party outdoors. Kaduna's weather was reliably dry and pleasant. We invited everyone we knew in Kaduna and every year the party increased in size. Our celebration planned for January 1966 was no exception.

I asked my British friend Mr. Boxer who was the manager of the football stadium to supply tables and chairs. A good Lebanese friend imported delicious grapes for us and stored a shipment of turkeys, chickens, and legs of lamb in his huge freezer. Rachel and

I sent out the invitations and a few ladies volunteered to help with the cooking. Everything was set. We would have a smoothly run grand party.

The day before the party Mr. Boxer delivered all the tables and chairs and his men arranged them on our property. The women started cooking all the meat and other dishes in their kitchens. By the time Rachel and I went to bed that night we were exhausted. We quickly fell asleep knowing that our party would be a resounding success.

Loud booms shattered the dead of the night. Rachel and I wondered if soldiers were in training and throwing grenades or target shooting at a firing range.

In the early morning, a glorious sun rose in a cloudless sky. The phone rang and my Lebanese friend destroyed my beautiful vision of a lovely day. In broken English, he said that there had been lots of shootings in the town and the Premier had been assassinated. Soldiers with guns stood in front of his property. He couldn't go outside. We had to forget about the party. No one was safe. All the Northerners were in mourning.

I told Rachel and the servants. Our cook said that he had seen soldiers on the road near the front of our house. The telephone rang again. Dr. Bonda told me to hurry to the hospital. I quickly dressed and raced out to the car. When I entered the main road, I was stopped at a roadblock. Soldiers approached me with their guns drawn. They ordered me from the car and demanded that I open the trunk before they told me to raise my hands. As one soldier inspected the car and the trunk, another soldier demanded to know where I was going.

I said that I was a doctor. I had been summoned to the hospital to work. They muttered that work must go on before they told me to proceed.

I navigated through two more roadblocks until I finally reached the front of the hospital where more soldiers stood guard at the gate. They sent me to the doctors' lounge where I joined other staff members who nervously watched army officers sitting in chairs casually sipping tea. An army officer finally stood up and addressed us. He said that the army had been forced to root out the dishonest and inefficient government. It had put an end to the corrupt civilian administration.

The officer announced that General Ironsi who was the Supreme Commander of the Army was Nigeria's new ruler. He said that this honest general would turn Nigeria into a great country that benefited the great Nigerian people. General Ironsi would not tolerate any corruption, drug use, or disobedience. The officer ordered us to follow the Supreme Commander's decrees and orders, or we would be severely punished with the possibility of death. He said our work must go on without interruption.

The army officers left the hospital, but some of their soldiers stayed behind to watch us with their guns ready to fire. Except for the Ibos and the other Christian Nigerians, our staff was bewildered. I went to my office and sat in silence until the chief surgical nurse and the chief operating nurse came to see me with tears in their eyes.

When I asked them what happened in the night they sobbed and said that there had been an army coup d'état. They heard that General Ironsi had ordered officers and soldiers into the houses of Yoruba officers. They had killed all the Yoruba officers who refused to join their coup before they stormed the Premier's house. They killed his bodyguards and assassinated the Premier. Other ministers had fled, and no one knew where they were hiding. They had vanished.

Dr. Bonda called me into his office. He asked me if the surgical clinic was open. I said that I didn't think anyone would come today. He told me to stop thinking. He ordered me to open the clinic. He repeated the mantra that work must go on.

No one arrived at our clinic, so we stood around listening to martial music on the radio until a broadcaster reported that General Ironsi had confronted the Prime Minister last night. He had ordered the Prime Minister to stand up and hear his death sentence for committing treason against the people of Nigeria. General Ironsi shot him several times before the soldiers dragged his body from the room. An Ibo nurse in our clinic smiled, but the rest of us stared in silence.

Dr. Bonda summoned the senior staff to his office where the Permanent Secretary had arrived to tell us that the transfer of power wouldn't affect anyone at the hospital. We should continue to do our work and serve the people. The Permanent Secretary who was aware of my friendships with the former leaders took me aside. After he told me not to despair, he said that our telephones were tapped. He talked to a few other doctors before he left the hospital.

I went back to my office and called Rachel. She said that she and our daughters were fine, but Mrs. Ganguly who was the wife of an Indian army officer had telephoned her. She told Rachel that terrible things were happening in the barracks at the defense academy. Rachel said that she had invited the couple to move into our guest wing. She added without the slightest trace of irony that we had plenty of food. I called Mrs. Ganguly and also invited her and her husband to stay at our house. She said that all the Indian officers had left the academy and moved in with their friends.

Before I went home for the night, I learned that Ibo soldiers had also gone to the Governor's House. They had forced Sir Ali Ibrahim and his family to move into a civilian residence. Dr. Bonda also told us that the Premier of Western Nigeria had been assassinated after he had refused to join the coup. The Ibos had taken control of all of Nigeria.

I asked our Indian guest Colonel Ganguly how the Ibos officers could force Northern soldiers to kill their Muslim commanders. He said that soldiers were always brainwashed. They were trained to obey the orders of their superior officers, under all circumstances, even after a coup.

That evening an ambulance with its siren blaring raced into our driveway. An Ibo nurse hurried to our front door. He said that a wounded major had metal fragments lodged in his neck. Everyone, including the major, worried that he would bleed to death. The nurse said that the wounded major would only allow me to operate on him. I would have to perform the surgery with local anesthesia.

I was stuck in an awful dilemma. This major was a murderer. His soldiers had been involved in the death of my friend the Premier. If I operated on this man, my Northern friends would consider me a traitor. But the Ibos would kill my family and me if I refused to assist him.

I told the nurse that I needed permission from the Permanent Secretary before I could operate on such an important official. I asked him to tell the major to be kind enough to wait. I had to secure the proper authorization and the operating room at the hospital. We should plan to operate on the major in the morning.

I couldn't sleep all night. I felt helpless and prayed to God for a way out of operating on this man. The next morning when I arrived at the hospital, I learned that the major had been transferred to Enugu, which was the capital of Eastern Nigeria. I thanked God and my lucky stars.

Two days after the coup I continued to face a series of road-blocks every time I traveled between my house and the hospital. On the third day, the new military governor came to the hospital to address our staff. He described the powers and virtues of the new Supreme Commander and reminded us that General Ironsi would not tolerate corruption, drugs, and licentiousness.

Days later the Governor invited me for tea at his residence. After I endured roadblocks that were guarded by suspicious soldiers who repeatedly searched me and my car, I was finally allowed into the Governor's compound. During the restrained conversation, the Governor said that he was pleased that I didn't need to operate on the Ibo major. He knew that the surgery would be problematic for me. He asked me if he could do anything to make my work easier during this difficult time.

I thought a moment before I told the Governor that the road-blocks and repeated searches were destroying my mental peace. I traveled frequently because I was the surgeon in charge of the civilian hospital and the military hospital. The next day I received a card stamped with the Governor's official seal. He had authorized my right to travel alone or with my family without any restrictions.

~ 97 ~

COUNTERPLAN

As TIME PASSED NOT A single Western government protested Nigeria's coup. Foreign governments accepted the military takeover of the country. In Kaduna, the Ibos, who finally ruled the country, walked tall. However, few members of our staff wanted to follow the orders of any of the Ibo doctors in our hospital.

One afternoon the chief pharmacist who was a good friend of the Northern leaders came to see me in my office. He said that times were hard. He hoped that God would soon end this sad state of affairs. The pharmacist talked briefly about the Northern ministers and other leaders who had fled Kaduna the night of the coup. He said that everyone was safe, but some of them needed medical attention. He thought that my friends would try to visit me at night. He handed me a box of medical supplies and left my office.

That evening the Emir of Zunguru tapped on my backdoor. He was pale and breathing heavily. After I helped him inside the house my friend told me that Northern supporters had taken most of the leaders to safety where a local militia watched over them. Some of their allies were also watching my house because I was at risk.

The Emir who was running a high fever had acute pharyngitis and possibly pneumonia. I gave him medicine for seven days and told him to come back if he wasn't feeling better.

The next few days more Northern leaders came to our backdoor at night for medical help. I kept the back of our house dark and examined them in our pantry. No one ever saw them, but everyone in the house knew what was going on. When Colonel Ganguly said that I was putting my family in danger, I explained to our guest that I couldn't forsake my friends. They had been good to me every time I asked for their help.

After a few weeks, the military government pardoned every deposed leader who agreed to accept the authority of the new regime. Once the pardon went into effect the Emir of Zunguru came to thank me for my help. He told me that the former leaders planned to undo the Ibo mischief. Before he left my house the Emir reminded me that Ibos were watching my house and tapping my telephone. He told me not to worry. His people would keep us safe.

Rachel and I were invited to a cocktail party at the Governor's House that would honor the Supreme Commander General Ojukwu when he came to Kaduna. Before the Supreme Commander arrived in Kaduna people feared that either Northerners would assassinate the general or the general's soldiers would kill Northern leaders. Everyone was jittery.

On the day of the cocktail party when Rachel and I drove toward the Governor's House fully armed soldiers repeatedly stopped us and searched our car. Soldiers in camouflage hid in the bushes that grew along the border of the governor's property. While we dined and sipped our drinks the general's officers circulated the lawn and told everybody that our lives would improve under the rule of the Supreme Commander.

General Ironsi looked spiffy in his ceremonial uniform when he marched onto a platform and listened to his loyal officers cheer "Long Live the Supreme Commander!" But apprehension unnerved the crowd. Everyone was relieved when we could finally go home.

Over time I started working two days a week at the military hospital. Colonel Oba told me that he had a new reason to fear the Ibos at the hospital. They hated him because he had refused to join their insurrection. But his superiors still refused to transfer his family to Western Nigeria.

One day Colonel Obo said that he thought that the military governor was a loyal Northerner. Why else would he put so many Northern military officers into sensitive government positions? His reasoning made me see the governor in a new light. I wondered if Colonel Oba's supposition was correct.

Sometime later the Emir of Zunguru came to talk to me at our house. He said that he planned to travel through Northern Nigeria with the other leaders and talk to Muslim families who had sons serving in the army. The leaders knew that every Northerner loved his land as much as life itself. They also knew that Northerners were aware that the Southerners coveted their land. Once Northern families understood that the Ibo government wanted to seize the farms of their Muslim enemies, they would go visit their sons serving in the army. They would tell them to sneak out of their barracks and kill Ibo officers as they slept in their homes. When enough terrified Ibo officers and soldiers fled to Eastern Nigeria the Northerners would retake control of the army and launch a full-scale counter-coup.

The Emir said that he was leaving Kaduna in the morning. If anyone asked me where he had gone, he wanted me to say that the

Emir had returned to Zunguru. There was nothing left for him to do in Kaduna. My friend walked toward the front door and pointed to a car sitting on the street not far from our driveway. He said that Ibo spies were inside that car. They followed him everywhere, but he knew that he was safe. Well-armed Northerners were watching the Ibos. The Emir removed the top from his walking stick and pulled out a hidden sword. He smiled and said that this weapon was his best defense.

~ 98 ~

RUMORS

THE NEXT TIME I WENT to the military hospital a medical officer hurried me to a ward to examine a new patient. A young officer had nasty wounds on his right arm and his chest, but they weren't life-threatening. After I told the medical officer the correct way to treat the soldier a doctor who had been my former medical student pulled me aside. He lowered his voice and said that three Ibo officers had been attacked in their homes last night. Two officers were killed. He pointed to the ward and said that I had just examined the third officer. He didn't think the attackers were outsiders. He thought that they belonged to a nearby army unit. I wondered if the counterinsurgency had begun.

The next morning a military ambulance pulled to stop in front of the civilian hospital. Military personnel rushed a uniformed man who was covered in blood into the surgery clinic. A medical officer asked me to treat the injured man. As I examined a large gash that had sliced open his abdomen a colonel told me that once I finished the surgery, he was taking the patient back to the military hospital.

After I completed the operation, I wanted the man to spend some time in our recovery room; but the Permanent Secretary called and informed me that we had no jurisdiction over military patients in our civilian hospital. The military personnel whisked their patient away.

The attacks on Ibo officers continued night after night. Colonel Ganguly and his wife who had returned to their house on the defense academy compound said that they kept waking up to the sound of shouts and gunshots. Twice, they had watched in horror as houses belonging to Ibo officers went up in flames. The Ibo families who lived on the base were terrified. Similar attacks on Ibos occurred on army bases throughout Northern Nigeria and in parts of Western Nigeria.

One day the chief pharmacist came to see me again. I saw his worried look as he closed my office door. He said that some Northern soldiers had found a list in the house of an Ibo captain that identified Northern Nigerians and expatriates whom they planned to murder. They were going to bury their victims in a trench by the side of a road outside the city.

The pharmacist pointed to my name when he showed me the list. He said that the Ibos were targeting me because I was a loyal friend of the North. But they would never get me. Northerners were guarding everyone on the list. He promised me that Northerners always took good care of their friends.

Rachel was stunned when I told her about the Ibo hit list. She wanted us to get out of Nigeria and immigrate to Canada. She didn't think that the Ibos would back down even if they were pushed out of power. In her estimation, Nigeria was headed for a civil war. No one would be safe. She wanted us to leave.

I had recently met with my friend who was a senior member

of the Public Service Commission. He said that I had job security for at least fifteen more years. The commission had also promised me a significantly high salary increase if I agreed to stay in Nigeria. I was in such a favorable career and financial position. But Rachel was right. Nigeria was unstable. The Ibos even wanted to end my life.

Some friends who were in the Canadian Peace Corps assured Rachel and me that their country would be a perfect place for us. Canada had good educational and medical systems and doctors earned excellent incomes. We would do well in their country.

I also talked to the Irish anesthetic Dr. Brown who was a trustworthy friend. He said that if we planned to leave Nigeria, we should go while I was still young. I would need time to get established in Canada, but he was confident that I would eventually get work as a surgeon in a small town or maybe in the city of Halifax. He also thought that our two girls were the right age to make a successful transition to Canada's fine educational system.

I wrote to Dr. Ram Krishnan, who had moved to Nova Scotia with his family. I told him about our interest in immigrating to Canada and asked him for his advice. He wrote back that he and his family were happily settled in a lovely Nova Scotia valley. He was confident that I would eventually make the specialist list in Canada, but even as a family practitioner, I could perform many surgical operations. He assured me that I would have a rewarding professional life in his new country. He also believed that our children would benefit from Nova Scotia's excellent schools. He urged us to come to Canada.

The First Consul at the British Embassy was certain that I would receive permission to immigrate to Canada. He said his department would also grant my family "returning resident" status so that we could return to the United Kingdom. I would also receive my British pension and other benefits in Canada since I was a Special List B officer, but he worried about the transfer of my assets to Canada. The Nigerian government didn't let anyone transfer more than 500 pounds from the country. While the Colonial Service paid my salary and additional inducement allowance directly into my London bank account, I still had a significant amount of money from my private practice in Nigeria. I had to find a solution.

~ 99 ~

NEW PROBLEMS

THE VIOLENCE BETWEEN THE IBO and Muslim forces intensified. Pitched gunfights broke out at many army bases, including the base in Kaduna. The huge number of injuries forced me to spend more time at the military hospital. Fortunately, my hardworking Egyptian assistant at the civilian hospital was so competent that he could perform most operations without me.

As military officers and soldiers were killed or injured rumors spread throughout Nigeria and increased the country's instability. My Nigerian friends told me that Northern agents who listened to private telephone conversations between Ibo politicians and Western diplomats or oil executives no longer trusted any Western power. They were aware that the British and the Americans only wanted access to the oil buried in Ibo territory. They weren't interested in anything else.

A few days later when I saw my friend Malam Lawan, I mentioned that my name was on an Ibo liquidation list. He nodded. He said that his name was on the same list. During all this time masked soldiers continued their nighttime attacks against Ibo officers. After Ibos killed some senior Yoruba officers in Kaduna because they had refused to support the coup, Colonel Oba worried about the safety of his family. He was certain that he had only survived because he wasn't in Kaduna the night of the attack. He wished his superiors would transfer his family to Western Nigeria.

I felt bad for Colonel Oba. He was vulnerable because few Yoruba officers and soldiers worked at the hospital. The next morning the Colonel told me that so many Ibo officers in Kaduna's armored vehicle brigade had been murdered that the military was going to transfer the rest of the brigade and its tanks to Eastern Nigeria. They didn't want this unit to fall into the hands of the Northerners. When people in the city heard about this plan they protested and forced the army to keep the brigade at the Kaduna army base.

Early one morning a medical officer from the military hospital called me while I was getting ready for work. Two Ibo officers had been seriously wounded. They were in stable condition, but he wanted me to come treat the two men. I told the military officer that I would see them after I completed my morning rounds at the civilian hospital.

I arrived at our hospital before any other doctors were on the ward. My senior surgical nurse said that an old man with a strangulated inguinal hernia needed to see me. The elderly man's son had brought him to the hospital. The son said that his father had started to complain about severe abdominal pain three days ago. He had also been vomiting. He said that his father felt better this morning, but he still couldn't keep anything in his stomach.

The elderly man was dehydrated. His abdomen was distended; his pulse and temperature were elevated. He told me that he hadn't passed any urine for 10 hours and hadn't passed any gas for two days. The poor man was extremely sick. I thought that his strangulated hernia had become gangrenous.

I knew that the nurses would have to treat his dehydration and get his kidneys to function before I could operate on him. I asked the senior surgical nurse to call my Egyptian assistant and tell him to hurry to the hospital.

When he arrived, I described the elderly man's condition and our ongoing treatment to my assistant. I asked him to monitor the patient and keep me informed. I also left instructions for the senior surgical nurse to perform an hourly suction to keep the patient's stomach empty. I told my assistant that I would operate on the elderly man as soon as he improved, but I was worried that the patient might not recover.

I hurried to the military hospital where I spent two hours treating the severe injuries of the two injured officers. Once I was confident they would survive, I returned to the civilian hospital. Dr. Bonda was leaving the surgical ward. He ignored me and headed to his office. My assistant told me that the old man had passed away fifteen minutes ago. I told his son that we had tried hard to save his father's life, but God had other plans. The son who was a devout Muslim understood that death was always in Allah's hands. He was grateful that the Egyptian doctor and the senior nurse had stayed with his father until he had taken his final breath. The son added that a Nigerian doctor had come and stood by his father's bed. But he had just stared at his father's body before he walked out of the ward without saying anything to him as he watched over his father.

After I expressed my sympathy to the son once again, I went to speak with the senior surgical nurse and my assistant who had begun treating another patient. After they finished their examination the three of us went to my office. Just after we sat down Dr. Bonda interrupted us. He handed me a letter and told me to read it aloud.

Dr. Bonda's letter accused me of negligence for my failure to examine and treat a seriously ill elderly patient who had died in our hospital. He reprimanded me for leaving the patient under the care of an inexperienced physician while I went to look after officers at the military hospital and sip tea with the commander of that institution. My actions revealed a complete lack of compassion for the poor and needy people of Nigeria. Dr. Bonda asked the officials at the Ministry of Health to discipline me for my unacceptable behavior.

When I told Dr. Bonda that I had examined the patient and that he had been treated according to my instructions. The doctor said that he had visited the ward. He had seen my assistant treating the patient. He didn't see me in that room or my car in the parking lot. The nurses on the ward hadn't seen me either. He wondered if I had used Indian magic to make myself invisible.

The senior surgical nurse told Dr. Bonda he was talking nonsense. Why hadn't he spoken to him since he was the senior surgical nurse? He could have told the doctor that Dr. Ray had done everything possible to save the patient. Or why hadn't Dr. Bonda spoken to the other surgical nurses on the ward? All these nurses knew that I had examined the patient. Or why hadn't he talked to the patient's son who had sat the entire time by his father's bedside? Why had he only spoken to the day duty nurses who had come onto the ward after Dr. Ray had left the hospital? Dr. Bonda grabbed the letter and said that he was sorry. He hurried from my office.

As I drove home that day I thought about this doctor and his authoritarian behavior. Nigeria had changed so quickly. I no longer had the goodwill or the protection of the people who were in power. Once I reached our house, I fixed myself a drink and continued thinking about my vulnerability. I remembered my years in England when unfair people had created problems for me. Back then I was never afraid because one or two honorable people always stood up for me. I also knew that the law was on my side back then and the rule of law would prevail. Even in Nigeria when the country was under colonial rule I could rely on a few well-placed British officers and Nigerian officials who defended me when Headquarters wanted to throw me out of the Colonial Service. Fairness had prevailed.

But times had changed. After I arrived in Nigeria I had sided with the powerful Northern leaders. I had no interest in changing my allegiance. The deposed leaders were my friends. I would continue to offer them my help.

By now almost everyone knew that I planned to leave Nigeria. My old friends wanted me to stay in their country, but they understood my situation. I had to take care of my family. I needed to further my medical career in a fair-minded country that honored the rule of law.

~ 100 ~

Countercoup!

That evening while I was thinking deeply about my past and my future someone knocked on our front door. The First Consul from the American Embassy said that he had come to pay his wife's medical bill. I invited him into our house and offered him a drink. When he asked if I was immigrating to Canada with my family, I said that this was my intention. But I was still sorting out the details.

He said that everything looked good. My immigration papers were in order. I asked him how he knew this. He said that it was his job to know these things. He asked if I knew that the Nigerian government restricted the transfer of foreign exchange from the country. Did I also know that Nigerian pounds were of little value in Canada? He added that I would have just as much trouble transferring money from England to Canada.

I felt uncomfortable. I didn't want to discuss financial matters with this man. I barely knew him. He announced that he could help me with money transfers if I would be willing to do something in exchange for him. I asked him what he had in mind.

He said that Supreme Commander General Ironsi wanted to suppress some troublesome soldiers in Kaduna. But first, he needed the names of the two wounded officers whom I had treated at the military hospital. If I gave the First Consul the names of these men, the American government would transfer all my money from Nigeria and England to my account with the Bank of Nova Scotia in Halifax. Uncle Sam would also pay the fees for the transfers.

The offer offended me. I asked the First Consul why he needed me to give him this information. Why didn't he go ask the commander who was in charge of the military hospital? Colonel Oba could easily supply the two names.

The First Consul smiled. He said that the Americans preferred to ask me for help. They questioned the loyalty of the Yoruba commander and the Northern medical officers who worked in the military hospital. This American representative who was also my neighbor was asking me to violate my moral principles. I thanked him, but I told him that I would never violate my medical oath.

The First Consul blushed. He said that he had wanted me to provide these names so that America could help Nigeria. He paid the bill for his wife's treatment and left my house.

As I watched the man walk down our driveway and disappear into the dark, I wondered why he took his walk at night. No one ever did this in our neighborhood. Kaduna was much too dangerous during these perilous times.

I couldn't sleep that night. I worried about the powerful forces that were unexpectedly trying to manipulate me. I was afraid that the Americans would steal my assets. I would be a pauper in Canada.

The next day my good friend Malam Lawan came to my office. After he closed the door, he asked me why the First Consul from the American Embassy had come to my house last night. When I said that my neighbor had come to pay his wife's medical bill Malam Lawan agreed that this was the official reason. But he said that the truth was hidden in the darkness of the night. He reminded me that Northerners were watching my house to keep me safe. The American Consul's visit had made them suspicious. My friend said that this man had wanted to keep his visit secret, which was why he had acted as if he had walked into my house. But Northern agents had followed the American's movements once he left my driveway. My neighbor had actually parked his car at his friend's nearby house.

After I discussed the First Consul's attempt to bribe me, I told Malam Lawan that his involvement in political intrigues surprised me. He said that everyone was involved in political intrigues these days. He brought up the Ibos who were promising the Americans the rights to their oil and using their common bond of Christianity to get them behind their decision to create an independent Ibo state in Eastern Nigeria. He also discussed the Ibo's failed attempt to transfer Kaduna's armored unit to the Eastern capital of Enugu. The Ibos had hoped to strengthen their military power inside their territory. Malam Lawan thanked me for refusing to help the First Consul. When the Northerners took back Nigeria, he promised that they would try to help me transfer my assets to Canada.

As the attacks on Ibo officers continued through the North and Western parts of Nigeria, I reluctantly agreed to extend my tour another six months. I needed more time to figure out a way to get my money to Canada.

After a long absence, the Emir of Zunguru finally visited me at our house. He said that the Emir of Sokoto was caring for Sir Ahmadu Bello's family. The Premier's assassination had left his family destitute. My good friend looked into my eyes before he said that the Northerners were ready to act.

On July 29, 1966, we heard marshal music on the radio in the hospital before a broadcaster announced the assassination of the Supreme Commander General Ironsi. We soon learned that his chief of staff Lt. Colonel Yakubu Gowon along with some other trusted officers had betrayed the general. After they captured him, they had supposedly tortured the military ruler before they finally took his life. Lt. Colonel Yakubu Gowon seized control of the government and ordered Northern soldiers to launch a full-scale attack against Ibo officers and soldiers living on army bases in Kano and Kaduna and in the capital of Lagos.

In Kaduna, after hundreds of Ibos crowded onto a train that traveled to the East, Northerners posted soldiers at the station and told them to kill any Ibos who tried to leave the city. Northerners also attacked Kaduna Sabongari. They looted Ibo homes and killed the occupants before they set their houses on fire. Attacks against the Ibos spread throughout Kaduna. All night we watched flames light up the star-filled sky and listened to frightening wails and screams that wrenched the air. Kaduna's local authorities never intervened. Some of them were evidently willing participants.

When I went to the hospital the next morning, I saw stacks of bodies and countless injured Nigerians crowding the wards, halls, and verandas. I soon noticed that Northerners on the staff seemed reluctant to show kindness or sympathy toward any Ibo victims. Most of the Ibos died without treatment. When I told the staff that we had to take care of everyone my senior surgical nurse said that no one was sitting idle. He led me into the examining room where I saw nurses looking after wounded people. I went into the operating room and saw my Egyptian assistant performing surgery on a victim. I felt as if I were reliving my experience in Bengal during the "Great Calcutta Killing." I was surrounded by the horrid consequences of human hatred and cruelty.

For eight long hours, I operated on one patient after another. By the end of the day, our staff was so exhausted that I told everyone to take an hour to rest and eat before we continued to care for the injured. During our break, I learned that angry mobs had killed Ibo staff members of our hospital, including Mr. Ibe. This man, whom I had known for so many years, had managed to send his family to Eastern Nigeria, but he wasn't spared.

At midnight when we finally stopped working, I realized that my staff had ignored my earlier plea. They had only treated patients from the North. Seriously injured Ibos were left to die. I wished that I had helped select the patients for treatment, but I had been too busy caring for victims inside the operating room. I also knew that most likely I would have been killed if I had tried to intervene.

The murders and arson continued for four days before an eerie quiet settled into place. Was it just a lull? No one knew. By then our medical staff was exhausted. I knew that my memories of this mindless carnage would never fade away. These endless days of madness would remain as vivid to me as the Calcutta killings that had occurred so many years ago.

~ 101 ~

FINAL TOUR

AN INDIAN DOCTOR WHO LIVED in nearby Zaria called me during the last night of the riots. He said that a gang of Northerners had caught his Ibo servant and his servant's wife after they fled from their quarters. The Northerners had returned to the doctor's house to get the couple's children who had been left behind. The men told the doctor and his wife that they had no quarrels with them, but they had to hand over the servant's children, or they would take them from his house by force. When the crowd started shouting "Allahu Akbar" the terrified doctor feared that the crowd would harm his young son who was also inside their house. He and his wife gave up the Ibo children.

I didn't remind the doctor that I had told him long ago to get rid of his Ibo servants. Instead, I comforted him. I said that these awful killings and riots were unfortunately beyond our control. There was nothing he and his wife could have done to protect the servants or their children.

As I imagined the deaths of this poor Ibo family, I thought

about Simon. Someone had told me that he had started a popular restaurant in the Kano Sabongari, which was home to so many Ibos. Rachel and I cared for Simon. I hoped that he had survived this terrible massacre.

Rachel and I drove around Kaduna after the rioting. We were shocked that rioters had also torched so many buildings in the city's shopping district. People had told us to stay away from Sabongari, so we never saw the Ibo areas that had borne the brunt of the attack.

Early one morning my senior surgical nurse called and asked me to hurry to the hospital. He rushed me into the ward where an elderly man lay unconscious on a bed. He said that the man's family had brought him to the emergency room after he was hurt in a car accident. He was conscious when Dr. Bonda had treated him. The doctor had told the oldest son to take his father home to rest. He wasn't seriously hurt. If his father had any pain, he should give him an aspirin. The entire family stayed near the elderly man until midnight when they went to bed. They thought that he was fine, but he was unconscious in the morning. They rushed him back to the hospital.

When I examined the elderly man he failed to respond to any stimuli. He had no obvious injury to his chest, abdomen, or his limbs; but he had a small bruise and swelling in his right temporal region. His eyes were dilated and one eye failed to react to light.

I ordered blood work and an immediate x-ray of his head and neck, which showed that the man had a linear fracture in the temporal region, and he was suffering from a middle meningeal hemorrhage. He needed an immediate operation.

Once I arranged for cross-matching and units of blood I convinced our staff that we could do this challenging operation, which had never been performed in any Northern hospital. I explained to them that we had no other choice. If we didn't operate on the man, he wouldn't survive.

Dr. Brown decided to use a local anesthetic to intubate the patient and keep him oxygenated during the entire procedure. The matron also made a vital discovery when she found an old set of instruments that had been designed for craniotomies. I unexpectedly had the delicate equipment that would enable me to operate more safely on the injured man.

When I explained the surgical procedure to the family, I was grateful that some of his relatives were well-educated. They understood the risk, but they told us to proceed. Once I started the operation, I had to remove a huge blood clot and much more bone than I had anticipated. I was relieved that we had three units of blood. We used them all. I was also fortunate that our operating room had a diathermy machine, which helped me cauterize the bleeding blood vessels.

When we completed the surgery, the matron, the anesthetist and I took turns staying with our patient in the recovery room until the next morning. The elderly man regained consciousness around noon. But on the second night, he needed IV diuretics to relieve intracranial pressure. But finally, our efforts paid off.

While the elderly man slowly recovered in the hospital, I noticed that every important Northern Nigerian came to visit him. Kaduna's military governor and commanding officer, all the permanent secretaries, and my friend Sir Ali Ibrahim stopped by to wish him well.

After the elderly man went home Dr. Bonda came to my office and closed the door. He claimed that I was responsible for his transfer to one of the worst hospitals in the province. He hoped that I was happy. I told Dr. Bonda that I knew nothing about his transfer. But

Dr. Bonda refused to believe me, not even when I said that I had never talked to anyone in the Ministry of Health.

After Dr. Bonda left my office, I thought about his unfortunate misdiagnosis of the elderly man. He had made a serious blunder, but his mistake should have warranted nothing more than a reprimand, not a transfer. When I learned that Dr. Bonda's punishment was the result of an internal inquiry at the Ministry of Health, I realized that once again I was witnessing the capricious state of the rule of law in Nigeria. Dr. Bonda, who was a Christian, had lost his power and his protection after the countercoup. The doctor had been correct to be wary of the Muslim Northerners, even though they had never proven a connection between him and the Ibos. But suspicion was reason enough to punish the Christian doctor.

I decided that I could no longer stay in Nigeria. I would leave Nigeria with my family at the end of my tour. A subsequent incident convinced me that this was the correct decision. One day a nurse called me from the hospital while I was at home eating lunch with Rachel. An administrative officer had been in an automobile accident and needed my attention.

As I headed toward the hospital a Nigerian woman who was traveling with her children sped into an intersection and hit my car. The woman wasn't injured, but her two children suffered minor abrasions. She willingly gave me her home phone number before I drove to a nearby house for help. The woman who answered the door was a nurse. She promised to tend to the family so that I could get to the hospital. After I treated the injured officer for a superficial wound, I went back to see the nurse who had cared for the Nigerian family. She said that she had cleaned a couple of minor abrasions and covered them with band-aids. I considered the matter closed.

I went to my Greek friend's repair shop to get an estimate of the cost of fixing my Mercedes. He loaned me a car and advised me to talk to the other car owner before I authorized any repairs. I called the Nigerian lady who said that her husband would contact me.

A few days later while I was in the surgical clinic a clerk handed me a letter from the husband's attorney. The lawyer claimed that I was driving above the speed limit, and I had ignored his client's car as it entered the intersection. My reckless behavior had caused the accident. The lawyer also accused me of driving my car without proper insurance.

These false assertions infuriated me. I knew that I had been driving below the speed limit. I was also driving on the main road, which gave me the right of way. The lady who was traveling on a side street should have stopped her car before she entered the intersection. I didn't have my new insurance papers, but I remembered that I had paid for my insurance extension a few months ago.

I went to see my Greek friend and asked him to look at my insurance file. He recalled leaving a note for his former clerk who had asked him to send me my new insurance document along with the premium payment receipt once it arrived in the office. My friend searched my file, but he couldn't find his note or any of the documents. Someone had removed them.

I asked my friend how the attorney could have known that I didn't have car insurance. He shrugged and said that his Ibo clerk had disappeared during the riots. His new clerk interrupted us. He said that someone had called and asked if I had insurance on the Mercedes. The clerk had told the man that he couldn't find a record of insurance in my file.

My Greek friend prepared a new insurance receipt. He also wrote a letter that explained that the original set of insurance documents had disappeared along with his former clerk who had fled during the recent disturbances. My friend told me not to worry. Everything would be resolved.

When I told Malam Lawan about this incident, he called me the next day to say that the matter was settled. Each party would repair his own car and forget that the accident ever occurred. I was relieved and grateful. But this incident was the last straw. It was time for my family to move to Canada.

~ 102 ~

FAREWELL, NIGERIA!

THE DAY THE CANADIAN HIGH Commission granted our family the right to immigrate to Canada I wrote a letter of resignation to the Ministry of Health. At my resignation interview, the members of the Public Service Commission offered to increase my salary if I would agree to stay in Nigeria. I thanked them, but I said that it was time for us to move. The commission reluctantly accepted my decision.

Days later I met with Sir Ali Ibrahim who understood my reasons for leaving Nigeria. He said that he was returning to his home in Maiduguri. He no longer wanted to be involved in politics. Sir Ali Ibrahim wished me good luck. He hoped that I would make a wonderful life for my family in Canada. Sir Ali Ibrahim was the only Nigerian official who advised me to do what was best for my family. He also didn't ask me to promise to come back.

The new Governor Colonel Hassan invited me to have tea with him at the Governor's House. I felt strange sipping tea with the colonel in this room where I had once sat with the former governor Sir Ali Ibrahim. Colonel Hassan surprised me when he said that the assassination of Premier Sir Ahmadu Bello had deeply saddened him. He explained that his father, who had been an emir, was close friends with the Premier.

I told the Governor that I had been forced to destroy a beautiful album of photographs of the Northern leaders that his father had presented to me. I had treasured this special gift. But my friends from the North had warned me that if Ibo officers found the album in my possession, they would punish me. The Governor said that I had done the right thing. I had been on the Ibo hit list. He shifted the conversation and asked me if I would remove a tumor from his neck before I left Nigeria. Of course, I agreed to treat him.

After we finished our tea, the Governor asked his Aide de Camp to take me in a jeep along the road that led from Kaduna to Jos. Just outside the city the Aide de Camp stopped and pointed to a long trench that was freshly covered with turned-over soil. He said that the Ibos had planned to dump the bodies of their enemies into these trenches. Instead, many traitorous Ibos were buried here after the riots. A chill went down my spine as I stared at the long mound of dirt along the roadside. If the Ibos had succeeded with their plan, I wondered how many of my friends would have ended up in these trenches. And what about me?

Days later I successfully removed the tumor from Colonel Hassan's neck. The operation was relatively easy. My real challenge was keeping the Governor safe while he was under our care in the civilian hospital. No political leader was free from threats in Nigeria.

I had to meet with the Permanent Secretary at the Ministry of Health to finalize my family's travel plans to Canada. We were entitled to first-class sea passage to England or India, but I hoped that the Permanent Secretary would grant us first-class sea passage from England to Canada. I told him that once we reached England the fare to India would cost more than the fare to Canada.

A few days later a senior officer at the Ministry of Health contacted me to say that the Permanent Secretary had approved our travel plans to Canada. But the old Scottish officer who was the senior accountant at the Ministry of Finance had rejected the authorization. I arranged to meet with the Nigerian Permanent Secretary who ran this department. I told him that his senior accountant had rejected my family's travel plans to Canada. He looked through my file and told me not to worry. True to his words he authorized our journey and gave us a month-long stopover in England.

I still needed to find a way to transfer my assets to Canada. When I met with the bank manager in Kaduna, he said that he could only authorize the transfer of 500 Nigerian pounds into my bank account in Halifax. The bank would need to release the remainder of my money in yearly installments. The bank manager said that my British bank had similar restrictions. I was devastated. I wouldn't be able to support my family in Canada.

When I discussed my problem with my old friend the Emir of Zunguru he wished that he had the power to get the Governor of the Reserve Bank to grant me a special exemption. Three days later the Emir asked me to go with him to visit a mutual friend. His driver took us to a traditional Northern Nigerian home set inside a large compound. When we entered the house, I was surprised to see my distinguished elderly patient who had suffered from the meningeal hemorrhage. He looked healthy but tired.

The distinguished gentleman thanked me for saving his life. He invited us to sit and have a cup of tea and cookies with him. As we chatted together the kind man said that he might be able to help me with my financial problem. One week later I was sitting in my office at the hospital when the bank manager in Kaduna called me. He wanted me to come to see him immediately.

The bank manager took me into his office and read aloud a letter from the Governor of the Reserve Bank that authorized the transfer of all my assets from Nigeria to Canada. The bank manager had also received a copy of a letter that the Governor had written to his counterpart at the Bank of England. This second letter authorized the transfer of all my assets from the British bank to my bank in Canada. The bank manager asked me if I had received the original letters because they were addressed to me.

I raced back to the hospital and asked my clerk for the day's mail. I was overjoyed when I saw an envelope from the Governor of the Reserve Bank. I called the Emir of Zunguru who took me back to see my former patient. He was the Governor of the Reserve Bank of Nigeria. The elderly man was delighted to help me, but he asked me not to speak about this confidential transaction with anyone. When I got home, I shared this amazing coincidence with my beloved Rachel. Our voyage to Canada had finally become very real and inviting.

We had so much to do, and so little time left in Nigeria. I wrote to Jacob and told him about our decision to spend a month in London before we left for Canada. He invited us to stay with him and Hilda and their young daughter and son. He told us that Daniel had become a successful chartered accountant at an accounting firm and Joseph who was still at his old job was playing his violin in several music clubs in London. Everyone in Rachel's family was eager to see us.

I was relieved that my replacement at the hospital started work three weeks before my departure. The new surgeon immediately assumed all my duties, which gave Rachel and me more time to say goodbye to our friends in Kaduna and our friends who lived in nearby towns and cities. We also attended so many farewell celebrations. The hospital administration and the Ministry of Health arranged a wonderful official party, while some doctors and nurses organized an intimate event for us. The Permanent Secretary at the Ministry of Health declared that the winds of Africa would blow my family and me back to his country in a very short time.

Newspapers in Kaduna published long articles that showered me with praise and appreciation. One tribute pointed out that Nigerians normally preferred to see the backside of an expatriate officer, but they felt differently about me. Everyone knew that I cared for the Nigerian people and their country. All the generous press and celebrations filled Rachel and me with deep feelings of gratitude and joy. Perhaps, we were also overcome with emotion because the Northerners were finally in power.

A few days before we departed from Kaduna, we gave away lots of our furniture, utensils, and old clothing that we doubted we would ever need in Canada. We packed the rest of our possessions into huge wooden crates that had been built on our property. All this time I kept thinking about the ten and a half years that we had spent in Nigeria.

I had learned so much about this amazing country and myself. I had suffered from the conservative outlook and prejudice of the old timers in the Colonial Service, but I had earned the reliable trust and goodwill of the Northern Nigerian leaders and Nigerian people. Rachel and I had gone through anxious times marked by deep despair when my job seemed dangerously insecure during our first few years in this country. Many times, I had thought that I would be disgraced and forced to leave the Colonial Service. Many times, I believed that my career as a surgeon and doctor was in jeopardy.

But after so many struggles I had tasted victory. I had gained not only recognition and security, but I had received the honor and respect of the authorities.

I would never forget the few senior British officers who had defended me and defied the strong wills of their peers. These few officers who were convinced that the allegations against me were unjust had sided with me and the truth.

Rachel and I had experienced an extremely pleasant family life in this country where our two wonderful daughters had been born. Sheila and Monica were lovely young people. Many fine teachers had helped them build solid foundations. I felt confident that they would continue their fine education in Canada.

I thought about Nigeria, which was a diverse country with many special people. I worried about tribal and religious distrust and hatred. The country needed to unite, or its future would remain uncertain. Some people of good will believed that all Nigerians could live together in harmony and experience mutual prosperity. They were certain that they would live to see genuine reunification that would draw together Nigeria's different cultural and religious groups. But I knew that currently, the country's Muslim majority suppressed these hopeful voices and also their vision. Neither the coup nor the countercoup had resolved anything.

I doubted that the Ibos would accept a federal government that was administered by the dominant Northern army officers. The Ibos would probably press for an independent state and try to create a country that they called Biafra in Eastern Nigeria. I feared that the larger Northern army, which had more firepower, would march east and subdue any Ibo attempt to gain independence. The Northerners wanted a unified country. They would never relinquish ownership of the black gold in Ibo territory.

On the day of our departure, we drove to the airport to take a plane to Lagos. Many people, including dignitaries, were waiting to say goodbye to us. Some well-wishers sang farewell songs, other people held up big signs that said, "No goodbye, only au revoir. We shall meet again."

As the plane took off, I stared out the window at Kaduna one last time and became lost in my private thoughts. A man carrying a large envelope approached me. I saw my name written boldly on the front. He saluted me and handed me the envelope. I pulled out a letter that was signed by all the ex-ministers of Northern Nigeria. It expressed their grief that I was leaving their beloved land. They said that they didn't have the heart to come and say goodbye to me, but they wished me a long happy life with my family in Canada. They asked me to remember that wherever I traveled in the world I carried their good will and best wishes with me.

During our sea voyage from Lagos to Liverpool, I stared into the Atlantic Ocean every night. Nothing seemed real to me, no land mass existed in any direction. I only heard the enormous waves that thrashed back and forth against the side of our boat, but I felt the presence of that land where I had lived for a decade. My eyes felt misty at times. I knew that I was leaving Nigeria, but a part of Nigeria would remain with me forever.

I wondered if I was coming to the end of the long road that led to a final home in Canada. I didn't know if our immigration would work out for us. I was 44-years-old, but I didn't know if my restless mind could ever end its quest for something new. Maybe I had a wandering soul that could never be completely content or tranquil if I stayed in one place.

But I hoped and prayed that Rachel would get a permanent happy home. She deserved it. I also hoped that Sheila and Monica would receive an excellent education in Canada. I wanted my two lovely daughters to reach their full potential in their new home. I knew that I owed this to both of them. This was their true birthright.

EPILOGUE

BY THE TIME MY FATHER, Krishna Das Ray, who was known throughout his life as K. D. Ray, left Nigeria for Canada his career had spanned three continents. He had chosen to settle his family on a fourth continent where once again he would need to overcome the suspicion directed at a newcomer. He understood that this move to Canada was mainly for the benefit of his two daughters, so he was pleased that we received an excellent education in Nova Scotia.

Each of us excelled and fulfilled the promise of our lives. I became a successful gastroenterologist, and my sister, Sheila, became a successful judge. K.D.'s surgical career also blossomed. After seventeen years of professional service in his final homeland, the Medical Society of Nova Scotia bestowed him with a rare honor when it recognized his contribution to the practice of surgery and admitted him as a Senior Member of their society.

After he retired, he continued to pursue his love of people, the arts, archeology, and history. He and my mother Rachel traveled extensively. He also wrote and published a book entitled *India: A*

Journey Through the Ages, cataloged by the Library of Congress in Washington. This book has been placed in the collection of the Trinity College Library at Oxford University in England.

When he was in his early eighties, he sat down at his computer and began typing this autobiography. He had hoped to publish this incredible memory of a life lived in turbulent times. Unfortunately, while editing his memoirs, he became ill and died before it could be completed. On his deathbed he made me promise to at least print this manuscript. My mother completed the edit. At the urging of friends, I began the process of fulfilling his wishes.

K.D. Ray lived to celebrate his sixtieth wedding anniversary with his beloved Rachel. As he stood before his friends and family with Rachel at his side, he shared thoughts and feelings that reflected the essence of who he was: "I shall conclude by saying something you all know, learning never stops. Love, compassion, and affection for all must be learned and practiced every day of our lives. I can assure you I am trying."

He passed away at the age of ninety-one in 2014.

~Monica Ray

ACKNOWLEDGEMENTS

I AM SO GRATEFUL TO have my father's story brought to life in this book. It was a labor of love for my dad to write the manuscript and for me to turn it into a publishable form. I am thankful for the support of my husband, Robert Kronenberg, and my mother, Rachel Ray, who read various versions along the way and provided helpful comments and suggestions. This was especially challenging for my mother who did this with greatly reduced eyesight using a video magnifier, which makes her efforts all the more significant. And, of course, the moral support and suggestions from my son Alan Ray Kronenberg and my sister Sheila Ray were invaluable.

I also would like to thank Cheryl Benton, my wonderful editor and publisher, and Susan Herbst for the beautiful book cover and interior design.

I know my father would be pleased that we honored his wish for his story to become a published book. We are grateful to have his legacy live on.

~Monica Ray

ABOUT THE AUTHOR

KRISHNA DAS RAY, AFFECTIONATELY KNOWN as K.D. Ray, was born in India in 1924. After earning his medical degree in India, he moved to London to become a Fellow of the Royal College of Surgeons. His career then took him to Nigeria, where he served as an officer and physician in the British Colonial Service for a decade. Eventually, Dr. Ray settled in Nova Scotia with his family, where he dedicated seventeen years to his profession. His exceptional contributions to surgery were recognized by the Medical Society of Nova Scotia, which honored him as a Senior Member.

A passionate world traveler, Dr. Ray had a keen interest in history, art, and archaeology. He delved deeply into the cultures of middle, central, and south Asia, and authored the book *India: A Journey Through the Ages*, cataloged by the Library of Congress and housed in the Trinity College Library at Oxford University. His memoir, *Echoes Across Continents*, was completed shortly before his passing in 2014 at the age of ninety-one.

www.ingramcontent.com/pod-product-compliance
Lightning Source LLC
Chambersburg PA
CBHW021208130626
46554CB00004B/1133